Query Processing
for Advanced Database Systems

THE MORGAN KAUFMANN SERIES IN
DATA MANAGEMENT SYSTEMS

Series Editor, Jim Gray

ATOMIC TRANSACTIONS
Nancy Lynch, Michael Merritt, William Weihl, and Alan Fekete

QUERY PROCESSING FOR ADVANCED DATABASE SYSTEMS
Edited by Johann Christoph Freytag, David Maier, and Gottfried Vossen

TRANSACTION PROCESSING: CONCEPTS AND TECHNIQUES
Jim Gray and Andreas Reuter

UNDERSTANDING THE NEW SQL: A COMPLETE GUIDE
Jim Melton and Alan R. Simon

BUILDING AN OBJECT-ORIENTED DATABASE SYSTEM: THE STORY OF O_2
Edited by François Bancilhon, Claude Delobel, and Paris Kanellakis

DATABASE TRANSACTION MODELS FOR ADVANCED APPLICATIONS
Edited by Ahmed K. Elmagarmid

A GUIDE TO DEVELOPING CLIENT/SERVER SQL APPLICATIONS
Setrag Khoshofian, Arvola Chan, Anna Wong, and Harry K. T. Wong

THE BENCHMARK HANDBOOK FOR DATABASE AND TRANSACTION
PROCESSING SYSTEMS, *SECOND EDITION*
Edited by Jim Gray

CAMELOT AND AVALON: A DISTRIBUTED TRANSACTION FACILITY
Edited by Jeffrey L. Eppinger, Lily B. Mummert, and Alfred Z. Spector

DATABASE MODELING AND DESIGN: THE ENTITY-RELATIONSHIP
APPROACH
Toby J. Teorey

READINGS IN OBJECT-ORIENTED DATABASE SYSTEMS
Edited by Stanley B. Zdonik and David Maier

READINGS IN DATABASE SYSTEMS
Edited by Michael Stonebraker

Query Processing
for Advanced Database Systems

Edited by

Johann Christoph Freytag
David Maier
Gottfried Vossen

MORGAN KAUFMANN PUBLISHERS
San Mateo, California

Senior Editor: *Bruce M. Spatz*
Production Manager: *Yonie Overton*
Assistant Editor: *Douglas Sery*
Final Formatting/Output: *SuperScript Typography*
Cover Design: *Patty King*
Icon Design: *Wells Larson Associates*
Printer: *R.R. Donnelley & Sons*

This book has been author-typeset using LaTeX macros provided by the publisher.

Morgan Kaufmann Publishers, Inc.
Editorial Office:
2929 Campus Drive, Suite 260
San Mateo, CA 94403

97 96 95 94   5 4 3 2 1

Library of Congress Cataloging in Publication Data is available for this book.
ISBN   1-55860-271-2
ISSN   1046-1698

In Memoriam
Peter Lyngbaek

Contents

3   Query Optimization in Object Bases: Exploiting Relational Techniques

A. Kemper and G. Moerkotte   **63**

4   Optimization of Complex-Object Queries in PRIMA - Statement of Problems

H. Schöning   **99**

10 Implementation of the Object-Oriented Data Model TM

H. J. Steenhagen and P. M. G. Apers   **273**

11 Extensible Query Optimization and Parallel Execution in Volcano

G. Graefe R. L. Cole, D. L. Davison,
W. J. McKenna, R. H. Wolniewicz   **305**

Preface

The chapters of this book provide an excellent snapshot of current research and development activities in the area of query processing and optimization. They supply potential answers to many questions that have been raised for new types of database systems and at the same time reflect the variety of the different approaches taken. The book acts both as a reference for the state of the art in query processing for the "next generation" of database systems, and as a good starting point for anybody interested in understanding the challenging questions in the area. Furthermore, the book will help the reader to gain an in-depth understanding of why efficient query processing is needed for future database systems.

This book puts together selected contributions from a week-long workshop on "Query Processing in Object-Oriented, Complex-Object and Nested Relation Databases," which was held at the *Internationales Begegnungs- und Forschungszentrum für Informatik*, Schloss Dagstuhl, Germany, in June 1991. The workshop brought together academic and industrial researchers from eight different countries, among them **Peter Lyngbaek** of HP Labs, Palo Alto, California. We all were deeply sorry to learn of Peter's premature death shortly after the workshop. As the Dagstuhl workshop was probably the last scientific event Peter could attend, we dedicate this book to him.

This book would not have been possible without the patience and dedication of the many authors involved. Special thanks go to the staff at Morgan Kaufmann and in particular to Bruce Spatz, the Senior Editor of this book, for ongoing support and pleasant cooperation.

J.C. Freytag   D. Maier   G. Vossen

Introduction

Over the last decade relational database technology has emerged as the dominant technology for information storage and retrieval. Experience with relational database systems has demonstrated that **efficient query processing** is one of the key elements for maximizing the benefits of this technology.

Relational database systems allow the user to access the data in a *declarative manner*. That is, the user's only specifies *what* should be retrieved from the database. It is the responsibility of the database system to determine *how* this request should be evaluated against the database. Therefore the database system has to generate a *procedural* query evaluation program (QEP) from the declarative user query without changing the user's intention.

The challenge of generating an efficient QEP highlights the importance of query processing in relational database systems. A query processing algorithm must generate the best plan possible – or at least avoid generating the worst plan – for any given query from the available choices for a QEP using information on the internal representation of data in the database. This generation process is driven by a search strategy and guided by cost functions and statistics about the stored data. The search strategy determines the number of alternatives that are generated, and their respective order. The cost functions and statistics provide a basis for comparing different alternatives of (partially) generated query evaluation plans by taking into account information about value ranges and value distributions for the data stored in the database. Besides determining the best strategy for accessing the data, any query processing algorithm must also determine the join order and the join strategies between different relations. The choice heavily depends on the size of the (intermediate) relations and the available access strategies.

In addition to generating optimal query evaluation plans – this process is also called "physical plan generation" – query processing includes others aspects of handling, manipulating, and specifying the user's request. In particular, with the increasing complexity of user requests the need for **rewriting** or **transforming** a query into a form that is more amenable for generating a query evaluation plan has become apparent. Such logical transformations take into account "rewriting rules" for transforming the query without changing its intention. Based on additional information that is derived from integrity constraints or other sources of information available to the database system, rewriting can result in less complex queries that allow the system to generate more efficient query evaluation plans.

Other aspects of query processing include the design and study of formalisms on which to perform query processing effectively. This work focuses on developing external and internal frameworks for handling and expressing user requests, such as query algebras, studying their expressive power, and understanding the translations between different formalisms, respectively. Query processing also includes the design of application interfaces, such as graphical interfaces, and the embedding of database requests into existing programming languages.

This variety of query processing tasks also influences the implementation of query processing components, their structure, and their relationships and interdependencies. Therefore, the design of appropriate architectures for query processors on which to base concrete implementations is also part of query processing.

Recently, the field of database systems has gone through a stage of transformation with the appearance of many new database models and technologies. This development includes extended relational systems, deductive database systems, database systems based on semantic models, and structural and behavioral object-oriented database systems. Such systems use database technology to address a wide variety of new application domains and user needs.

These efforts have yielded more than just new data models or paper systems. There are now working prototypes, and in some cases, initial commercial offerings representing those different types of systems. Their initial focus has been greater expressivity and supporting modes of access of new database applications, such as computer-aided design (CAD), office information systems, or computer-aided software engineering (CASE). However, these new systems are still weak in an area where current relational systems excel: efficient querying via a declarative language.

The need to provide such a capability in new database systems is widely acknowledged, but the challenges are many:

1. New data model features such as added base types, ordered type constructors (e.g., lists and arrays), object identifiers and user-defined data types require that algebraic formalisms used to represent queries for optimization and evaluation be extended.

2. Set-at-a-time processing must be adapted to tolerate variations resulting from additional data model features. Relational query processing exploits the homogeneity of large collections of data to carry out set-at-a-time processing. While new database systems are designed to support such large collections, heterogeneity creeps in from a variety of sources: different levels of nesting or repetition, multiple implementations for a type or a method, subtype hierarchies and union types, to name a few.

3. Query optimizers must be constructed so that they can be extended in parallel with the models and access methods. Many of these systems provide for extensibility by the application programmer, database designer or DBMS implementor.

4. The encapsulation provided by class- and type-definition mechanisms found in some of these systems obscures the global knowledge required by a query optimizer to deduce alternative execution. This raises the question whether processing strategies exist that allow the system to manage these two conflicting concepts in such a way that they can coexist. Based on requirements or user specifications one might give preference to (1) maintain encapsulation, (2) provide global knowledge for exhaustive optimization, or (3) an intermediate approach between these two extremes (i.e., not giving up encapsulation completely thus not gaining complete global knowledge of the request). In any case, the ideal strategy of how to bring together encapsulation and optimization remains an open topic for further research.

5. To support efficient execution of user requests in object-oriented, complex object, or nested relation database systems, new kinds of access structures need to be offered and explored. Furthermore, relationships between objects at the logical level might impact the organization of objects at the storage level. Such physical organization needs to be maintained over time. Here the question arises: what kinds of concepts, data structures, and algorithms are necessary to achieve optimal storage and processing of objects?

6. Most relational optimization is done at compile time based on cost estimates that are derived by cost functions. The question is whether such a static model is adequate for models with much richer concepts than the relation model, i.e., whether there are alternative ways of optimizing user requests, such as some kind of run-time optimization that exhibit a more dynamic behavior to take better into account the existing object organization and to adapt more easily to possible changes at various levels.

7. A semantically rich environment, such as those presented by new application areas, provides more information than is traditionally included in the processing of user requests. This is particularly true for information embedded in the semantic concepts offered by the various new data models. Most relational systems focus on physical optimization, i.e., taking into account the physical layout of data on disk, possibly supported by auxiliary structures such as indexes. Considering such semantically rich environments leads to a kind of logical optimization that goes beyond current optimization in most relational systems. The challenge is to determine what kind of optimizations are possible and what kind are desirable for these advanced database models.

8. All these new aspects raise the immediate question as to whether current architectures for query processing components in relational systems are also adequate also for implementing such components for advanced database systems. The higher complexity in query processing might suggest alternative architectures that go beyond simply extending existing ones to the new requirements.

New developments in the area of database systems are integrated with, and influenced by, concepts and techniques from traditional (relational) databases, object-oriented programming languages, logic, and parallel hardware. In this sense, the chapters in this book provide a representative survey of the field, since they reflect these diverse sources in a variety of ways. Indeed, this book is an excellent snapshot of currently available answers to the various challenges posed by the role of query processing and optimization in advanced database applications.

When looking at the recent developments in database area, we can identify different approaches that have influenced the current development of future database technology. One group of research activities bases its extensions and changes on the existing relation model and its implementation in various products and prototypes. The goal is to extend the relational framework with additional concepts in an "evolutionary" manner. That is, by building on available experience, new concepts and new functionality are added to the model and to corresponding existing relational database systems.

Another group of research activities takes object-oriented concepts as implemented in object-oriented programming languages as the basis for their extensions. Incrementally, database features and database functionality are added to provide the same capabilities as relational systems, such as a (declarative) query language and transaction management. In some cases this has resulted in user interfaces and implementations that differ considerably from those of relational database systems.

The third group of research activities relies heavily on concepts and implementation techniques that have been developed for logic programming and deductive systems in general. The use of rules or calculus-oriented languages and deduction-based techniques as an important technique for evaluating complex requests reflects the logic-based approach. In many ways, this approach complements and extends the relational approach as far as the model and the language are concerned.

We have organized the chapters into four groups according to the different approaches to make the material more accessible for the reader. Besides the groups reflecting the affect of the relational approach, the logic-based approach, and the object-oriented approach, we added a fourth group that contains contributions in the area of indexing and performance measurements. The chapters of the latter group differ from those of the other groups in that they discuss system- and implementation-oriented aspects.

Part I, called *Extending Relational Approaches*, shows how relational languages as well as relational query processing and optimization techniques may be extended beyond the limits of a flat data model. These enhancements can be achieved by either adding new functionality, for example abstract data types (ADTs), to existing query languages such as SQL, or by extending the representation of the data in relations, i.e., allowing complex objects or nested relations. Specifically, **Kulkarni** et al. describe an ADT-based type system that has been proposed for inclusion in Version 3 of the SQL Standard. **Mitschang** and **Pirahesh** discuss another extension of SQL called SQL/XNF, intended to support complex objects which are stored in a relational database. **Schöning** introduces the reader to alternative query evaluation strategies as employed in the *PRIMA* experimental complex object database system. **Kemper** and **Moerkotte** investigate to what extend relational optimization techniques can be applied to object-oriented query processing. Finally, **Demuth** et al. show how to generalize algebraic optimization from the relational to a structurally object-oriented data model.

Part II reflects the *Logic-based Approaches*. This group shows that expressive logic languages demand new kinds of optimization techniques to guarantee efficient evaluation. Furthermore, since logic approaches have focused primarily on query or manipulation languages rather than on data structuring and data representation, the synthesis of logic and object-oriented concepts becomes an important challenge. Understanding the power and the limits of various different frameworks that have been proposed in the logic context has always been of great interest to this community. The chapters of this group reflect these challenges that come with the logic-based approach. **Jeusfeld** and **Staudt** investigate query optimization in *ConceptBase*, an experimental system integrating structural object-orientation and deductive capabilities. **Lausen** and **Marx** present a subset of *F-logic* as a sample language that embeds object-oriented features into the computational formalism of deductive databases. **Gyssens**, **Saxton** and **Van Gucht** generalize Tarski's "calculus of relations" by a tag operation and discuss various properties of the resulting language. They demonstrate that object creation, a common new feature in advanced data models, can be simulated nicely in a logical setting.

Part III, called *Object-Oriented and Complex Object Approaches*, focuses on query languages in object-oriented database systems, the optimization of queries and the architecture and implementation of a query processing component in object-oriented database systems. Although the proposals and solutions made in all chapters draw from the experience in the relational domain, they all heavily emphasize the object-oriented aspect. In particular, **Cluet** and **Delobel** propose a unifying formalism for algebraic query rewriting, and optimization based on class extensions. **Steenhagen** and **Apers** describe the implementation of a novel object-oriented data model called *TM* using an algebraic database language based on functional programming. **Maier** et al. first survey core functions of object-oriented databases, their impact on query processing in general, and current system solutions, and then present an architecture of a query processing system which they design and implemented in a prototype for an object-oriented database system. **Graefe** et al. describe an optimizer generator as a means to simplify the implementation of query processing components. Rather than building optimizers from scratch for new requirements, they exploit the rigorous structure of this component by providing a specification language to describe the capabilities of the optimizer that is to be generated. Graefe et al. also discuss how query evaluation plans for parallel hardware systems may be generated.

As already mentioned, Part IV discusses *Access Methods, Physical Design, and Performance Evaluation.* It provides discussions and solutions on how to support the access to objects efficiently, how to treat physical schema design in an object-oriented database environment, and what to expect from object-oriented database systems with respect to performance. First, **Bertino** gives a detailed account of indexing techniques that have been proposed for object-oriented databases. **Scholl** discusses alternatives for physical design of object-oriented databases, their use in a design optimizer, and their affect on a query optimizer. Finally, **van den Berg** and **Kersten** analyze dynamic query optimization under distinct distributions of data.

By including the major areas that currently influence the direction for future database systems, this book reflects the advances and an overview of the emerging concepts in the areas of query processing and query optimization for several new types of database systems. Despite many differences the hope is that the contributions will help to identify commonalities between these various types. If this has been accomplished, individual solutions can be generalized and then tailored to the specific requirements of different kinds of database systems and applications.

It is our hope that with this book we raise the confidence that query processing and optimization will continue to support the declarative approach efficiently for the new types of systems also in the future. Since declarative concepts support the programmer's and user's efforts to manage the ever increasing complexity of their information processing environment, it is important to continually improve concepts that allow the transformation of declarative requests into efficient procedural programs. Improving query processing and optimization as documented in this book contributes towards that goal.

PART I

Extending Relational Approaches

1

ADT-based Type System for SQL

Krishna Kulkarni
Jonathan Bauer
Umeshwar Dayal
Mike Kelley
Jim Melton

Abstract

Currently, most database vendors support the database language SQL, adopted by both ANSI and ISO as the database language standard. An examination of the type system associated with the SQL language reveals many serious shortcomings for developing complex applications. This paper reports on an effort to add an extensible type system to SQL. The type system is based on the notion of abstract data types. The types in this system are abstract (obey strict encapsulation), immediate (users can define types using only the SQL constructs), and first-class (user-defined types have the same status as predefined types). In addition, the type system supports both value and object semantics, and the usual notions of subtypes and supertypes, parameterized types, polymorphic functions and dynamic binding. The paper also covers the initial change proposals that we have submitted to both ANSI and ISO for incorporation into SQL3.

1.1
Introduction

The database language SQL has become both a *de facto* and a *de jure* standard for database access. SQL is a non-procedural query language that operates on data structures in the form of "tables", based on the relational data model. For serious application programming, SQL programs are expected to be used in conjunction with programs written in other host languages, such as COBOL, PL/I, Pascal, C, *etc.*

Because of its non-procedural nature, SQL has gained tremendous popularity for developing data-intensive applications. The number of implementations claiming conformance with SQL has been growing over the last few years. Correspondingly, the number of applications built using SQL has also grown rapidly. In fact, the Third-Generation Database System Manifesto describes SQL as *"intergalactic dataspeak"* [Stonebraker et al. 1990].

The first version of this standard, SQL-86, was published in 1986 by both ANSI [ANSI 1986] and ISO [ISO 1987]. This standard was largely based on the SEQUEL 2 language developed as part of IBM's System R project [Chamberlin et al. 1976]. SQL-86 provided for creation and manipulation of data organized as table structures, but it lacked many features such as referential integrity and schema manipulation. In 1989, a revised version of the standard, SQL-89, was published [ANSI 1989], [ISO 1989]; this version enhanced the earlier version with a definition for basic referential integrity.

A substantial revision of the SQL standard under the informal name of "SQL2" is nearing completion [ISO 91]. SQL2 provides for increased orthogonality and new functionality. New functionality in SQL2 includes: additional data types; cast specifications (explicit data type conversions); the concepts of information schema, domains, temporary tables, character repertoires, collations, table/column constraints and assertions; new options to enforce referential integrity; better error handling; additional join operators; new cursor options; and facilities to drop or alter schema objects. SQL2 is expected to be published as SQL-92 standard in 1992. Work has also started under the informal name of "SQL3" for evolving the language beyond SQL2 [Melton 1991]. SQL3 is expected to be completed in the 1995-96 timeframe.

The type system offered by the SQL language is rather limited. As a result, it is very hard to model complex applications using SQL. In order to make the language applicable for a wide class of applications, we and others (from organizations such as Oracle, IBM, HP, *etc.*) in the ANSI committee have been working on incorporating an extensible type system based on the notion of abstract data types. As the work has progressed, we have prepared a number of change proposals that extend the type system in an incremental fashion and submitted them to the ANSI committee responsible for SQL standardization (X3H2). Some of the proposals have been submitted to ISO also.

This paper describes the progress we have made so far in extending the type system of SQL. All the change proposals reported here have been accepted by the X3H2 committee for incorporation into the SQL3 draft standard. We would, however, like to caution readers that the paper may not reflect the current state of the language, as it is undergoing continuous change. Also, this paper does not reflect a number of change proposals that have been submitted by other committee members and accepted by ANSI. In addition, any or all the extensions reported here are subject to revision, either by us or by other X3H2 committee members.

The rest of the paper is organized as follows: Section 1.2 describes the type system of the existing SQL standard, followed by a brief discussion of its shortcomings. Section 1.3 provides a review of the previous research in overcoming those shortcomings. Section 1.4 describes the salient features of our proposed type system, starting with a discussion of the concept of abstract data types as we use it in this paper, followed by the description of the complete type system we envision for SQL. Section 1.5 describes the progress we have made so far in introducing this type system into the SQL3 draft standard. Section 1.6 provides a brief comparison of our work with some of the earlier research efforts.

1.2
Type System of SQL

SQL-89 provides a fixed set of predefined types — character, numeric, decimal, integer, smallint, float, real, and double precision. SQL2 extends this set of predefined types with character varying, date, time, timestamp, interval, bit, and bit varying. Both SQL-89 and SQL2 also allow the definition of a single kind of data structure, *table*, which is a multiset of tuples. The types of the tuple attributes are restricted to one of the predefined types.

If we compare the type system of SQL with the type system of any modern programming language, we see many serious shortcomings. Firstly, other than the table constructor, SQL provides no support for defining complex data structures that are commonly found in programming languages. For example, though the table constructor is equivalent to a multiset of tuple structures, there is no explicit support for multiset and tuple constructors. There is also no support for set, array, or list constructors.

Secondly, SQL does not cleanly separate type definition from data definition. For example, it is not possible to define a table type independently of declaring a table to be of that type. Also, the type system is highly non-orthogonal. For instance, an attribute of a table cannot itself be a table structure. Other examples of non-orthogonality of the language include the fact that persistence is allowed only for table structures but not for any other types.

1.3
Previous Research

Of late, it is becoming increasingly clear that the relational data model and query languages based on the relational data model are not sufficiently expressive nor are they convenient for many complex applications such as computer-aided design, office automation, *etc.* [Stonebraker et al. 1990]. There have been many efforts to extend the relational data model to deal with such complex applications. To date, such extensions have been based on two broad approaches:

1. Support for non-first normal form relations [Jaeschke and Schek 1982], [Fischer and Thomas 1983], [Abiteboul and Bidoit 1988], [Roth et al. 1987], nested relations [Schek and Scholl 1986], [Colby 1989], [Gyssens et al. 1989], [Korth and Roth 1989], and extended non-first normal form relations [Pistor and Anderson 1986], [Dadam et al. 1986], [Bancilhon et al. 1987]: All these efforts attempt to generalize the attribute types to complex types such as sets, lists, and relations.

2. Support for abstract data types [Osborn and Heaven 1986], [Stonebraker 1986], [Linnemann et al. 1988], [Wilms et al. 1988], [Gardarin et al. 1989], [Ingres 1989]: These efforts let users introduce application-specific data types which are then used for defining attribute types.

In dealing with complex applications, a somewhat different approach was taken by so-called *semantic data models* [Hull and King 1987], [Peckham and Maryanski 1988]. Though there is no precise definition of a semantic data model, a few key concepts are common to almost all semantic data models. Semantic data models model an application in terms of *entities*, each having a set of *attributes* and possessing a unique *identity* that is distinct from its attribute values. They also introduced constructors such as *aggregation*, *grouping* or *association*, and *generalization* for creating complex structures.

Recently, a number of systems supporting *object-oriented data models* are gaining attention for developing complex data-intensive applications [Zdonik and Maier 1989], [Kim and Lochovsky 1989], [Hughes 1991]. In general, object-oriented database systems attempt to combine the advances in programming languages, especially object-oriented languages, with database system concepts. Though there are many proposals for a definitive object-oriented data model [Atkinson et al. 1990], [Beeri 1990], [ANSI 1991a], there is yet no single accepted definition. However, they all support an extensible type system, data abstraction, subtyping, and late binding.

There is currently a debate between proponents of the relational data model who advocate an evolutionary approach and the proponents of object-oriented data models who advocate a revolutionary approach. We believe that future database systems need to integrate the advances in relational, semantic and object-oriented systems. We further believe that such an integration can be achieved by extending the SQL type system into an extensible type system found in many object-oriented languages. In this paper, we report on just such a type system.

1.4
Proposed Type System for SQL

The following subsections describe the salient features of our type system.[1] The type system is based on the notion of abstract data types, subtype-supertype hierarchies, parameterized types, polymorphism, and dynamic binding.

1.4.1   Abstract Data Types

The concept of abstract data types was developed in the field of programming languages in the 1970s [Guttag 1977]. The earliest language to incorporate the notion of abstract data types was SIMULA. Many modern object-oriented programming languages, *e.g.*, Smalltalk, C++, Trellis, Eiffel, are also based on the concept of abstract data types.

An *abstract data type (ADT)* is the specification of behavior of similar objects, called *instances* of that ADT. An important aspect of ADTs is the separation of the *interface* of the type from its *implementation*. The *interface (of an ADT)* defines the behavior of an ADT, specified through a set of operation signatures. Some of the operations associated with an ADT might be realized by means of data that is stored in a database, while other operations might be realized as executable code (functions) which implements the manipulations that can be performed on an object. Stored data together with the data structures and code that implements the behavior of an ADT is its *implementation*.

Each ADT instance has an associated *value*, which is the stored data pertaining to an ADT instance. The value of an ADT instance is also called its *state*. The *representation (of an ADT)* is the data structure used to represent the value of an ADT instance. This data structure may be defined using any known data type, including other ADTs.

Encapsulation is a mechanism to conceal the details of an ADT's implementation from users of the ADT. A *type definer* specifies the interface and

---

[1]Many of the concepts in this proposed type system owe their origin to the OODAPLEX language, designed by one of the authors [Dayal 1990].

implementation of an ADT. Hence, implementation of an ADT is visible to type definers. A *type user* uses a given ADT to define other types, to declare program variables, or to create instances of that ADT. Type users can manipulate the value of an ADT instance only through the operations defined on the ADT (its interface). The implementation of an ADT is not visible to type users, and hence, type users are not affected if the implementation of an ADT they are using is changed or if there are multiple implementations of an ADT.

Operations on an ADT are classified into four categories:

1. *Observer operations*: Operations that do not change the state of an ADT instance and may return one or more values that are derived from the state of one or more ADTs.
2. *Mutator operations*: Operations that change some part of the state of an ADT instance. They may do so by directly manipulating the value of an instance of an ADT.
3. *Constructor operations*: Operations that create new instances of an ADT, and make them part of the database.
4. *Destructor operations*: Operations that remove an instance of an ADT from the database.

We do not *formally* distinguish between observer and mutator operations, but it is often convenient to have a mental idea of the difference. We call operations that may be either observers or mutators (but not constructors or destructors) *actor operations*.

1.4.2 Values and Objects

Unlike most object-oriented programming languages, we classify ADTs into two broad categories, *value ADTs* and *object ADTs*, based on the semantics associated with those ADTs. For a clear discussion of difference between values and objects, we refer the reader to MacLennan [MacLennan 1982] and Beeri [Beeri 1990]. Paraphrasing MacLennan:

1. Values are atemporal, in the literal sense of being timeless; they are neither created nor destroyed. The best examples of values are mathematical entities, such as integer, real, complex numbers, *etc.* On the other hand, objects have a definite lifetime; they can be created and destroyed.

2. Values are immutable; they cannot be altered. When a variable x
   is assigned the value of 2, and later 1 is added to x, the number 2
   is not changed. What is changed is the number that x denotes (or
   contains). Since values are immutable, it is irrelevant whether different program segments share the same value or different "copies"
   of the value. Thus, it is meaningless to talk about the sharing of
   values.

   On the other hand, objects are mutable, *i.e.,* their state can
   change in time. Since objects are mutable, it is a crucial question
   whether they are shared or not. A change made to an object by
   one user should be made visible to all the other users who share
   that object.

3. Values are self-identifying, *i.e.,* each value is uniquely determined
   by the value itself. It is not meaningful to speak of this 2 or that
   2; there is only one 2 (it is, of course, possible to make copies of a
   representation of a value).

   On the other hand, every object is different from every other
   object, even if they have the same state, *i.e.,* the same "value."
   Each object has a unique name or identity that distinguishes it from
   any other object. An object's identity remains invariant throughout its lifetime (the notion of object identity is discussed extensively
   in [Khoshafian and Copeland 1986]).

   There is a distinction between value equality and identity
   equality for objects, whereas for values, they are one and the same.
   In fact, the default equality for values is based on the equality of
   values, while for objects, default equality is based on the equality
   of their identities.

It is possible to design a language that provides only objects (for example, Smalltalk). The problem with such languages is that it is up to the
programmer to keep track of the different instances of what were intuitively
the same value so that he or she does not accidentally update a shared value.
It is also possible to design a language that provides only values (for example,
applicative languages such as pure LISP). The problem with such languages
is the difficulty in handling state changes of shared objects. For example, it is
not uncommon to see application programs pass large data structures representing the state of the computation from one function to the next, resulting
in less clarity and poor performance.

However, most programming languages confuse values and objects, usually treating the instances of atomic data types as values and instances of non-atomic data types as objects. We believe that a language should support both values and objects and the means to use them in appropriate ways. Some applications will need complex data types with the benefit of data abstraction, but will not necessarily want to treat them as objects. For example, instances of types such as date, time, complex number, *etc.*, naturally have unchanging values and there is no need to pay the overhead associated with objects for such types.

We also believe that the application semantics, not the language designer, should decide which types are values and which are objects. If users are modelling an abstraction that is atemporal and immutable, such as dates and complex numbers, then they should use values; if they are modelling an abstraction that exists in time and is mutable, such as employees or departments, then they should use objects.

The notion of object identity is fundamental to object ADTs. Besides enabling the modelling of network structures, providing object identities for instances of object ADTs helps in removing many explicit join operations from the query formulations. It is *possible* to simulate object identity using values associated with objects, but doing so would require the existence of surrogates or some simulation of them that are guaranteed to be immutable; it would also require that (probably complex) referential integrity constraints be defined to keep multiple values in synchrony when those values are intended to represent a single object. We believe that providing object-like capabilities by such means would be awkward.

In summary, value ADTs may be viewed as having the following observable characteristics:

1. Instances of value ADTs are self-identifying; default equality of instances of value ADTs is based solely on whether they have the same value. Users may define other type-specific notions of equality.
2. Instances of value ADTs are immutable; that is, their values can never change.
3. Since instances of value ADTs are immutable, sharing of value ADT instances has no logical consequence.

On the other hand, Object ADTs may be viewed as having the following observable characteristics:

1. Instances of object ADTs have unique identity that is distinct from their values; default equality of instances of object ADTs is based solely on whether they are the same object (*i.e.*, have the same object identity under all circumstances). Users may also define other type-specific notions of equality.

2. Instances of object ADTs are mutable; that is, their values can be changed.

3. Instances of object ADTs are sharable; that is, an instance of an object ADT can be shared among many users. Changes made to an instance of object ADT are visible among all sharers.

1.4.3   Other Features

Our type system is extensible, *i.e.*, using the facilities provided by our type system, users can freely define application-specific ADTs. User-defined types may be value types or object types. Types in our type system are similar to *manifest types* of Maier [Maier 1991]. In particular, types in our type system have the properties of manifest types, as listed by Maier:

1. Abstract — Implementation of a type is hidden from clients of the type, be they other types, application programs, or end users.

2. Immediate — Type definition facilities are directly accessible to any database programmer, *i.e.*, new types can be defined using only the DDL and DML of the database system.

3. First-class — User-defined types are first-class citizens, *i.e.*, instances of user-defined types are on the same footing as instances of built-in types.

We also allow users to parameterize type definitions with both value and type parameters. This facility provides additional extensibility for the type system. A representative set of *type constructors* such as sets, multisets, tuples, lists, arrays, *etc.* are provided as built-in parameterized types. Type equivalence in our model is based on name equivalence.

We allow subtypes of types to be defined, leading to subtype-supertype hierarchies, thus encouraging reuse of type definitions. We further allow definitions of polymorphic functions and specify rules for both static and dynamic binding of function invocations to appropriate implementations. With our type system in place, SQL qualifies to be a *strongly typed language, i.e.,* all variables and expressions in SQL are typed, and all expressions are guaranteed to be type consistent although the exact run-time type of the object to which the expression evaluates is unknown at compile time.

All types in our type system, both built-in and user-defined, are abstract in that they consist of an interface and an implementation. Built-in types such as integer, real, Boolean, and built-in type constructors such as tuples, sets, multisets, *etc.* are abstract data types in that they have a system-supplied interface and implementation. They can be manipulated only by the functions defined for them, and users of these types need not be aware of how they are implemented; *e.g.,* an integer may be represented in 2's complement or 1's complement, a set may be implemented by an array, a bitmap, or a list. In addition, built-in types and type constructors are immutable (*i.e.,* no mutator functions are defined for them). The standard functions (including equality) are defined for all built-in types.

As in Beeri's model [Beeri 1990], there are no explicit references or pointer types in our model. As Beeri argues in [Beeri 1990], *"A conceptual model does not deal with storage implementation, where objects and references to them differ. Nor is there a need to manipulate objects and references to them differently. Just as in everyday language, whenever we use a name of, or a reference to, an object, we are denoting the object itself. There is no need to declare the 'dept' component of employees to be of type 'ref Dept'; the type 'Dept' suffices."* Hence, in our model, there is no difference in accessing an attribute which is of object type or of value type.

In keeping with the explicit deletion model adopted by most DBMSs, we allow instances of object ADTs to be explicitly deleted through destructor operations, in contrast to the garbage collection model adopted by some object-oriented languages. Invocation of a destructor operation results in deletion of the object from the database, possibly accompanied by various cleanup actions specified in the body of the destructor operation. Currently, we do not define referential integrity-like syntax or semantics for object ADTs, thus leaving any references to destroyed objects "dangling."

1.5
SQL3 Change Proposals

One of the most effective ways to evolve a standard (indeed, the *only* way in the SQL standardization process) is to write a detailed change proposal that documents which pieces of the existing standard need to be changed and what those changes are. Since evolving the existing type system of SQL to the proposed type system described above in one change proposal would have resulted in a tremendously large proposal, we decided to evolve the SQL type system in a series of change proposals.

In the following subsections, we describe four of the major change proposals we have written so far. These correspond to:

1. Basic ADT facility
2. Subtype-supertype hierarchies
3. Parameterized types
4. Polymorphism

All these proposals have been incorporated into the SQL3 draft standard. Note that, since their acceptance, other X3H2 committee members have changed the language. As a result, some of the syntax may not correspond to what is described here.

This paper does not cover the changes to the type system required to provide for collections of object ADT instances nor the changes to the DML of SQL to deal with such collections. One possible approach is to extend the notion of "table" to act as a multiset of object ADT instances. With this change, most of SQL DML can be used, with some syntactic modification, to manipulate the collection of object ADT instances. ANSI X3H2 committee has recently accepted a proposal made by Oracle along these lines [ANSI 1991b].

In parallel to the efforts on extending the SQL type system, our colleagues at Digital have been working on adding procedural extensions to the language in the form of multi-statement SQL functions, control and looping constructs, assignment statement, and exception handling facilities. Because of these procedural extensions, it is possible to specify implementations of ADT operations without having to escape to host programming languages. Work on adding common type constructors such as set, multiset, list, array, *etc.* and on further procedural extensions is underway.

Currently, we have retained the existing SQL restriction that tables are the only persistent structures. This restriction will be eliminated in the near future so that SQL3 can support the notion of *orthogonal persistence* [Atkinson et al. 1990].

1.5.1 Basic ADT facility

As a first step in introducing the type system described in Section 1.4, our first change proposal concerned the mechanism to define abstract data types. Since SQL3 already had the CREATE TYPE statement, we did not need any new syntax. However, we now require the user to tag the CREATE TYPE statement with VALUE or OBJECT to indicate which kind of ADT is being defined. We also require ADT functions to be defined directly in SQL rather than in a host programming language. We believe letting ADT functions to be defined outside SQL, *i.e.,* using host programming languages, leads to serious performance and safety problems.

Though an ADT's representation in our model can be in terms of any type known to the system (including types defined using type constructors), we currently require the representations to be in terms of tuple structures whose attributes can be of any type. In order to provide for strict encapsulation, we have restricted the access to an ADT's representation to references that are lexically scoped in the ADT's type definition. As a consequence, the ADT representation cannot be passed to external procedures. The reason for limiting access to references in the type definition is to localize the impact of changes. In this way, the definer of a rectangle ADT can change the representation of a rectangle, knowing that, so long as he or she preserves the semantics of the ADT operations, no client of the ADT will be affected.

Users can optionally specify functions for equality and less-than comparison of instances of the ADT being defined. Users can also specify implicit cast functions that convert an instance of the type being defined to an instance of another type and vice-versa.

We also provide for *overloading* where different functions are allowed to have the same name. For example, with overloading, one can define a NAME function for both the EMPLOYEE and DEPT abstract data types. To help the compiler determine which function is denoted by a particular use of the name, the argument lists of overloaded functions must differ in some way. Hence, either the data types of the formal parameters or the number of parameters they have must be different. (See Section 1.5.3 for the actual rules.)

Below, we give an example of a value ADT definition.

```
CREATE VALUE TYPE RATIONAL;

  REPRESENTATION IS
    TUPLE
      ( NUM INTEGER,
        DEN INTEGER );

    EQUALS RAT_EQ;

    LESS THAN RAT_LT;

  CONSTRUCTOR FUNCTION RATIONAL (:N INTEGER, :D INTEGER)
                      RETURNS RATIONAL;
    :R RATIONAL
    BEGIN
      :R.NUM := :N;
      :R.DEN := :D;
      RETURN :R;
    END;

  ACTOR FUNCTION NUM (:R RATIONAL) RETURNS INTEGER;
    RETURN :R.NUM;

  ACTOR FUNCTION DENOM (:R RATIONAL) RETURNS INTEGER;
    RETURN :R.DEN;

  ACTOR FUNCTION NORMALIZE (:R RATIONAL) RETURNS RATIONAL;
    RETURN <code to calculate the normalized value goes here>

  ACTOR FUNCTION RAT_EQ (:R1 RATIONAL, :R2 RATIONAL)
                                RETURNS BOOLEAN;
    RETURN (:R1.NUM * :R2.DEN = :R2.NUM * :R1.DEN);

  ACTOR FUNCTION RAT_LT (:R1 RATIONAL, :R2 RATIONAL)
                                RETURNS BOOLEAN;
    RETURN (:R1.NUM * :R2.DEN < :R2.NUM * :R1.DEN);
```

```
ACTOR FUNCTION RAT_DOUBLE (:R1 RATIONAL)
                                RETURNS RATIONAL;
  RETURN TUPLE (:R1.NUM * 2, :R1.DEN);


END VALUE TYPE RATIONAL;
```

The specification and implementation of objects ADTs is identical to the specification and implementation of value ADTs, except for the following differences:

1. The optional keyword OBJECT is used in the interface definition of object ADTs, while the required keyword VALUE is used in the interface definition of value ADTs.
2. The body of the constructor operations for an object ADT contains a NEW statement for allocating an object in the database.
3. Mutator operations can be specified for object ADTs.
4. Destructor operations can be specified for object ADTs.

Below, we provide an example of an object ADT definition:

```
CREATE OBJECT TYPE PERSON;

  REPRESENTATION IS
    TUPLE
      ( NAME VARCHAR,
        ADDRESS ADDRESS,
        BIRTHDATE DATE
      );

  EQUALS DEFAULT;

  LESS THAN NONE;

  CONSTRUCTOR FUNCTION PERSON (:N VARCHAR, :A ADDRESS, :B: DATE)
                    RETURNS PERSON;
    :P PERSON;
    BEGIN
```

```
     NEW :P;
     :P.NAME := :N;
     :P.ADDRESS := :A;
     :P.BIRTHDATE := B;
     RETURN :P;
   END;


 ACTOR FUNCTION AGE (:P PERSON) RETURNS INTEGER;
   RETURN <code to calculate the age goes here>;


 ACTOR FUNCTION CHANGE_ADDRESS (:P PERSON, :A ADDRESS);
   BEGIN
     :P.ADDRESS := :A;
   END;


 DESTRUCTOR FUNCTION REMOVE_PERSON (:P PERSON);
   BEGIN
     -- various other cleanup actions, if required
     DESTROY :P;
   END;


END OBJECT TYPE PERSON;
```

1.5.2   Subtype-Supertype Hierarchies

Types in our type system can be related through subtype-supertype relationships. A *subtype* is a named type defined by an abstract data type definition that contains a *subtype clause* starting with the keyword UNDER. Type T_b is called a *supertype* of T_a iff T_a is a subtype of T_b. Below, the following code defines a STUDENT type as a subtype of the PERSON type we introduced earlier:

```
CREATE OBJECT TYPE STUDENT UNDER PERSON;

 REPRESENTATION IS
   TUPLE
     ( STUDENT_ID INTEGER,
       MAJOR VARCHAR,
```

```
      YEAR INTEGER
   );

EQUALS DEFAULT;

LESS THAN NONE;

CONSTRUCTOR FUNCTION STUDENT (:N VARCHAR, :A ADDRESS,
                             :B: DATE, :ID INTEGER,
                             :M VARCHAR, :Y INTEGER
                             )
                             RETURNS STUDENT;

   :S STUDENT;
   BEGIN
     NEW :S;
     :S.NAME := :N;
     :S.ADDRESS := :A;
     :S.BIRTHDATE := B;
     :S.STUDENT_ID := :ID;
     :S.MAJOR := :M;
     :S.YEAR := :Y;
     RETURN :S;
   END;

ACTOR FUNCTION CHANGE_MAJOR (:S STUDENT, :M VARCHAR);
   BEGIN
     :S.MAJOR := :M;
   END;

DESTRUCTOR FUNCTION REMOVE_STUDENT (:S STUDENT);
   BEGIN
     -- various other cleanup actions, if required
     DESTROY :S;
   END;

END OBJECT TYPE STUDENT;
```

A subtype can define constructor, actor, and destructor operations like any other ADT. Because of overloading allowed in the model, a subtype can define operations that have the same name as operations defined on other types, including its supertypes. The argument matching rules for polymorphic functions are used to detect ambiguous cases (see Section 1.5.3).

If T_a is a subtype of T_b, then an instance of T_a can be used wherever an instance of T_b is expected, *i.e.*, every instance of T_a is also an instance of T_b.[2] In particular, if O is a function with parameter P of type T_b, then an invocation of O can use an instance of type T_a as the actual parameter P. For example, if STUDENT is a subtype of PERSON, an instance of STUDENT can be operated on by all operations that are applicable to PERSON.

In general, an instance can be associated with more than one type. We require that every instance be associated with exactly one *most specific type*, which is defined by the property that every other type associated with the instance is a supertype of the most specific type. The most specific type of an instance at run time is used to select the actual function to execute (*dynamic binding*). For example, suppose RECTANGLE is a subtype of POLYGON with the operation *perimeter* defined on both types. In an execution of a call such as *perimeter(x)*, the most specific type of the contents of x at run time is used to determine which version of *perimeter* to invoke.

Since each instance must have at most one specific type associated with it, a given instance cannot belong to other sibling types of its most specific type. However, there may be situations where such a facility is required. For example, the same person may be both a student and an employee in a college. To handle such situations, we allow a type to have more than one direct supertype. For example, we can define a type STUDENT_EMPLOYEE which is a subtype of both STUDENT and EMPLOYEE types. A person who is both a student and an employee can be modelled as an instance of the STUDENT_EMPLOYEE type. This way an instance can always be associated with a single most specific type.

If type T_a is declared to be a subtype of another type T_b, then T_a is called a *direct subtype* of T_b. If T_a is a direct subtype of T_b, then T_b is called a *direct supertype* of T_a. A subtype definition has lexical access to the representation of all of its direct supertypes (but only within the ADT definition that defines the subtype of that supertype). Effectively, the representations of all direct supertypes are copied to the subtype's representation with same name and data type. If more than one supertype has representation components

---

[2]This is termed *inclusion polymorphism* in the literature — see Section 1.5.3.

with the same name, there is a need to distinguish them when they are inherited. To resolve such name clashes, we allow the inherited components to be renamed. For example, if both STUDENT and EMPLOYEE have a NAME representation component, and if we define a STUDENT_EMPLOYEE type as a subtype of both STUDENT and EMPLOYEE types, users can rename one or both the inherited NAME representation components. The following example illustrates this:

```
CREATE OBJECT TYPE STUDENT_EMPLOYEE
   UNDER STUDENT (WITH NAME AS S_NAME), EMPLOYEE

REPRESENTATION IS
  TUPLE (
       .

       .

         );

       .

       .



END OBJECT TYPE STUDENT_EMPLOYEE;
```

1.5.3   Polymorphism

Polymorphism means the "ability to take several forms." Cardelli and Wegner define *polymorphic languages* as languages in which some values and variables may have more than one type [Cardelli and Wagner 1985]. Polymorphic functions are functions whose operands can have more than one type. Polymorphic types are types whose operations are applicable to operands of more than one type. Polymorphism is a useful property, as it permits writing programs that work not only for a range of existing types, but also for types to be added later, thus enhancing software reusability.

Our type system supports all four types of polymorphism described by Cardelli and Wegner:

1.   Overloading: In this form of polymorphism, different functions are allowed to have the same name and the context is used to decide

which function is denoted by a particular use of the name.

2. Coercion: In this form of polymorphism, an argument of a given type is converted to the type expected by a function to avoid type errors. For example, an integer value can be used where a real is expected, and vice versa. Possible type coercions may be defined by the system for predefined types or defined by the users through SQL's CAST functions.

3. Inclusion: This form of polymorphism allows objects of a subtype to be uniformly manipulated as if belonging to their supertype, as discussed in Section 1.5.2.

4. Parametric: In this form of polymorphism, a polymorphic function (or type) has an implicit or explicit type parameter. Such functions (or types) are also known as *generic* functions (or types). We discuss parametric polymorphism in Section 1.5.4.

Argument Matching Rules for Polymorphic Functions

As in C++, we adopt the rule that, for any particular function invocation, there must be a single "best match" [Ellis and Stroustrup 1990]. If there is no single best match, the invocation is ambiguous and thus not allowed.

The procedure for determining the best-matching function has two steps. The first step is to find, for each argument, all functions that have the best match. A function with the best match for the argument in question is determined by the following type conversion scheme:

1. no conversion (i.e., an exact match) is better than
2. an implicit conversion to a supertype (where the "closest" type up the tree is preferred), which in turn is better than
3. an implicit SQL-defined CAST, which in turn is better than
4. an implicit user-defined CAST.

The next step is to take the intersection of sets of functions obtained in the first step. For a single best match to exist, the intersection must have exactly one member.

Best match rules can be illustrated with the following example: suppose there is an ADT X with the following functions:

```
FUNCTION F(:p1 X, :p2 INTEGER)
FUNCTION F(:p1 X, :p2 REAL)
```

and an ADT Y with the following function:

```
FUNCTION F(:p1 Y, :p2 REAL)
```

Further, assume that the ADT X has a cast function that specifies a user-defined CAST from INTEGER to X. The set of best matches for each argument of the invocation of F(1,1) is calculated as follows:

```
set for 1st argument:      F(X,INTEGER), F(X,REAL)
set for 2nd argument:      F(X,INTEGER)
```

where the conversion from INTEGER to X is used in all three cases. The intersection of these two sets is F(X,INTEGER), so the resolution of the call F(1,1) is F(CAST(1 TO X),1).

As an example of an ambiguous case, consider the same ADT X with the following two functions:

```
FUNCTION F(:p1 X, :p2 INTEGER)
FUNCTION F(:p1 INTEGER, :p2 X)
```

If the user again invokes F with integer values 1 and 1, the set of best matches can be calculated for each argument as follows:

```
set for 1st argument:      F(INTEGER,X)
set for 2nd argument:      F(X,INTEGER)
```

Since the intersection of these sets is empty, the call F(1,1) is ambiguous.

Another case of ambiguity arises in case a type has multiple supertypes. For example, suppose type D is a subtype of both B and C which are in turn are subtypes of A. Further, suppose that there are three functions F, defined as:

```
FUNCTION F(:p1 A) RETURNS A
FUNCTION F(:p1 B) RETURNS B
FUNCTION F(:p1 C) RETURNS C
```

The best match for the invocation of F(d) where 'd' is of type D yields a set containing the two functions F(:p1 B) and F(:p1 C) and hence is ambiguous. Even the invocation F(a) where 'a' is of type A is ambiguous as the value of the variable 'a' could, at runtime, be of type D.

Such ambiguous cases are detected at compile time by considering all possible cases that might occur at runtime. The rationale is that this approach is safer than the detection of ambiguity at runtime. Accordingly, the rules we propose are:

1. Each of the runtime cases must be unambiguous, that is, the compile-time ambiguity rules described above must hold and identify for each case a unique function.
2. The set of identified functions must specify RETURNS data types such that they all share a common supertype.

Based on the rules above, an invocation of F is checked for all possible argument types, A, B, C, and D. Since there is no single best match for type D, invocation will fail to compile. An easy way to fix the problem is to define another function, say,

```
FUNCTION F(:p1 D) RETURNS D
```

Each of the four cases now resolve to a single best-match function. Also, the result types of all the four best match functions share a common supertype, A. Hence, the compilation succeeds.

As a consequence of above argument matching rules, some of the existing applications may break whenever a new subtype is defined with multiple direct supertypes and two or more of those supertypes have functions with the same name. In such cases, the types or the applications must be modified.

1.5.4   Parameterized Types

A parameterized type is an ADT with one or more parameters. The notion of parameterized types is already present in SQL, where many of the predefined SQL data types are parameterized. For instance, SQL allows the data type FLOAT to have a parameter indicating the number's precision.

It is important to extend the ability to parameterize types to user-defined types as well. For instance, suppose one wants to define a LABEL data type representing the textual label for geometric objects. It is often not possible to specify *a priori* the maximum number of characters allowed for a label. In such cases, it is important to be able to specify the maximum number of characters for a label as a parameter to the LABEL ADT.

In the above example, a *value* serves as the parameter for the type definition. Users sometimes need the ability to specify a *type* as a parameter to the type definition. For instance, one might want to define a QUEUE ADT that works for elements of any type specified by the users of the QUEUE ADT. We allow for both kinds of parameterized types.

In providing the parameterized type facility, we have adopted the approach taken in languages such as Ada and C++, *viz.*, the so-called *type generator* approach. In this approach, a parameterized type definition is treated as a type "macro" that is essentially expanded each time there is a reference to the type. The advantage of this approach is that it allows for static type checking.

Since parameterized type definitions are merely templates for generating new non-parameterized types, we call them *type template definitions*. The type generated by a particular instantiation of a type template is called a *generated type*. Note that a generated type may correspond to a nested invocation of type templates. For instance, if there are two type templates: POINT(::coord_type) and SEQUENCE(::any_type), users can generate a type that is SEQUENCE(POINT(INTEGER)).

Type template definition

A type template definition looks much like a regular abstract data type definition. However, a type template definition contains the keyword TEMPLATE and a list of template parameters. Each parameter is required to be associated with either a data type or the keyword TYPE. The former indicates the parameter is a value of the specified data type, while the latter indicates that the parameter is a type. The body of a type template may also contain the distinguished name ::GEN_TYPE which refers to the name of the type being generated. This is illustrated in the following example:

```
CREATE OBJECT TYPE TEMPLATE POINT(::T TYPE)
  REPRESENTATION IS
    TUPLE
      ( XVAL ::T,
        YVAL ::T );

    EQUALS DEFAULT;
    LESS THAN NONE;

    CONSTRUCTOR FUNCTION POINT(:X ::T, :Y ::T)
                          RETURNS ::GEN_TYPE;
      :P ::GEN_TYPE;
      BEGIN
        NEW :P;
        :P.XVAL := :X;
        :P.YVAL := :Y;
      RETURN :P;
    END;

    ACTOR FUNCTION SAME_PLACE (:P1 ::GEN_TYPE,
                               :P2 ::GEN_TYPE)
                          RETURNS BOOLEAN;
    RETURN (:P1.XVAL=P2.XVAL AND P1.YVAL=P2.YVAL)

    DESTRUCTOR FUNCTION REMOVE(:P ::GEN_TYPE);
    BEGIN
    -- various other cleanup actions, if required
      DESTROY :P;
    END;

END OBJECT TYPE TEMPLATE POINT;
```

Note that the equality operation used in the implementation of the SAME_PLACE function above is specific to the type that acts as the actual parameter in a particular instantiation of POINT. Since we adopt the macro expansion approach, the type parameter is known at compile time, and the compiler will have no problem in picking the appropriate equality operation.

As in regular ADTs, a type template may be defined as a subtype of other ADTs. For example, suppose a set of IMAGE types that vary based on image size is to be defined. If there is already a BLOB type, one can define the IMAGE type template as:

```
CREATE TYPE TEMPLATE IMAGE(::size INTEGER)
  UNDER BLOB(::size)
  REPRESENTATION IS(...)
```

There is another way in which subtype-supertype relationships and type templates interact. For instance, suppose there are two types PERSON and EMPLOYEE, where the former is a supertype of the latter and a type template SEQUENCE. There may be cases where it is desirable to treat the generated type SEQUENCE(EMPLOYEE) as a subtype of the generated type SEQUENCE(PERSON). However, there may be other cases where the two generated types have no relationship. Currently, the SQL3 draft assumes there is no relationship between the two types.

1.6
Comparison with Previous Work

There have been many efforts to add ADTs to relational systems in the past [Osborn and Heaven 1986, Stonebraker 1986, Linnemann et al. 1988, Wilms et al. 1988, Gardarin et al. 1989]. Typically, ADTs in these approaches are not really abstract in that the representation of an ADT is not properly encapsulated. The definer of an ADT is expected to know the underlying representations of all ADTs referenced directly or indirectly by the operation. ADTs in these approaches are also not immediate in that the operations for an ADT are expected to be written in an external host language, not the DDL and DML of the database itself. Because ADTs in these approaches are not immediate, users are forced to make a tradeoff between safety and performance of the system. ADTs in these approaches are also not first-class since instances of user-defined ADTs cannot be made persistent unless they are attributes of a table. Also, the type system in these approaches did not support the concept of object identity or the concept of type constructors such as sets, lists, *etc.*

In contrast to these approaches, many other efforts attempted to generalize the attribute types of tables to complex types such as sets, lists, and relations, so-called non-first normal form or nested relational models [Jaeschke and Schek 1982, Fischer and Thomas 1983, Abiteboul and Bidoit 1988, Roth et al. 1987, Schek and Scholl 1986, Colby 1989, Gyssens et al. 1989, Korth and Roth 1989, Pistor and Anderson 1986, Dadam et al. 1986, Bancilhon et al. 1987]. All these efforts fail to provide for data abstraction and an extensible type system.

The type system described in this paper closely resembles the type systems found in many object-oriented database systems, *e.g.*, Iris [Fishman et al. 1987], ORION [Banerjee et al. 1988], EXODUS [Carey et al. 1988], GemStone [Maier et al. 1986], O2 [Lecluse et al. 1988], Objectivity/DB [Objectivity 1990], ENCORE [Zdonik 1991] , GOM [Kemper et al. 1991], PDM [Manola and Dayal 1986], Relational Object Model [Scholl and Schek 1990], *etc.* All these models try to combine object-oriented concepts such as data abstraction, inheritance, *etc.* with the concept of bulk types and operators of the relational data model. Other efforts that follow an approach somewhat similar to ours are: ESQL [Finance and Gardarin 1991], Intelligent SQL [Khoshafian 1990a] and OSQL [Lyngbaek et al. 1991].

1.7
Conclusions

The programming language notions of types and abstraction provide significant power to both application modelling and application development. We have demonstrated that it is possible to incorporate an ADT-based type system into SQL in an upward-compatible way. We have described the major elements of such a type system and some of the steps we have taken in realizing those elements in the standards framework.

Though we have introduced significant extensions to the SQL type system towards an extensible type system, there is still a lot of work to be done. We are currently working on adding type constructors such as sets, multisets, lists, arrays, and tuples. Other issues pertaining to the usability of the language concern facilities for general-purpose computation, extensions to the query language to deal with collections of object ADT instances, constraints, triggers, views, recursion, and authorization mechanisms.

We believe that our type system meets most of the criteria set forth in both the Third-Generation Database System Manifesto [Stonebraker et al. 1990] and the Object-Oriented Database System Manifesto [Atkinson et al. 1990]. In particular, our type system meets the following mandatory features of the Object-Oriented Database System Manifesto: complex objects, object identity, encapsulation, type hierarchies, overriding, overloading and late binding, extensibility, and ad hoc query facility. We also provide the optional feature of multiple inheritance. With the provision of other mandatory features such as classes, class hierarchies, and orthogonal persistence where objects of all types are allowed to be persistent, SQL3 will meet all the criteria set forth in the Object-Oriented Database System Manifesto.

Acknowledgment

We would like to acknowledge the assistance of Andrew Eisenberg, Rivka Ladin, and Ken Moore in refining some of the ideas reported in this paper.

Bibliography

[Abiteboul and Bidoit 1988] S. Abiteboul and N. Bidoit. Non First Normal Form Relations to Represent Hierarchically Organized Data. *Proc. of ACM Symp. Principles of Database Systems*, pp. 191-200, 1984.

[ANSI 1986] American National Standards Institute. ANSI X3.135-1986, *Database Language SQL*, 1986.

[ANSI 1989] American National Standards Institute. ANSI X3.135-1989, *Database Language SQL*, 1989.

[ANSI 1991a] American National Standards Institute. X3/SPARC/DBSSG/ OODBTG Final Report, September 1991.

[ANSI 1991b] American National Standards Institute. Tables and Subtables as Sets of Objects (by D. Beech and H. Rizvi). *X3H2-91-142rev1*, 1991.

[Atkinson et al. 1990] M. Atkinson, F. Bancilhon, D. DeWitt, K. Dittrich, D. Maier, and S. Zdonik. The Object-Oriented Database System Manifesto. In *Deductive and Object-Oriented Databases*, W. Kim, J.M. Nicholas, and S. Nishio (editors), Elsevier Science Publishers, 1990.

[Bancilhon et al. 1987] F. Bancilhon et al. FAD, A Simple and Powerful Database Language. *Proc. of VLDB Conf.*, pp. 97-105, 1987.

[Banerjee et al. 1988] J. Banerjee, W. Kim, and K.C. Kim. Queries in Object-Oriented Databases. *Proc. of International Conf. on Data Engineering*, pp. 31-38, 1988.

[Beeri 1990] C. Beeri. Formal Models for Object-Oriented Databases. In *Deductive and Object-Oriented Databases*, W. Kim, J.M. Nicholas, and S. Nishio (editors), Elsevier Science Publishers, 1990.

[Cardelli and Wagner 1985] L. Cardelli and P. Wegner. On Understanding Types, Data Abstraction, and Polymorphism. *ACM Computing Surveys*, 17(4):471-522, 1985.

[Carey et al. 1988] M.J.Carey, D.J.DeWitt, and S.L.Vandenberg. A Data Model and Query Language for EXODUS. *Proc. of ACM SIGMOD Conf.*, pp. 413-423, 1988.

[Chamberlin et al. 1976] D.D. Chamberlin et al. SEQUEL 2: A Unified Approach to Data Definition, Manipulation and Control. *IBM Journal of Research and Development*, 20(6):560-575, 1976.

[Colby 1989] L. Colby. A Recursive Algebra and Query Optimization for Nested Relations. *Proc. of ACM SIGMOD Conf.*, pp. 273-283, 1989.

[Dadam et al. 1986] P. Dadam et al. A DBMS Prototype to Support Extended NF2 Relations: An Integrated View on Flat Tables and Hierarchies. *Proc. of ACM SIGMOD Conf.*, pp. 356-367, 1986.

[Dayal 1990] U. Dayal. Queries and Views in an Object-Oriented Data Model. *Proc. of 2nd International Workshop on Database Programming Languages*, R. Hull, R. Morrison, and D. Stemple (editors), pp. 80-102, Morgan Kaufmann, 1990.

[Ellis and Stroustrup 1990] M. Ellis and B. Stroustrup. The Annotated C++ Reference Manual. *Addison-Wesley*, 1990.

[Finance and Gardarin 1991] B. Finance and G. Gardarin. A Rule-Based Query Rewriter in an Extensible DBMS. *Proc. of Seventh International Conference on Data Engineering*, pp. 248-256, 1991.

[Fischer and Thomas 1983] P. Fischer and S. Thomas. Operations for Non First Normal Form Relations. *Proc. of IEEE COMPSAC Conf.*, pp. 464-475, 1983.

[Fishman et al. 1987] D. Fishman et al. Iris: An Object-Oriented Database Management System. *ACM Trans. on Office Information Systems*, 5(1):48-69, 1987.

[Gardarin et al. 1989] G. Gardarin et al. Managing Complex Objects in an Extensible DBMS. *Proc. of VLDB Conf.*, pp. 55-65, 1989.

[Guttag 1977] J. Guttag. Abstract Data Types and the Development of Data Structures. *Communications of ACM*, 20(6):396-404, 1977.

[Gyssens et al. 1989] M. Gyssens, J. Paredaens, and D. Van Gucht. A Uniform Approach toward handling Atomic and Structured Information in the Nested Relational Database Model. *J. ACM*, 36(4):790-825, 1989.

[Hughes 1991] J.G. Hughes. *Object-Oriented Databases*. Prentice-Hall, 1991.

[Hull and King 1987] R. Hull and R. King. Semantic Database Modelling: Survey, Applications, and Research Issues. *ACM Computing Surveys*, 19(3):201-260, 1987.

[Ingres 1989] Ingres Object Management Extension for the Unix and VMS Operating Systems, Release 6.3, 1989.

[ISO 1987] International Organization for Standardization ISO 9075-1987 *Database Language SQL*, 1987.

[ISO 1989] International Organization for Standardization ISO 9075:1989 *Database Language SQL*, 1989.

[ISO 91] ISO91 International Organization for Standardization ISO DIS 9075:1991 *Database Language SQL*, 1991.

[Jaeschke and Schek 1982] G. Jaeschke and H. Schek. Remarks on the Algebra of Non First Normal Form Relations. *Proc. of ACM Symp. Principles of Database Systems*, pp. 124-138, 1982.

[Kemper et al. 1991] A. Kemper, G. Moerkotte, H.D. Walter, and A. Zachmann. GOM: A Strongly Typed, Persistent Object Model with Polymorphism. *Proc. of BTW*, Springer-Verlag, pp. 198-217, 1991.

[Khoshafian and Copeland 1986] S. Khoshafian and G. Copeland. Object Identity. *Proc. of ACM Conf. on Object-Oriented Programming Systems, Languages, and Applications*, pp. 406-416, 1986.

[Khoshafian 1990a] S. Khoshafian. Intelligent SQL. *Proc. of the Object-oriented Database Task Group Workshop*, pp. 136-164, May 22, 1990.

[Kim and Lochovsky 1989] W. Kim and F.H. Lochovsky (editors). *Object-Oriented Concepts, Databases, and Applications*, Addison-Wesley Publishing Company, 1989.

[Korth and Roth 1989] H. Korth and M.A. Roth. Query Languages for Nested Relational Databases. In *Nested Relations and Complex Objects in Databases*, Springer-Verlag, 1989.

[Lecluse et al. 1988] C. Lecluse, P. Richard, and F. Velez. O2, an Object-Oriented Data Model. *Proc. of ACM SIGMOD Conf.*, pp. 424-433, 1988.

[Linnemann et al. 1988] V. Linnemann et al. Design and Implementation of an Extensible Database Management System Supporting User Defined Data Types and Functions. *Proc. of VLDB Conf.*, pp. 294-305, 1988.

[Lyngbaek et al. 1991] P. Lyngbaek et al. OSQL: A Language for Object Databases. *Hewlett-Packard Technical Report*, HPL-DTD-91-4, 1991.

[MacLennan 1982] B.J. MacLennan. Objects in Programming Languages. *ACM SIGPLAN Notices*, 17(12):70-79, 1982.

[Maier et al. 1986] D. Maier et al. Development of an Object-Oriented DBMS. *Proc. of ACM Conf. on Object-Oriented Programming Systems, Languages, and Applications*, pp. 472-482, 1986.

[Maier 1991] D. Maier. Comments on the Third-Generation Data Base System Manifesto. *Unpublished Report*, 1991.

[Manola and Dayal 1986] F. Manola and U. Dayal. PDM: An Object-Oriented Data Model. *Proc. of International Workshop on Object-Oriented Database Systems*, 1986.

[Melton 1991] J. Melton (editor). Database Language SQL3. *ISO-ANSI Working Draft*, 1991.

[Objectivity 1990] *Objectivity/DB System Overview*. Objectivity Inc., 1990.

[Osborn and Heaven 1986] Osborn, S. and Heaven, T. The Design of Relational Database System with Abstract Data Types for Domains, *ACM Trans. on Database Systems*, pp. 357-373, 1986.

[Peckham and Maryanski 1988] J. Peckham and F. Maryanski. Semantic Data Models. *ACM Computing Surveys*, 20(3):153-189, 1988.

[Pistor and Anderson 1986] P. Pistor and F. Anderson. Designing a Generalized NF2 Model with an SQL-Type Language Interface. *Proc. of VLDB Conf.*, pp. 278-285, 1986.

[Roth et al. 1987] M.A. Roth, H.F. Korth, and D.S. Batory. SQL/NF: A Query Language for -1NF Relational Databases. *Information Systems*, 12(1):99-114, 1987.

[Schek and Scholl 1986] H.J. Schek and M.H. Scholl. The Relational Model with Relation-valued Attributes. *Information Systems*, 11(2):137-147, 1986.

[Scholl and Schek 1990] M.H. Scholl and H.J. Schek. A Relational Object Model. *Proc. of International Conf. on Database Theory*, pp. 89-105, 1990.

[Stonebraker 1986] M. Stonebraker. Inclusion of New Types in Relational Database Systems. *Proc. of IEEE Data Engg. Conf.*, pp. 262-269, February 1986.

[Stonebraker et al. 1990] M. Stonebraker, L.A.Rowe, B. Lindsay, J. Gray, M. Carey, M. Brodie, P. Bernstein, D. Beech. Third-Generation Data Base System Manifesto. *ACM SIGMOD Record*, 19(3), 1990.

[Wilms et al. 1988] Wilms, P., Schwartz, P., Schek, H. and Haas, L. Incorporating Data Types in an extensible architecture. *Proc. of International Conf. on Data and Knowledge Bases*, pp. 180-192, 1988.

[Zdonik and Maier 1989] S.B. Zdonik and D. Maier (editors). *Readings in Object-Oriented Database Systems*. Morgan Kaufmann, 1989.

[Zdonik 1991] S.B. Zdonik. ENCORE: An Object-Oriented Approach to Database Modelling and Querying. *IEEE Data Engineering Bulletin*, 14, 1991.

2

Integration of Composite Objects into Relational Query Processing: The SQL/XNF Approach

Bernhard Mitschang
Hamid Pirahesh

2.1
Introduction

Complex database applications, such as design applications, multi-media and AI applications, and even enhanced business applications can benefit significantly from a database language that supports composite objects. The data used by such applications are often shared with more traditional applications, such as cost accounting, project management, etc. Hence, sharing of the data among traditional applications and complex object applications is important.

Our approach, called SQL Extended Normal Form (short SQL/XNF) provides a general framework that supports novel processing models based on composite objects. Especially, it enhances relational technology by a composite object facility, which comprises not only extraction of composite objects from a shared database, but also adequate browsing and manipulation facilities provided by an appropriate application programming interface. Further on, the language allows sharing of the database among normal form SQL applications and complex object applications. SQL/XNF provides sub-object sharing and recursion, all based on its powerful composite object constructor concept, which is closed under the language operations. SQL/XNF DDL and DML are a superset of SQL, and are downward compatible with SQL.

In this paper we concentrate on query processing issues for composite objects. We discuss the main ideas underlying the integration of composite object processing into a relational framework and contrast this to common relational query processing. We also report on the realization of these concepts in our implementation of SQL/XNF as an extension to the Starburst DBMS.

2.2
Motivation

Complex applications, such as design applications, multi-media and AI applications, and even enhanced business applications ask for a database processing model that is different to the conventional ones. The idea is to have a processing model that naturally supports in each state of application processing the actual processing context or 'working set.' Such a **context** defines the amount of data needed to perform a specific application task. E.g., VLSI design is done one step at a time using different tools: a synthesis tool is used to transform logic description of a chip into chip structure data, which is then used by the planning tool to design the floorplan that, in turn, is fed into the chip assembly tool in order to get out the mask layout that is needed for chip manufacturing. The process model adopted by each tool is characterized by first reading its input data, then working in this context, and finally writing its output data (that in most cases is then input data of the subsequent tool that takes over). Similar scenarios exist in mechanical CAD, geographic applications (i.e., geographic information systems), and even in software engineering: each tool selects its input data (e.g., the surface geometry of an airplane, the street maps for the downtown area of Berlin, the software module ' index manager' of DB2), i.e., context data of say 10MBytes, out of a shared database in the TBytes range covering all the applications' CAD data.

Zooming into the data that defines a context for a tool, we recognize that a context consists of components that are related to each other according to the applications' semantics. E.g., the (input) context for the chip planning tool describes the structure of the 'cell under design' consisting of components defining the sub-cells together with their area estimations, and components giving the net data as well as the pin data that define the connections between the sub-cells relating sub-cell components through pins on the same net [Wiederhold 1986]. Similarly, geometric models [Mortenson 1985] like CSG (constructive solid geometry), BREP (boundary representation), or spline-based geometry representations are used in CAD applications, and topology-based models [Guenther 1991] prevail geography applications in order to represent the context data. This analysis characterizes a context as a so-called **composite (or complex) object** (shortly, **CO**) consisting of several components (possibly from different types) with relationships in between. In the following, we prefer the notion of composite object in order to emphasize that a CO is composed of multiple interrelated components; still it can show a complex inner structure that is transparent at the CO level. Of course different tools and applications may have different COs that may overlap. Therefore COs are mostly 'views' (**object views** or **structured views**) composed from a shared database.

The provision of a context requires from the application program the specification of the context data (and data structures) and from the underlying database management system (DBMS) efficient delivery of the component and relationship data. This means for the DBMS to provide, on the one hand, an adequate interface that allows the application program to define its contexts in form of declaratively (and not procedurally) specified composite objects. On the other hand, the DBMS has to extract the CO, i.e., its components and relationships, out of the shared database through efficient subsetting, i.e., qualification, and structuring. Once a context is extracted (and loaded), the application program works with the context data, mostly navigating by means of the relationships defined. When the context is properly defined there is no object-faulting any more. This contrasts the processing model most object-oriented systems apply, that is, after having specified some object as 'starting points' the applications navigate over the object network using the relationships (pointers or references) installed. There, object-faulting is not precluded as is in the context-based processing model described above.

Since relational technology is generally accepted and widely used in traditional as well as in engineering applications, a lot of data is already stored in relational databases and accessed through those applications. Even more data is being transferred from flat files and navigational DBMSs such as IMS and DBTG-type systems to relational systems. The major goal and driving force in doing this is sharing of data between multiple application types, i.e., among traditional applications and CO applications.

From a practical point of view there is a need to bridge the gap between a relational store (i.e., data stored in relational DBMSs) and the CO abstraction level mentioned before. The XNF approach provides solutions to this problem offering a CO interface to relational data and handling CO at the application interface. In order to do this, the XNF approach must comprise

- a sound language and data model that unifies composite objects and relational concepts,

- an application programming interface that adequately supports navigation and manipulation, and

- an efficient implementation approach.

In this paper we concentrate on query processing issues for composite objects. We discuss the main ideas underlying integration of composite object processing into a relational framework and contrast this to common relational query processing. We also report on the realization of these concepts in our implementation of SQL/XNF as an extension to Starburst DBMS [Haas 1990]. The rest of the paper is organized as follows: Section 2.3 describes the XNF approach to composite objects. Then, in Section 2.4, we repeat the main steps and issues in relational query processing, and Section 2.5 talks about processing of CO queries. Issues in query representation as well as rewrite optimization are the main focus. Section 2.6 draws a line to related work and gives an outlook to future work after having summarized the main achievements of XNF and its realization in Starburst. For the course of the paper it is assumed that the reader is familiar with SQL syntax and semantics [ISO-ANSI 1989].

2.3
SQL/XNF Approach to Complex Objects

In bridging the gap between relational data and CO abstraction, XNF has to handle COs that are stored in relational DBMSs. This means, the components and the relationships that are part of a CO definition must incorporate the relational data or, speaking the other way around, components and relationships have to be derived from the relational data, i.e., from the tuples stored in flat tables. In the words of [Lee 1990], the COs have to be instantiated form relations by evaluating view queries.

The major achievements of the XNF approach to be described in this chapter are:

- sharing of components both within and between objects, thus permitting an (component) object to play multiple roles in relationships to other or the same objects,

- recursive COs, where an object may have subobjects that, in turn, may have subobjects, arbitrarily deep, enabling, e.g., bill-of-material processing or management of organization hierarchies,

- CO views, allowing different COs to be defined over the same shared data.

- retention of benefits from the relational model, like declarative queries over COs, closure of the model w.r.t. its query language, and provision of a consistent extension of the relational data model,

- CO abstraction, that is, data contained in existing relational DBMSs can be presented to applications at an appropriate level of abstraction.

2.3.1   Basic Concepts, Syntax, and Semantics

Instead of the relational view concept (with its by default normalized result relation), we would rather apply a more ER-likeconcept [Chen 1976] and have the components of the view kept separate and the relationships in between made explicit in order to reach the desired CO representation. Even modern systems like IBM's Repository Manager or the set of Bachmann's tools [Bachman 1989] rely on an ER-based view to the applications' (composite) data. This way of thinking is at the heart of the XNF approach and embodied in XNF's powerful **CO constructor** that constitutes an XNF query. These queries define CO views (i.e., structured views), which can be seen as an extension to the SQL view concepts towards multi-table views that are organized as collections of inter-related rows. In the context of XNF, these CO views are known as **XNF views** that are defined through XNF queries. Unless otherwise noted, both terms are treated interchangeable in the following discussions. The basic building blocks for an **XNF query** are:

- **XNF tables** are nothing different than tables in the relational model. These normal form (NF) tables have attributes and are populated by corresponding tuples that are derived from the underlying (relational) database. In general table expressions are used to define these tables. For graphical representation, tables are drawn as nodes in the form of rectangles.

- **XNF relationships** are similar to the relationships known from the ER approach but, analogously to XNF tables, derived from the base data. A relationship is defined between its partner tables by means of a **predicate**. In contrast to many ER models, we allow n-ary relationships since we can relate more than two partner tables in a relationship. The notion of roles (same as in ER models [Chen 1976]) is known, since partners can play certain roles w.r.t. a relationship. In addition there might be attributes defined for the relationship. Relationships are populated by so-called **connections** that represent the relations existing between the corresponding partner tuples. Speaking in relational terms, we can say that connections are tuples that show the foreign keys of the partner tuples they reference and the relationship attributes if defined. Drawing this analogy is very useful, because we can treat relationships very similar to tables. For this reason, the term table or component table refers to both, unless otherwise noted. For graphical representation purposes, relationships are drawn as small black diamonds connected to the nodes that represent their partners.

The CO constructor is a proper extension to SQL by a compound query statement that allows the specification of a collection of tables, populated with the records one needs to see, and of the relationships among the resulting records. An XNF query is identified by the keywords OUT OF and consists of the following parts:

- definitions for the component tables, identified by the keyword SELECT,

- definitions for the relationships, identified by the keyword RELATE, and

- specifications for the output, identified by the keyword TAKE.

Component and relationship definitions make out XNF's CO constructor. With this, an XNF query simply reads like this:

'OUT OF ... the CO (that is constructed by the CO constructor)

TAKE ... the parts projected (that define the resulting CO)'

As an introduction to XNF syntax and semantics, let us discuss the example CO 'deps-k55' given by Figure 2.1. The upper part of Figure 2.1 shows on the left the schema and on the right the instance level for CO 'deps-k55', whereas the lower part of Figure 2.1 gives the corresponding query that defines this compelx object.

As shown by this sample XNF query, the nodes, i.e. the component tables, are derived through standard SQL queries. Syntactic shortcuts (see definition of xemp, xproj, and xskills component table) are provided for sake of brevity. In our example the base tables departments (DEPT), employees (EMP), projects (PROJ), and skills (SKILLS) are used for derivation. The relationship tables that make up the edges show a different syntax, but basically also apply SQL queries for their definition. In order to read the query in a convenient way, we have given role names (VIA clause) to the parent partners of the relationships. Based upon the relationship predicates (given in the WHERE clauses), the relationships (identified by the key word RELATE) defined establish for any given department connections to the employees it EMPLOYS, to the projects it HAS, and to the skills that either one of its employees POSSESSES or one of its projects NEEDS, or both.

By means of the USING clause, a relationship may use data not only from its partner tables but also from other tables. For example, the two relationships empproperty and projproperty define many-to-many relationships that are derived from the mapping tables EMPSKILLS and PROJSKILLS. The EMPSKILLS (PROJSKILLS) table holds information about skills possessed (needed) by an employee (project). Mapping tables are the typical way of modeling many-to-many relationships in relational DBMSs. Therefore, these tables are only important for the processing of the relationship and for the establishment of the derived connections, but they are not needed in the result of the XNF query, hence they do not appear at the CO abstraction level.

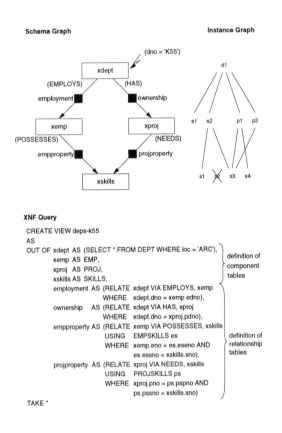

FIGURE 2.1
Sample CO 'deps-k55'

Retrieval of such an XNF CO results in retrieval of the tuples defined by the XNF tables and provision for the relationship information defined by the XNF relationships. Of course not all the tuples of XNF tables are meaningful for a specific CO. In the above example, obviously, only those tuples, for which there is an existing connection, are meaningful components w.r.t. the CO. That is, only those components that are reachable within the CO are important for the CO. This concept, named reachability, restricts to only the relevant components of a CO. Reachability says that each component of a CO must be reachable from another component of the same CO through a relationship instance that also has to exist in that CO. The so-called roots (or root components, e.g. department tuples (xdept)) are reachable by definition, since they define the anchors of the COs.

So far, an XNF CO specifies a heterogeneous set of records with different record formats. If a component tuple is multiply used within a view then it exists, of course, only once in the view, but it participates in multiple connections (possibly from different relationships). Therefore the important notion of **object sharing** is a fundamental part of the XNF CO concept. Sharing of components can occur either because of (n:m) relationships (then it is also called instance sharing) or because of overlapping relationship definitions (then called schema sharing). Both types of sharing are naturally incorporated into XNF and can coexist. Schema sharing can be made visible by the so-called **schema graph**, which is built from the XNF tables used as nodes and the XNF relationships being the edges (see Figure 2.1). The graph visualizes the structural (as well as schema or type level) aspects of the corresponding CO. It is a very simple but expressive presentation form that is very useful when working with queries involving XNF views. Due to the reachability feature, there is a notion of parent and child partners w.r.t. relationships. This defines a direction to the relationships, which in turn makes the whole schema graph a directed graph. The arrow that is used to draw the edges gives the direction. Nodes having no incoming edge (i.e., these nodes are no child partners in any relationship) are termed root nodes. If the schema graph shows cycles, the XNF query specifies a **recursive CO**, otherwise it defines a non-recursive CO. Those nodes having more than one incoming edge are shared between their partners. This makes up schema sharing and it is referred to as **non-disjoint (shared) COs**. At the instance level we can view the nodes' tuples and the relationships' connections as being organized in a so-called **instance graph** that is built in analogy to the corresponding schema graph (see Figure 2.1).

XNF COs may be combined, projected, and restricted. Combination is simply done by definition of a relationship between any node of one CO and a node of another. Projection is defined by listing all the nodes and combining relationships to be retained. The star '*' is used as a special syntactic construct for projection of all the components with their attributes and all the relationships defined. Restriction can be done through additional predicates on the node tables and the relationships. All retrieval and manipulation operations of the XNF language work at the XNF level, taking into account the given graph structure and the heterogeneous tuple set. Since the result of an XNF query consists of a set of component tables and relationship tables, an XNF query (or XNF view) can be used as input for a subsequent XNF query or view definition. Because all operations stay in the framework defined by XNF queries (or XNF views), the model is closed under its language operations.

2.3.2   API for XNF

Once an XNF query is processed and the CO consisting of components and relationships has been extracted, the application programs want to work with the CO through an adequate application programming interface (API) that supports manipulation and navigation along the given relationships. At the moment two kinds of APIs are envisioned:

- The **structure loader** loads the data in the desired format into an application-provided data space. This supports applications that, for some reasons, have specific format requirements. Manipulation and browsing of the CO is done by mechanisms provided in the application programming environment, e.g., in a C++ environment browsing can be efficiently accomplished by pointer dereferencing.

- Alternatively, a **cursor-based API** allows for individual component-oriented access. Here, each root node has a cursor associated that can be OPENed and FETCHed in order to produce successive instances of the root node. In addition, direct as well as indirect child nodes will have also cursors attached that are automatically (re-)OPENed with each FETCH from its parent cursors. Using these (hierarchical) cursors, the entire CO can be traversed.

Of course there are other kinds of API conceivable and currently under investigation, but for the purpose of this paper the above given abstract view to a CO API is sufficient.

2.3.3   Implementation Strategy and Overview

As shown in Figure 2.2 SQL/XNF can be seen as a language processor that creates COs and their constituting components and relationships by derivation/instantiation from relational data. Likewise to sharing of the (NF) database between traditional SQL applications and XNF applications, these two types of applications do also share their base 'relational engine' (that is the DBMS software, e.g., an SQL DBMS). This kind of architecture allows on the one hand the traditional SQL application to run unchanged in its known environment. On the other hand, the XNF application can work at the CO level through the XNF interface that is realized by the XNF language processor. XNF queries are translated to (optimized) NF queries that are executable by the underlying relational engine. This way, XNF's CO processing is integrated into the relational framework (not an on-top solution) , thus benefiting from the wealth of available relational technology (e.g., representation structures for queries, query rewrite and optimization, storage and access structures etc.).

2.4
Relational Query Processing

Before talking about query processing for (XNF) COs, we want to give a better understanding of relational query processing. As our sample system, we use the Starburst Extensible Database System that is best described in [Haas 1990]. Most interesting are the relational language processor being described next and the internal representation structure for queries that will be presented thereafter.

2.4.1   Starburst's Language Processor CORONA

Processing of the data manipulation language is done by first, compilation of the query, and secondly, execution. Starburst consists of two components that match these two stages: the query language processor CORONA [Haas 1989], and the data man-ager CORE [Lindsay 1986]. CORONA compiles queries (written in an extended SQL version) into calls to the underlying CORE services to fetch and modify data. Roughly speaking, CORE and CORONA correspond to System R's [Astrahan 1976] RSS (Relational Storage System) and RDS (Relational Data System).

As depicted in Figure 2.3, there are five distinguishable stages of query processing in CORONA; each stage is represented by a corresponding system component. An incoming SQL query is first broken into tokens and then parsed into an internal query representation called **Query Graph Model** (shortly **QGM**). Only valid queries are accepted, because semantic analysis is also done in this first stage. During query rewrite, the QGM representation of the query is transformed (rewritten by transformation rules) into an equiva-

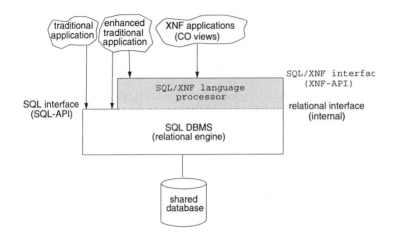

FIGURE 2.2
General Architecture of the SQL/XNF Language Processor

lent one that (hopefully) leads to a better performing execution strategy when
processed by the subsequent stage of plan optimization. Plan optimization
chooses a possible execution strategy based on estimated execution costs, and
writes the resulting Query Execution Plan (QEP) as the output of the compilation phase. This evaluation plan is then repackaged by the plan refinement
stage for more efficient execution by the Query Evaluation System (QES). At
runtime QES executes the QEP against the database. Thereby, each QES
routine interprets one QEP operator, which takes one or more streams of
tuples as input and produces one or more streams as output.

2.4.2   Starburst's Query Graph Model

The query graph model is an internal semantic network that describes
the query during all stages of compilation. Since Starburst was designed to
be an extensible database system also w.r.t. language extensions, the design
of QGM had to be able to cope with these kind of extensions. Therefore
orthogonality and flexibility were among the cornerstones of the QGM design.

From a logical point of view QGM can be understood as a kind of entity-

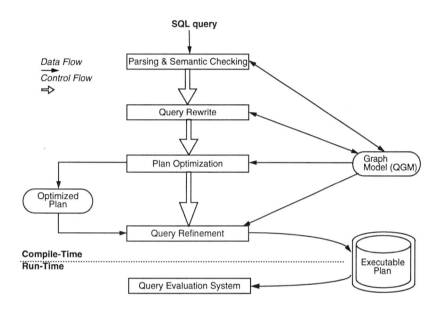

FIGURE 2.3
Stages of Query Processing

relationship model that maintains attributes of query entities (e.g., base tables, derived tables, columns predicates) and the relationships in between
(e.g., columns belonging to tables, predicates defined over columns and constants, predicates restricting tables). Thus, QGM can be regarded as the
'schema' for a main memory database that stores information about a query.
For a complete description of QGM and of the query transformations it permits for rewriting, we refer to [Hasan 1988]. Here we want to introduce some
basic concepts through a detailed discussion of the Starburst SQL query and
its corresponding QGM structure given in Figure 2.4.

QGM is based on the notion of table abstraction. That is, queries are
represented as a series of high level operations (e.g., SELECT, GROUP BY,
INSERT, UPDATE, DELETE, UNION, INTERSECTON) on either base tables (i.e., physically stored ones) or derived tables. An operation consists of

a head and a body: the head describes the output table and the body shows
how this table has to be derived from other tables the body refers to. In our
graphical notation we represent the operation by a box that consists of a big
rectangle that is labeled with the operation's name and that also covers the
operation's body, and small rectangles on the top that make up the operation's head. Scanning a table produces a stream of tuples that has properties
such as order, duplicates or no duplicates, cost etc., which are used by the
optimization step.

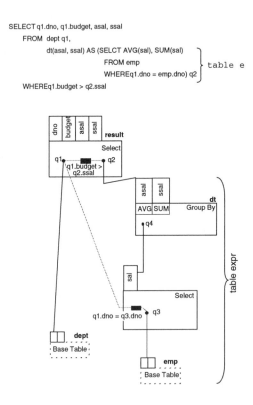

FIGURE 2.4
Sample Query and Corresponding QGM Structure

The query from Figure 2.4 retrieves for each department (range variable q1 over base table dept) the department number (dno) and department budget (budget) as well as the computed average salary (asal) and the

sum of all salaries (ssal) of the employees working for this department, if the department budget is greater than the derived sum of salaries. This query uses the language concept of derived tables: the table dt is such a derived table that is computed by a table expression given by the inner SELECT...FROM...WHERE construct that, in turn, uses the correlation concept for associating employees to their valid departments. As shown by the range variable q2 being defined over table dt, derived tables and base tables are treated the same. These logical parts of the query are easily detectable in the corresponding QGM graph. The upper QGM box is labeled 'Select' and realizes a SELECT operation, which might perform selection, projection, and join. This box represents the outer SELECT...FROM...WHERE construct. The head of this box shows the result table (here the columns dno, budget, asal, and ssal) of the query. The body consists of two vertices (called set formers) q1 and q2 that realize the two table references of the FROM clause. These set formers range over their associated tables, i.e., q1 ranges over the base table dept and q2 over the derived table dt. This is drawn as edges (called range edges). The other edge that connects q1 and q2 (called the qualifier edge and drawn as a dotted edge) gives the join predicate from the WHERE clause. The rest of this QGM graph is devoted to derive the table dt. The lowest box also labeled 'Select' ranges over the base table emp (indicated by the internally introduced set former q3) and retrieves the employees that work for the department specified by the qualifier edge that governs the correlation to q1, i.e., to the departments. The box labeled 'Group By' uses the set former q4 that ranges over the previously discussed table. The operation associated with this kind of box is grouping of tuples from the input table (referred to by set former q4) and application of aggregate functions (AVG and SUM) to each group.

At an abstract level we can interpret the QGM graph being generated like this: For each tuple within the tuple stream that comes out of the 'Base Table' box, the result box has to do two tasks. First the derived table dt has to be generated w.r.t. the actual department. In order to do this, the 'Group By' box has to be evaluated, which needs the output stream from the lowest 'Select' box. This box, i.e., operator, is responsible for selection of those employees that relate to the actual department given by the correlation predicate. Secondly after table dt has been derived, the join and the qualification are performed in order to derive the result table for this query graph.

2.5
Composite Object Processing

For a moment let us reconsider the things said before, and then let us put the pieces together: From Section 2.4 we have learned how to derive the result table from an (SQL) query, and the message from Section 2.3 was that COs are instantiated from the underlying relational database by derivation of the component node tables and the component relationship tables. So, CO processing in a relational framework simply means derivation of the CO's component tables; and in order to do this, we will use the techniques introduced in the previous section.

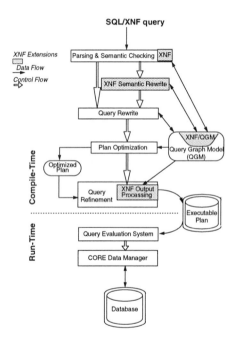

FIGURE 2.5
Stages of XNF Query Processing

2.5.1   Overview of XNF Language Processing

The XNF language processor (cf. Section 2.3.3) is developed as an extension to Starburst's CORONA. The distinguished stages of XNF query processing are shown in Figure 2.5. Those features that are different to the ones used in the traditional Starburst CORONA (and shown in Figure 2.3) are shaded and all the common ones are shown unchanged. Figure 2.5 already exposes that the XNF language processor is truly an extension to CORONA's standard SQL processor. Basically we can distinguish three consecutive steps in XNF compilation. In order to emphasize more on the integration of CO processing into the relational framework, and for better understanding of the specific extensions we explain the corresponding components and their in-going and out-coming data structures. This discussion will clearly disclose that the extensions only affect the compilation part: parsing, semantic check-ing, and rewrite as well as the internal query representation (i.e., QGM) have to be adapted to XNF needs.

1. XNF semantic routine processing

   The crucial extension to the language was the CO constructor. Since this extension affected the language grammar, both the language parser and the semantic checking had to be extended correspondingly. In the same way, as the old processor created during this phase the internal query representation, i.e., a normal form QGM graph, the XNF processor has to create the XNF QGM graph that has to incorporate the XNF query semantics. In order to do this, a new operator had to be installed for QGM. The purpose of this **XNF operator** is to reflect the semantics of the language's CO constructor. Therefore, this XNF operator had to be able to incorporate n$\geq$1 incoming tables and to produce m$\geq$1 output tables being the result node and edge tables of the CO constructed. For the rest of the paper we will call the QGM for the SQL queries NF QGM, and the one that contains the XNF operator the XNF QGM, and if the difference between both does not really matter, then we simply call it QGM. In addition to this, the top operator had to be adapted, too. The purpose of this operator is to deal with query parameters (like host variables and query constants) and to provide a basis for the API cursors; all QGM graphs have a single top operator. A description on how an XNF QGM graph for a sample query looks like will be given in the next section.

2. XNF semantic rewrite

   In this step the translation from XNF QGM and XNF semantics to NF QGM and NF semantics has to be accomplished. Speaking in other words, this component has to get rid of the XNF operator and replace

it by NF operators. In this step we exploit that the components, i.e.,
the building blocks, of COs are derived tables.

3. Query rewrite and plan optimization
   Since the previous step already produced a clean NF QGM (that reflects
   the CO query semantics), the resulting compilation work can be done
   by the components from the SQL language processor. That is, the
   now NF QGM graph is taken and transformed by the query rewrite
   component to a semantically equivalent one that, in general, allows more
   efficient evaluation strategies to be chosen for the QEP when being
   processed by plan optimization and query refinement component. All
   these components are shared between the XNF language processor and
   the SQL language processor.

From a software engineering point of view, we decided to have two query
rewrite components: one for the XNF part and the already existing one for
the traditional SQL part. Both components apply the same transformation
techniques, i.e., rule-based rewriting, and both use the same rule representation mechanism as well as the same rule engine (for more information on this
see [Hasan 1988]). This decision entailed faster and easier implementation as
well as a clear distinction of responsibilities: all rewrite transformations that
must know about XNF context and semantics were packaged into the XNF
semantic rewrite component, and all others were put into the (NF) rewrite
component. In result we got less complex tasks to be performed by these
components.

2.5.2   Query Representation

In the first stage of XNF query compilation the internal query representation is built by means of the XNF semantic routines. As already mentioned,
this XNF QGM uses the XNF operator in order to incorporate XNF query
semantics. For the XNF query from Figure 2.1 we have shown the corresponding XNF QGM graph in Figure 2.6. Again, those parts that are exclusively
XNF QGM are shaded, while the NF QGM parts are kept un-shaded. In the
following we will explain how such a query graph is built from a given query.

Since an XNF query consists of three building blocks, there are also
three semantic routines associated that construct the final XNF QGM graph
in three subsequent phases:

(0) QGM initialization
When it is recognized by the parser that there is an XNF query (i.e.,

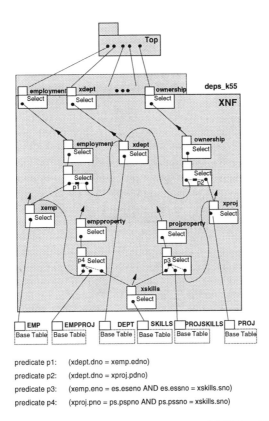

predicate p1:   (xdept.dno = xemp.edno)

predicate p2:   (xdept.dno = xproj.pdno)

predicate p3:   (xemp.eno = es.eseno AND es.essno = xskills.sno)

predicate p4:   (xproj.pno = ps.pspno AND ps.pssno = xskills.sno)

FIGURE 2.6
XNF QGM for the Example Query

when reading the key word 'OUT OF'), then the initialization routine
is invoked. This semantic routine initializes QGM by installation of the
XNF operator, which is drawn as a box labeled 'XNF.' If the query
is named, then this XNF box gets the query's name; in our example
the name of the XNF view deps-k55. Similar to the other boxes, the
XNF box also consists of head and body: the head describes the output
tables that constitute the XNF CO, and the body shows how these
tables are derived from other tables the body refers to. Furthermore,
the initialization routine adds the top operator in form of a box labeled
'Top.'

(1) Derivation structures for XNF component tables

The semantic routines within this phase fill out the body of the XNF box. Each table definition in the OUT OF clause invokes a semantic routine that defines parts of the final QGM. There is a routine for XNF tables and another one for XNF relationships:

- An XNF table is defined as a derived table over some base tables. Therefore the corresponding semantic routine creates a 'Select' box that refers to the base tables it is derived from. Since these steps are in the context of SQL, the semantic routine represents this, using NF QGM constructs. For example, the XNF table xdept is represented by a 'Select' box (within the body of the XNF box) that refers to the base table dept represented by a 'Base Table' box and that, in this case, also has a qualifier restricting the departments to those with location 'ARC.'

- An XNF relationship is also a derived table that is always based on a table expression. First, we represent the table expression by a 'Select' box, and then we derive from that the relationship table through a 'Select' box that refers to that table expression. A relationship's table expression at least has to relate its partner tables through the relationship predicate. For example, the table expression for the XNF relationship employment relates the xdept partner to the xemp partner by the relationship predicate, whose qualifier edges refer to the xdept and xemp boxes (i.e., tables). The 'Select' box labeled employment refers to the 'Select' box that represents that table expression, thus defining the derivation of the XNF relationship employment. The other XNF relationships are constructed the same way. In our example both the empproperty and the projproperty relationships refer in addition to their partner tables to another table that is used in the corresponding table expression.

(2) Consideration of node and edge restrictions

In Section 2.3 we have only mentioned that it is possible to restrict XNF tables and relationships. This is not exemplified, but the way this works out should be clear: these restrictions are simply added as a predicate (i.e., as a qualifier edge) to the 'Select' box that represents the subject for restriction.

(3) Handling projection

Each element in the TAKE clause is subject to projection. For each one, we create an 'output' box (labeled 'Select') that contains all the output columns and, in case of relationships, the role and the partner information. These output boxes are connected to the 'Top' box, and they refer to the boxes that represent the XNF tables and relationships. For sake of simplicity, we have omitted to draw all the 'output' boxes. But those boxes of the XNF body, which are referred to by 'output' boxes, are drawn with an arrow pointing from their head to the head of their XNF box.

The above explanations revealed that the XNF constructor can be represented more or less by means of NF-QGM operators. This already shows that the XNF extensions fit into the rest of NF QGM, and that it vastly exploits the basic building blocks provided by NF QGM. Therefore, interpretation of any XNF QGM graph goes similar to the interpretation of an NF QGM graph (cf. Section 2.4.2): basically, we can view the (body of an) XNF operator as a block that comprises its components, which constitute the CO giving a notation for derivation/instantiation the components from the base data.

For an XNF QGM graph no QEP can be created and with this there is also no query evaluation by QES, because neither plan optimization nor query refinement can deal with the XNF operator. In order to get into this track we have to transform an XNF QGM graph into a semantically equivalent NF QGM graph. This is done by the XNF semantic rewrite, as already mentioned before. This component first gets rid of the XNF operator, and secondly it has to install reachability, because when we interpret the body of an XNF operator with NF QGM semantics, we then recognize that reachability is not manifested. Both transformations are done via corresponding rules that are executed by the rule engine, which is shared with NF-based query rewrite. After this 'compilation' down to the level of NF QGM, NF-based query rewrite takes over. In our design we clearly separated the rewrites that need to be done while XNF semantics is still given from those transformations that work on plain NF QGM. In order to cope with the (natural) complexity of XNF QGM, we also used some simplification rules that are also known to NF-based rewriting: removal of unused boxes, and box merge. The first one cuts a query graph down to only relevant and used boxes, whereas the latter one condenses the graph. For example, when we look again to Figure 2.6 we can see that there are lots of boxes that refer only to one single other box (e.g., the pair of boxes that is used for representation of XNF relationships): in most cases these pairs can be merged into one resulting box.

2.6
Conclusion, Outlook, and Related Work

In this paper we revealed that, from a practical point of view, next generation database systems are under duress for sharing data among traditional applications and CO applications. This means that there is a need to bridge the gap between a relational store (i.e., data stored in relational DBMSs) and the CO abstraction level. The XNF approach provides solutions to this problem

- by offering a CO interface through a sound language and data model that unify CO and relational concepts, and

- through provision of an API handling COs properly at the application interface.

Since the efficiency of the system is crucial, and because relational data and relational applications are omnipresent, we decided to base the implementation on the wealth of existing relational technology. That is, we integrated CO processing into the relational framework: XNF queries are translated to relational queries, optimized, and then executed by a relational engine. In order to do this, we basically had to introduce one single operator, the XNF operator, and its translation to the level of relational queries. The benefits of this approach are manifold and the most important ones are

- exploitation of proved relational technology as well as acceptance of newly developed one, like parallelization in query processing [DeWitt 1990, Graefe 1990, Lorie 1989, Pirahesh 1990],

- DBMS software sharing (e.g., compiler, rule engine, QGM, relational engine, i.e., query runtime system), and

- data sharing among relational abstractions and CO abstractions.

In contrast to our integration approach stands the on-top approach followed by Wiederhold and described in [Barsalou 1989, Lee 1990]. There an object-oriented program is interfaced with databases through instantiation of objects from relational databases by evaluation of view queries. The system model applied has three elements: the object type model that defines the structure of the objects, the relational data model for storage of base data, and the view model that contains the relational query and defines a mapping between objects and relations. That view model is restricted only to an acyclic select-project-join query. Basically this approach is comparable to XNF but major differences are obvious. First, XNF has with its CO constructor a more powerful view concept (multi-table views), which, secondly, provides an abstraction level that considerably reduces the final mapping (if needed at all) to the application's favorable processing format. With this, XNF does not bind itself to only object-oriented application interfaces as is done in [Lee 1990]. In contrast, XNF is open to different application environments; this is especially important since there are different object-oriented models that need this kind of CO support. Thirdly, DBMS software could be considerably shared (and not replicated at different processing levels) due to the integration of XNF processing and relational processing. Fourthly, viewed from the other side, we can use XNF as another (and what we think, better) kind of view model within the system model of [Lee 1990], thus profiting from the framework defined (i.e., the object type model, the corresponding compiler etc.).

There are various other approaches to modeling and management of COs as extensions to the relational model. Lorie's [Lorie 1984] COs are defined by special columns (assigning an identifier to a row, containing the parent identifier, and referencing another row). Joins among parents and children are supported by system-maintained access paths (called maps) on a per-CO basis. Although this approach integrates CO processing into the relational framework, its usages are limited because of the restrictions of the data model to more or less hierarchical COs that are statically defined in the database schema. As liberation from these restrictions and towards more degrees of flexibility, we can view the MAD model [Mitschang 1989] that supports network-like as well as recursive COs. This Molecule Atom Data model specifies its COs (called molecules) on a reference basis in the CO/molecule query and not in the schema. With this, more flexibility is achieved, because COs are now similar to views defined over the underlying database by means of a CO query. Compared to the XNF approach, the MAD approach is less flexible, because the molecule building references must exist in the database, and therefore also in the schema; remember that the relationships in XNF can be defined on an ad-hoc basis in the query by a predicate. Again, and in contrast to XNF, any membership in a MAD relationship must be explicitly specified by referencing the two partner tuples. Query processing in MAD [Haerder 1992] is also based on a set of operators, which are different from the known relational ones due to the molecule semantics applied. Another approach that provides more flexibility as compared to Lorie's is the NF2 approach [Schek 1986]. By now it is implemented in several prototypes and extended in several ways [Dadam 1986, Linnemann 1988, Pistor 1986, Schek 1990]. This nested relation approach is targeted towards hierarchical COs by generally placing components with the parent component. In general, access to sub-components goes through the parent. Sharing of components between parents is done by listing of foreign keys (or logical references), which implies that access is done on a join basis as in relational systems. Flexibility is achieved through specific operations that can flatten out or restructure the nestings given in the database schema. Because of these model specific operations, the implementation reflects an extended relational engine. As in the other approaches, and in contrast to XNF, membership in a relationship is explicitly set.

What we call the navigational approach is the way many object-oriented systems deal with COs. In most cases they directly represent the relationships between the components through pointers mostly defined and managed by methods. Of course this approach to CO is not as flexible as XNF's, since on the one side only those relationships that are predefined in the static schema can be navigated on, and on the other side membership in a relationship must be explicitly set. Other approaches to COs [Stonebraker 1991, Hudson 1989] define their COs through object attributes that are evaluated in order to specify the object's sub-components. If query languages are considered (e.g., RELOOP [Cluet 1989]), then these languages show similarities to languages like MQL (MQL is the molecule query language of the MAD model [Haerder 1992]) and XNF. Therefore, there is considerable confidence that query processing concepts for COs play an integral part in OO query processing as well as in query processing for deductive database languages [Lanzelotte 1991a, 1991b, Cheiney 1992].

Acknowledgements

The cooperation of the whole Starburst staff is greatly acknowledged. Special thanks are due to Bruce Lindsay, Peter Pistor, and Norbert Suedkamp, who all helped in our joint effort of getting the good stuff into XNF, while streamlining the syntax. G. Lohman improved the optimizer to handle our complex queries, and G. Wilson provided valuable implementation experiences on his work on an earlier prototype.

Bibliography

[Astrahan 1976] Astrahan, M., et al. "System R: Relational Approach to Data Base Management Systems." *ACM TODS*, **1**, **1**, pp. 97–137.

[Bachman 1989] Bachman, C. "A Personal Chronicle—Creating Better Information Systems, with Some Guiding Principles." *IEEE Transactions on Knowledge and Data Engineering* **1**, pp. 17–32.

[Barsalou 1989] Barsalou, T., Wiederhold, G. "Knowledge-Based Mapping of Relations into Objects." *Computer Aided Design*.

[Cheiney 1992] Cheiney, J., Lanzelotte, R. "A Model for Optimizing Deductive and Object-Oriented DB Requests." In *Proc. of Data Engineering Conf*, Phoenix.

[Chen 1976] Chen, P.P. "The Entity Relationship Model: Toward a Unified View of Data." *ACM TODS*, **1**, **1**, pp. 9–36.

[Cluet 1989] Cluet, S., Delobel, C., Lecluse, C., Richard, P. "RELOOP: An Algebra-Based Query Language for an Object-Oriented Database System." In *First International Conference on Deductive and Object-Oriented Databases*, Elsevier, Kyoto, Japan.

[Dadam 1986] Dadam, P., Kuespert, K., et al. "A DBMS Prototype to Support Extended NF2 Relations: An Integrated View on Flat Tables and Hierarchies." In *Proc. of the ACM SIGMOD Conf.*, Washington D.C., Mayu 1986, pp. 356–367.

[DeWitt 1990] DeWitt, D.J., Ghandeharizadeh, S., Schneider, D.A., Bricker, A., Hsiao, H.-I., Rasmussen, R. "The Gamma Database Machine Project." *Knowledge and Data Engineering*, **2**, **1**.

[Graefe 1990] Graefe, G. "Volcano, an Extensible and Parallel Query Evaluation System." Research Report University of Colorado at Boulder, CU-CS-481-90.

[Guenther 1991] Guenther, O., Schek, H.-J. (eds.). "Advances in Spatial Databases." *Proc. 2nd Symposium*, SSD.

[Haas 1989] Haas, L., Freytag, J.C., Lohman, G., Pirahesh., H. "Extensible Query Processing in Starburst." In *Proc. of the ACM SIGMOD Conf.*, Portland, pp. 377–388.

[Haas 1990] Haas, L., Chang, W., Lohman, G. et al. "Starburst Mid-Flight: As the Dust Clears." *Special Issue on Database Prototype Systems, IEEE Transactions on Knowledge and Data Engineering*, **2**, **1**, pp. 143–160.

[Haerder 1992] Haerder, T., Mitschang, B., Schoening, H. "Query Processing for Complex Objects." *Data and Knowledge Engineering*, **7**, pp. 181–200.

[Hasan 1988] Hasan, W., Pirahesh, H. "Query Rewrite Optimization in Starburst." IBM Almaden Research Center, Research Report RJ 6367.

[Hudson 1989] Hudson, S.E., King, R., "CACTIS. A Self-Adaptive, Concurrent Implementation of an Object-Oriented Database Management System" *ACM TODS*, **14**, **3**, pp. 291–321.

[ISO-ANSI 1989] ISO-ANSI "Working DraftDatabase Language SQL2 and SQL3".

[Keller 1991] Keller, T., Graefe, G., Maier, D. "Efficient Assembly of Complex Objects." In *Proc. of the ACM SIGMOD Conf.*, Denver, pp. 148–157.

[Lanzelotte 1991a] Lanzelotte, R., Cheiney, J. "Adapting Relational Optimization Technology to Deductive and Object-oriented Declarative Database Languages." Workshop on Database Programming Languages, Greece.

[1991b] Lanzelotte, R., Valduriez, P., Ziane, M., Cheiney, J. "Optimization of Nonrecursive Queries in OODB's." In *Second Int. Conf. on Deductive and Object-Oriented Databases*, Munich.

[Lee 1990] Lee, B.S., Wiederhold, G. "Outer Joins and Filters for Instantiating Objects from Relational Databases through Views." CIFE Technical Report, Stanford University.

[Lindsay 1986] Lindsay, B., McPherson, J., Pirahesh, H. "A Data Management Extension Architecture." In *Proc. of the ACM SIGMOD Conf.*, San Francisco, pp. 220–226.

[Linnemann 1988] Linnemann, V., Kuspert, K. "Design and Implementation of an Extensible Database Management System Supporting User Defined Data Types and Functions." In *Proc. of the 14th VLDB Conference*, Los Angeles, CA.

[Lohman 1991] Lohman, G., Lindsay, B., Pirahesh, H., Schiefer, B. "Extensions to Starburst: Objects, Types, Functions, and Rules." *Communications of the ACM*, **34**, **10**, pp. 94–109.

[Lorie 1984] Lorie, R, Kim, W., et al. "Supporting Complex Objects in a Relational System for Engineering Databases." IBM Research Report, San Jose, CA.

[Lorie 1989] Lorie, R., Daudenarde, J., Hallmark, G., Stamos, J., Young, H. "Adding Intra-Transaction Parallelism to an Existing DBMS: Early Experience." *Data Engineering*, **12**, **1**.

[Mitschang 1989] Mitschang, B. "Extending the Relational Algebra to Capture Complex Objects." In *Proc. of 15th Int. VLDB Conf., Amsterdam*, pp. 297–306.

[Mortenson 1985] Mortenson, M.E. "Geometric Modeling." *John Wiley and Sons*.

[Pirahesh 1990] Pirahesh, H., Mohan, C., Cheng, J., Liu, TS, Selinger, P. "Parallelism in Relational Data Base Systems: Architectural Issues and Design Approaches." In *Proc. of the Int. Symposium on Databases in Parallel and Distributed Systems*, Dublin.

[Pistor 1986] Pistor, P., Andersen, F. "Designing a Generalized NF2 Data Model with an SQL-type Language Interface." In *Proc. of 12th Int. Conf on VLDB*, Kyoto.

[Schek 1986] Schek, H.J., Scholl, M.H. "The Relational Model with Relation-Valued Attributes." *Information Systems*, **2**, **2**, pp. 137–147.

[Schek 1990] Schek, H.-J., Paul, H.-B., Scholl, M.H., Weikum, G. "The DASDBS Project: Objectives, Experiences, and Future Prospects." In *IEEE Transactions on Knowledge and Data Engineering*, **2**, **1**, pp. 25–43.

[Stonebraker 1991] Stonebraker, M., Kemnitz, G. "The POSTGRES Next-Generation Database Management System." In *Special Issue on Database Prototype Systems, IEEE Transactions on Knowledge and Data Engineering*, **2**, **1**, pp. 78–93.

[Wiederhold 1986] Wiederhold, G., El Masri, R. "The Structural Model for Database Design." *Entity-relationship Approach to System Analysis and Design*, North-Holland, pp. 237–257.

[Zdonik 1990] Zdonik, S. Maier, D. ed. *Readings in Object-Oriented Database Systems*, Morgan Kaufmann Publishers.

3

Query Optimization in Object Bases: Exploiting Relational Techniques

Alfons Kemper
Guido Moerkotte

Abstract

There exists a large body of knowledge—gathered over a period of almost two decades—in relational query optimization. In this paper we investigate to what extent the relational optimization techniques can be applied to object-oriented query processing. As a "testbed" we chose our object-oriented database GOM which incorporates two very general indexing structures: *access support relations* which materialize frequently traversed path expressions and *generalized materialization relations* which maintain precomputed function results. These two indexing structures provide a good "yardstick" for analyzing a query optimizer since they subsume many other access support schemes proposed in the literature. In the analysis of rule-based query optimization we contrast two different internal query representation languages that were developed for rule-based optimization in GOM: (1) the procedurally oriented term language and (2) an object algebra representation that is based on relational algebra with a few extensions. The two representation languages are illustrated by way of optimizing an example query, step by step. Our initial approach to algebraic optimization reveals that the starting point for the optimization process is crucial. Therefore, we propose the so-called *most costly normal form (MCNF)* as the initial algebraic representation of object queries. Re-optimizing the example query illustrates that this starting point leads to a more structured approach (1) to query rewriting and (2) to generating alternatives during the optimization process.

3.1
Introduction

Object-oriented database systems are emerging as the "next generation" database technology—especially for advanced engineering applications, e.g., mechanical CAD/CAM. Compared to the relational model, the object-oriented model(s) offer substantially higher expressiveness by incorporating the *structural* and the *behavioral dimension* in a unifying framework. Nevertheless, the acceptance of this new database technology will largely depend on the performance that can be achieved. Database users, in particular engineers, are generally not willing to trade performance for functionality. Therefore, the development of effective optimization techniques for object-oriented systems will largely determine their fate in the commercial market place.

In this paper we set out to investigate one of the core optimization concepts: the optimizer for declarative queries, commonly called the *query optimizer*. There exists a large body of knowledge—accumulated over a period of almost two decades—within the relational framework. Obviously, it would be worthwhile investigating whether this knowledge can be exploited in an object-oriented context.

Our work is carried out on the basis of the object-oriented database model GOM [Kemper et. al 1991]. GOM is a good candidate for this research since it incorporates the most salient features of object-oriented database models, as described in the "Manifesto" [Atkinson et. al 1989]. In addition, GOM provides two very general indexing methods, which—of course—have to be incorporated into query optimization:

- *access support relations (ASRs)* [Kemper and Moerkotte 1990a] enhance the performance of object access via arbitrarily long reference chains leading from one object to another object or a set of other objects. Access support relations generalize other indexing schemes, e.g., links [Härder 1978], binary join indexes [Valduriez 1987], path indexes for object models [Maier and Stein 1986, Bertino and Kim 1989], and path indexes for the nested relational model [Keßler and Dadam 1991].

- *generalized materialization relations (GMRs)* can be utilized to maintain precomputed results of those functions that are frequently used in search predicates. [Kemper, Kilger, and Moerkotte 1991] introduces this optimization method for object-oriented databases.

These two very general access support structures provide a good "yardstick" for evaluating the quality of a query optimizer by analyzing how well these structures are exploited in the optimized query evaluation plan.

A principal question in the design of a query optimizer concerns the internal representation of the query during the optimization process. In this paper we contrast two representation formats that were developed in GOM for rule-based query rewriting: (1) a procedurally oriented term representation [Kemper and Moerkotte 1990b] and (2) an object algebra that resembles relational algebra—with a few extensions accounting for the characteristics of object-oriented query processing. Both representations exhibit distinct advantages: the term representation is more amenable to incorporation of procedurally oriented constructs, e.g., for specifying the exploitation of access support structures. The object algebra, on the other hand, has the advantage of being more closely related to relational query optimization formats and, thus, may lead to easier incorporation of relational techniques.

The analysis of the two representation formats is based on performing the step-wise optimization of a rather complex example query. Our investigation reveals that the starting point, i.e., the initially generated internal representation of the declarative user query is crucial for a well structured query optimization process. We propose a normal form into which all queries are initially translated: the *most costly normal form (MCNF)*. This normal form has a positive impact on the design of optimizer strategies in that it allows clear definition of several steps of optimization. As a side effect, this structuring allows the easy and systematic generation of alternative branches that are to be investigated by the optimizer.

The remainder of this paper is organized as follows. In Section 3.2 our object model GOM is surveyed briefly. Then, in Section 3.3 the object-oriented query language GOMql, which is based on the relational language QUEL, is introduced. In Section 3.4 the access support structures that were developed for GOM are explained briefly. In Section 3.5 the two query representation formats, object algebra and term language, are introduced. In Section 3.6 the rule-based optimization of a term expression is illustrated by way of a complete example. The two different internal query representation formats are contrasted, the most costly normal form is defined, and the optimizer strategy is outlined. Section 3.7 concludes this paper.

3.2
Our Object Model GOM

3.2.1   Main Concepts

This research is based on an object-oriented model that unites the most salient features of many recently proposed models in one coherent framework. In this respect, the objective of GOM can be seen as providing a syntactical framework of the essential object-oriented features identified in the "Manifesto" [Atkinson et. al 1989]—albeit the GOM model was developed much earlier. Similarly, Zdonik and Maier developed the so-called Reference Model in [Zdonik and Maier 1989]. The features that GOM provides are relatively *generic*, so that the results derived for this particular data model can easily be applied to a variety of other object-oriented models. This genericity helps to overcome the diversity of existing object-oriented models which is due to the lack of a commonly adopted base model—which, for example, helped

in the relational database area to focus the research in one direction. More
specifically, GOM provides the following object-oriented concepts:

- *object identity*, i.e., each object owns an unchangeable object identifier
  that is used to uniquely identify (reference) the object.

- *complex values*, which—contrary to objects—do not possess an identity.

- *type constructors*, i.e., GOM supports tuple-, set-, and list-constructors.
  Building upon these, the user is free to define his or her own constructors
  utilizing the generic type concept.

- *subtyping* in conjunction with *inheritance*, i.e., the subtype inherits all
  features—properties and operations—of the supertype(s).

- *strong typing*, that is, the type safety of all programs is verified at compile time.

- *object instantiation*, i.e., objects are created by instantiating types.

In addition to types, GOM provides for (complex) *sorts*. The main difference
between types and sorts is that the instances of the former are objects whereas
the instances of the latter are values.

A traditional relation can be modeled by a sort and its extension is a
value.

There exist the following *base sorts*: BOOL, INT, FLOAT, STRING,
and OID. Thus, the set of object identifiers (OIDs) is viewed as a base sort.
For typing purposes, it is divided into subsets containing identifiers for objects
of a certain type. For more details see [Kemper et. al 1991].

3.2.2 The Running Example

In this subsection we will introduce an example object base, called *Company*. This database will be used throughout the paper to illustrate our optimization concepts. The type definitions are shown in Figure 3.1. Since no
public clause is supplied in any of the type definitions, all attributes and
operations are visible. We further assume all defined types to be persistent.
For each type, we maintain a type extension. These extensions also contain
all instances of subtypes.

A (small) database extension based on the above schema is shown in
Figure 3.2. The labels id_j for $j = \{1, 2, 3, \ldots\}$ denote the object identifiers
(OIDs), which are system-wide unique. References via complex attributes are

type EMP **is**
  body
    [Name: STRING;
    WorksIn: DEPT;
    Salary: INT;
    JobHistory: HISTORY;]   !! assuming *HISTORY*
  operations   !! being defined elsewhere
    declare skill: → INT;
  implementation
    define skill **is**
      ...   !! derived from the *JobHistory*
end type EMP;

    type DEPT **is**
      body
        [Name: STRING;
        Mgr: MANAGER;
        Profit: INT;]
      operations
        declare avg_skill: → FLOAT;
      implementation
        define avg_skill **is**
          ...   !! compute the average skill of
          ...   !! employees within this department
      end type DEPT;

    type MANAGER
      supertype EMP **is**
      body
        [BackUp: EMP;]
    end type MANAGER;

FIGURE 3.1
Type Definitions of our Running Example

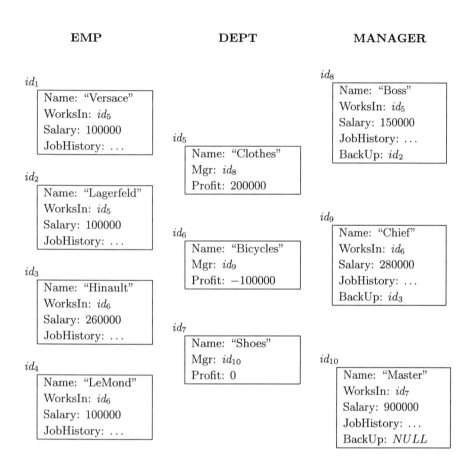

FIGURE 3.2

Example Extension of the Object Base *Company*

maintained uni-directionally in GOM—as in almost all other object models, e.g., O2, GemStone, etc. For example, in an extension of the above schema there exists a reference in the form of a stored OID from an *EMP*loyee to his *DEPT*, but not vice versa. These references are maintained by storing the unique OID of the referenced object in the referencing attribute or variable.

3.3
Query Language

For our object model we developed a QUEL-like [Stonebraker 1985] query language along the lines of the EXCESS object query language that was designed as the declarative query language for the EXTRA object model that is described in [Carey, DeWitt, and Vandenberg 1988]. We assume that every query returns a relation (see [Ullmann 1987]). This relation is a complex value that may then be assigned as a value to an object. More detailed information on this topic and a more thorough treatment of the semantics of our object model as well as of the query language can be found in [Kemper and Moerkotte 1991].

3.3.1   Abstract Syntax

As complex sorts we only have tuples denoted by $[\tau_1, \ldots, \tau_n]$ for $n > 0$ and τ_i being base sorts, sets denoted by $\{\tau\}$, and lists denoted by $< \tau >$ where τ is a base or a tuple sort (see [Kemper and Moerkotte 1991] for more details). In order not to run into any problems concerning the uniqueness of attribute names, we assume a tuple to be ordered and use numbers for their identification. On tuple sorts the operator "∘" denotes concatenation. This operator will be used for both function composition and tuple concatenation. This overloading can easily be resolved by looking at the argument types.

To build *terms*, there exist basic functions for arithmetic and string manipulation as well as the possibility to apply built-in and user-defined operators. The most important built-in operator is attribute access, denoted by "."—whose successive application on tuple structured objects leads to so-called *path expressions*. To build predicates we have the following *comparison operators*:

$$\begin{aligned} \text{binary operators} \quad &: \quad =, \neq, <, >, \geq, \leq, in \\ \text{unary operator} \quad &: \quad empty \end{aligned}$$

A *predicate* is either an application of a comparison operator to (a) term(s) or an application of a user-defined function returning a Boolean value. From predicates we build *Boolean expressions* by applying the usual Boolean connectives AND, OR, and NOT.

We are now ready to define our query language. In GOM a query is a **retrieve** expression returning a complex value, i.e., a relation.

Let x_i be variables, T_i type names, e_j expressions, and S a Boolean expression called the *selection predicate*. Then, a query has the following form:

> **range** $\quad x_1 : T_1, \ldots, x_n : T_n$
> **retrieve** $e_1, \ldots, e_m$
> **where** $\quad S(x_1, \ldots, x_n)$

In fact, GOMql is more powerful in that the T_i are not restricted to type names only but may, instead, represent general set typed or set valued expressions [Kemper and Moerkotte 1991]. Note, however, that our current implementation of the GOM query language facilitates single-target queries only ([Kemper and Moerkotte 1990b]). We have chosen the query language above because it is well suited to show its mapping to the (slightly extended) relational algebra and the optimization within the algebra. The T_i could also be lists but so far we have only considered sets as results.

3.3.2 The Running Example

In our example query we want to retrieve—and subsequently fire—the managers of departments that generate losses and, at the same time, pay at least one of their employees an exorbitant salary (exceeding 200000). Since we do not want to fire highly skilled managers we additionally require that the skill of the managers is less than 4. In addition to the manager, i.e., the manager OID, we want to retrieve the manager's skill relative to the average of skill (*avg_skill*) of all employees in his or her department. In GOMql the query can be stated as follows:

> **range** $\quad e :$ EMP, $d :$ DEPT
> **retrieve** $d.$Mgr, $d.$Mgr.skill$/d.$avg_skill
> **where** $\quad d = e.$WorksIn **and**
> $\qquad\quad d.$Profit < 0 **and**
> $\qquad\quad e.$Salary > 200000 **and**
> $\qquad\quad d.$Mgr.skill < 4

3.4
Access Support Structures

3.4.1   Access Support Relations

Access support relations (ASRs) have been introduced as an index structure to support the evaluation of *path expressions*. A very special case is reviewed briefly here. More detailed information can be found in the original papers [Kemper and Moerkotte 1990a] and [Kemper and Moerkotte 1992].

Definitions

A path expression has the form

$$o.A_1. \cdots .A_n$$

where o is a tuple structured object with an attribute A_1 and $o.A_1. \cdots .A_i$ refers to an object or tuple value having an attribute A_{i+1}. More formally:

DEFINITION 3.1   *Path Expression*

Let $t_0, \ldots, t_n$ be (not necessarily distinct) types. A (generic) path expression on t_0 is an expression $t_0.A_1. \cdots .A_n$ if and only if for each $1 \leq i \leq n$ the type t_{i-1} is defined as **type** t_{i-1} **is** $[\ldots, A_i : t_i, \ldots]$*, i.e., t_{i-1} is a tuple with an attribute A_i of type t_i*[1].

Thus we concentrate on the case where none of the path attributes is set valued—even though ASRs in their general form allow set-valued attributes as well ([Kemper and Moerkotte 1990a]).

As we will see, the information contained in a path can be held in a relation. Consequently, we will use relation extensions to represent access paths. The next definition maps a given path expression to the declaration of the underlying access support relation.

DEFINITION 3.2   *Access Support Relation (ASR)*

Let $t_0, \ldots, t_n$ be types, $t_0.A_1. \cdots .A_n$ be a path expression. Then the access support relation $[\![t_0.A_1. \cdots .A_n]\!]$ is of arity $n + 1$ and has the following form:

$$[\![t_0.A_1. \cdots .A_n]\!] : [S_0, \ldots, S_n]$$

The domain of the attribute S_i is the set of identifiers (OIDs) of objects of type t_i of Definition 3.1 for $(0 \leq i \leq n)$. If t_n is an atomic type

---

[1]Meaning that the attribute A_i can be associated with objects of type t_i or any subtype thereof.

then the domain of S_n is t_n, i.e., values are directly stored in the access support relation.

We distinguish several possibilities for the extension of such relations. To define them for a path expression $t_0.A_1. \cdots .A_n$, we need n auxiliary relations $[\![t_0.A_1]\!], \ldots, [\![t_{n-1}.A_n]\!]$.

DEFINITION 3.3 *Auxiliary Binary Relations*

For each A_i $(1 \leq i \leq n)$, i.e., for each attribute in the path expression, we construct the auxiliary binary relation $[\![t_{i-1}.A_i]\!]$. The relation $[\![t_{i-1}.A_i]\!]$ contains the tuples $(id(o_{i-1}), id(o_i))$ for every object o_{i-1} of type t_{i-1} and o_i of type t_i such that $o_{i-1}.A_i = o_i$. If t_n is an atomic type, then $id(o_n)$ corresponds to the value $o_{n-1}.A_n$. Note, however, that only the last type t_n in a path expression can possibly be an atomic type.

Let us now introduce different possible extensions of the access support relation $[\![t_0.A_1. \cdots .A_n]\!]$. We distinguish four extensions:

1. The *canonical* extension, denoted $[\![t_0.A_1. \cdots .A_n]\!]_{can}$ contains only information about complete paths, i.e., paths originating in t_0 and leading (all the way) to t_n. Therefore, it can only be used to evaluate queries that originate in an object of type t_0 and "go all the way" to t_n.

2. The *left-complete* extension $[\![t_0.A_1. \cdots .A_n]\!]_{left}$ contains all paths originating in t_0 which must not necessarily lead to an object in t_n, but possibly ending in a *NULL*-value.

3. The *right-complete* extension $[\![t_0.A_1. \cdots .A_n]\!]_{right}$, analogously, contains paths leading to t_n, but possibly originating in some object o_j of type t_j that is not referenced by any object of type t_{j-1} via the A_j attribute.

4. Finally, the full extension $[\![t_0.A_1. \cdots .A_n]\!]_{full}$ contains all partial paths, even if they do not originate in t_0 or do end in a *NULL*-value.

DEFINITION 3.4 *Extensions*

Let $\bowtie$ ($\,\rlap{\sqsupset}\bowtie$, $\bowtie$, $\bowtie\llap{\sqsubset}\,$) denote the natural (outer, left outer, right outer) join on the last column of the first relation and the first column of the second relation. Then the different extensions are obtained as follows:

$$[\![t_0.A_1. \cdots .A_n]\!]_{can} := [\![t_0.A_1]\!] \bowtie \ldots \bowtie [\![t_{n-1}.A_n]\!]$$

$$[\![t_0.A_1.\cdots.A_n]\!]_{full} := [\![t_0.A_1]\!] \bowtie \cdots \bowtie [\![t_{n-1}.A_n]\!]$$

$$[\![t_0.A_1.\cdots.A_n]\!]_{left} := (\cdots ([\![t_0.A_1]\!] \bowtie [\![t_1.A_2]\!]) \cdots \bowtie [\![t_{n-1}.A_n]\!])$$

$$[\![t_0.A_1.\cdots.A_n]\!]_{right} := ([\![t_0.A_1]\!] \bowtie \cdots ([\![t_{n-2}.A_{n-1}]\!] \bowtie [\![t_{n-1}.A_n]\!]) \cdots)$$

Aside from extensions, we also allow decomposition of access support relations which is not treated here. We further do not discuss the storage structure of access support relations but again refer to the original literature.

Let us now define the *applicability* of a given access support relation for evaluating some path expression:

DEFINITION 3.5   *Applicability*

An access support relation $[\![t_0.A_1.\cdots.A_n]\!]_X$ *under extension* X *is applicable to a path* $s.A_i.\cdots.A_j$ *with* $s \leq t_{i-1}$ *under the following condition—depending on the extension* X:

$$Applicable([\![t_0.A_1.\cdots.A_n]\!]_X, s.A_i.\cdots.A_j) =$$
$$\begin{cases} X = full & \wedge & 1 \leq i \leq j \leq n \\ X = left & \wedge & 1 = i \leq j \leq n \\ X = right & \wedge & 1 \leq i \leq j = n \\ X = can & \wedge & 1 = i \leq j = n \end{cases}$$

Here $s \leq t_{i-1}$ *denotes that type* s *has to be identical to type* t_{i-1} *or a subtype thereof.*

The Running Example

Let us reconsider the path expression of our schema *Company* (now we indicate the types of the subpaths by the underbraces):

$$P \equiv \underbrace{\underbrace{EMP.WorksIn}_{DEPT}.Mgr}_{MANAGER}$$

For this path the canonical extension $[\![EMP.WorksIn.Mgr]\!]_{can}$ looks as follows:

$[\![\mathbf{EMP.WorksIn.Mgr}]\!]_{\mathbf{can}}$		
OID_{EMP}	OID_{DEPT}	$OID_{MANAGER}$
id_1	id_5	id_8
id_2	id_5	id_8
id_3	id_6	id_9
id_4	id_6	id_9
$\ldots$	$\ldots$	$\ldots$

This extension contains all complete paths corresponding to the underlying path expression.

3.4.2 Function Materialization

In this subsection we describe one (further) piece in the mosaic of access support structures that we incorporated in our experimental object base system GOM: the *materialization of functions*, i.e., the precomputation of function results (see [Kemper, Kilger, and Moerkotte 1991] and the more detailed presentation in [Kemper, Kilger, and Moerkotte 1992] for further information).

Materialization—just like indexing—is based on the assumption that the precomputed results are eventually utilized in the evaluation of some associative data access. Function materialization is a dual approach to *Access Support Relations*, which constitute materializations of heavily traversed path expressions that relate objects along attribute chains.

Definitions

The main definition needed within this paper concerned with the optimization of GOMql queries utilizing materialized functions is the one for *generalized materialization relations*:

DEFINITION 3.6 *Generalized Materialization Relations (GMRs)*

Let $t_1, \ldots, t_n, t'_1, \ldots, t'_m$ be types and $f_1, \ldots, f_m$ side-effect-free functions with $f_j : t_1, \ldots, t_n \to t'_j$ for $1 \leq j \leq m$. The generalized materialization relation $\langle\!\langle f_1, \ldots, f_m \rangle\!\rangle$ for the functions $f_1, \ldots, f_m$ is of arity $n + m$ and has the following form:

$$[O_1 : t_1, \ldots, O_n : t_n, f_1 : t'_1, \ldots, f_m : t'_m]$$

The attributes $O_1, \ldots, O_n$ store the arguments, i.e., values if the argument type is atomic or references to objects if the argument type is complex; the attributes $f_1, \ldots, f_m$ store the results or, if the result type is complex, references to the result objects. In this paper we restrict our discussion to functions having complex argument types and atomic result types. However, our concepts scale up to arbitrary functions [Kemper, Kilger, and Moerkotte 1992]. To keep the overhead in case of an update as low as possible, special attention has to be paid to the invalidation and rematerialization procedures [Kemper, Kilger, and Moerkotte 1991, Kemper, Kilger, and Moerkotte 1992].

The Running Example

Consider the database extension in Figure 3.2. Recall functions *skill* and *avg_skill* associated with the object types *EMP* and *DEPT*, respectively:

skill: $EMP \rightarrow INT$
avg_skill: $DEPT \rightarrow FLOAT$

Their computation requires to iterate over the whole sets of employees and departments, hence there computation is quite complex and materialization pays off.

The extensions of the GMRs $\langle\!\langle skill \rangle\!\rangle$ and $\langle\!\langle avg\_skill \rangle\!\rangle$ with all results valid are depicted below.

$\langle\!\langle skill \rangle\!\rangle$	
$O_1{:}EMP$	$skill{:}INT$
id_1	4
...	...
id_8	5
id_9	3
id_{10}	10

$\langle\!\langle avg\_skill \rangle\!\rangle$	
$O_1{:}DEPT$	$avg\_skill{:}FLOAT$
id_5	5.32
id_6	7.50
id_7	6.77

Using this information together with the information in Figure 3.2 we are able to give an answer tuple for our example query: $[id_9, 0.4]$.

3.5
The (Internal) Query Representation Formats
3.5.1   The Algebra

The main motivation for introducing the object algebra—which constitutes a slightly enhanced relational algebra—is to show that GOMql queries can be captured by it and, since it consists mainly of the relational operators, that relational optimization strategies can be applied as is. Further, we will show that it is even possible to express the utilization of the above access support methods within the algebra. In particular, we show how to incorporate ASRs and GMRs in the next section where optimization in the presence of these is discussed. Since we will not review all the relational optimization techniques we restrict the part of our algebra represented here to the minimum. It should be obvious how to include special operators to deal with, for example, NULL values and quantifiers, by incorporating the appropriate operators from the relational area.

Definitions

Aside from the basic operations to build tuple constants ("$[\cdot]$") and set constants ("$\{\cdot\}$"), the operators for tuple access ($x.n$ retrieves the n-th attribute of tuple x) and for set manipulation ("$\cup$", "$\setminus$", "$\cap$", "*fetch*", which retrieves the element of a singleton set) the algebra consists of the usual *selection*, *projection*, and *join* operations as well as a new operator *ext* that retrieves the extension, i.e., the set of object identifiers of the instances of the given type. Their declarations as polymorphic operators are as follows ([von Bültzingsloewen 1990]):

$$
\begin{aligned}
\sigma_{g:\tau_1 \to BOOL} \quad &: \quad \{\tau_1\} \quad &\to \quad \{\tau_1\} \\
\pi_{g:\tau_1 \to \tau_2} \quad &: \quad \{\tau_1\} \quad &\to \quad \{\tau_2\} \\
\bowtie_{g:[\tau_1,\tau_2] \to BOOL} \quad &: \quad \{\tau_1\}, \{\tau_2\} \quad &\to \quad \{[\tau_1,\tau_2]\} \\
\bowtie_{g:\tau_1 \circ [\tau_2] \to BOOL} \quad &: \quad \{\tau_1\}, \{\tau_2\} \quad &\to \quad \{\tau_1 \circ [\tau_2]\} \\
\bowtie_{g:\tau_1 \circ \tau_2 \to BOOL} \quad &: \quad \{\tau_1\}, \{\tau_2\} \quad &\to \quad \{\tau_1 \circ \tau_2\} \\
\\
ext(\tau) \quad &: \quad \quad &\to \quad \{\tau\}
\end{aligned}
$$

Here, τ and τ_i are either sort or type variables.

The functions appearing in the subscripts of the operators will be written using λ-notation. Note that, contrary to the relational algebra, the operators appearing within the subscripts are allowed to be general functions defined as an λ-expression, and not just those accessing attribute values. As a consequence the projection operator resembles a general *map* operator.

The $\bowtie$ operations will be used to "join" the extensions of types. Since these extensions are not tuples, but instead sets of object identifiers we apply $\bowtie$ in order to join two of them. This results in a set of tuples with two components. Joining a third extension to this result requires the application of $\bowtie$. This way we can perform in a left-to-right order a join of any number of extensions. Sometimes the ordinary join $\bowtie$ is still needed. All three joins will be overloaded (denoted by $\bowtie$) and always be processed from left to right. Overloading is resolved by first applying $\bowtie$. If its application is not possible we apply $\bowtie$, last we apply $\bowtie$. We will abbreviate $\bowtie_{\lambda x.true}$ by $\bowtie$.

The Running Example

Our example query can be translated into the following algebraic expression:

$\pi_{\lambda x.[x.2.\mathrm{Mgr},x.2.\mathrm{Mgr.skill}/x.2.\mathrm{avg\_skill}]}$
  $\sigma_{\lambda x.(x.2=x.1.\mathrm{WorksIn}\ \mathbf{and}\ x.2.\mathrm{Profit}<0\ \mathbf{and}\ x.1.\mathrm{Salary}>200000\ \mathbf{and}\ x.2.\mathrm{Mgr.skill}<4)}$
   $(ext(\mathrm{EMP}) \bowtie ext(\mathrm{DEPT}))$

3.5.2   The GOM Term Language

This section reviews the GOM term language and gives the algebraic definitions of its most important constituents. Building upon the term language, a set of transformation rules has been defined and a rule-based optimizer was implemented ([Kemper and Moerkotte 1990b, Kemper and Moerkotte 1990c]).

The Term Language Operators

Path Term   A path term is used to retrieve the attribute value at the end of a path. Thus for v of type t_0, $v.A_1$ of type t_1, ..., $v.A_1.\cdots.A_n$ of type t_n the **path** term

   $(\mathbf{path}\ v\ A_1 \ldots A_n)$

is defined as

   $fetch(\pi_{\lambda x.(x.A_1.\cdots.A_n)}(\{v\}))$.

This expression is equivalent to

$fetch($
  $\pi_{\lambda x.(x.n+1)}$
   $\sigma_{\lambda x.(x.1=v)}$
    $(ext(t_0) \bowtie_{\lambda x.(x.1.A_1=x.2)} ext(t_1) \bowtie_{\lambda x.(x.2.A_2=x.3)} \cdots$
     $\bowtie_{\lambda x.(x.n.A_n=x.(n+1))} ext(t_n)))$

Path expressions constitute a major difference between relational and object-oriented databases. In the former they are not supported whereas in the latter they are among the most basic and most frequently used expressions. Thus, the above equivalence is not present in relational databases but can be exploited for optimization purposes in object-oriented databases.

On the other hand, note that the standard relational technique of reordering joins applied to the second expression coincides with optimizations proposed in several papers ([Banerjee, Kim, and Kim 1988, Jenq et. al 1990, Kim et. al 1988]). Although the latter is more general in that it can deal with arbitrary or generalized path expressions that are not just linear chains of attributes, the stated optimization techniques can still be derived from relational join reordering as we will see in Section 3.6.2.

Retrieve Term   The **retrieve** operator is often seen as one of the reasons for the term language being low level as opposed to algebras. The reason is that the proposed implementation of the **retrieve** operator's evaluation is a nested loop. Nevertheless, the definition of this operator can be given in purely algebraic terms. More specifically, we can define

$$(\textbf{retrieve} :\textbf{B} \ ((x_1 \ t_1) \dots (x_n \ t_n)) \ :\textbf{S} \ sel\_pred \ :\textbf{P} \ proj\_list)$$

as

$$\pi_{\lambda x.proj\_list'} \sigma_{\lambda x.sel\_pred'}(ext(t_1) \bowtie \cdots \bowtie ext(t_n))$$

where $proj\_list'$ and sel_pred' are derived from $proj\_list$ and sel_pred, respectively, by modifying them such that the accesses to variables are replaced by accesses to components of the tuples obtained by the joins.

In the definition above we have restricted ourselves to the case where the binding list contains elements that are tuples of the form (*variable type*). In general, the second component can be any term—even a single-valued expression—to which the variable is bound. This binding mechanism can also serve a similar purpose as in SQL: resolving binding ambiguities that might occur, e.g., in the case of nesting access support relation accesses. If necessary, any operator in the term language can be enhanced by a binding clause. An example will be shown later in the paper.

Getasr Term   The **getasr** operator

$$(\textbf{getasr} \ [\![t_0.A_1.\cdots.A_n]\!]_X \ :\textbf{S} \ sel\_pred \ :\textbf{P} \ proj\_list)$$

is defined as

$$\pi_{\lambda x.proj\_list'}(\sigma_{\lambda x.sel\_pred'}(\llbracket t_0.A_1.\cdots.A_n \rrbracket_X))$$

where the expressions *proj_list'* and *sel_pred'* are modified such that they reflect the correct redirection of attribute accesses, i.e., each attribute access to the access support relation is preceded by an x.

In fact, we are a little bit sloppy in the usage of the getasr operator since in the original version it is able to cope with the actual physical representation including the utilization of indexes on the accessed ASR. The **getgmr** operator, which retrieves data from a generalized materialization relation (GMR), is defined analogously.

The Running Example

The translation of our example query into the GOM term language results in the following initial term:

(**retrieve :B** ((*e* EMP) (*d* DEPT))
         :S (**and** (= *d* (**path** *e* WorksIn))
                (< (**path** *d* Profit) 0)
                (> (**path** *e* Salary) 200000)
                (< (**path** *d* Mgr).skill 4))
         :P ((**path** *d* Mgr) (/ (**path** *d* Mgr).skill *d*.avg_skill)))

Note that *skill* is not an attribute but instead is an operation to be computed. Thus it cannot be included in the **path**-expression. The same holds for *avg_skill*.

3.6
The Optimization Process

As should be clear from the definition of our algebra, all the techniques developed for relational query optimization can be considered for object-oriented query optimization as well. Note that it is not the goal of this paper to review the optimization techniques for relational query optimization. (For a more thorough survey see, e.g., [von Bültzingsloewen 1990, Freytag 1987, Jarke and Koch 1984, Lehnert 1988].)

Instead, we come to the most critical experiments of this paper. The main question we are trying to answer by the following two experiments is how to provide a basis for exploiting the knowledge of relational query optimization for object-oriented query optimization. Obviously, there exist two possibilities to do so. First, one could perform a technical integration by simply changing the internal representation of an existing object-oriented query optimizer to an algebra, transforming its rewrite rules to the algebraic representation and then adding the proposed rewrite rules for relational query optimization to its rule base. This approach will be pursued within the next subsection. A consequence of this approach is that one must be able to mirror the object-oriented optimization within the algebra. We will do so and show the result. However, we will identify several disadvantages of this approach preventing the useful integration of relational optimization knowledge. One problem occurring is that the relational algebra transformations treat all the expressions which are subscripts to the algebra operators as black boxes. Therefore, additional transformations are needed to transform the subscripts into algebra operators or to transform the subscripts themselves. We will refer to this approach as the *syntactic integration* of relational and object-oriented query processing.

In the second approach, the integration does not take place at the technical level but must first take place at the "intellectual" level. By this we mean that the designer of the object-oriented query optimizer must first learn—at an abstract level—some basic ideas of relational query optimization in order to grasp its spirit. Next one is asked to transform this spirit to object-oriented query optimization. From then on the integration of both approaches into one useful approach to object-oriented query processing is straightforward. As we will see this approach results in a very clear optimization process allowing a clean optimizer and optimizer strategy design. We call this approach the *semantic integration*. This second experiment is carried out in Subsections 3.6.2 and 3.6.3.

3.6.1 Mimicking Term-Based Optimization Within the Algebra

In this section it is shown that it is possible to mimic the object-oriented query optimization process performed within the GOM optimizer within the algebra. This indicates the possibility of integrating relational and object-oriented query processing.

In order to facilitate the understanding of the optimization process it is useful to state the overall optimization strategy. The GOM optimizer strategy as currently employed is represented as a heuristic net. It is interpreted at optimization time. This interpretation enhances flexibility. A full account of this subject is beyond the scope of the paper, hence, only the restricted part relevant to the example is given. The optimization process for the running example will pass through 4 phases:

1. extending and splitting path expressions such that the available access support relations become applicable,

2. introducing the applicable access support relations and generalized materialization relations,

3. moving selections inwards,

4. moving projections inwards.

Each phase consists of possibly several steps. For example, Phase 1 consists of the two steps extending and splitting. Each step has a certain set of rules attached to it. Since the statement of the rules requires a good deal of formalism to be introduced, only the results after each application are illustrated—we trust that the reader is able to roughly figure out how the rules are specified. Note that several rules may be applied within one step. For further details we refer to the original literature.

Another characteristic of the GOM optimization process is that rewriting first takes place at inner terms and then proceeds to outer terms. In particular, the rule application first concentrates as much as possible on the selection clause (**:S**) of the **retrieve** term.

Original query   We restate the original query in term and algebraic representation:

(**retrieve :B** ((e EMP) (d DEPT))
        :S (**and** (= d (**path** e WorksIn))
               (< (**path** d Profit) 0)
               (> (**path** e Salary) 200000)
               (< (**path** d Mgr).skill 4))
        :P ((**path** d Mgr) (/ (**path** d Mgr).skill d.avg_skill)))

$\pi_{\lambda x.[x.2.\text{Mgr},x.2.\text{Mgr.skill}/x.2.\text{avg\_skill}]}$
$\sigma_{\lambda x.(x.2=x.1.\text{WorksIn and } x.2.\text{Profit}<0 \text{ and } x.1.\text{Salary}>200000 \text{ and } x.2.\text{Mgr.skill}<4)}$
$(ext(\text{EMP}) \bowtie ext(\text{DEPT}))$

For the subsequent optimization we assume the existence of the access support relation $\llbracket \text{EMP.WorksIn.Mgr} \rrbracket_{can}$. For simplicity of notation we will omit the subscript *"can"* within the ASR-specification. Further, the optimization process will take advantage of the generalized materialization relations $\langle\langle\text{skill}\rangle\rangle$ and $\langle\langle\text{avg\_skill}\rangle\rangle$.

The first phase of the optimization process consists of the two steps of extending and splitting path expressions such that the given access support relation becomes applicable (see Def. 3.5). Loosely speaking, these steps cut and paste path expressions until the materialized path *EMP.WorksIn.Mgr* is derived.

Extending paths/variable removal   In the term representation extending leads to the following (equivalent) term expression:

(**retrieve** :B ((e EMP))
   :S (**and** ($<$ (**path** e WorksIn Profit) 0)
       ($>$ (**path** e Salary) 200000)
       ($<$ (**path** e WorksIn Mgr).skill 4))
   :P ((**path** e WorksIn Mgr)
      (/ (**path** e WorksIn Mgr).skill (**path** e WorksIn).avg_skill)))

Note that not only all occurrences of d within the :S clause have been replaced by (**path** e WorksIn) but also the occurrence of d within the :B clause has been removed. This step could, of course, be deferred until the end of this optimization phase.

The same transformation step applied to the algebraic representation yields:

$$\pi_{\lambda x.[x.\text{WorksIn.Mgr},(x.\text{WorksIn.Mgr.skill}/x.\text{WorksIn.avg\_skill})]}$$
$$\sigma_{\lambda x.(x.\text{WorksIn.Profit}<0 \text{ and } x.\text{Salary}>200000 \text{ and } x.\text{WorksIn.Mgr.skill}<4)}$$
$$(ext(\text{EMP}))$$

If the removal of d had been deferred the whole transformation would have taken place within the subscripts. Nevertheless, we can speak of a "subscript driven" optimization step since the transformations at the algebra level are only adjustments, whereas the relevant information and the triggering part are contained in the subscript. We will see that this finding is also true for the subsequent optimization steps. It is important to note that this is a phenomenon not present only within the GOM optimizer.

Splitting and variable insertion   Remember that the transformation process first concentrates as much as possible on the selection predicate, i.e., the

:S clause. This concentration prevents the introduction of the applicable access support relation $[\![EMP.WorksIn.Mgr]\!]_{can}$ into the projection (**:P**) clause of the term above. Within the selection clause the access support relation is not yet applicable since the call to the method *skill* immediately succeeds the path. Thus, we split at this location:

(**retrieve :B** ((e EMP) (m MANAGER))
         :S (**and** (< (**path** e WorksIn Profit) 0)
                  (> (**path** e Salary) 200000)
                  (= (**path** e WorksIn Mgr) m)
                  (< m.skill 4))
         :P (m (/ m.skill (**path** e WorksIn).avg_skill))))

Contrary to the extending step where a variable could be eliminated from the term, we had to introduce a new variable m to hold the manager obtained at "the end" of the path (**path** e WorksIn Mgr) in order to be able to compute his or her skill, subsequently.

    Within the algebraic representation, this step results in the following:

$$\pi_{\lambda x.[x.2,(x.2.skill/x.1.WorksIn.avg\_skill)]}$$
$$\sigma_{\lambda x.(x.2=x.1.WorksIn.Mgr \text{ and } x.1.WorksIn.Profit<0 \text{ and } x.1.Salary>200000 \text{ and } x.2.skill<4)}$$
$$(ext(\text{EMP}) \bowtie ext(\text{MANAGER}))$$

Again, this step constitutes a "subscript driven" transformation.

Utilization of the ASR   Due to the above two steps we are now able to replace the path traversal (**path** e WorksIn Mgr) by an access to the access support relation $[\![EMP.WorksIn.Mgr]\!]_{can}$. For the term representation this replacement results in:

(**retrieve :B** ((e EMP) (m MANAGER))
         :S (**and** (**in** (e m) (**getasr** $[\![EMP.WorksIn.Mgr]\!]$
                                 :S (**true**) **:P** (#1 #3)))
                  (< (**path** e WorksIn Profit) 0)
                  (> (**path** e Salary) 200000)
                  (< m.skill 4))
         :P (m (/ m.skill (**path** e WorksIn).avg_skill))))

And in the algebra we obtain:

$$\pi_P \sigma_S(ext(\text{EMP}) \bowtie ext(\text{MANAGER}))$$

where

$P \equiv \lambda x.[x.2, (x.2.\text{skill}/x.1.\text{WorksIn.avg\_skill})]$

$S \equiv \lambda x.(x \in \pi_{\lambda x.[x.1,x.3]}(\llbracket \text{EMP.WorksIn.Mgr} \rrbracket) \text{ and}$
$\qquad x.1.\text{WorksIn.Profit} < 0 \text{ and}$
$\qquad x.1.\text{Salary} > 200000 \text{ and}$
$\qquad x.2.\text{skill} < 4)$

Utilization of GMRs   After having introduced the access support relation, the replacement of function invocations by GMR accesses is performed. The ordering among these two steps is arbitrary since they do not interfere. For the introduction of the GMR access two variables are necessary. The first, d, iterates over the departments whereas the second, s, holds as a result the skill of a manager. Introducing the variables and replacing the calls to *skill* and *avg_skill* by GMR accesses yields—after several elementary steps—the following term expression:

(**retrieve :B** ((e EMP) (m MANAGER) (d DEPT) (s INT))
    :S (**and** (**in** (e d m s) (**join** (**getasr** $\llbracket$EMP.WorksIn.Mgr$\rrbracket$
                 :S (**true**)
                 :P (#1 #2 #3))
            (**getgmr** $\langle\!\langle$skill$\rangle\!\rangle$
                 :S (**true**)
                 :P (#1 #2))
          :J (= #3 #4)
          :P (#1 #2 #3 #5)))
     (< (**path** d Profit) 0)
     (> (**path** e Salary) 200000)
     (< s 4))
    :P (m (/ s (**fetch** (**getgmr** $\langle\!\langle$avg_skill$\rangle\!\rangle$
              :S (= #1 d)
              :P #2)))))

Note that the binding of s to *INT* does not result in any problem if the term is processed further. Actual execution of the term above would run into problems due to the huge range of (computer representable) integers. Actually, it is impossible to directly mimic this step within the algebra. Nevertheless, ignoring the problems we will introduce a cross product with the extension of the integers and get rid of this construct in later steps. Thus, we obtain:

$$\pi_P \, \sigma_S(ext(\text{EMP}) \bowtie ext(\text{DEPT}) \bowtie ext(\text{MANAGER}) \bowtie ext(\text{INT}))$$

where

$$P \equiv \lambda x.[x.3, (x.4/fetch(\pi_{\lambda y.(y.2)} \sigma_{\lambda y.(y.1=x.2)}(\langle\!\langle\text{avg\_skill}\rangle\!\rangle)))]$$

$$S \equiv \lambda x.(x \in \pi_{\lambda x.[x.1,x.2,x.3,x.5]}([\![\text{EMP.WorksIn.Mgr}]\!] \bowtie_{\lambda x.(x.3=x.4)} \langle\!\langle\text{skill}\rangle\!\rangle)$$
$$\text{and } x.2.\text{Profit} < 0$$
$$\text{and } x.1.\text{Salary} > 200000$$
$$\text{and } x.4 < 4)$$

Moving selection predicates inwards   We now come to the more conventional optimization techniques as already employed within the relational optimization process. Moving selection predicates inwards is one of the common heuristics that can often be applied successfully.   Applying it to the example yields:

(**retrieve :B** ((*m* MANAGER) (*d* DEPT) (*s* INT))
   :S (**in** (*d m s*) (**join** (**getasr** [[EMP.WorksIn.Mgr]]
            :S (**and** (< (**path** #2 Profit) 0)
               (> (**path** #1 Salary) 200000))
          :P (#2 #3))
         (**getgmr** $\langle\!\langle$skill$\rangle\!\rangle$
            :S (< #2 4)
            :P (#1 #2))
        :J (= #2 #3)   !! revised column numbering
        :P (#1 #2 #4)))
    :P (*m* (/ *s* (**fetch** (**getgmr** $\langle\!\langle$avg_skill$\rangle\!\rangle$
              :S (= *d* #1)
              :P #2)))))

and

$$\pi_P \sigma_S(ext(\text{DEPT}) \bowtie ext(\text{MANAGER}) \bowtie ext(\text{INT}))$$

where

$$P \equiv \lambda x.[x.2, (x.3/fetch(\pi_{\lambda y.(y.2)} \sigma_{\lambda y.(y.1=x.1)}(\langle\!\langle\text{avg\_skill}\rangle\!\rangle)))]$$

$$S \equiv \lambda x.(x \in \pi_{\lambda x.[x.1,x.2,x.4]}$$
$$((\pi_{\lambda x.[x.2,x.3]}$$
$$\sigma_{\lambda x.(x.1.\text{Salary}>200000 \text{ and } x.2.\text{Profit}<0)}$$
$$([\![\text{EMP.WorksIn.Mgr}]\!]))$$
$$\bowtie_{\lambda x.(x.2=x.3)}$$
$$(\sigma_{\lambda x.(x.2<4)}$$
$$(\langle\!\langle\text{skill}\rangle\!\rangle)))$$

Moving projections inwards and removing retrieves   Again, this step consists of several rule applications. Within the term language several parts of the selection predicate can be moved to the binding list, resulting in smaller bindings to be explored if executed by a nested loop. This step is always required for variables that are bound to "infinite" sorts such as integer. If the selection predicate becomes empty (true) by this step, the outer retrieve can be removed and the resulting term representing the query is gained by moving the projection of the retrieve to the projection of the expression within the binding list.

Within our example there exists only one term within the selection predicate. It expresses variable bindings for all variables bound within the binding list. Its removal from the binding list results in a selection predicate equivalent to true. Since it is possible to move the projection of the outer retrieve to the expression within the binding list, the retrieve can totally be removed. We get

(join (getasr [[EMP.WorksIn.Mgr]]
          :S (and (< (**path** #2 Profit) 0)
                        (> (**path** #1 Salary) 200000))
            :P (#2 #3))
      (getgmr ⟨⟨skill⟩⟩
              :S (< #2 4)
              :P (#1 #2))
  :J (= #2 #3)
  :P (#2 (/ #4 (**fetch** (**getgmr** ⟨⟨avg_skill⟩⟩
                                  :B (d #1)
                                  :S (= d #1)
                                  :P #2)))))

Here, we see an example for the use of the binding clause **:B** within a non-**retrieve** term. Its usage is necessary here since the column number #1 would otherwise be ambiguous.

Within the algebra the equivalent of the expressions above replaces the cross product of the extensions by the access support relation access as performed within the selection operation of the selection. The result is as follows:

$\pi_{\lambda x.[x.2,(x.4/fetch(\pi_{\lambda y.(y.2)}\sigma_{\lambda y.(y.1=x.1)}(\langle\langle\text{avg\_skill}\rangle\rangle)))]}$
    $((\pi_{\lambda x.[x.2,x.3]}$
        $\sigma_{\lambda x.(x.1.\text{Salary}>200000 \text{ and } x.2.\text{Profit}<0)}$
            $([[\text{EMP.WorksIn.Mgr}]]))$
    $\bowtie_{\lambda x.(x.2=x.3)}$
    $(\sigma_{\lambda x.(x.2<4)}$
        $((\langle\langle\text{skill}\rangle\rangle)))$

We will now have a closer look at both optimizations, especially at the one performed within the algebra. Here, there is one important point to note: the optimization rules are mostly performed within the selection predicate of the selection operator or within the projection operations within the projection operator, i.e., in both cases the rewriting takes place within the subscripts of the algebraic operators. This subscript rewriting is not the clean algebraic optimization we are used to in the relational context. One goal of the next subsection is to remedy this situation.

Another observation is that often new domains (extensions) are introduced together with variables which are subsequently dropped and then reintroduced again. This seems to be a rather unstructured approach which will be remedied in the next subsection, as well.

3.6.2   The Most Costly Normal Form

In the previous section we have seen that algebraic optimization is not as readable as expected. One could argue that readability is no problem since the terms are only to be read by the optimizer; but, nevertheless, there exist reasons why readability is important. Not only the optimizer becomes harder to debug and errors more difficult to find, but also the search for optimization rules and the organization of the optimizer, i.e., the development of its strategy and pruning heuristics, is hindered.

As seen in the previous section, one of the main drawbacks is that the optimization takes place mostly within the subscripts. This rewriting of subscripts will be overcome by selecting another starting point, the term derived initially from the translation of the query into the algebra. This choice is crucial for the optimization process. A good starting point can be seen as a good heuristic to organize the optimization.

In object-oriented query processing it seems quite common to translate the query into an internal representation as close to the original query as possible ([Banerjee, Kim, and Kim 1988], [Cluet and Delobel 1992], and also [Kemper and Moerkotte 1990b]). This observation is also true for relational query processing where, for example, an SQL query is translated into a $\pi\sigma\bowtie$ -expression. But this representation exhibits another property that the initial internal representation of object-oriented queries lacks: it is a very costly term. Considering the following metaphor this seems a good heuristic. Optimization starts from the highest mountain from a cost point of view and then explores several ways down to the cost valleys. If one is not sure about the right way to the deepest valley, alternatives have to be explored. We will adopt this idea for object-oriented query processing and propose a very costly starting point. There exists another argument of equally importance for $\pi\sigma\bowtie$-expressions as starting points: they permit more transformations to be applied easily.

Parts of the idea can already be found in [Cluet and Delobel 1992] where some queries are translated into a $\pi\sigma\bowtie$ expression. In the context of extensible query optimization the idea is also utilized in [Becker and Güting 1992]. Our starting point will exhibit one additional projection directly following the $\bowtie$. Thus, it consists of a sequence $\pi\sigma\pi\bowtie$. First all the extensions whose instances are needed for the query evaluation are joined. More specifically, the cross product is taken. Then a projection follows which enhances each tuple of the resulting relation by further information needed in order to evaluate the selection predicate solely on the basis of this result. Then the selection follows evaluating the selection predicate of the query on each tuple resulting from the projection. Last, a projection onto the required result takes place. We call the thus derived query representation the *most costly normal form (MCNF)*.

For our example we get

$$\pi_{\lambda x.[x.7,x.8/x.6]}$$
$$\sigma_{\lambda y.(y.1=y.3 \wedge y.4=y.7 \wedge y.2>200000 \wedge y.5<0 \wedge y.8<4)}$$
$$\pi_{\lambda z.[z.1.\text{WorksIn},z.1.\text{Salary},z.2,z.2.\text{Mgr},z.2.\text{Profit},z.2.\text{avg\_skill},z.3,z.3.\text{skill}]}$$
$$(ext(\text{EMP}) \bowtie ext(\text{DEPT}) \bowtie ext(\text{MANAGER}))$$

with all join predicates being $\lambda x.true$. For the rest of this section we will stick to this convention.

3.6.3   Optimizer Strategy and Generating Alternatives

This normal form allows a clear optimizer strategy, and thus a clear optimizer design. Note that we are not talking about heuristics that are used to prune the search space of alternatives. Instead, a strategy divides the optimization process into several steps performed sequentially or under any other control procedure. Whenever a step may generate alternatives, heuristics may be useful to favor or discard some of them.

Another aspect treated within this section is the systematic generation of alternatives; a problem often neglected in object-oriented query processing.

The control strategy we propose is a hybrid of the current GOM optimizer strategy and the one described in [Becker and Güting 1992]:

1. Decompose any operation. For example, selection predicates with **and** are decomposed into two selections and so forth.

2. Introduce access support relations and generalized materialization relations, which may necessitate some join reordering first. If it is not clear that their introduction results in a performance gain, alternatives have to be generated.

3. Order the join operations—possibly generating alternatives.

4. Reassemble the path expressions and remove any redundant joins.

5. Improve the algebraic expression by pushing selections and the projections inwards and removing redundant join expressions.

6. Recombine operations—which is the inverse of the first step.

Again, we illustrate the optimization process starting with the most costly normal form and following the strategy above with the running example. This time, we will also illustrate that generating alternatives — which is the key to any effective optimization procedure — can be performed very systematically.

Step 1   results in:

$$
\begin{aligned}
\pi_{\lambda x.[x.7,x.8/x.6]} \\
\sigma_{\lambda y.(y.1=y.3)} \\
\sigma_{\lambda y.(y.4=y.7)} \\
\sigma_{\lambda y.(y.2>200000)} \\
\sigma_{\lambda y.(y.5<0)} \\
\sigma_{\lambda y.(y.8<4)} \\
\pi_{\lambda z.[z.1.\mathrm{WorksIn},z.1.\mathrm{Salary},z.2,z.2.\mathrm{Mgr},z.2.\mathrm{Profit},z.2.\mathrm{avg\_skill},z.3,z.3.\mathrm{skill}]} \\
(ext(\mathrm{EMP}) \bowtie ext(\mathrm{DEPT}) \bowtie ext(\mathrm{MANAGER}))
\end{aligned}
\tag{1}
$$

Step 2   Access support relations are introduced by replacing a sequence of joins of extensions by the appropriate access support relation—if the latter is applicable. For this step there may be some reordering of joins necessary. Further, the selection predicates have to be checked for the occurrence of the correct join predicates. For the example, assume that the introduction of the

GMRs clearly results in a performance increase whereas this is uncertain for the introduction of the ASR. Then two alternatives are generated:

$$\pi_{\lambda x.[x.7,x.8/x.6]}$$
$$\sigma_{\lambda y.(y.1=y.3)}$$
$$\sigma_{\lambda y.(y.4=y.7)}$$
$$\sigma_{\lambda y.(y.2>200000)}$$
$$\sigma_{\lambda y.(y.5<0)}$$
$$\sigma_{\lambda y.(y.8<4)} \qquad\qquad (2.a)$$
$$\sigma_{\lambda y.(y.3=y.9)}$$
$$\sigma_{\lambda y.(y.7=y.10)}$$
$$\pi_{\lambda z.[z.1.\text{WorksIn},z.1.\text{Salary},z.2,z.2.\text{Mgr},z.2.\text{Profit},z.5,z.3,z.7,z.4,z.6]}$$
$$(ext(\text{EMP}) \bowtie ext(\text{DEPT}) \bowtie ext(\text{MANAGER})$$
$$\bowtie \langle\!\langle\text{avg\_skill}\rangle\!\rangle \bowtie \langle\!\langle\text{skill}\rangle\!\rangle)$$

and

$$\pi_{\lambda x.[x.5,x.6/x.4]}$$
$$\sigma_{\lambda y.(y.1>200000)}$$
$$\sigma_{\lambda y.(y.3<0)}$$
$$\sigma_{\lambda y.(y.6<4)}$$
$$\sigma_{\lambda y.(y.2=y.7)} \qquad\qquad (2.b)$$
$$\sigma_{\lambda y.(y.5=y.8)}$$
$$\pi_{\lambda z.[z.1.\text{Salary},z.2,z.2.\text{Profit},z.5,z.3,z.7,z.4,z.6]}$$
$$([\![\text{EMP}.\text{WorksIn}.\text{Mgr}]\!] \bowtie \langle\!\langle\text{avg\_skill}\rangle\!\rangle \bowtie \langle\!\langle\text{skill}\rangle\!\rangle)$$

Within the above subscripts of the inner projection we have ordered the entries of the tuple to be created such that it first contains all necessary information on employees, followed by the information on departments and then the information on managers. Last, the first columns of the generalized materialization relations are included in order to provide the necessary information for the join predicates.

Step 3 We consider for expression (2.a) two different join orderings corresponding to forward traversal and mixed traversal of [Kim et. al 1988] and [Jenq et. al 1990]:

$$\pi_{\lambda x.[x.7,x.8/x.6]}$$
$$\sigma_{\lambda y.(y.1=y.3)}$$
$$\sigma_{\lambda y.(y.4=y.7)}$$
$$\sigma_{\lambda y.(y.2>200000)}$$
$$\sigma_{\lambda y.(y.5<0)}$$
$$\sigma_{\lambda y.(y.8<4)} \hspace{4cm} (3.a.1)$$
$$\sigma_{\lambda y.(y.3=y.9)}$$
$$\sigma_{\lambda y.(y.7=y.10)}$$
$$\pi_{\lambda z.[z.1.\text{WorksIn},z.1.\text{Salary},z.2,z.2.\text{Mgr},z.2.\text{Profit},z.5,z.3,z.7,z.4,z.6]}$$
$$(ext(\text{EMP}) \bowtie ext(\text{DEPT}) \bowtie ext(\text{MANAGER})$$
$$\bowtie \langle\!\langle\text{avg\_skill}\rangle\!\rangle \bowtie \langle\!\langle\text{skill}\rangle\!\rangle)$$

$$\pi_{\lambda x.[x.7,x.8/x.6]}$$
$$\sigma_{\lambda y.(y.1=y.3)}$$
$$\sigma_{\lambda y.(y.4=y.7)}$$
$$\sigma_{\lambda y.(y.2>200000)}$$
$$\sigma_{\lambda y.(y.5<0)}$$
$$\sigma_{\lambda y.(y.8<4)} \hspace{4cm} (3.a.2)$$
$$\sigma_{\lambda y.(y.3=y.9)}$$
$$\sigma_{\lambda y.(y.7=y.10)}$$
$$\pi_{\lambda z.[z.4.\text{WorksIn},z.4.\text{Salary},z.3,z.3.\text{Mgr},z.3.\text{Profit},z.7,z.5,z.2,z.6,z.1]}$$
$$(\langle\!\langle\text{skill}\rangle\!\rangle \bowtie ext(\text{DEPT}) \bowtie ext(\text{EMP})$$
$$\bowtie ext(\text{MANAGER}) \bowtie \langle\!\langle\text{avg\_skill}\rangle\!\rangle)$$

We do not consider any reordering for (2.b), which thus equals (3.b).

Step 4 In query (3.a.1) we reassemble the path *EMP.WorksIn.Mgr* since a forward traversal of references is cheaper than performing the joins. Reassembling the path yields:

$$\pi_{\lambda x.[x.5,x.6/x.4]}$$
$$\sigma_{\lambda y.(y.1>200000)}$$
$$\sigma_{\lambda y.(y.3<0)}$$
$$\sigma_{\lambda y.(y.6<4)}$$
$$\sigma_{\lambda y.(y.2=y.7)} \hspace{4cm} (4.a.1)$$
$$\sigma_{\lambda y.(y.5=y.8)}$$
$$\pi_{\lambda z.[z.1.\text{Salary},z.1.\text{WorksIn},z.1.\text{WorksIn.Profit},z.3,z.1.\text{WorksIn.Mgr},z.5,z.2,z.4]}$$
$$(ext(\text{EMP}) \bowtie \langle\!\langle\text{avg\_skill}\rangle\!\rangle \bowtie \langle\!\langle\text{skill}\rangle\!\rangle)$$

This step might again be called "subscript driven," which is unavoidable since the equivalence of path expressions and joins has to be expressed. We have a flow of the relevant information from the joins to the subscripts. Obviously, this step complements the creation of the most costly normal form.

There is no path to be reassembled for (3.a.2) but we can eliminate the redundant access to the extension of *MANAGER*, which results in:

$$
\begin{aligned}
&\pi_{\lambda x.[x.4,x.8/x.6]} \\
&\quad \sigma_{\lambda y.(y.1=y.3)} \\
&\qquad \sigma_{\lambda y.(y.2>200000)} \\
&\qquad\quad \sigma_{\lambda y.(y.5<0)} \\
&\qquad\qquad \sigma_{\lambda y.(y.8<4)} \\
&\qquad\qquad\quad \sigma_{\lambda y.(y.3=y.9)} \\
&\qquad\qquad\qquad \sigma_{\lambda y.(y.4=y.7)} \\
&\qquad\qquad\qquad\quad \pi_{\lambda z.[z.4.\mathrm{WorksIn},z.4.\mathrm{Salary},z.3,z.3.\mathrm{Mgr},z.3.\mathrm{Profit},z.6,z.1,z.2,z.5]} \\
&\qquad\qquad\qquad\quad (\langle\!\langle\mathrm{skill}\rangle\!\rangle \bowtie\ ext(\mathrm{DEPT}) \bowtie ext(\mathrm{EMP}) \bowtie \langle\!\langle\mathrm{avg\_skill}\rangle\!\rangle)
\end{aligned}
\tag{4.a.2}
$$

There is no path to be reassembled nor are there any redundant joins in (3.b). Let (4.b) equal (3.b).

Step 5 This step consists of pushing the selections inwards and moving the access to the GMR $\langle\!\langle\mathrm{avg\_skill}\rangle\!\rangle$ to the outer projection.

$$
\begin{aligned}
&\pi_{\lambda x.[x.2,x.3/fetch(\pi_{\lambda y.(y.2)}\sigma_{\lambda y.(y.1=x.1)}(\langle\!\langle\mathrm{avg\_skill}\rangle\!\rangle))]} \\
&\quad ((\sigma_{\lambda y.(y.\mathrm{Profit}<0)} \\
&\qquad \pi_{\lambda z.(z.\mathrm{WorksIn})} \\
&\qquad\quad \sigma_{\lambda y.(y.\mathrm{Salary}>200000)}(ext(\mathrm{EMP}))) \\
&\quad \bowtie \lambda x.(x.1.\mathrm{Mgr}=x.2) \\
&\quad (\sigma_{\lambda y.(y.2<4)}(\langle\!\langle\mathrm{skill}\rangle\!\rangle))))
\end{aligned}
\tag{5.a.1}
$$

$$
\begin{aligned}
&\pi_{\lambda x.[x.1,x.2/fetch(\pi_{\lambda y.(y.2)}\sigma_{\lambda y.(y.1=x.3)}(\langle\!\langle\mathrm{avg\_skill}\rangle\!\rangle))]} \\
&\quad (\sigma_{\lambda y.(y.2<4)}(\langle\!\langle\mathrm{skill}\rangle\!\rangle) \\
&\quad \bowtie \lambda x.(x.1=x.3.\mathrm{Mgr}) \\
&\quad \sigma_{\lambda y.(y.\mathrm{Profit}<0)}(ext(\mathrm{DEPT})) \\
&\quad \bowtie \lambda x.(x.3=x.4.\mathrm{WorksIn}) \\
&\quad \sigma_{\lambda y.(y.\mathrm{Salary}>200000)}(ext(\mathrm{EMP})))
\end{aligned}
\tag{5.a.2}
$$

Of course, the last join in the above expression could be reduced to a semijoin utilizing the $\in$ predicate.

$$\pi_{\lambda x.[x.3,x.5/fetch(\pi_{\lambda y.(y.2)}\sigma_{\lambda y.(y.1=x.2)}(\langle\!\langle\!\langle\text{avg\_skill}\rangle\!\rangle\!\rangle))]}$$
$$(\sigma_{\lambda y.(y.1.\text{Salary}>200000 \wedge y.2.\text{Profit}<0)}([\![\text{EMP.WorksIn.Mgr}]\!]_{can})$$
$$\bowtie_{\lambda x.(x.3=x.4)}$$
$$\sigma_{\lambda y.(y.2<4)}(\langle\!\langle\!\langle\text{skill}\rangle\!\rangle\!\rangle))$$

(5.b)

Step 6 recombines selections. In our example there is no recombination possible. The algebraic expression (5.b) mostly resembles the result of the previous subsection. For the derivation of the equivalent of (5.b) in the previous subsection, tranformations in all six steps were necessary. Here, the number of relevant steps was diminished to only three steps. Paying attention to the fact that the introduction of GMRs and ASRs accounted for one step in the latter optimization process the gain is still 2/3. Taking into account that the search space increases roughly exponential in the number of transformations to be carried out, the saving above becomes highly relevant.

For the evaluation of the above expressions note that a sequence of type $\pi\sigma\pi(ext(t))$ can be performed by a single *scan* operator applied to the objects of type t.

3.7
Conclusion

In this paper we investigated to what extent the relational query optimization techniques can be exploited for object-oriented query optimization. It turned out that the so-called "semantic integration" through the *most costly normal form* results in a highly structured optimization strategy.

Since it should be clear by now that object-oriented query processing can benefit a lot from relational query processing, the question arises whether relational query processing can benefit from object-oriented query processing as well. Of course, since there is no behavior within relational databases, the methods developed for operator materialization cannot be applied. But things look different for the access support relations. They can be seen as the materialization of n-way joins where the projection takes place on the primary key of each relation. The different extensions of ASRs allow a broad utilization of ASRs, even if the query to be optimized does not span all n joins.

Further, it should be explored whether every index access can be expressed as an access to a special relation with a cost possibly different from the costs of accessing a non-index relation. A further step would be to also reflect physical properties within the algebra allowing to discard the two-step approach of first algebraic optimization and then index exploitation. There would be two advantages of this approach. First, one could avoid the generation of many alternatives, since indexes are not considered during algebraic optimization and their utilization may depend on its outcome. Second, the query optimizers would have to deal with a single representation—which would be amenable to a well-structured design.

Acknowledgment

This work was supported by the German Research Council DFG under contracts SFB 346 and Ke 401/6-1.

We thank K. Peithner, A. Roemer, and R. Waurig for careful reading of a first draft and for many fruitful discussions. R. Waurig implemented the term-language-based GOM query optimizer. Further, we acknowledge gratefully the fruitful comments of the editors J. C. Freytag, D. Maier, and G. Vossen.

Bibliography

[Atkinson et. al 1989] Atkinson M., Bancilhon F., DeWitt D. J., Dittrich K. R., Maier D., and Zdonik S. "The object-oriented database system manifesto." In *Proc. of the Conference on Deductive and Object-Oriented Databases (DOOD)*, pp. 40–57, Kyoto, Japan.

[Banerjee, Kim, and Kim 1988] Banerjee J., Kim W., and Kim K. C. "Queries in object-oriented databases." In *Proc. Int. Conf. on Data Engineering*, pp. 31–38.

[Becker and Güting 1992] Becker L. and Güting R. H. "Rule-based optimization and query processing in an extensible geometric database system." *ACM Trans. on Database Systems*, **17**(2), pp. 247–303.

[Bertino and Kim 1989] Bertino E. and Kim W. "Indexing techniques for queries on nested objects." *IEEE Trans. Knowledge and Data Engineering*, **1**(2), pp. 196–214.

[Carey, DeWitt, and Vandenberg 1988] Carey M. J., DeWitt D. J., and Vandenberg S. L. "A data model and query language for EXODUS." In *Proc. of the ACM SIGMOD Conf. on Management of Data*, pp. 413–423, Chicago, Il..

[Cluet and Delobel 1992] Cluet S. and Delobel C. "Towards a unifiction of rewrite based optimization techniques for object-oriented queries." In *Proc. ACM SIGMOD Conf. on Management of Data*, pp. 383–392, San Diego, CA.

[Freytag 1987] Freytag J. C. "A rule-based view of query optimization." In *Proc. of the ACM SIGMOD Conf. on Management of Data*, pp. 173-180, San Francisco, CA.

[Härder 1978] Härder T. "Implementing a generalized access path structure for a relational database system." *ACM Trans. Database Syst.*, **3**(3), pp. 285–298.

[Jarke and Koch 1984] Jarke M. and Koch J. "Query optimization in database systems." *ACM Computing Surveys*, **16**(2), pp. 111–152.

[Jenq et. al 1990] Jenq P., Woelk D., Kim W., and Lee W. "Query processing in distributed ORION." In *Proc. Int. Conf. on Extended Database Technology (EDBT)*, Venice, Italy.

[Kemper, Kilger, and Moerkotte 1991] Kemper A., Kilger C., and Moerkotte G. "Materialization of functions in object bases." In *Proc. of the ACM SIGMOD Conf. on Management of Data*, pp. 258–268, Denver, CO.

[Kemper, Kilger, and Moerkotte 1992] Kemper A., Kilger C., and Moerkotte G. "Function materialization in object bases: design, realization, and evaluation." To appear in *IEEE Trans. Knowledge and Data Engineering*.

[Kemper and Moerkotte 1990a] Kemper A. and Moerkotte G. "Access support in object bases." In *Proc. of the ACM SIGMOD Conf. on Management of Data*, pp. 364–374, Atlantic City, NJ.

[Kemper and Moerkotte 1990b] Kemper A. and Moerkotte G. "Advanced query processing in object bases using access support relations." In *Proc. of The Conf. on Very Large Data Bases (VLDB)*, pp. 290–301, Brisbane, Australia.

[Kemper and Moerkotte 1990c] Kemper A. and Moerkotte G. "Advanced query processing in object bases: A comprehensive approach to access support, query transformation and evaluation." Technical report No. 27/90, University of Karlsruhe, Computer Science Department, 7500 Karlsruhe, F. R. G.

[Kemper and Moerkotte 1991] Kemper A. and Moerkotte G. "A formal model for object-oriented databases." Technical report, University of Karlsruhe.

[Kemper and Moerkotte 1992] Kemper A. and Moerkotte G. Access support relations: an indexing method for object bases. *Information Systems*, **17**(2), pp. 117–145.

[Kemper et. al 1991] Kemper A., Moerkotte G., Walter H. D., and Zachmann A. "GOM: a strongly typed, persistent object model with polymorphism." In *Proc. of the German Conf. on Databases in Office, Engineering, and Science (BTW)*, pp. 198–217, Kaiserslautern, Springer-Verlag, Informatik-Fachberichte Nr. 270.

[Keßler and Dadam 1991] Keßler U. and Dadam P. "Auswertung komplexer Anfragen an hierarchisch strukturierte Objekte mittels Pfadindexen." In *Proc. of the German Conf. on Databases in Office, Engineering, and Science (BTW)*, pp. 218–237, Kaiserslautern, Springer-Verlag, Informatik-Fachberichte Nr. 270.

[Kim et. al 1988] Kim K. C., Kim W., Woelk D., and Dale A. "Acyclic query processing in object-oriented databases." In *Proc. of the Entity Relationship Conf.*, Italy.

[Lehnert 1988] Lehnert K. *Regelbasierte Beschreibung von Optimierungsverfahren für relationale Datenbankanfragesprachen*. PhD thesis, Technische Universität München, 8000 München, Germany.

[Maier and Stein 1986] Maier D. and Stein J. "Indexing in an object-oriented DBMS." In Dittrich K. R. and Dayal U., editors, *Proc. IEEE Intl. Workshop on Object-Oriented Database Systems*, Asilomar, Pacific Grove, CA, pp. 171–182. IEEE Computer Society Press.

[Stonebraker 1985] Stonebraker M., editor. *The INGRES Papers: Anatomy of a Relational Database System*. Addison Wesley, Reading.

[Ullmann 1987] Ullman J. D. "Database theory: past and future." In *Proc. ACM Symp. on Principles of Database Systems*, (PODS), pp. 1–10.

[Valduriez 1987] Valduriez P. "Join indices." *ACM Trans. Database Syst.*, **12**(2), pp. 218–246.

[von Bültzingsloewen 1990] von Bültzingsloewen G. *SQL Anfragen: Optimierung für parallele Bearbeitung (Optimization of SQL-queries for parallel processing)*. FZI Berichte Informatik, Springer-Verlag, 1992.

[Zdonik and Maier 1989] Zdonik S. and Maier D. "Fundamentals of object-oriented databases." In Zdonik S. and Maier D., editors, *Readings in Object-Oriented Databases*, pp. 1–32. Morgan Kaufmann Publishers.

4

Optimization of Complex-Object Queries in PRIMA - Statement of Problems

Harald Schöning

Abstract

The molecule-atom data model allows the dynamic construction of complex objects using an identifier-reference concept. The model and its implementation in the PRIMA system are sketched. Then, with the help of some sample queries, some alternatives for query evaluation are discussed. The decision among the possible algorithms cannot be based on the standard statistics such as distribution of an attribute value. The kind of information needed is the correlation between graph properties and attribute values. In order to accelerate access, its components may be read in parallel. Using a maximum degree of parallelism for this purpose has disadvantages if the complex object does not qualify with respect to the condition included in the query. Criteria for an optimal degree of parallelism still have to be found.

4.1
Introduction

The support of complex objects has become a strong requirement for advanced database management systems. There have been several proposals for so-called structurally object-oriented database management systems which focus on complex object handling facilities. In addition, the object-oriented database systems also cover several aspects of complex objects management. In this paper we will consider a specific structurally object-oriented database management system called PRIMA, which provides an elaborated complex-object data model with a variety of underlying storage structures. The data model together with the storage structures and the parallelism offered by the system architecture give several degrees of freedom for the choice of query evaluation algorithms. We focus on a basic operator in PRIMA and demonstrate the possible evaluation methods. In order to determine the optimal combination of choices one has compare the costs of several alternatives which heavily depend on the graph structure of the underlying database. Statistically capturing this graph structure seems to be a hard problem.

The rest of the paper is organized as follows. Section 4.2 gives a short overview of the molecule-atom data model provided by PRIMA. The architecture of PRIMA is sketched in Section 4.3. Section 4.4 gives an overview of the query processing in PRIMA. Section 4.5 focuses on the basic operator in molecule construction and discusses the choices to be made during optimization. Section 4.6 gives a short conclusion.

4.2
Basic Features of the Molecule-Atom Data Model

The molecule-atom data model (MAD model [Mitschang 1988a]) was introduced to support the use of dynamically defined complex objects. Complex object types (molecule types) are defined in terms of their components, which may be either complex object types or basic object types (atom types). An atom type consists of some attribute types, and therefore may be compared to a relation in the relational model. The corresponding objects, called atoms, are similar to tuples. We allow a richer selection of data types than most conventional database systems do. Particularly, the two special data types IDENTIFIER and REFERENCE are used to explicitly express binary relationships between atoms. The *IDENTIFIER* attribute, which is present in each atom exactly once, contains a system-defined primary key (surrogate) to uniquely identify the atom. *REFERENCE* attributes contain one or more IDENTIFIER values, all pointing to atoms of the same atom type (typed references). At the schema level, there must be a corresponding "back reference" for each REFERENCE attribute, i.e., if atom type $\mathcal{A}$ has a REFERENCE attribute pointing to atom type $\mathcal{B}$ (for short, "REFERENCE attribute to $\mathcal{B}$"), then atom type $\mathcal{B}$ must contain a corresponding REFERENCE attribute to $\mathcal{A}$. Symmetry is also required at the instance level. If the REFERENCE attribute of atom a contains the value of the IDENTIFIER attribute of atom b the corresponding REFERENCE attribute of atom b has to contain the value of the IDENTIFIER attribute of a. This structural integrity is enforced by the operations of the MAD model. Thus, there is a means to reflect 1:1, 1:n, and n:m relationships among atoms in a direct and symmetric way. The relationships between atoms, which are manifested by the values of the REFERENCE attributes, lead to the so called atom network. As described so far, the MAD model is similar to the entity-relationship model [Chen 1976].

The relationships installed by REFERENCE attributes can be used to define molecule types. The notation `A.bref-B.cref-C` means, for example, that for each atom a of type $\mathcal{A}$ all atoms of type $\mathcal{B}$ ("$\mathcal{B}$ atoms") that are referenced by a's REFERENCE attribute *bref* and all $\mathcal{C}$ atoms referenced by attribute *cref* of these $\mathcal{B}$ atoms are grouped to a molecule. This definition assigns a direction to the relationships between $\mathcal{A}$ and $\mathcal{B}$, and $\mathcal{B}$ and $\mathcal{C}$ respectively. We call such a directed relationships within one molecule a link. Hence, a molecule can be seen as a directed subgraph of the atom network having one root, the so-called *root atom* (in contrast to the *component atoms*).

If $\mathcal{A}$ has only one REFERENCE attribute to $\mathcal{B}$, A-B may be written instead of `A.bref-B`.

Besides hierarchical structures as introduced above, the MAD model also allows network-like and recursive molecule type definitions. When an atom type has more than one predecessor in the molecule type graph, an atom of this type belongs to a corresponding molecule only if it has references to at least one atom of each of the predecessor types that also belongs to that corresponding molecule (AND semantics). Recursive molecule types repeat a component molecule type at several recursion levels. Recursion level 0 of a recursive molecule consists of a molecule of the component molecule type. All molecules of the component molecule type that are referenced by the recursion defining REFERENCE attribute of a component molecule at level i form level i+1 of the recursion. If a component molecule appears at more than one level of recursion, it belongs to only the lowest numbered one. Thus, cycles in the recursive molecule are avoided, and the termination of the operator computing the transitive closure is guaranteed. Figure 4.1 illustrates some molecule types and corresponding molecules for a sample database. Several features should be observed:

- Molecules vary in size. For instance, one of the molecules of type A-B-C in Figure 4.1 consists of only one atom. This structural incompleteness is caused by the fact that a REFERENCE attribute has an empty value. Cardinality restrictions may be specified in the database schema which prohibit empty or undefined values for REFERENCE attributes.

- The links from an atom to its descendants may vary from molecule to molecule (consider atom b_1 in molecule type A-(B,D)-C). The molecule-atom data model directly reflects sharing of components among molecules (i.e., molecules overlap[1]). Furthermore, if there are several paths to an atom in a molecule graph, this atom is not replicated, but included only once in the molecule.

Sets of molecules can be inserted, deleted, updated or retrieved (selected) using the SQL-like molecule query language (MQL). In this paper, we concentrate on the SELECT-statement, which is the most complex statement.

---

[1] To emphasize the single molecules, molecule overlapping is not shown graphically in Figure 4.1. However, some molecules do overlap (for instance, the molecules of type C-B-A share atom a_2).

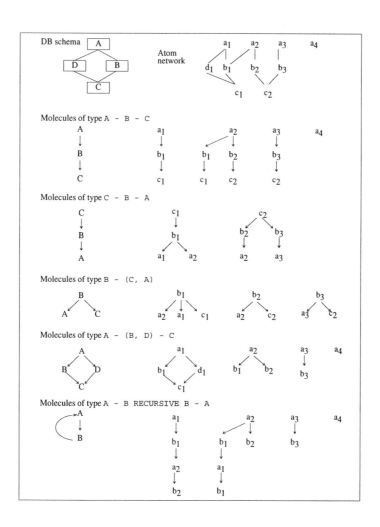

FIGURE 4.1

Example of molecules for various molecule type definitions

It is used to extract a set of molecules of a certain type from the database. Its general form is

```
SELECT <projection clause>
FROM   <molecule type definition clause>
WHERE  <restriction clause>
```

The *molecule type definition clause* determines the environment (molecule type) to work on. Besides the facilities for molecule type definition which were introduced so far, a Cartesian Product of molecule types may be defined by enumerating the participating molecule types separated by a comma.

The *restriction clause* contains a condition ranging over the environment molecule type. It may be of arbitrary complexity, and may contain quantifiers and SELECT-statements (nested subqueries). Only those molecules that fulfill this condition (molecules that *qualify*) are members of the result set. If no restrictions are to be imposed, "WHERE <restriction clause>" may be omitted. The following quantifiers may occur in a condition: EXISTS, EXIST_EXACTLY (n), EXIST_AT_LEAST (n), EXIST_AT_MOST (n), FOR_ALL.

The projection clause specifies which parts of the molecules should appear in the result. According to this clause, atoms or attributes are removed from the qualifying molecules. A value-dependent projection is possible ("qualified projection") and can be specified using a SELECT-statement with the special molecule type definition clause "RESULT". The last query in Figure 4.2 shows an example of a qualified projection. All molecules of type C-B-A belong to the result. Of these molecules, however, atoms of types $\mathcal{B}$ are included in the result only if there are exactly two links to atoms of type $\mathcal{A}$. Atoms of type $\mathcal{C}$ are always included in the molecule, while atoms of type $\mathcal{A}$ never are.

The result of a SELECT query is a set of molecules of the type specified in the molecule type definition clause, which qualify under the conditions of the restriction clause and have undergone the projection specified in the projection clause. Figure 4.2 shows a sample atom network and some queries together with their resulting sets of molecules.

This short introduction to MQL neglects many aspects of our query language as well as of our data model [Mitschang 1988b, Mitschang 1989, Schöning 1989]. Nevertheless, it will be sufficient to understand the discussions in the following sections.

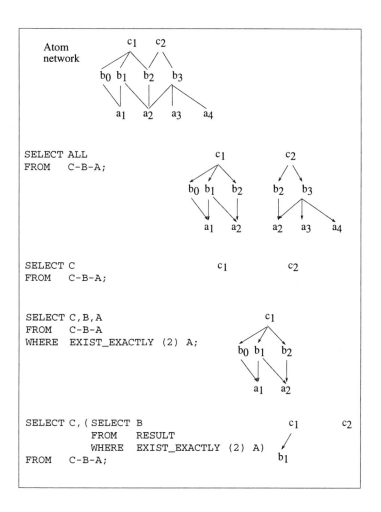

FIGURE 4.2

Some queries with their results based on a sample atom network

4.3
The PRIMA Architecture

So far, we have sketched some features of the MAD model. In the following, we present a short overview of its implementation within the PRIMA system [Härder et al. 1987, Härder 1988]. Our implementation model for PRIMA (Figure 4.3) distinguishes three different layers for mapping molecules, which

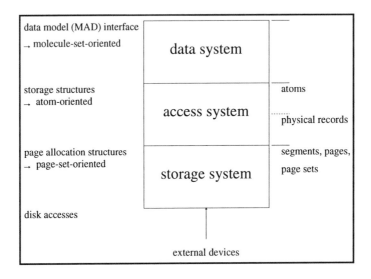

FIGURE 4.3
Implementation model of PRIMA

are visible at the MAD interface, onto blocks stored on external devices:

- The main task of the *data system* is to execute MQL statements. For this purpose, the user-submitted MQL statements are transformed into semantically equivalent query evaluation plans (QEPs). This step comprises compilation and optimization. Subsequently, these QEPs are evaluated, yielding the desired result (execution phase).

- The *access system* [Sikeler 1989] provides an atom-oriented interface similar to the tuple-oriented interface of the Research Storage System

(RSS) of System R [Chamberlin 1981]. However, the access system is more powerful than RSS as outlined in the following. It allows for direct access and manipulation of a single atom as well as navigational atom-by-atom access to either homogeneous or heterogeneous atom sets. Manipulation operations (insert, modify, and delete) and direct access (retrieve) operate on single atoms identified by the value of their IDEN-TIFIER attribute.

Different kinds of scan operations are introduced as a concept to manage a dynamically defined set of atoms, to hold a current position in such a set, and to successively deliver single atoms. The *atom-type scan* delivers all atoms in a system-defined order based on the basic storage structure that always exists for each atom type. Similarly, the *sort scan* processes all atoms according to a specified sort criterion thereby utilizing the basic storage structure. However, since sorting an entire atom type is expensive and time consuming, a sort scan may be supported by an additional storage structure called sort order. A sort order consists of a homogeneous atom set materializing a sort operator, i.e. a redundant copy of the atoms of one atom type, physically stored in the specified order. The *access-path scan* provides an appropriate means for fast value-dependent access based on different access path structures such as B-trees, grid files, and R-trees. The *atom-cluster-type scan* as well as the *atom-cluster scan* speed up the construction of frequently used molecules by allocating all atoms of a corresponding molecule in physical contiguity using a tailored storage structure called atom-cluster type [Schöning and Sikeler 1989]. An atom-cluster type corresponds to a hierarchical molecule type. Thus, it clusters a heterogeneous set of atoms according to the directed type graph. Clustering is done in addition to the storage in the basic storage structure, i.e., the atom-cluster type is a redundant storage structure. Furthermore, clusters may overlap. Thus, an atom may be contained in several clusters of the same or another atom-cluster type.

- The *storage system* as the lowest layer of PRIMA pursues two major tasks: It manages the database buffer and organizes the external storage devices, thus being responsible for the data exchange between main storage and disk storage. For this purpose, the database is divided into various segments consisting of a set of logically ordered pages. All pages of a segment are of equal size, and can be chosen for each segment independently to be 1/2, 1, 2, 4, or 8 kbytes, being kept fixed during the lifetime of a segment. Thus, the page size may be adapted to the specific access pattern of the segment in order to diminish either the conflict rate or the number of I/O operations. The five page sizes, however, are not sufficient when considering the mapping process performed by the access system. Therefore, page sequences are introduced as predefined page sets supported by physical clustering. A page sequence is a set of logical consecutive pages of a segment that contain (from the viewpoint of the access system) a single object spanning these pages [Deppisch et al. 1986].

This short overview of the PRIMA architecture should be sufficient as a basis for the following discussions.

4.4
Query Processing in the Data System

When an MQL statement is given to the data system, it is compiled into an equivalent QEP forming a directed graph. The vertices of this graph are labeled with operators, while its edges correspond to the data flow among the operators. The leaves of the QEP represent the operator *construction of simple molecules* (CSM), which builds up hierarchical, non-recursive molecules fulfilling some qualifications by using access system calls. The other vertices stand for operators such as *recursion, Cartesian product*, etc. Figure 4.4 shows a simple example of a QEP for a query containing a Cartesian Product (indicated by two molecule type definitions which are separated by a comma). In the resulting molecules, atoms of type $\mathcal{D}$ are omitted. The QEP may be subject to transformations by the optimizer, which is expected to generate a more efficient QEP by choosing appropriate access paths, selecting specific methods for each operator, and so on. Some of the possible choices for the CSM operator are discussed later.

When a QEP is executed, the operations indicated by its leaves are involved first, i.e., CSM operations are started. Whenever a molecule has been constructed, it is handed in a pipelined way to the next operator as indicated by the edges in the QEP. The root operator of the QEP produces the final result set of molecules [Härder et al. 1988]. Each node of a QEP may be evaluated on another processor. Hence, the data driven approach chosen here saves inter-processor communication, since no control messages have to

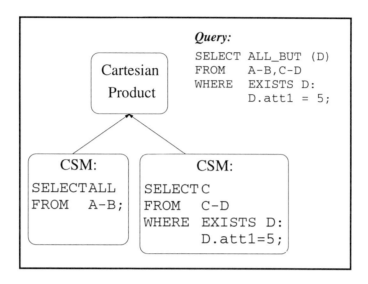

FIGURE 4.4
Sample query and corresponding QEP

be passed. In Volcano [Graefe 1990] there are OPEN, NEXT, CLOSE calls which manage a control-driven evaluation of a QEP as long as no processor boundaries are crossed. Otherwise, evaluation is done data-driven, but this fact is masked by a specialized operator. A consequence of this approach, however, is that parallelism has to be pre-planned, i.e., embedded in the QEP, which is not the case in PRIMA, where run-time assignment of operator evaluation and even migration of the corresponding tasks from one processor to another is possible.

All other operators get their input (directly or transitively) from the CSM operator in a pipelined way. Often, however, CSM is the only operator in a QEP, since in many cases the complex object facilities are sufficient to model the application's objects without explicit join or other higher operators. Therefore, it is necessary to direct one's attention to the optimization of the execution of the CSM operator. CSM constructs a set of molecules characterized by the following MQL query:

```
SELECT P(M)
FROM   M
WHERE  Q(M);
```

M is the definition of a non-recursive hierarchical molecule type, P(M) is a coherent subgraph of M (projection), containing the root atom type of M, and Q(M) is a restriction on M that can be determined by the consideration of a single molecule. As a consequence, Q(M) is not allowed to contain any sub-queries.

Conceptually, CSM scans the root atom type of M. For each atom of this type, CSM fetches the successor atoms according to M, then their successor atoms, and so on. When the whole molecule is fetched, it is checked against Q(M). If it qualifies, the molecule is postprocessed according to P(M) and added to the result set. This viewpoint, however, is only conceptual. In the following section we will show how CSM may be computed more efficiently.

4.5
Evaluating CSM

As mentioned above there are several algorithms to compute the result of a CSM operator. In the sequel we discuss some of the possible choices. For several sets of choices, we still lack criteria to determine the best one.

Two phase approach

Obviously, it would be inefficient to construct a molecule completely before evaluating the restriction, if only parts of the molecule are referenced in the corresponding expression. One should first consider a coherent minimal subgraph of M that is sufficient to decide Q(M). For this purpose, we introduce two phases of a molecule's construction: the *checking phase* checks the qualification of the molecule with respect to the restriction, the *completion phase* completes its components, i.e., reads those parts of the molecule that do not contribute to the result of the expression in the restriction clause. For example, for the query

```
SELECT ALL
FROM   A-(B,C)
WHERE  FOR_ALL C: C.Att1=5;
```

in the checking phase one would scan atom type $\mathcal{A}$. For each atom a of type $\mathcal{A}$, one then reads the atoms c of type $\mathcal{C}$ referenced by a, until one of them does not fulfill the condition `c.att1=5` or all are read and fulfill the condition. In the latter case, in the completion phase the atoms of type $\mathcal{B}$ referenced by a have to be read. In the completion phase, the order of accesses to atoms of the atom types that still have to be read does not matter, because all orders lead to the same amount of I/O. In the checking phase, however, the order of access is important.

Top-down or bottom-up

The condition Q(M) of the restriction clause may reference several atom types. Let us assume that Q has the following shape:

$$Q(M) = Q_1 \quad \text{AND} \quad Q_2 \quad \text{AND} \quad Q_3... \quad \text{AND} \quad Q_n.$$

In the checking phase, all these parts of the restriction clause have to be evaluated to TRUE if a molecule qualifies. For the evaluation of a part Q_i of Q(M), only the atoms of a subset of the atom types have to be considered, i.e.atoms of the atom types mentioned in Q_i. We call this set of atom types $\mathcal{R}$ (Q_i).

One approach to evaluate the restriction clause is the *top-down approach*: All atoms of the root atom type are read. For each root atom, each part Q_i of Q(M) is considered. For each atom type in $R(Q_i)$, the atoms referenced by the root atom type are read. If Q_i evaluates to TRUE, the next Q_i is considered. Note that the set of atoms which has to be taken into account is determined by the root atom's references. If the root atom type $\mathcal{R}$ does not directly reference an atom type $\mathcal{A}$ in R (Q_i), then all atoms of atom types on the path from $\mathcal{R}$ to $\mathcal{A}$ also have to be read. Obviously, a molecule may be skipped, if a Q_i evaluates to FALSE. Hence, an optimal order of the Q_i has to be found which minimizes the I/O effort needed to decide the disqualification of a molecule. This order cannot be determined by sorting the Q_i by their selectivity, because a very selective Q_i should not be put in the first place if one has to read the whole molecule to evaluate it.

If there is only one atom type in R (Q_i) a *bottom-up approach* may be more efficient. This approach starts with atoms of the only atom type in R (Q_i) that fulfill Q_i. These may be accessed with the help of an access path. From these atoms, references are followed towards the root atom type. For each atom of the root atom type which is identified in this way, the rest of Q(M) is evaluated as described before. The following query illustrates that the decision for either the top-down or the bottom-up approach is data-dependent:

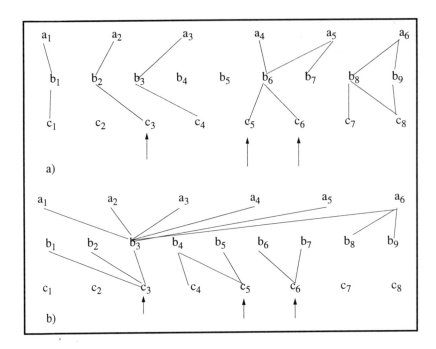

FIGURE 4.5

Figure 5: Sample atom networks

```
SELECT ALL
FROM    A-B-C
WHERE  EXISTS C: C.att1=7;
```

Consider the atom network of Figure 4.5a. The atoms of type C with $C.att1=7$ are marked by an arrow. Proceeding top-down leads to the construction of six molecules (reading atoms $a_1, b_1, c_1, a_2, b_2, c_3, a_3, b_3, c_4, a_4, b_6, c_5, c_6, a_5, b_7, a_6, b_8, b_9, c_7, c_8$, i.e. 20 atoms), but only three of them qualify. Starting from the C atoms and following the references bottom-up, however, leads to the three root atoms of the qualifying molecules (thereby reading atoms $c_3, b_2, a_2, c_5, b_6, a_4, a_5, b_7, c_6$, i.e. 9 atoms if there is an appropriate access path on atom type C. Otherwise, C has to be scanned and another 5 atoms have to be read). In this case, all atoms which were read belong to the result. Consider the atom network of Figure 4.5b now, where the opposite is true: Top-down evaluation yields only qualifying molecules (reading 10 atoms), while bottom-up evaluation reads some atoms of type $\mathcal{B}$ and $\mathcal{C}$ that do not belong to the result (16 atoms are read if an access path exists, 21 otherwise). For the atom network of Figure 4.5a, a bottom-up evaluation is the better choice, while for the atom network of Figure 4.5b top-down is more profitable. In this example, there was only one Q_i, but in general there are several. If the root atoms qualifying with respect to one Q_i have been found, the remaining Q_i have to be checked for the corresponding molecules. Again, there is a choice of evaluating the conditions top-down (starting from the remaining root atoms) or bottom-up (computing the intersection of the sets of root atoms found). Note that a bottom-up evaluation does not read all atoms of the considered atom types which may belong to a qualifying molecules. Hence, it has to be followed by a top-down completion of the molecule (In Figure 4.5a, atom b7 is read in the course of this completion).

A bottom-up evaluation is not possible if a molecule may qualify without having atoms of the atom type in R (Q_i) (structurally incomplete molecule). Hence, if a the qualification is quantified with one of the quantifiers FOR_ALL, NOT EXISTS, or EXIST_AT_MOST bottom-up evaluation is possible only if the database schema does not allow structural incompleteness for the atom type under consideration.

To summarize, one has to determine the optimal order of the evaluation of the sub-conditions as well as the strategy for the evaluation (bottom-up or top-down). Hence, we consider more strategies than just linear traversal [Kim et al. 1988]. For the cost computations one needs knowledge about the selectivity of the sub-conditions (i.e., how many molecules qualify with respect to the sub-condition) and the I/O effort needed to read the data needed to evaluate a sub-condition bottom-up or top-down. The selectivity depends on the network-structure of the data. Note that in the both network structures shown in Figure 4.5 the selectivity of the condition is different, although the same number of atoms of atom type $\mathcal{C}$ qualifies with respect to the condition C.att1=7. Obviously, the I/O effort also depends on the network structure. Therefore, it is crucial to have an accurate estimation of the number of atoms of a certain atom type which are directly or transitively referenced by atoms of another atom type.

How can this number be estimated? Note that in both atom networks shown in Figure 4.5 there is the same number of references from atoms of type $\mathcal{A}$ to atoms of type $\mathcal{B}$, and from atoms of type $\mathcal{B}$ to atoms of type $\mathcal{C}$.

Hence, knowing only the number of references linking two atom types is not sufficient for a satisfactory estimation. A more accurate estimation may be possible, if the transitive reference behavior is known (i.e., the number of atoms of atom type $\mathcal{A}$ transitively referenced by atoms of atom type $\mathcal{C}$ in our example). However, in a database with many atom types, this statistic obviously would explode in size. Furthermore, in our example there may be a correlation between the values of att1 of atoms of type $\mathcal{C}$ and the number of atoms of type $\mathcal{B}$ referenced by these atoms.

Depth-first or breadth-first

Up to now, we have assumed that top-down evaluation considers one sub-condition after the other. However, the evaluation of several sub-conditions may be overlapped. We illustrate this by another example. The query

```
SELECT A
FROM   A-B-C
WHERE  EXISTS B: B.att1=7 AND FOR_ALL C: C.att2=8;
```

allows two different top-down evaluation methods. In both cases we start reading an atom of type $\mathcal{A}$ (one for each molecule). In the next step, we either read all atoms of type $\mathcal{B}$ and check them against the condition, and then check all the atoms of type $\mathcal{C}$ (breadth-first), or we read only one atom b of type $\mathcal{B}$, check it against B.att1=7, then read the atoms of type $\mathcal{C}$ referenced by b, and check against C.att2=8 before reading the next atom of type $\mathcal{B}$ (depth-first). The two alternatives resemble the "nested loop retrieval method" and the "sort domain retrieval method" [Kim et al. 1988]. Whether breadth-first or depth-first is the better choice depends not only on the selectivities of the predicates, but again on the correlation of attribute values and graph properties of the molecules.

Amount of parallelism to be used

The next problem arises from the fact that PRIMA is capable of parallelizing its actions. Consider the query

```
SELECT ALL
FROM   A-(B,C)
WHERE  EXISTS B: B.att1 = 8 AND EXISTS C: C.att1 = 9;
```

We could scan the atom types $\mathcal{B}$ and $\mathcal{C}$ in parallel, and check the condition for each atom. This parallelism leads to an improvement compared to the

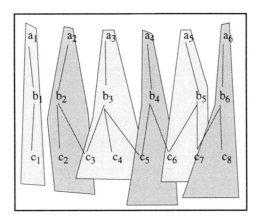

FIGURE 4.6
Atom clusters of type `A-B-C`

sequential version, if there are only few disqualifying molecules. For each disqualifying molecule, however, it is likely that more atoms of the molecule are read before the molecule construction is discarded than in the sequential version. We could specify every degree of parallelism between 1 (sequential) and the maximum. For example, we could read two atoms of type C and three of type B in parallel, and then evaluate the condition. Again, we lack a criterion for the optimal degree of parallelism.

Use of atom clusters

As mentioned above, one can store heterogeneous sets of atoms in physical contiguity (atom cluster). Such an atom cluster corresponds to a molecule of a specific type, which must be hierarchical. In PRIMA, this is a redundant storage structure, i.e., the atoms belonging to an atom cluster are also stored in another storage structure (called the basic storage structure). Hence, one has to decide whether to use the atom cluster or not for the computation of a specific query.

Figure 4.6 shows a sample database consisting of atom types A, B and C, and the effect of an atom cluster definition `A-B-C`. Some of the atom clusters overlap. Consider now the following query:

```
SELECT ALL
FROM    A-B-C
WHERE   EXIST_EXACTLY (2) C: C.att1=3;
```

Obviously the atom-cluster type can be used to efficiently compute this query because we can immediately decide which atoms of type C belong to the molecule and hence decide the qualification condition. Compared to the top-down approach the use of atom-cluster types saves accesses to the external storage. Bottom-up evaluation is not appropriate. Because of the quantifier EXIST_EXACTLY it would identify a superset of the qualifying molecules which may be much larger than the result set. For the opposite direction of molecule definition the atom clusters cannot be used, as demonstrated in the following query:

```
SELECT ALL
FROM    C-B-A
WHERE   EXIST_EXACTLY (2) A: A.att1=3;
```

If in this query the quantifier is modified to **EXISTS** the atom cluster type may be used to identify the root atoms of qualifying molecules. While in these cases the decision of whether to use the atom cluster or not are quite obvious, there are more difficult cases. One of them occurs, when the atom cluster is only partially covered by the query's molecule type, as in the following example:

```
SELECT ALL
FROM    A-B-D;
```

When the atom cluster is used, the atoms of A and B are read in one step, but also are the atoms of type C, which are not needed. It is not clear whether it is better to use the atom clusters or not. Similarly, the following query can be evaluated in several ways:

```
SELECT ALL
FROM    A-B-C
WHERE   EXISTS C: C.att1=6;
```

We could scan the atom clusters to find qualifying molecules, or we could apply the condition C.att1=6 to the atoms of type C (potentially supported by an appropriate access path), and then navigate bottom-up to the corresponding atoms of type A. Here, the decision again must be based on the graph properties in correlation with the attribute values. Additional one must be aware that in the case of an atom-cluster-type scan, some C atoms are read multiply because of the overlapping of atom clusters.

Note that the query containing the quantifier `EXIST_EXACTLY` could not be computed as easily by the second approach, because starting with a qualifying atom c of type C does not guarantee that the atoms of type A that are transitively referenced by c are root atoms of qualifying molecules.

In this section, we have considered several choices of algorithms that are available for the evaluation of the CSM operator. We saw that in many cases there are no obvious criteria that allow a decision among the algorithms at hand.

4.6
Conclusions

When considering the evaluation of queries in the molecule-atom data model, one has to focus mainly on an efficient computation of the CSM operator, because this is the basic operator that appears in every query. The CSM operator constructs hierarchical non-recursive molecules which qualify according to a restriction. Optimization problems mainly arise from the efficient evaluation of this restriction. The goal of optimization is to find a strategy which delivers the qualifying molecules with a minimal I/O overhead.

Standard optimization techniques (like those developed to optimize sequences of join operators) do not apply for CSM. While determining the root atoms of qualifying molecules may be done bottom up, a top-down traversal has to follow in order to complete the molecule. Hence, in some cases one has to traverse a molecule type graph twice: bottom-up to find a set of root atoms (or a superset thereof) and top-down to complete the molecule.

The decisions required in the course of optimization are

- determine a sequence of evaluation for the sub-conditions of the overall restriction,

- for each sub-condition, decide whether it should be evaluated top-down or bottom-up,

- decide which sub-conditions are to be evaluated in depth-first manner,

- find the optimal amount of concurrent (parallel) evaluation of sub-conditions,

- check for supporting redundant storage structures for the sub-conditions and decide about their usage.

We found that the decisions mentioned above heavily depend on the graph structure of the database. We also showed that in our case an abstraction of the graph properties in the form "number of connections between two node types", "number of nodes of each type", etc. is not sufficient. The kind of information really needed here is the dependencies between attribute values and graph properties.

This paper's purpose is to direct attention to the problems mentioned above, not to present the solutions found so far [Schöning 1992]. In particular, there seems to be a need for a more accurate statistical model for graph structures. We believe that this is also a requirement for optimization in object-oriented database systems because the processing model of such systems as well as their data structures are quite similar to that of PRIMA.

We did not consider the other operators that may occur in a QEP of the PRIMA system. Some of these are "standard" operators (i.e., very similar to relational operators), and optimization mechanisms developed for other systems may be adapted. Among the more interesting operators is the *construction of recursive molecules*, which also can be computed by a huge variety of algorithms. Because of the differences in the definition of recursion between the MAD model [Schöning 1989] and other systems, we have investigated this operator in more detail [Schöning 1992].

Bibliography

[Chamberlin 1981] Chamberlin, D.D. et al. "A History and Evaluation of System R." *CACM*, **24:10**, pp. 632-646.

[Chen 1976] Chen, P.P. "The Entity-Relationship-Model—Toward a Unified View of Data." *ACM TODS*, **1:1**, pp. 9-36.

[Deppisch et al. 1986] Deppisch, U., Paul, H.-B., and Schek, H.-J. "A Storage System for Complex Objects." In *Proc. Int. Workshop on Object-Oriented Database Systems*, Asilomar, pp. 183-195.

[Graefe 1990] Graefe, G. "Encapsulation of Parallelism in the Volcano Query Processing System." In *Proc. Int. Conf. on Management of Data SIGMOD '90*, Atlantic City, NJ, pp. 102-111.

[Härder 1988] Härder, T. (ed.) *The PRIMA Project—Design and Implementation of a Non-Standard Database System*, SFB 124 Research Report No. 26/88, University Kaiserslautern.

[Härder et al. 1987] Härder, T., Meyer-Wegener, K., Mitschang, B., Sikeler, A. "PRIMA—A DBMS Prototype Supporting Engineering Applications." In *Proc. 13th VLDB*, Brighton, 1987, pp. 433-442.

[Härder et al. 1988] Härder, T., Schöning, H., Sikeler, A. "Parallelism in Processing Queries on Complex Objects." In *Proc. Int. Symp. on Databases in Parallel and Distributed Systems*, Austin, Texas, pp. 131-143.

[Kim et al. 1988] Kim, K.-C., Kim, W., Woelk, D., Dale, A. "Acyclic Query Processing in Object-Oriented Databases." In *Proc. 7th Int. Conf. on the Entity/Relationship Approach*, Roma, Italy, pp. 193-210.

[Mitschang 1988a] Mitschang, B. "Towards a Unified View of Design Data and Knowledge Representation." In *Proc. 2nd Int. Conf. on Expert Database Systems*, Tysons Corner, Virginia, pp. 33-49.

[Mitschang 1988b] Mitschang, B. *Ein Molekül-Atom-Datenmodell für Non-Standard-Anwendungen—Anwendungsanalyse, Datenmodellentwurf und Implementierungsaspekte*, Ph.D. Thesis (in German), University Kaiserslautern.

[Mitschang 1989] Mitschang, B. "Extending the Relational Algebra to Capture Complex Objects." In *Proc. 15th Int. Conf. on Very Large Data Bases*, Amsterdam, pp. 297-305.

[Schöning 1989] Schöning, H. "Integrating Complex Objects and Recursion." In *Proc. 1st Int. Conf. on Deductive and Object-Oriented Databases*, Kyoto, pp. 535-554.

[Schöning 1992] Schöning, H. *Anfrageverarbeitung in Komplexobjekt-Datenbanksystemen*, Ph.D. Thesis (in German), University Kaiserslautern.

[Sikeler 1989] Sikeler, A. "Supporting Object-Oriented Processing by Redundant Storage Structures" In *Proc. Int. Conf. on Computing and Information (ICCI'89)*, Toronto, Canada.

[Schöning and Sikeler 1989] Schöning, H., Sikeler, A. "Cluster Mechanisms Supporting the Construction of Complex Objects." In *Proc. FODO '89*, LNCS 367, pp. 31-46. Berlin: Springer-Verlag.

5

Algebraic Query Optimization in the CoOMS Structurally Object-Oriented Database System

Birgit Demuth
Andreas Geppert
Thorsten Gorchs

Abstract   ITHACA[1] is a system for the development of advanced application software. The kernel of ITHACA includes a (persistent) object-oriented programming language, Cool[2], and a structurally object-oriented database system CoOMS[3]. Additionally, CoOMS is also intended for use as a stand-alone database system. Like any other database system, CoOMS has to support efficient and optimized access to large sets of objects. These objects, in turn, may be structured in an arbitrarily complex manner. Thus, while some rules of relational algebraic optimization carry over to CoOMS, additional optimization mechanisms are necessary in the presence of inheritance hierarchies and complex objects.

5.1
Introduction

Object-oriented data models [Atkinson et. al 1989] aim at support for more sophisticated means to model real-world entities, in comparison to classical models. To that end, they support inheritance and specialization hierarchies, complex objects, orthogonal type constructors, and the definition of behaviour of objects, to name some features. Furthermore, modern database systems also have to offer a declarative language for descriptive and ad-hoc access to objects. Additionally, access to large collections of objects has to be efficient, thus requiring queries to be optimized. Optimization usually is carried out in two steps: first, algebraic optimization is performed, which uses algebraic properties to transform queries into semantically equivalent, but cheaper ones. Second, non-algebraic optimization takes physical characteristics such as the presence of access paths or indexes into account.

Algebraic optimization is well-understood for relational systems; there, an algebra is given for the semantics of (e.g., SQL) queries, algebraic equivalences have been specified, and heuristic rules were discovered when it is beneficial to apply those equivalences for the transformation of queries. However, the "objects" in question are very simply structured (sets of tuples). Thus, while the equivalences (and rules) carry over to new data models, they are

---

[1]Integrated Toolkit for Highly Advanced Computer Applications
[2]Combined Object-Oriented Language.   Cool is a trademark if Siemens-Nixdorf Informationssysteme
[3]Cool Object Management System

by no means sufficient. Namely, algebraic optimization has to take complex objects and type hierarchies into account.

CoOMS is a *structurally object-oriented database system* [Dittrich 1991], i.e., it supports complex objects and (generic) operations on them, but not the modelling of arbitrary object behaviour. However, full object-orientation is achieved through the coupling of CoOMS with the object-oriented programming language Cool [Schröer 1991]. On the structural side, NO^2, the data model of CoOMS, provides for object identity and a distinction between objects and values, completely orthogonal value constructors, and general as well as *is_part_of* references. Additionally, *is_a* relationships (i.e. type hierarchies) can be represented.

CoOMS, as usual, distinguishes between algebraic and non-algebraic optimization. Algebraic optimization takes idempotence, commutativity, associativity, and distributivity properties of operations into account. Some optimization rules (based on these properties) carry over from the relational algebra, while other rules are related to the specific features of NO^2; thus we specify inheritance, subobject, and navigational rules. Non-algebraic optimization, as the second optimization phase in the query transformation process, includes access path selection as well as generation of a query execution plan in a "classical" manner and will be done by the CoOMS query manager. The cost criterion of optimization rules is to "move" as few objects as possible between secondary storage and main memory, since CoOMS is intended to be used in the area of information processing systems. Thus, queries are supposed to access many, but "small" objects.

The remainder of the paper is organized as follows: the NO^2 data model is introduced in the next section. Section 5.3 describes algebraic optimization based on the properties of the NO^2 algebra. The fourth section gives an overview of the overall project. Section 5.5 compares our work to related research.

5.2
The NO² Data Model

5.2.1   NO² Data Structures

In this section, we describe the data structures conforming to the NO^2 data model [Dittrich, Geppert, and Goebel 1990].

Objects and Values NO^2 distinguishes between *objects* and *values*. Any object is uniquely identified by an *object identifier* (OID). This identifier is generated and assigned by the system, cannot be altered by users and is not reused even if the object ceases to exist [Koshafian and Copeland 1986]. Apart from its identifier, each object has a value. While objects can exist in their own right, values cannot. Furthermore, since objects possess identity, they can be shared. Values do not have identity and thus cannot be shared.

Values are either basic or complex. Basic values are integers, reals, boolean, long fields and so forth. Complex values are constructed from existing (basic or complex) values using the constructors

- set,

- tuple,

- list, and

- array.

Both set and tuple have the usual meaning, with the exception that tuple attributes—in contrast to SQL—need not have atomic domains. Lists are ordered sequences that may grow or shrink dynamically, while arrays are of fixed and value set specific length (i.e., no dynamic arrays). Values from the same domain are collected into *value sets*. An *object type* is specified by a name and a value set (defining the permitted structure of the objects), and has an *extension* that contains all the existing objects or instances of the type associated to them.

Object Structures NO^2 provides for two kinds of references in order to establish object structures. First, NO^2 supports *general references*, which are "general" in the sense that the database system does not attribute any specific semantics to them. Second, *subobject* (or is-part-of) references are supported. Semantically, these references express the fact that objects consist (beyond having arbitrary other values) of other objects and are thus called structured objects (complex objects, composite objects). Operators are provided that treat complex objects (i.e., objects together with all their direct and indirect subobjects) "in their entirety". Furthermore, similar to ORION [Kim, Bertino, and Garza 1989], subobjects are

- sharable or exclusive, and

- dependent or independent.

A sharable subobject can be contained in more than one complex object, while an exclusive one cannot. The existence of a dependent subobject depends on the existence of the complex object it is contained in (e.g., propagation of deletion to dependent subobjects). By combination of these properties, four kinds of subobjects are obtained. While objects may (transitively) contain objects of the same type as subobjects (i.e., recursive types), cyclic subobject references on the instance level are not permitted.

In summary, NO^2 provides for a rich collection of value constructors and two kinds of references for the modelling of object structures. As in AIM-P [Pistor and Andersen 1986] and O$_2$ [Deux 1990], value constructors in NO^2 are completely orthogonal to each other.

Type Hierarchies and Inheritance NO^2 also supports *type hierarchies* and *inheritance*. A type may be specified as a subtype of another type in two ways:

1. T1 may be more specific as T2 in the sense that T1 has more attributes than T2. Naturally, this case is restricted to types with tuple value sets. T1 *inherits* the value sets (i.e., attributes) from T2 (and possibly other types) and may define further ones. This case is called *structure extension*.

2. T1 can inherit the value set of T2 but specialize some components (e.g. integers to a subrange of integers). This case is is termed *value restriction* and is not necessarily restricted to tuple value sets.

In both cases, an *is-a* relationship between T1 and T2 holds. Furthermore, NO^2 supports *substitutability*, i.e., whenever an instance of T2 is required, an instance of T1 may be specified instead.

For an example, see the schema as depicted in Figure 5.1. Rectangles represent object types. Normal arrows are used for subobject references, those with hollow heads represent general references, and dashed arrows express *is_a* relationships. Furthermore, list value sets are represented by angle brackets enclosing the element value set, while curly brackets represent sets.

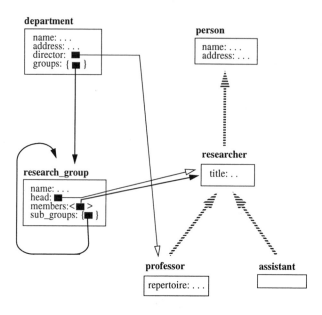

FIGURE 5.1
Sample NO^2 Schema

5.2.2   *Quod*, the NO^2 Query Language

Quod [Geppert, Goebel, and Dittrich 1990], the query language of NO^2, provides for access to databases in an SQL-like, declarative style. Like in SQL, queries are structured into a *select*, a *from*, and an optional *where* clause. The result of a query can be a collection of (existing) objects or values, or a single object or value. If queries are supposed to have object-generating effects, it has to be stated explicitly.

The exact structure of a query result is specified in the *select* clause. Unlike SQL, this clause may in turn contain queries itself. In the *from* clause, extensions are specified against which the query is to be executed. Additionally, variables may be defined that can be bound to lists or sets and which may be used in *select* or *where* clauses. Finally, *where* clauses have the usual meaning of restricting the result to those objects or values that fulfill some given condition.

A variety of built-in operators is provided for the construction of and access to objects and values. Objects, for example, may be tested for identity or "dereferenced" in order to access their values. For sets and lists, there exist constructors, operators such as union or difference, cardinality, accessors, and flatten. For tuples, operators for construction, access to attributes, and concatenation are supported. Further operators provide for sorting or grouping sets and lists (and thereby support the conversion of sets into lists).

A further feature of *Quod* is *recursive queries*. Due to general or subobject references, recursive types (types which—directly or indirectly—reference themselves) can be specified. Consequently, structures may result whose nesting depth is not known beforehand. Thus, recursive queries (or, more precisely, the possibility to construct generalized transitive closures) is a requirement. For instance, if objects may contain instances of the same type as subobjects, a recursive query can be used to transitively retrieve all subobjects for a set of specific instances of that type.

Example: All researchers who have a PhD and live in Dresden.
select *
from r in researcher
where r.title = "PhD" and r.address.city = "Dresden"

Example: The name of all researchers heading a group with more than three members, together with the set of their subordinates.
select [head: gr.head.name, members: select r.name
                            from r in gr.group.members]
from gr in research_group
where length(gr.members) > 3.

5.2.3   The NO^2 Algebra

The Algebra Domain The NO^2 algebra [Geppert et. al 1990] is a *many-sorted algebra* [Goguen, Thatcher, and Wagner 1978]. Roughly speaking, there is one sort for each basic value set, i.e., for integers and so forth, especially including a sort for object identifiers. Object types are represented by the cartesian product of the object identifier sort and the value set of the type. Hence, objects are modelled as pairs (*object identifier, value*), where the value is an element of the sort corresponding to the value set of the object type. Furthermore, each complex value set (tuples, sets, etc.) object type formally correspond to one sort. An object type extension is a set of objects (a subset of the cartesian product of object identifiers and the value set). For this case, we assume that the extension of an object type (logically, but presumably not physically) contains all the instances of all the type's subtypes as well; thus an object may be a member of multiple extensions.

object operators	$\pi_O(.)$	projection to oid
	$\pi_V(.)$	projection to value
	$\pi_D(.)$	dereference operator
set operators	$\{\,.\,\}$	constructor
	pick (.)	projection
	$\sigma_S[\lambda s.formula](.)$	selection
	$\iota_S[\lambda s.expression](.)$	image
	$\phi_S(.)$	flatten for sets
	$.\cup.$	set union
	$.\,/\,.$	set difference
	card (.)	set cardinality
tuple operators	$[a_1: v_1, ..., a_n: v_n]$	tuple construction
	$\pi_T[att\_name](.)$	tuple projection
list operators	$<., list >$	list construction
	$\pi_F(.)$	projection to first element
	$\pi_R(.)$	projection to tail
	$+_L (., .)$	list concatenation
	$\sigma_L[\lambda s.formula](.)$	list selection
	$\iota_S[\lambda s.expression](.)$	list image
	$\phi_L(.)$	flatten for lists
	length (.)	length of lists
array operators	$[x_1 , ..., x_n]$	array construction
	$\pi_A [n] (.)$	array projection

TABLE 5.1
Algebraic Operators

Algebraic Operators   Generic, algebraic operators are defined for the various kinds of value sets. They can be classified as constructors, projection operators performing access to components of a complex value, selection, and iteration.

For objects, three operators exist. Applied to a general reference, *deref* returns the referenced object, i.e., given an object identifier, this operator returns the corresponding object. When applied to an object, the other two operators return the identifier and the value of an object, respectively. Note that there is no object constructor supported by the algebra.

Unlike the relational algebra, operators are provided for single tuples instead of for sets of tuples. Tuple values can be constructed using the constructor ("[ ]"), while tuple projection returns a single attribute value of an attribute. Furthermore, projection of tuples to tuples containing a subset of the attributes can be expressed as the combination of tuple construction and projection.

Since the difference between lists and sets is solely the ordering of elements for lists, both have operators with comparable semantics. For both sets and lists, constructors ("{ }" and "< >") and cardinality (or length, respectively) are provided. The flatten operator can be applied to sets or lists, its effect is to remove one level of nesting (i.e., it converts, say, a set of sets into a set). Furthermore, set-theoretic union and difference are applicable to sets while concatenation ($+_L$) can be applied to lists. However, the most powerful operators are selection and image. Selection transforms a set (or list) into a set (or list) consisting of the elements of the input collection fulfilling a specific condition. Image (or filter) transforms a collection into a collection, where a specified algebraic operation is applied to each element of the input collection.

Due to the ordering of lists, further operators can be applied to them, but not to sets. Projection is supported for singleton sets ("pick" operator). Lists can be projected to their first element or to the tail (the list without its first element); projection of the ith member is an abbreviation of repeated application of projection to the tail followed by projection to the first element.

For arrays, only construction and projection is supported. Since arrays have to be of fixed length, selection would not be well-defined, since the size of an array resulting from a selection can not be known beforehand.

Cartesian product operators in the sense of the relational algebra can be defined as abbreviations of other operators for sets and lists (X_S and X_L), respectively.

Table 5.1 summarizes the algebraic operators. As an example for an algebraic expression, the first query from above is equivalent to the following algebraic expression:

$$\sigma[\lambda s.\pi_T[address](\pi_V(s)) = "Dresden"]$$
$$(\sigma[\lambda t.\pi_T[title](\pi_V(t)) = "PhD"](researcher)$$

5.3
Algebraic Optimization

Prerequisites Essential prerequisites for algebraic optimization of NO^2 queries are algebraic laws valid for the defined operators, allowing algebraic expressions to be transformed into semantically equivalent, but more efficiently executable, ones. In our approach we consider two queries to be equivalent if they return the same values in the same structure. There is a large set of algebraic laws in NO^2 including

- idempotence

- commutativity

- associativity

- distributivity

of unary and binary operators [Demuth et. al 1991]. The following set of optimization rules represents semantically equivalent query transformations. In our notation, we write $S, S1, S2, S3$ for an *object type extension* or a *set* of values, $L, L1, L2, L3$ for a *list* of values, and $p, p1, p2$ for *selection predicates* respectively *formulas* in set or list selection.

Relational Rules   The following set of rules is particularly derived from the well-known algebraic optimization technique in relational systems. So we called these rules *relational.* Rule R1 is based on the definitions of formulas

RULE R1	Compounding of operations on the same object type extension or value set to a selection with a formula in selection
R1.1	$\sigma_S[p1](\sigma_S[p2](S)) \Rightarrow \sigma_S[p1 \wedge p2](S)$
R1.2	$\sigma_L[p1](\sigma_L[p2](L)) \Rightarrow \sigma_L[p1 \wedge p2](L)$
R1.3	$\sigma_S[p1](S) \bigcup \sigma_S[p2](S) \Rightarrow \sigma_S[p1 \vee p2](S)$
R1.4	$\sigma_S[p1] \setminus \sigma_S[p2](S) \Rightarrow \sigma_S[p1 \wedge \neg p2](S)$
R1.5	$S \setminus \sigma_S[p](S) \Rightarrow \sigma_S[\neg p](S)$
R1.6	$S \bigcup \sigma_S[p](S) \Rightarrow S$

in set and list selection. Its effect is to avoid the redundant creation and manipulation of intermediate results whenever object type extensions or value sets are retrieved repeatedly.

Example: The algebraic expression

$$\sigma_S[\lambda s.\pi_T[address](\pi_V(s)) = \text{``}Dresden\text{''}]$$
$$(\sigma_S[\lambda t.\pi_T[title](\pi_V(t)) = \text{``}PhD\text{''}](researcher))$$

will be transformed to

$$\sigma_S[\lambda s.(\pi_T[address](\pi_V(s)) = \text{``Dresden''} \wedge \pi_T[title](\pi_V(s)) = \text{``PhD''})]$$
$$(researcher)$$

Algebraic equivalences allow selections to be pushed down before cross product, set, or list operations to attempt to minimize the number of objects or values retrieved (see Rule R2).

RULE R2 Pushing down selections   valid for
R2.1 Pushing down set selections
$\sigma_S[p](S1 \; op \; S2) \Rightarrow \sigma_S[p](S1) \; op \; S2$ if p valid for S1
$\sigma_S[p](S1 \; op \; S2) \Rightarrow S1 \; op \; \sigma_S[p](S2)$ if p valid for S2 $op \in \{\bigcup, \backslash\}$
$\sigma_S[p1 \wedge p2 \wedge p3](S1 \; op \; S2) \Rightarrow$ $\sigma_S[p3](\sigma_S[p1](S1) \; op \; \sigma_S[p2](S2)$ if p1 valid for S1, p2 valid for S2,   and p3 valid for (S1 op S2)
R2.2 Pushing down list selections $\sigma_L[p](L1 \; op \; L2) \Rightarrow \sigma_L[p](L1) \; op \; L2$ if p valid for L1
$\sigma_L[p](L1 \; op \; L2) \Rightarrow L1 \; op \; \sigma_L[p](L2)$ if p valid for L2 $op \in$ $\{+_L\}$
$\sigma_L[p1 \wedge p2 \wedge p3](L1 \; op \; L2) \Rightarrow$ $\sigma_L[p3](\sigma_L[p1](L1) \; op \; \sigma_L[p2](L2)$ if p1 valid for L1, p2 valid for L2,   and p3 valid for (L1 op L2)

Rule R3 for image pushdown also minimizes the number of values before application of set or list operations. It is based on the distributivity of unary over binary operators. Because the image function f(s) often is an NO^2 projection operation, the rule is similiar to the (relational) projection pushdown one. Optimizing sequences of cross product, set or list operations is handled

RULE R3 Pushing down images	valid for
R3.1 Pushing down images for sets $l_S[\lambda s.f(s)](S1 \ op \ S2) \Rightarrow$ $l_S[\lambda s.f(s)](S1) \ op \ l_S[\lambda s.f(s)](S2)$	$op \in \{\bigcup, \backslash\}$
R3.2 Pushing down images for lists $l_L[\lambda s.f(s)](L1 \ op \ L2) \Rightarrow$ $l_L[\lambda s.f(s)](L1) \ op \ l_L[\lambda s.f(s)](L2)$	$op \in$ $\{+_L\}$
preconditions: (1) function argument must be from an attribute with unique property (2) function must be defined both for S1 and S2 respectively L1 and L2	

RULE R4 Optimizing sequences of binary operations
R4.1 Set operations before cross product $(S1 X_S S2) \ op \ (S1 X_S S3) \Rightarrow S1 X_S (S2 \ op \ S3)$ if $op \in \{\bigcup, \backslash\}$
R4.2 Sequence of same operations $(S1 \ op \ S2) \ op \ S3 \Rightarrow S1 \ op \ (S2 \ op \ S3)$ if $op \in \{X_S, \bigcup\}$ and $card(S1 \ op \ S2) > card(S2 \ op \ S3)$

by Rule R4, which is founded on the algebraic properties

- distributivity of binary operators

- associativity.

Further query transformations are possible by applying the commutativity law for set union and set intersection. Increase in the efficiency of such query transformations is given by the minimization of intermediate value sets. The underlying heuristic rules can be formalized as follows

$$card(S1 \setminus S2) < card(S1 \bigcup S2) < card(S1 \ X_S \ S2)$$

and

$$card(L1 -_L L2) < card(L1 \ X_L \ L2)$$

not to mention that values created by a cross product are "longer" than values created by set or list operations.

A last relational rule that is not exactly described here summarizes a lot of algebraic equations to simplify complex NO^2 expressions and to eliminate redundant object and value accesses in that manner. Such query transformations will be interesting in cases of preceding transformations in the optimization process. Either equal subexpressions (that means the same sequence of algebraic operators on the same object type(s)) will be recognized and executed only once by creating a temporary value set, or well-known algebraic laws such as $S1 \bigcup S1 \Rightarrow S1$ will be applied. We call these transformations *trivial* set and list operations. Furthermore, we can give many trivial transformation rules for formulas in selection.

Inheritance Rules   As one facet of subtyping, the extension of a subtype is supposed to be a subset of the supertype's extension: $E1 \subseteq E2$. Based

RULE I1	Elimination of operations in a type hierarchy
I1.1	$l_S[\lambda s.f(s)](S1) \bigcup l_S[\lambda s.f(s)](S2) \Rightarrow l_S[\lambda s.f(s)](S1)$
I1.2	$\sigma_S[p](S1) \bigcup \sigma_S[p](S2) \Rightarrow \sigma_S[p](S1)$
precondition:	S2 is a subtype of S1

on this subset relationship, we specify *inheritance rules* for queries involving generalizations of object types. Thus, Rule I1 eliminates set or list operations and images or selections in type hierarchies.

Example: The query "Find all names of researchers and professors" can be expressed by

$$l_S[\lambda s.\pi_T[name](\pi_V(s))](researcher) \bigcup l_S[\lambda t.\pi_T[name](\pi_V(t))](professor)$$

This algebraic expression will be transformed by Rule I1.1 to

$$l_S[\lambda s.\pi_T[name](\pi_V(s))](researcher)$$

under the condition that *professor* is a subtype of *researcher*.

Navigational Rules   According to the definition of the NO^2 algebra domain, object identifiers (used for genreal references) are treated as a specific value set. General references to existing objects are useful to navigate through complex object structures. Thus, we look for optimization rules for queries that access objects via general references; those are termed *navigational rules*. Here we specify only one rule. Rule N1 can be applied under the condition

RULE N1 Pushing down projection before selection
$l_S[\lambda s.\pi_D(f(s))](\sigma_S[\lambda s.p](S2)) \Rightarrow$ $\sigma_S[\lambda s.p](l_S \lambda s.\pi_D(f(s))](S2))$
preconditions: (1) f(s) is an idempotent function   (2) attributes of image and selection must coincide

that attributes for image and selection coincide.

Example: The query "Find every head of a research group who is also a member of the respective group" can be expressed by

$$l_S[\lambda t.\pi_D(t.head)](\sigma_S[\lambda s.\pi_D(s.head) \text{ in } s.members](research\_group)).$$

This expression will be transformed by Rule N1 to

$$\sigma_S[\lambda s.s \text{ in } s.members](l_S[\lambda t.\pi_D(t.head)](research\ group))$$

The optimization effect is the elimination of duplicate projection, that means, minimization of redundant accesses to objects via general references. Further rules could beneficially exploit the presence of default inverse references.

RULE S1 Pushing down projection before selection
$l_S[\lambda s.s.subobj](\sigma_S[p](S2)) \Rightarrow \sigma_S[p](l_S[\lambda s.s.subobj](S2))$
precondition: attributes of image and selection must coincide

Subobject Rules   Similar to general references, object type extensions are valid basic value sets that allow the modelling of complex object structures. Queries with such involved subobject types shall be optimized by so called *subobject rules*. We feel that there are different possibilities to increase the effiency of execution of NO^2 expressions on subobjects. Rule S1 is a query transformation like the navigational rule N1. Another one is the shifting of

RULE S2 Nesting of operations
$l_S[\lambda t.f(t)](\phi_S(l_S[\lambda s.s.subobj](S))) \Rightarrow$ $\phi_S(l_S[\lambda s.(l_S[\lambda t.f(t)](s.subobj))](S))$
precondition: attributes of image and selection must coincide

flatten and nesting of operations (see Rule S2). In our notation, the value set *subobj* is an extension of an object type.

Example: The query "Select names of all existing subgroups" can be expressed by

$$l_S[\lambda s.\pi_T[name](\pi_D(s))](\phi_S(l_S[\lambda t.\pi_T[subgroups](\pi_V(t))](research\ group)))$$

and will be transformed by Rule S2 to

$$\phi_S(l_S[\lambda s.l_S[\lambda z.\pi_T[name](\pi_V(z))](\pi_T[subgroups](\pi_V(s)))](research\ group))$$

The Optimizer Internally, algebraic expressions are represented as *operator trees*. Hence, algebraic optimization is performed on these operator trees. The semantic of the root of such a tree is to create the result of the corresponding algebraic expression, while inner nodes represent (algebraic) operators and leaf nodes correspond to constants or extension names. Since the left sides of the algebraic optimization rules are unique, the optimizer can apply at most one rule in any case. If a rule matches a subtree of the operator tree, the algebraic transformation is performed (i.e., the subtree is replaced with a tree representing the right side of the rule).

During the step following algebraic optimization, the operator tree is transformed into an efficient query execution plan that is based on scans and exploits available access paths. The selection of adequate access paths is subject to *non-algebraic optimization*.

5.4
Project Overview

The work presented in this paper is part of the ITHACA project currently under development by several partners and funded as Technology Integration Project within the European Community ESPRIT II program. The

ITHACA project aims at building a development environment for large-scale applications in the domain of advanced information processing systems, office systems and selected CAx systems. A general ITHACA architecture is shown in Figure 5.2.

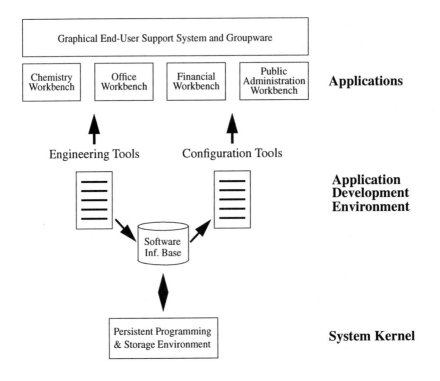

FIGURE 5.2

The ITHACA approach to application engineering

The system consists of the following major components:

- an object-oriented software information base,

- an application development environment,

- an object-oriented system kernel.

The object-oriented software information base is used to store information that constitutes the basic building blocks with which developers work. It cooperates closely with the tools of the application development environement. Particular consideration is given to providing support for an object-oriented life cycle and methodology geared towards streamlining the configuration process called by the applications.

The system kernel of ITHACA is formed by three parts (see Figure 5.4): the storage subsystem CoOMS, the language subsystem which contains

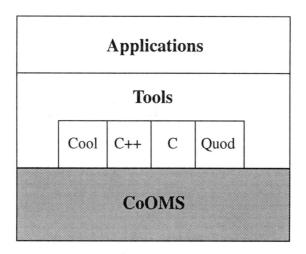

FIGURE 5.3
The General Architecture of the ITHACA system kernel

object oriented programming languages like CooL and C++, and interactive query facilitites like Quod. The third part of the kernel is the tool subsystem consisting of a debugger, a filter/browser, a library, graphical user interfaces, and the like. This kernel comprises a persistent, object-oriented programming languages, an integrated structurally object-oriented database system, and an appropriate runtime system. The system kernel is designed so that it integrates both object-oriented as well as procedural programming languages. In addition, application developers are provided with a filtering and browsing system, a high-level, interactive multi-language debugger, a configuration tool and a graphical user interface. The CoOMS database system considers both requirements of the object-oriented world and typical database functionality as provided by traditional database systems.

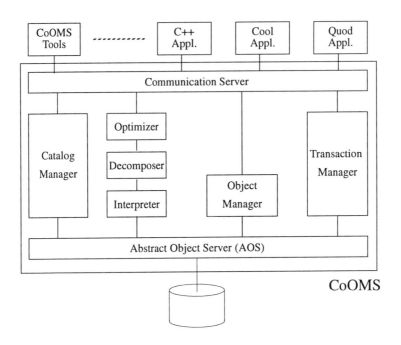

FIGURE 5.4
CoOMS Architecture

Although CoOMS is designed as a layered system (see Figure 5.4), it also tries to exploit object-oriented mechanisms in a straightforward way. Thus, CoOMS can be viewed as a number of components, where a component in turn is a collection of types (or classes), and where components interact by exchanging messages. We believe that designing and implementing CoOMS "as object-oriented as possible" eases future extensions and modifications. The implementation of CoOMS is based on an *abstract object server* (AOS) that provides for operations on physical objects (byte containers), basic transaction management, and physical access paths. Algebraic optimization is performed by the optimizer component, while the task of the decomposer is the selection of access paths and the generation of query execution plans. These query execution plans are then interpreted by the interpreter component. Finally, the object manager is responsible for direct, non-declarative access to and manipulation of single objects.

To a large extent, CoOMS is implemented in the volatile version of Cool. Some components (e.g., providing for interaction with the operating system) are implemented in C, encapsulated in Cool procedure calls.

5.5
Comparison to Related Work

The data model of NO^2 uses concepts known from various other models. For example, orthogonality of constructors is also present in HDBL [Pistor and Andersen 1986] and O_2 [Deux 1990]. The same kinds of subobject references (there called *composite objects*) are proposed by ORION [Kim, Bertino, and Garza 1989], where object and value constructors are less orthogonal in ORION.

Since the data models of HDBL, O_2 and NO^2 are quite similar as far as the various kinds of orthogonal value constructors are concerned, operations provided by *Quod* can also be found in the query languages of the former two models. Recursion (i.e., generalized transitive closure) has been proposed and proven successful in other structurally object-oriented data models ([Schiefer and Rehm 1989, Schoening 1989]).

The design of the algebra has to cope with the permissible data structures and operations defined on them. Thus, as a first requirement, in contrast to the relational algebra [Maier 1983] or the nested relational algebra [Schek and Scholl 1986], the algebra has to cope with orthogonally constructed and irregular structures. [Abiteboul and Beeri 1988] proposes an algebra for "complex objects", i.e., orthogonally constructed sets and tuples. However, there is no support for objects and lists in this approach. [Gueting, Zicari, and Choy 1989] also proposes a many-sorted algebra, thus allowing for the inclusion of operators like *count* or *card*. Finally, an algebra similar to our approach has recently been proposed for the EXTRA/EXCESS data model [Vandenberg and DeWitt 1991].

An algebra is especially useful to represent queries for optimization and evaluation. Because we consider a structurally object-oriented data model, we do not have the problem of optimizating queries including methods. Other algebraic formalisms for structurally object-oriented data models have been suggested in several projects ([Osborn 1988, Straube 1991, Vandenberg and DeWitt 1991, Zdonik 1988]).

5.6
Conclusion

In this paper, we first have presented the structurally object-oriented data model NO^2, including the data definition facilities, a descriptive query language, and an algebraic formalization. As far as algebraic optimization is concerned, rules and equivalences known from the relational algebra carry over. New rules have been specified for inheritance (or more precisely, subtypes) as well as object structures specific to NO^2. Finally, a short impression of the project context and the implementation of CoOMS has been given.

Bibliography

[Abiteboul and Beeri 1988] S. Abiteboul, C. Beeri. *On the Power of Languages for the Manipulation of Complex Objects.* Technical Report 846, INRIA, 1988.

[Atkinson et. al 1989] M. Atkinson, F. Bancilhon, D. DeWitt, K. Dittrich, D. Maier and S. Zdonik. *The Object-Oriented Database Manifesto.* Proc. Intl. Conf. on Deductive and Object-Oriented Databases, 1989.

[Demuth et. al 1991] B. Demuth, T. Gorchs, K.-H. Müller, F. Schönefeld, E. Spudulite. *Query Optimization in the NO^2 Data Model.* Technical Report, Technische Universität Dresden, 1991.

[Deux 1990] O. Deux. *The Story of O_2.* IEEE Transactions on Knowledge Bases and Data Engineering 2:1, 1990.

[Dittrich, Geppert, and Goebel 1990] K.R. Dittrich, A. Geppert, V. Goebel. *The NO^2 Data Definition Language.* Technical Report, Institut für Informatik, Universität Zürich, 1990.

[Dittrich 1991] K.R. Dittrich. *Object-Oriented Database Systems: The Notions and the Issues.* In K.R. Dittrich, U. Dayal, A.P. Buchmann (eds.): On Object-Oriented Database Systems. Springer-Verlag, 1991.

[Geppert et. al 1990] A. Geppert, K.R. Dittrich, V. Goebel, S. Scherrer. *An Algebra for the NO^2 Data Model.* Technical Report, Institut für Informatik, Universität Zürich, 1990.

[Geppert, Goebel, and Dittrich 1990] A. Geppert, V. Goebel, K.R. Dittrich. *Quod: A Query Language for NO^2.* Technical Report, Institut für Informatik, Universität Zürich, 1990.

[Goguen, Thatcher, and Wagner 1978] J.A. Goguen, J.W. Thatcher, E.G. Wagner. *An Initial Algebra Approach to the Specification, Correctness, and Implementation of Abstract Data Types.* In R.T. Yeh (ed.): Current Trends in Programming Methodology, Vol. IV. Prentice Hall, Englewood Cliffs, New Jersey, 1978.

[Gueting, Zicari, and Choy 1989] R.H. Gueting, R. Zicari, D.M. Choy. *An Algebra for Structured Office Documents.* ACM Transactions on Office Information Systems 7:4, 1989.

[Kim, Bertino, and Garza 1989] W. Kim, E. Bertino, J.F. Garza. *Composite Objects Revisited.* ACM-SIGMOD Intl. Conf. on Management of Data, 1989.

[Koshafian and Copeland 1986] S. Khoshafian, G. Copeland. *Object Identity.* Conf. on Object-Oriented Programming Languages, Systems, Languages, and Applications, 1986.

[Maier 1983] D. Maier. *The Theory of Relational Databases.* Computer Science Press, Rockville, 1983.

[Osborn 1988] S.L. Osborn. *Identity, Equality and Query Optimization.* Lecture Notes in Computer Science 334, Springer-Verlag, 1988.

[Pistor and Andersen 1986] P. Pistor, F. Andersen. *Designing a Generalized NF^2 Model with an SQL-Type Language Interface.* Intl. Conf. on Very Large Data Bases 1986.

[Schek and Scholl 1986] H.-J. Schek, M.H. Scholl. *The Relational Model With Relation-Valued Attributes.* Information Systems 11:2, 1986.

[Schiefer and Rehm 1989] B. Schiefer, S. Rehm. *Eine Anfragesprache fuer ein strukturell-objectorientiertes Datenmodell.* GI Conf. on Databases for Office, Engineering, and Scientific Applications, 1989.

[Schoening 1989] H. Schoening. *Rekursion im MAD-Modell: Rekursiv-molekuele als Objekte des Datenmodells*. GI Conf. on Databases for Office, Engineering, and Scientific Applications, 1989.

[Schröer 1991] F.W. Schröer. *The Cool 0.3 Language Description*. Project Report ITHACA.SNI.90.L1 #3, Siemens-Nixdorf Informationssysteme, Berlin, 1991.

[Straube 1991] D.D. Straube. *Queries and Query Processing in Object-Oriented Datebase Systems*. PhD Thesis, University of Alberta, 1991.

[Vandenberg and DeWitt 1991] S.L. Vandenberg, D.J. DeWitt. *Algebraic Support for Complex Objects with Arrays, Identity, and Inheritance*. ACM-SIGMOD Intl. Conf. on Management of Data, 1991.

[Zdonik 1988] S.B. Zdonik. *Data Abstraction and Query Optimization*. In K.R. Dittrich (ed.): Advances in Object-Oriented Database Systems, Lecture Notes in Computer Science 334, Springer-Verlag, 1988.

PART II

Logic-based Approaches

6

Query Optimization in Deductive Object Bases

Manfred Jeusfeld

Martin Staudt

Abstract

Deductive object bases are extended database systems which amalgamate structural object-orientation with logical specification. Queries in such a system are regarded both as classes and as deduction rules. Besides a general architecture for query processing in deductive object bases, two specific query optimization techniques are presented: semantic query optimization with structural axioms of the object base, and view maintenance optimization. The approach has been formalized in the language Telos and implemented in the system ConceptBase.

6.1
Introduction

Traditionally, databases are systems for storing and accessing large amounts of shared persistent data in a secure way. Database research has always been concerned with providing efficient methods for these tasks. One major conjecture was that data should be independent from specific application programs. This point of view has been materialized by the relational-style databases. They provide a simple and very attractive data model, and *declarative* query languages. Compared to complete programming languages, a query language is usually rather limited – a limitation that has an important benefit: it is easier to prove properties of queries. One such property is guaranteed termination. Another is the ability to decide whether two expressions are equivalent. The latter is a prerequisite for query optimization. While relational (and deductive) databases were very successful partly because of their query optimizers, they can fail for complex applications like design [Maier 86]. The reason for this failure is the too simple data model which is unable to adequately describe the data structures manipulated by such applications. Another drawback is the total negligence of operational properties of data, also known as abstract data types [Guttag 75]. Object-oriented databases address these problems by their richer type (or class) system and - at least a few of them - by their ability to store operations or *methods* together with the data. At first glance, the added complexity implies some obstacles for query optimization. For instance, a complete programming language for methods introduces undecidability when methods are used within queries (like e.g. in O_2 [Bancilhon et al. 89]). The notion of complex objects offers a multitude of nested structures that can all hold the same kind of data. This makes it a more difficult task to combine such data. [Shaw and Zdonik 90] propose a whole array of different equality operators depending on the nesting depth of objects. The problem arises from the distinction between objects given by their identifier and objects given by their (composite) value (see also [Beeri 90]).

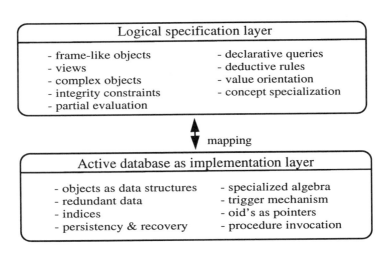

FIGURE 6.1
Architecture of a deductive object base

This paper pleads for a deductive style of object bases achieved in a two layer architecture (see Fig. 6.1). The top layer of such an object base system consists of declarative expressions, i.e., frame-like object specifications, views (esp. for complex objects), deductive rules, general integrity constraints, and a query language. All of these items are firmly based on a first-order theory of object bases. This layer corresponds to a modified view of databases as systems for *managing a model of knowledge about the world in an accessible and accurate manner for users*. Some basic optimization techniques for the logical layer are simplification methods [Nicolas 82, Blakely et al. 89], recursion optimization [Bancilhon and Ramakrishnan 86], and semantic query optimization [Jarke 84, Chakravarthy et al. 90]. They have in common that optimized formulas are obtained by partially evaluating either integrity constraints or update specifications with queries. The bottom layer contains

the implementations of the logical expressions. Object names are mapped
to object identifiers which behave similar to virtual memory addresses. The
basic optimization techniques at this level are rewritings of algebraic expressions (e.g., [Freytag 87, Graefe and DeWitt 87]), and redundant data, esp.
indices (e.g., [Kemper and Moerkotte 90]). An integrated trigger mechanism at the implementation layer meets the requirements for *active database
systems* whose active components enable the creation and execution of data
manipulation operations in a production rule like way. In our view and also
in our implementation these action rules are compiled automatically from
the specifications at the logical layer [Jeusfeld and Krüger 90]. Other approaches propose semi-automatical derivation methods with user interaction
for purposes of integrity checking [Ceri and Widom 90] and view maintenance
[Ceri and Widom 91].

We claim that such a two layer architecture is able to combine both de-
ductive-relational query optimization and the advantages of an object-oriented
data model. This claim is justified as follows:

- Section 6.2 defines *deductive object bases* as a special case of deductive databases with integrity constraints. Object-oriented abstraction
  principles like object identity, classification, and specialization become
  axioms of a first-order database theory.

- Queries can be defined as classes whose instances are the answer to the
  query (Section 6.3). Such a view allows to *classify queries* into the class
  hierarchy of the object base. A mapping of queries to deductive rules
  precisely defines the semantics of such queries.

- The *increased structure* of object bases can be used to perform semantic
  query optimization based on the structural axioms of the object model.
  Section 6.4.1 shows, as an example, the exploitation of the attribute
  typing axiom in order to eliminate class membership predicates.

- Trigger mechanisms from deductive integrity checking methods are used
  to optimize views, i.c., queries whose answers are maintained consistent
  with the object base (Section 6.4.2). The mechanism works in combination with (recursive) deductive rules. An additional benefit of *maintained views* is that they can help to optimize ad-hoc queries which are
  subclasses to the view.

The interplay of these logic-based optimization techniques with the algebraic and indexing techniques is sketched in the introduction to Section 6.4.

Experiences gained from an implementation within the deductive object base ConceptBase [Jarke 91] are reported in Section 6.5.

6.2
Object Bases as Deductive Databases

Most query optimization techniques have been developed for relational and deductive databases. On the other hand, the relational model has intrinsic weaknesses [Jackson 90] and performance comparisons [Duhl and Damon 88] indicate that object-oriented databases can beat their relational counterparts, esp. when following references. This section presents object bases to be special cases of deductive databases of the form (EDB,IDB,IC). EDB is the extensional database of base relations, IDB is a set of deductive rules, and IC is a set of integrity constraints. The formulas in IDB $\cup$ IC have to be range-restricted [Nicolas 82] which is a widely accepted sufficient condition for domain independence (see [Bry 88, Moerkotte and Lockemann 90] for more details). To ensure unique perfect models, we also assume that the set IDB is stratified [Ceri et al. 90b]. The next subsection defines the extensional database for deductive object bases. Then, the object-oriented principles are defined by axioms based on the extensional object base. The uniform representation of classes and instances requires an adaptation of the notion of stratification for defining the semantics of deductive rules.

6.2.1   The Extensional Object Base

The definition of the structure of an object base has considerable impact on the possible operations on it. For relational-style databases these operations are restricted to tuple updates on the base relation of the EDB. More demanding applications like software design, computer supported cooperative work, and others are characterized by two requirements that are hard to fulfill by relational-style databases:

- Updates on the database schema are frequent as the knowledge of the application domain is evolving. A data model that makes schema updates a cumbersome task is not appropriate.

- The data structures to be processed by the application tend to be dynamic in size rather than fixed as for first normal form tuples. Delivering exactly the required data structures for the application program is a precondition for a seamless integration of a database with the application.

For the reasons mentioned before we adopt an object model originally proposed for the requirements engineering of information systems: the knowledge representation language Telos [Mylopoulos et al. 90]. In Telos classes, instances, attributes, instantiation and specialization relationships are uniformly represented as quadruples:

DEFINITION 6.1

Let ID, LAB, LAB ⊆ ID, be countable sets of identifiers or labels, resp. Then a finite set

$$OB \subseteq \{P(o, x, l, y) | \; o, x, y \in ID, l \in LAB\}$$

is called an (extensional) **object base**. *The elements of OB are referred to as* **objects**.

In fact, this definition of an object base is like a total decomposition of a relational database into binary relations [Abrial 74] with two important differences:

1. Each binary "tuple" gets an object identifier which enables references from and to it.
2. The "relation name" is an argument of the quadruple. This allows quantification over such labels without leaving first order logic.

The intuition behind an object $P(o, x, l, y)$ is that there is a relation l between objects x and y. This relationship is itself an object with identifier o. In a graphical representation, *individual* objects, $P(o, o, l, o)$, are drawn as nodes. The other objects are links (attributes). Two special labels are reserved: $P(o, x, in, c)$ denotes that the object x is an instance of the (class) object c, and $P(o, c, isa, d)$ defines c to be a subclass of d. The semantics are defined by axioms of the object base theory (see next subsection).

In contrast to types in programming languages [Cardelli and Wegner 85] classes do not express sufficient conditions for class membership but only necessary ones. This is especially true for the attributes of a class: an instance of a class may instantiate these attributes but is not obliged to do so (provided there are no additional integrity constraints demanding that).

Figure 6.2 shows a sample Telos object base on patients and drugs. The class `Patient` has an attribute labeled `takes` to the class `Drug`. Both `Male-Patient` and `OldPatient` are subclasses of `Patient` where the former has an instance called `Sam`. `Sam` has two attributes `drug1` and `drug2` which are both

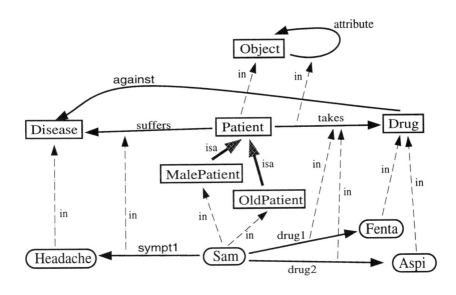

FIGURE 6.2

Object base for the drug example (graphical representation)

instances of the `takes` attribute class. The destinations `Fenta` and `Aspi` are instances of the class `Drug`. It should be noted that the graph does not contain oid's but only labels. An object base for Fig. 6.2 is summarized in Fig. 6.3.

A frame-like representation of objects and their properties is solely based on object labels (the third component of an object quadruple). The objects of Fig. 6.2 are mapped from the following frames:

```
Object Drug with
  attribute
    against: Disease
end

Object Patient with
  attribute
    takes: Drug;
    suffers: Disease
end

Object Disease
Object MalePatient isA Patient
```

$OB = \{$ $P(\#Pat,\#Pat,Patient,\#Pat),\ P(\#MP,\#MP,MalePatient,\#MP),$
             $P(\#isa1,\#MP,isa,\#Pat),\ P(\#OP,\#OP,OldPatient,\#OP),$
             $P(\#isa2,\#OP,isa,\#Pat),\ P(\#Drug,\#Drug,Drug,\#Drug),$
             $P(\#Dis,\#Dis,Disease,\#Dis),\ P(\#tak,\#Pat,takes,\#Drug),$
             $P(\#suff,\#Pat,suffers,\#Dis),\ P(\#ag,\#Drug,against,\#Dis),$
             $P(\#Sam,\#Sam,Sam,\#Sam),\ P(\#in1,\#Sam,in,\#MP),$
             $P(\#in2,\#Sam,in,\#OP),\ P(\#Fen,\#Fen,Fenta,\#Fen),$
             $P(\#Asp,\#Asp,Aspi,\#Asp),\ P(\#in3,\#Fen,in,\#Drug),$
             $P(\#in4,\#Asp,in,\#Drug),\ P(\#dr1,\#Sam,drug1,\#Fen),$
             $P(\#dr2,\#Sam,drug2,\#Asp),\ P(\#in5,\#dr1,in,\#tak),$
             $P(\#in6,\#dr2,in,\#tak),\ P(\#Head,\#Head,Headache,\#Head),$
             $P(\#in7,\#Head,in,\#Dis),\ P(\#sy1,\#Sam,sympt1,\#Head),$
             $P(\#in8,\#sy1,in,\#suff)$ $\}$

FIGURE 6.3
Object base for the drug example (tuple representation)

```
Object OldPatient isA Patient
Object Fenta in Drug
Object Aspi in Drug
Object Headache in Disease

MalePatient,OldPatient Sam with
  takes
    drug1: Fenta;
    drug2: Aspi
  suffers
    sympt1: Headache
end
```

Labels for individual objects have to be globally unique. Attribute labels have to be unique within the same frame. The classes of an object are written before the object, superclasses are preceded by the key word isA. The attributes of an object are instantiated to the attributes of the class by grouping them under the class attribute label. We omit the formal definition, esp. the conflict resolution on multiply inherited attributes with identical labels. The object Sam shows that the attribute takes may be instantiated several times.

There are some objects whose oid has a meaning outside the object base. These objects are called *values* [Beeri 90]. Examples for (atomic) values are numbers and strings. We write values as objects of the form $P(v,v,v,v)$, i.e., individual objects whose label and oid are the same [Koubarakis et al. 89].

6.2.2   Deductive Object Base Theory

From the deductive database standpoint an object base (Def. 6.1) is an extensional database with a single relation. That situation is undesirable since each deductive rule and each integrity constraint would be affected by any update. This section presents an axiomatic definition of object-oriented abstraction mechanisms (partially taken from [Mylopoulos et al. 90] and [Koubarakis et al. 89]). Deductive rules and integrity constraints are expressed with three literals for instantiation, specialization, and attribute relationships. Stratification is then applied to a rewriting of the formulas where class object identifiers are used as predicate names.

The first axiom defines object identity. No two objects in the extensional object base may have the same identifiers.

$$\forall\, o, x_1, l_1, y_1, x_2, l_2, y_2 \; P(o, x_1, l_1, y_1) \wedge P(o, x_2, l_2, y_2) \Rightarrow \qquad (A_1)$$
$$(x_1 = x_2) \wedge (l_1 = l_2) \wedge (y_1 = y_2)$$

For individual objects the label (third component) must be unique within the object base, too. The next three axioms induce base solutions for the three literals for instantiation, specialization, and aggregation. These three literals are later used to formulate deductive rules and integrity constraints.

$$\forall\, o, x, c \; P(o, x, in, c) \Rightarrow In(x, c) \qquad (A_2)$$
$$\forall\, o, c, d \; P(o, c, isa, d) \Rightarrow Isa(c, d) \qquad (A_3)$$
$$\forall o, x, l, y, p, c, m, d \; P(o, x, l, y) \wedge P(p, c, m, d) \wedge In(o, p) \Rightarrow A(x, m, y) \quad (A_4)$$

Inheritance of class membership is a deductive rule. The *Isa* literal is defined to form a partial order on the set objects identifiers of an object base (another 3 axioms not shown here).

$$\forall\, x, c, d \; In(x, c) \wedge Isa(c, d) \Rightarrow In(x, d) \qquad (A_5)$$

The next axiom declares "weak" attribute typing in a Telos object base. Objects may instantiate the attributes of their classes only if the destination of the attribute belongs to the correct class.

$$\forall\, o, x, l, y, p \; P(o, x, l, y) \wedge In(o, p) \Rightarrow \qquad (A_6)$$
$$\exists\, c, m, d \; P(p, c, m, d) \wedge In(x, c) \wedge In(y, d)$$

Axiom A_4 provides a single literal $A(x, m, y)$ for all attribute accesses from an object x to its attribute value y (sometimes written as $x.m = y$). In object-oriented languages it is common to allow the use of the same attribute label m for different classes. The next axiom demands that for any object x the literal $A(x, m, y)$ is uniquely assignable to an attribute class with label m.

If there are two different attribute classes that x instantiates, then there must be a common subclass of them:

$$\forall\, x, m, y, c, d, a_1, a_2, u, v \; In(x,c) \wedge In(x,d) \wedge A(x,m,y) \qquad (A_7)$$
$$\wedge P(a_1, c, m, u) \wedge P(a_2, d, m, v)$$
$$\Rightarrow \exists\, e, a_3, w \; In(x,e) \wedge P(a_3, e, m, w) \wedge Isa(e,c)$$
$$\wedge Isa(d,e) \wedge Isa(a_3, a_1) \wedge Isa(a_3, a_2)$$

The rest of the axioms (unique labeling, refinement of attributes for subclasses, membership to predefined classes) are omitted for sake of readability (see [Jeusfeld 91]).

6.2.3   Deduction and Integrity

Deductive rules and integrity constraints are range-restricted first order formulas over the three literals *In, Isa,* and *A*. Range-restrictedness can be guaranteed by assigning the quantified variables to classes: $\forall\, x/C \; \varphi$ stands for $\forall x \; In(x,C) \Rightarrow \varphi$, and $\exists\, x/C \; \varphi$ stands for $\exists x \; In(x,C) \wedge \varphi$. This syntax is not a real restriction since variables in our model always refer to elements in the object base.

Efficiency and stratification in deductive databases depend on the number of base and deduced relations. The above definition offers one base relation P and three deduced relations *In, Isa, A*. That number is surely not satisfactory. Therefore, a restricted interpretation of deductive rules and integrity constraints is adopted. Firstly, an object base with only $A_2 - A_4$ as deductive rules delivers ground facts for the three predicates. Note that the axioms are range-restricted and stratifiable. For a ground fact $A(x, m, y)$, the closure axiom [Reiter 84] applied to A_4 guarantees the existence of an object $P(p, c, m, d)$ to which an attribute of x was instantiated to. We extend the deduction machine by a rule that delivers a fact $A.p(x, y)$ for each such p. Similarly, a fact $In.c(x)$ for each ground fact $In(x, c)$ is derived. The Isa-literal remains unchanged. These modifications extend the number of literals by all class and attribute identifiers.

Now, deductive rules and integrity constraints are rewritten such that they only contain $A.p$, $In.c$ and *Isa* literals. For the *In* literal, this rewriting is trivial provided the second component is a constant. Otherwise the formula is rejected (see [Jeusfeld and Jarke 91] for handling meta formulas which range over classes). The interesting case is the literal A. Let $A(x, l, y)$ be a literal occurrence in a formula φ where x is bound to class c. Then c' is defined to be the lowest superclass of c that has an attribute labeled l. If there is such a

c' at all, then it is uniquely defined due to axiom A_7. The following example shows that there are cases where no such class exists ($\#Obj$ is the identifier of the system class `Object` which has all objects as instances):

$$\forall\ x/\#Obj\ A(x, takes, 1000)$$

Such formulas are forbidden as deductive rules or integrity constraints. The refinement of attributes creates no further problems since axiom A_7 demands a specialization relation between those attributes. Thereby, instances of refined attributes will also be visible at their superclasses.

The text representation of deductive rules and integrity constraints uses labels instead of object identifiers. The mapping from labels is a compilation task and not subject of this paper. The administration of the formula strings is done within the object base: they are stored as instances of the predefined classes `DeductiveRule` and `IntegrityConstraint`. Both are attributes of `Object`. As an example, a constraint demanding a patient to have at least one symptom, is assigned to the class `Patient`:

```
Object Patient with
  attribute
    takes: Drug;
    suffers: Disease
  constraint
    sick: $ forall p/Patient exists d/Disease A(p,suffers,d) $
end
```

The string represents the formula

$$\forall\ p\ In.\#Pat(p) \Rightarrow \exists\ s\ In.\#Dis(s) \wedge A.\#suff(p, s)$$

which becomes part of the set IC in the *deductive object base* (OB,R,IC). R denotes the set of deductive rules and takes over the role of the IDB. The concerned attribute of $A(p, suffers, s)$ is $\#suff$. Note that the constraint may only become part of the deductive object base if the rewriting of the literals succeeds. Further examples with recursive deduction rules are in [Jeusfeld and Jarke 91].

6.3
Queries as Classes

Many proposals exist in the literature for query representation formats in the context of object-oriented databases and knowledge representation systems. One group uses query languages adapted from conventional databases, for example, SQL-like languages augmented by some typical object-oriented constructs (ORION [Banerjee et al. 88], Iris [Lyngbæk et al. 90], Starburst [Lohmann et al. 91], and O_2 [Bancilhon et al. 89]). Another group of query languages is based on first order logic with a link to deductive databases, e.g., [Abiteboul and Grumbach 91] and [Kifer et al. 90]. They investigate the relationship of complex objects and operations (given by their signature) with logical statements about the object base. Among the derivatives of the knowledge representation language KL-ONE the systems CLASSIC [Borgida et al. 89] and CANDIDE [Beck et al. 89] offer a frame format for queries. Queries are described as any other concept stored in the knowledge base (KB). Kernel of these systems is a subsumption algorithm which is used to store new objects and to evaluate queries by temporary placement in the KB. Candidates for answer objects are those objects positioned underneath the query concept within the concept and individual hierarchy of the KB. An important advantage of these classification based query languages is their close relation to the underlying data description language. The main concepts of the data model occur in the query language too which means clarity and user friendliness. In addition queries are seen as objects which can be stored in the KB and manipulated in any other way.

In [Staudt 90] this latter idea of query representation has been adopted and used to build a query language for the above outlined notion of an object base. Using the frame notation of the last section for objects a metaclass `QueryClass`[1] shall contain all possible queries which themselves are classes. Following the instantiation and classification principle instances of a query class are answers to the represented query. To express necessary and sufficient membership conditions for answer instances in query classes by which membership can be tested and answers be computed, we have on the one hand the possibility to specify structural constraints like in the above mentioned classification based query languages.

First, query classes can have superclasses to which they are connected by an isa link. These superclasses restrict the set of possible answer instances to the common instances of the super classes of the query class.

```
QueryClass Q1 isA MalePatient,OldPatient
```

Here `MalePatient` and `OldPatient` are assumed to be themselves subclasses of `Patient`. Since the two specialization relationships represent the

---

[1]An approach with similar properties has independently been proposed in [Abiteboul and Bonner 91].

only membership condition for `Q1` the answer consists of the intersection of the instances of both subclasses of `Patient`.

Second, query classes may have attributes of two different types. The first kind of attributes is inherited of one of the superclasses. If such an attribute is specified explicitly in a query class description this means that answer instances are given back with value instantiations of this attribute, similar to projection in relational algebra. In addition, this explicit specification includes a necessary condition for the instantiation of the attribute with an admissible attribute value by the answer instances. This necessary condition can be enforced by specializing the target class of the inherited attribute. Then an answer instance must instantiate the attribute with a value which is an instance of this more special class.

```
QueryClass Q2 isA MalePatient,OldPatient with
    attribute
        takes: Antibiotics
end
```

`Antibiotics` is assumed to be a specialization of class `Drug`. `Q2` inherits attribute `takes` from class `Patient` via direct superclass `MalePatient` or `OldPatient`. These answer instances are the common instances of both super classes which actually take drugs of the class `Antibiotics`.

Attributes for query classes of the second type are attributes whose instantiation value by an answer instance is computed during the query evaluation process. That means that a relation between the answer instance and the computed attribute value is not necessarily stored explicitly in the KB or deducible by a stored deduction rule but nevertheless part of the answer. The prescription how to deduce these attributes must be included in the definition of the query class and can obviously not be done in a structural way without loss of generality. So there is need for a supplementing formalism. As assertions (integrity constraints and deductive rules) are used in the data description language of the object base, typed first order logic expressions can be introduced as possible building elements for query classes.

```
QueryClass Q3 isA MalePatient,OldPatient with
    attribute
        wrong:Drug
    constraint
        wrongRule: $ A(this,takes,wrong) and
                     not exists d/Disease A(this,suffers,d)
                     and A(wrong,against,d) $
end
```

Within the formula `this` is a shorthand reference to the answer instances of `Q3`. The variable `wrong` is identified with the value of the corresponding attribute. So here the first order logic expression denotes a prescription for the deduction of the **wrong** attribute. **Q3** computes all old and male patients who take drugs against diseases they do not suffer from. The deduced values for the **wrong** attribute are part of the answer. In addition it is possible to include any other membership conditions for instances of a query class using the logical representation. The integration of structural and logical representation formalisms leads to a hybrid query language. KRYPTON [Brachman et al. 85], a derivative of KL-ONE and ancestor of Telos, uses both formalisms for its query language too, but in its data description language they are not combined into one closed format.

In order to avoid the reformulation of similar, more specialized queries, attributes of query classes can be parameterized. Substitution of a concrete value for an attribute or specialization of its target class by a subclass leads to a subclass of the original query class which implies a subset relationship of the answer sets. In the frame syntax, specialized classes are written as terms that define the substitution. For instance, **Q3** can be specialized by substituting the **wrong** attribute:

```
Q3(Fenta/wrong)
```

This query is a shorthand for a query class which has only those patients as answer instances which are instances of **Q3** and have the concrete drug **Fenta** as their **wrong** attribute. Another kind of substitution refines the attribute value class: **Q3(wrong:Antibiotics)** considers only those answer instances of **Q3** whose "wrong" drugs belong to the subclass **Antibiotics**.

The semantics of query classes is twofold: First, a query class is just a class object that has some attributes. Second, there is a mapping from the query class frame to a deductive rule that defines which objects are the answer to the query. Consider the frame

```
QueryClass Q isA C1,...,Ck with
  attribute
    a1: S1; ... am: Sm;
    b1: T1; ... bn: Tn
  constraint
    c: $ <formula text> $
end
```

We assume that **a1,...,am** are attributes which are refined from existing attributes with the same labels in classes **C1,...,Cm**. The attributes **b1,...,bn** are additional properties of **Q**. Let φ be the first-order formula represented by **<formula text>**. Then the query rule corresponding to the frame is:

$$\forall x, y_1, ..., y_m, z_1, ..., z_n \ In.\#C1(x) \land ... \land In.\#Ck(x) \land$$
$$In.\#S1(y_1) \land A.\#a1(x, y_1) \land ... \land In.\#Sm(y_m) \land A.\#am(x, y_m) \land \qquad (1)$$
$$In.\#T1(z_1) \land ... \land In.\#Tn(z_n) \land \varphi \Rightarrow Q(x, y_1, ..., y_m, z_1, ..., z_m)$$

The first argument x of Q is called the **answer variable** of the query rule. The other arguments are called **query attributes**. The constants $\#C1, \#S1, \#T1$ etc. are the object identifiers of the labels C1, S1, T1 etc., and $\#a1,...,\#am$ are the identifiers of the attributes labeled by a1,...,am. As formula (1) shows, the variables in $Q(x, y_1, ..., y_m, z_1, ..., z_m)$ are bound to objects in the object base. There is no "invention" of object identifiers for answers to queries as, for example, in [Hull and Yoshikawa 90].

Since query classes may be superclasses, or attribute value classes of other queries, class membership to queries is defined by a second rule.

$$\forall \ x, y_1, ..., y_m, z_1, ..., z_n \ Q(x, y_1, ..., y_m, z_1, ..., z_m) \Rightarrow In.\#Q(x) \qquad (2)$$

The evaluation of this rule leads to a set of ground instances of the literal Q which can be used to build up the answer instances of the query class Q in frame format. The two deductive rules for query class Q3 are

$$\forall x, y_1 \ In.\#MP(x) \land In.\#OP(x) \land In.\#Drug(y_1) \land A.\#tak(x, y_1) \land \qquad (3)$$
$$\neg \exists \ s \ In.\#Dis(s) \land A.\#\text{suff}(x, s) \land A.\#ag(y_1, s) \Rightarrow Q_3(x, y_1)$$

$$\forall \ x, y_1 \ Q_3(x, y_1) \Rightarrow In.\#Q3(x) \qquad (4)$$

The parameterization of query classes has a strong logical counterpart, the simplification of formulas [Nicolas 82]. For instance, the deductive rule for the specialized query class Q3(Fenta/wrong) is obtained by simplifying formula (3) with $In.\#Drug(\#Fen)$. This step instantiates the universally quantified variable y_1. The result is

$$\forall \ x \ In.\#MP(x) \land In.\#OP(x) \land A.\#tak(x, \#Fen) \land$$
$$\neg \ \exists \ s \ In.\#Dis(s) \land A.\#\text{suff}(x, s) \land A.\#ag(\#Fen, s) \Rightarrow Q'_3(x, \#Fen)$$

$$\forall \ x, y_1 \ Q'_3(x, y_1) \Rightarrow In.\#Q3'(x)$$

The simplification of the query (3) conforms well with the specialization axiom A_5 since $In.\#Q3'(x)$ implies $In.\#Q3(x)$. The same property holds for the attribute value class refinement, e.g. Q3(wrong:Antibiotics).

6.4
Query Optimization Methods

With the given object model and query language as prerequisite in the following two opportunities of query optimization in deductive object bases are presented. Figure 6.4 shows the general query optimizer architecture of a deductive object base [Jarke and Koubarakis 89].

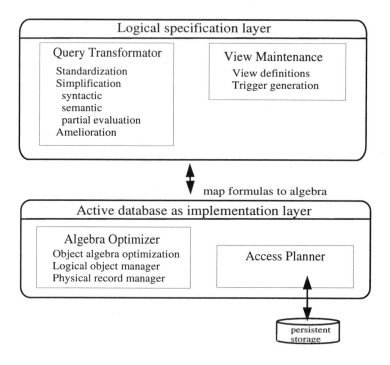

FIGURE 6.4

Architecture of a query optimization component for deductive object bases

The optimizer is subdivided into components for logical and algebraic query representations. The first one maps query declarations to algebra expressions which are then evaluated on the physically stored records. This mapping is accompanied by using different techniques of optimization to obtain necessary efficiency.

The query transformation component at the logical layer applies general rules, laws, and heuristics to optimize and map a user query. Three different aspects have to be distinguished. Standardization means mainly the introduction of a normal form used as a starting point for further transformations. Simplification can be understood in a syntactic (e.g., elimination of tautologies and redundancies) or semantic way (consideration of rules and integrity constraints) and includes partial evaluation methods. Amelioration covers issues such as recursion elimination and optimization, reuse of common subexpressions and application of general heuristics.

At the implementation layer besides the mapping to logical and physical storage structures optimizations for the special selected object algebra are performed. The access planning component takes quantitative statistical information about the current objectbase into account when optimizing the algebra expression resulting from the transformation step.

Finally, a view maintenance mechanism allows the use of materialized views which in fact are queries with stored answers and prevents unnecessary computations. Here we have an additional aspect of optimization which comprises the efficiency of the view maintenance algorithm. This last topic is discussed in Subsection 6.4.2. The following subsection concentrates on a semantic simplification technique using structural axioms of the underlying object model.

6.4.1   Structural Query Optimization

The deductive object base theory presented in Section 6.2 is characterized by an increased number of axioms when compared to deductive relational databases. The axioms are theorems, i.e. they are true in any consistent deductive object base (OB,R,IC). Therefore, they can always be used to simplify queries. In this section the exploitation of the attribute typing axiom A_6 is investigated.

Recalling the query rule formula (3), one observes a considerable number of class membership literals $In.c(x)$. They are introduced by the assignment of variables to classes, by the attribute value classes, and by the interpretation of superclasses as classes of the answer variable. Consider now an expression $A.p(x, y) \land In.c(x)$, and suppose that p is the oid of an object $P(p, c, m, d)$ in the extensional object base. Then, two cases can be distinguished:

1. $A.p(x, y)$ is derived from axiom A_4 (Section 6.2). Then there must be an object $P(o, x, l, y)$ with $In(o, p)$. The attribute typing axiom

A_7 then establishes the truth of $In(x, c)$.

2. $A.p(x, y)$ is derived from a deductive rule

$$\forall\ x/c', y/d'\ \varphi \Rightarrow A(x, m, y)$$

where $A(x, m, y)$ is rewritten to $A.p(x, y)$ (see Section 6.2). Then, c must be the lowest superclass of c' that has an attribute with label m. Then, $In.c'(x)$ is true, and as a consequence of axiom A_5 $In.c(x)$ follows.

In both cases, $In.c(x)$ is already guaranteed by $A.p(x, y)$, $P(p, c, m, d)$, and the axioms of the object base. A similar argument holds for $In.d(x)$ in a conjunction $Ap(x, y) \wedge In.d(y)$. Thus, any conjunction $A.p(x, y) \wedge In.c(x)$ or $A.p(x, y) \wedge In.d(y)$, resp., can be replaced with $A.p(x, y)$ provided p is the identifier of an object $P(p, c, m, d)$.

The query rule (3) for query Q3 serves as an example. Firstly, there is a conjunction $In.\#Drug(y_1) \wedge A.\#tak(x, y_1)$ where

$$P(\#tak, \#Pat, takes, \#Drug)$$

is in the object base. Thus, $In.\#Drug(y_1)$ can be canceled. Analogously, $In.\#Sympt(s) \wedge A.\#suff(x, s)$ reduces to $A.\#suff(x, s)$. The result is

$$\forall\ x, y_1\ In.\#MP(x) \wedge In.\#OP(x) \wedge A.\#tak(x, y_1)\ \wedge \qquad (5)$$
$$\neg\exists\ s\ A.\#suff(x, s) \wedge A.\#ag(y_1, s) \Rightarrow Q_3(x, y_1)$$

The first two instantiation literals are not redundant since they are subclasses of the class $\#Pat$, and membership to $\#Pat$ does not imply membership to $\#MP$ or $\#OP$. Whether the elimination of the instantiation literals yields a performance gain depends on the representation and evaluation algorithms. The point is that we now have the **choice** to use either the original or the reduced formula.

6.4.2   Complex Object View Optimization

A view is a query whose answer is used over a longer period of time. The view update problem is twofold. First, an update to the base data has to be efficiently propagated to the view in order to keep the answer consistent. Second, an update on the view has to be translated into updates on the base data. For *deductive* databases, views are seen as (materialized) deductive rules. In that framework, the first subproblem could be solved by re-evaluating the whole deductive rule on each update (this is much too costly). For the second subproblem, abduction has been proposed [Kakas and Mancarella 90]. In this section, we propose a deductive definition for views that takes the complex object principle into account. Simplification is proposed as an optimization technique for the first direction of view updates (*view maintenance*).

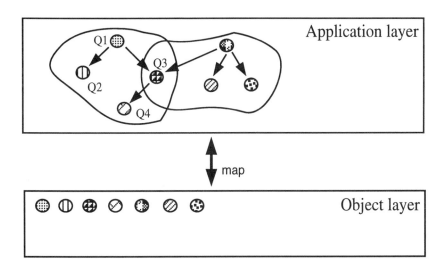

FIGURE 6.5
Molecules and atoms in PRIMA

While views in relational databases are just (derived) relations, the definition for object bases seems not that clear. For instance, the PRIMA object base system [Hübel and Mitschang 88] introduces the concept of *molecules*. These complex data structures are declared by means of SQL-like query statements on top of an object base of *atoms*. The definition of molecules depends on the application that manipulates them. Figure 6.5 shows two molecules which share a common atom. It is important to note that the molecule boundaries are prescribed by the application, not by the object base.

In a logic-based framework for an object base the usual representation for complex objects are complex terms [Ceri et al. 90a]. However, such representation forbids the direct use of deductive database methods that are based on a function-free horn logic. An alternative is shown in Def. 6.2.

DEFINITION 6.2

Let $Q_1, ..., Q_k$ be the conclusion predicates of query rules. Then, a rule

$$\forall\ v_1, ..., v_m\ Q_1(x_1, t_{11}, ..., t_{n_1 1}) \wedge Q_2(x_2, t_{12}, ..., t_{n_2 2}) \wedge ...$$
$$\wedge\ Q_k(x_k, t_{1k}, ..., t_{n_k k}) \Rightarrow Q(x_1)$$

*is called a **complex object view** iff all $x_i, i > 1$, appear at least once as a t_{rj} of a Q_j.*

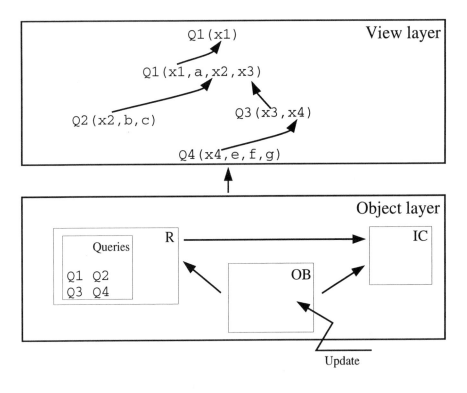

FIGURE 6.6
Complex object and update propagation

Figure 6.6 presents a typical example. The complex object identified by x_1 has an attribute a, and two part complex objects identified by x_2 and x_3. The complex object x_2 is not further decomposed, whereas x_3 has another part complex object x_4. The object layer of Fig. 6.6 shows the principal propagation of an update in the object base. The update is propagated to the simplified forms of deductive rules and integrity constraints. The idea is to use the same technique for the maintenance of the view.

The complex object rule in Definition 6.2 has two interpretations. The first is just the logical statement, i.e. all the ground facts $Q(x_1)$ that are derivable from the deductive object base. The set of these object identifiers can be seen as the set of pointers to the complex objects. The second interpretation is more algorithmic. The complex object rule is a statement which of the ground facts Q_i shall be stored and maintained in the view layer. All items contributing to a view are either ground facts of the object base or deductive rules, esp. queries are mapped to deductive rules. Therefore, methods from deductive database theory appear to be most appropriate to perform view maintenance optimization. The problem is as follows:

Given a sequence of updates

$$< op_1(P(o_1, x_1, l_1, y_1)), op_2(P(o_2, x_2, l_2, y_2)), ... >$$
$$(op_i \in \{Insert, Delete\})$$

find at lowest costs the induced update for a complex object $Q(x)$.

A subproblem is to find – starting from the object base update – the set of deductive rules that are affected by the update. The simplification method (e.g., [Bry et al. 88]) gives an answer to this question for integrity constraints:

Let $op(L)$ be an update and L' be a matching literal occurring in an integrity constraint φ. Then it is sufficient to check the simplified form $\varphi_{op(L)}$. If no matching literal occurs then the constraint is not affected by this update.

The simplification idea can be extended to deductive rules as well, see, e.g., [Olivé 91]. For each rule r and each update $op(L)$ that matches a literal L' occurring in the rule body a simplified rule $r_{op(L)}$ is generated. If L' is positive and $op=Insert$ then the evaluation of $r_{op(L)}$ yields a superset of the derived conclusions that are true due to the truth of L. Similar cases hold for negative L's and for delete operations. The original methods were proposed for deductive integrity checking for efficient computation of the derived facts that affect an integrity constraint.

A simple trick extends the upward propagation to complex object views: Include a formal constraint

$$\forall\ x/\#Obj\ Q(x) \vee \neg Q(x)$$

into the set IC of the deductive object base (OB,R,IC). Then, each insertion and deletion of a subobject $Q_i(x_i, ...)$ will be efficiently propagated from updates to the object base. To store the solutions in the view is a matter of implementation, see e.g. [Sellis et al. 89].

As an example, consider the following complex object view (see also Fig. 6.6). The query Q_3 is taken from Section 6.3.

$$\forall\ x_1, x_2, x_3, x_4, a, b, c, e, f, g\ Q_1(x_1, a, x_2, x_3) \wedge Q_2(x_2, b, c) \wedge \qquad (6)$$
$$Q_3(x_3, x_4) \wedge Q_4(x_4, e, f, g) \Rightarrow Q(x_1)$$

We assume that the view already contains the complex object identified by $\#drSm$:

$$Q_1(\#drSm, \text{``}Dr.med.Smith\text{''}, \#KlinAc, \#Sam)$$
$$Q_2(\#KlinAc, 5100, \text{``}KlinikumAachen\text{''})$$
$$Q_3(\#Sam, \#Asp)$$
$$Q_3(\#Sam, \#Fen)$$
$$Q_4(\#Asp, 17, 3)$$
$$Q_4(\#Fen, 7, 21)$$

With the example of Section 6.2, the update

$$< Delete(P(\#dr2, \#Sam, drug2, \#Asp)),$$
$$Delete(P(\#in6, \#dr2, in, \#tak)) >$$

deletes the literal $A.\#tak(\#Sam, \#Asp)$ due to axiom A_4. That derived update affects rule (5) for query Q3 (see Subsection 6.4.1). The simplified form for this update is

$$In.\#MP(\#Sam) \wedge In.\#OP(\#Sam) \wedge \qquad (7)$$
$$\neg \exists\ s\ A.\#suff(\#Sam, s) \wedge A.\#ag(\#Asp, s) \Rightarrow Q_3(\#Sam, \#Asp)$$

Assuming that the condition holds, we derive the deletion of $Q_3(\#Sam, \#Asp)$ which triggers the complex object view. The fact $Q_3(\#Sam, \#Asp)$ is removed from the view. In an implementation, facts with identical first component can be aggregated using a set data structure,. e.g.,

$$CO_3(\#Sam, \{\#Asp, \#Fen)\})$$

That gives us a restricted simulation of the set constructor found in other object bases. The update above would then effectively remove the element $\#Asp$ from the list. The dangling fact $Q_4(\#Asp, 17, 3)$ should then also be removed since it not longer contributes to the complex object. A small problem arises if the last fact of a predicate symbol is removed, e.g., $Q_3(\#Sam, \#Fen)$. Then, the condition of the view (6) fails, and $Q(\#Sam)$ is no longer true. In a strict interpretation, the complex object $\#Sam$ has to be totally removed from the view. Alternatively, one could interpret this situation by an empty set in the data structure:

$$CO_1(\#drSm, \{\text{``Dr.med.Smith''}\}, \{\#KlinAc\}, \{\})$$

Another optimization opportunity with views is to use their content as ranges for ad hoc queries. The general idea is to exploit subset relationships between answers to queries. If the query QA is a superclass of QB, then each answer to QB is also an answer to QA:

$$\forall x\ Q_B(x, ...) \Rightarrow Q_A(x, ...)$$

This result follows immediately from the transformation of superclasses in formula (1). If QB is queried frequently compared to QA then it makes sense to materialize the answer to QA for getting a finer range for the computation of the answer to QB. This materialization can be achieved by simply defining a view $\forall x\ Q_A(x, ...) \Rightarrow Q(x)$. An important application are the parameterized queries. They are superclasses of all their specializations. If the query class Q3 is materialized by a view

$$\forall\ x, y_1\ Q_3(x, y_1) \Rightarrow Q(x)$$

then ad-hoc specializations of Q3, e.g. Q3(Fenta/wrong) can scan the solutions of Q3 as a range and just check the additional condition $y_1 = \#Fen$.

6.5
State of Implementation

The object model described in Section 6.2 with deductive rules and integrity constraints and the presented optimization techniques are implemented in the deductive object base system ConceptBase [2] [Jarke 91] and its query

---

[2] In addition to the concepts mentioned in the previous sections, ConceptBase contains a temporal component for representing validity and system time for each object.

language CBQL [Staudt 90]. ConceptBase has been developed since 1987 at the Universities of Passau and Aachen. It is being used in a number of projects in Europe, the US, and Canada as a knowledge-based repository for design process information.

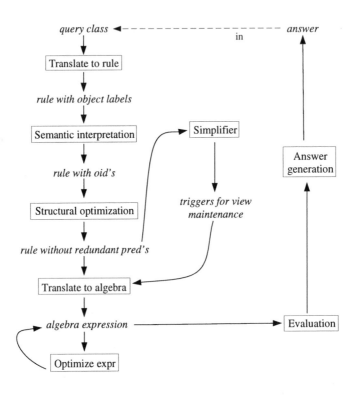

FIGURE 6.7
Query optimization in ConceptBase

The system consists of two parts: the kernel which realizes the object base administration mostly implemented in Prolog on SUN machines, and an X11-based usage environment for browsing, querying and editing of the object base. The communication between both parts and between the kernel and other application programs follows a client/server architecture.

The query optimizer of ConceptBase (see Fig. 6.7) accepts as input query classes which are transformed to a query rule according to Section 6.3. The constants which represent object labels are replaced by object identifiers, and the literals *In.A* are rewritten with the specialized literals. The resulting rule is then transformed by exploiting the structural axioms of the object base, esp. the attribute typing axiom. For queries which contribute to views, triggers for the view update are generated. The last transformation step is the translation to the object algebra. The algebra expression can then be evaluated over the object base. The algebra optimizer is currently simulated by a direct implementation of the base literals (P, In, A, Isa) on an extensible main memory-oriented object store [Gallersdörfer 90].

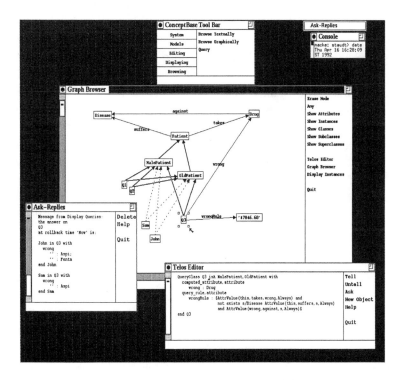

FIGURE 6.8
Screendump of a session with ConceptBase

Figure 6.8 shows the X11-based user interface of ConceptBase with the graphical browser and the object editor. The browser displays the object network of the drug example together with the query classes introduced in Section 6.3. Individuals and attributes are represented as nodes and labeled links, specialization and instantiation relationships as dotted and normal links. The query classes are stored as objects (and therefore browsing on classes is possible as on any other object). The frame representation of Q3 shown in the editor slightly differs from the format in Section 6.3. Deduced attributes of query classes belong to a special category computed_attribute. The literal *AttrValue* corresponds to the former *A* literal. The displayed situation is as follows: After selecting Q3 in the graph with menu item "Ask" Q3 is called to be evaluated i.e. the instances of Q3 together with values for the wrong attribute shall be computed. This task is transmitted to the ConceptBase kernel via an inter-process message. The answers are sent back to the usage environment and are displayed in the *Ask-Replies* window in their textual frame representation. In this example, Q3 has two instances of Patient as answer: Sam takes drug Aspi although he does not suffer from a symptom this drug is against. John doesn't need neither Aspi nor Fenta.

For queries, rules and constraints the actual implementation of ConceptBase contains different evaluable internal formats which can be chosen. Forward evaluation of deductive rules and integrity constraints triggered by class instantiations is done by a meta program interpreting an internal format of the formulas. Current implementation work concentrates on improving the evaluation of deductive rules (and queries) with the magic set format. Further efforts are directed towards the application of the view maintenance mechanisms via query classes to schema integration for heterogeneous databases [Klemann 91].

6.6
Conclusions

The aim of this paper was to demonstrate that a deductive kind of object bases offers optimization opportunities that fit well together with object-orientation. The Telos object model introduced in Section 6.2 is characterized by a total decomposition of information into quadruples forming the extensional object base. Instances, attributes, classes, instantiation and specialization links are uniformly treated as objects. As a consequence, updates on either of them are principally undistinguished. Based on this extensional object base, a first-order language for deductive rules and integrity constraints is defined. The interpretation is restricted by a stratification that is not applied to the original formulas but to a rewriting that replaces the fixed set of literals by literals based on object identifiers at the class level.

Our frame-like query language describes queries as classes with superclasses, attributes, and a logical statement that constrains the instances of the query class. The advantage of this notation – which is familiar with certain knowledge representation languages – is that users do not have to learn a special query language different from the data definition language. A mapping of the frame-like query classes to deductive rules defines the semantics of queries, and integrates well with (recursive) deductive rules. We only presented a small segment of query optimization at the level of logical formulas:

- Instantiation literals introduced by the class ranges of variables can be eliminated by applying the attribute typing axiom. Experiments indicate that the efficiency increase is about factor 2 - 5. But, the axioms of the object model hold in any object base. Thereby, this optimization can be applied to virtually any query, deductive rule, and integrity constraint inserted into the system.

- If complex objects are defined as function-free deductive rules, then well-known update propagation methods become applicable. We presented a definition that is able to simulate tuple and set constructors. Views can also be used to materialize queries that serve as ranges for ad-hoc queries specialized from them.

During the upward propagation of updates to views, a lot of intermediate updates on derived facts can be generated, each triggering another simplified rule. Surely, the proposed propagation method is not efficient enough if the amount of rules or their complexity exceeds a certain level. A possible solution is to restrict views and rules in a way that allows further optimization.

A major application of the deductive definition of complex objects is the software configuration problem [Rose et al. 91]. Software systems are composed from modules that are further decomposed. Updates to components have to be propagated downwards to submodules (this is a special abduction problem [Kakas and Mancarella 90]), and upwards to the modules (complex objects) that depend on the updated object (this is a special case of the view update problem in Section 6.4.2). Currently, we are investigating the special properties of complex objects in software configuration. Such properties are, for example, that integrity checking can be drastically simplified if the constraints only relate configured objects. Another research issue is to find a good mapping from the logical layer into the structural layer. We expect that the optimization methods based on rewritings of algebraic expressions can then be transferred to our storage system.

Acknowledgements

The authors would like to express their thanks to Matthias Jarke for his constant advice. Many thanks also to the participants of the Dagstuhl seminar for the vivid discussions and important hints.

Bibliography

[Abiteboul and Bonner 91] Abiteboul S. and Bonner A. "Objects and views." In *Proc. ACM-SIGMOD Int. Conf. on Management of Data*, pp. 238–247.

[Abiteboul and Grumbach 91] Abiteboul S. and Grumbach S. "A rule-based language with functions and sets." In *ACM Trans. on Database Systems* **16**(1), pp. 1–30.

[Abrial 74] Abrial J.R. "Data semantics." In *Data Base Management* (Klimbie and Koffeman, eds.), pp. 1–60. North-Holland.

[Bancilhon and Ramakrishnan 86] Bancilhon F. and Ramakrishnan R. "An amateur's introduction to recursive query processing strategies." In *Proc. ACM-SIGMOD Int. Conf. on Management of Data*, pp. 16–52.

[Bancilhon et al. 89] Bancilhon F., Cluet S., and Delobel C. "A query language for the O_2 object-oriented database system." Rapport Technique Altaïr 35-89.

[Banerjee et al. 88] Banerjee J., Kim W., and Kim K.C. "Queries in object-oriented databases." In *Proc. 4th Int. Conf. on Data Engineering*, pp. 31–38.

[Beck et al. 89] Beck H.W., Gala S.K., and Navathe S.B. "Classification as a query processing technique in the CANDIDE semantic data model." In *Proc. 5th Int. Conf. on Data Engineering*, pp. 572–581.

[Beeri 90] Beeri C. "A formal approach to object-oriented databases." In *Data & Knowledge Engineering* **5**, pp. 353–382.

[Blakely et al. 89] Blakely J.A., Coburn N., and Larson P.-A. "Updating derived relations: detecting irrelevant and autonomously computable updates." In *ACM Trans. on Database Systems* **14**(3), pp. 369–401.

[Borgida et al. 89] Borgida A., Brachman R.J., McGuiness D., and Resnick, L.A. "CLASSIC: A structural data model for Objects." In *Proc. ACM-SIGMOD Int. Conf. on Management of Data*, pp. 58–67.

[Brachman et al. 85] Brachman R.J., Gilbert V.P., and Levesque H.J. "An essential hybrid reasoning system: knowledge and symbol level accounts of KRYPTON." In *Proc. Int. Joint. Conf. on Artificial Intelligence*, pp. 532–539.

[Bry 88] Bry F. "Logical rewritings for improving the evaluation of quantified queries." In *Proc. 2nd Int. Symp. on Mathematical Fundamentals of Data Base Theory*.

[Bry et al. 88] Bry F., Decker H., and Manthey R. "A uniform approach to constraint satisfaction and constraint satisfiability in deductive databases." In *Proc. EDBT*, pp. 488–505.

[Cardelli and Wegner 85] Cardelli L. and Wegner P. "On understanding types, data abstraction, and polymorphism." In *Computing Surveys* **17**(4), pp. 471-522.

[Ceri and Widom 90] Ceri S. and Widom J. "Deriving production rules for constraint maintenance." In *Proc. 16th Int. Conf. on Very Large Databases*, pp. 566–577.

[Ceri and Widom 91] Ceri S. and Widom J. "Deriving production rules for incremental view maintenance." In *Proc. 17th Int. Conf. on Very Large Databases*, pp. 577–589.

[Ceri et al. 90a] Ceri S., Cacace F., and Tanca L. "Object orientation and logic programming for databases: a season's flirt or a long-term marriage?" In *Next Generation Information System Technology* (Schmidt and Stogny, ed.), pp. 124–143, *LNCS* 504, Springer-Verlag.

[Ceri et al. 90b] Ceri S., Gottlob G., and Tanca L. *Logic programming and databases*. Springer-Verlag.

[Chakravarthy et al. 90] Chakravarthy U.S., Grant J., and Minker J. "Logic-based approach to semantic query optimization." In *ACM Transactions on Database Systems* **15**(2), pp. 162–207.

[Duhl and Damon 88] Duhl J. and Damon C. "A performance comparison of object and relational databases using the Sun benchmark." In *OOP-SLA'88 Conference Proceedings*, pp. 153–163.

[Freytag 87] Freytag J.C. "A rule-based view of query optimization." In *Proc. ACM-SIGMOD Int. Conf. on Management of Data*, pp. 173–180.

[Gallersdörfer 90] Gallersdörfer R. *Implementation of a deductive object base using abstract data types* (in German). Diploma thesis, Universität Passau, Germany.

[Graefe and DeWitt 87] Graefe G. and DeWitt D.J. "The EXODUS optimizer generator." In *Proc. ACM-SIGMOD Int. Conf. on Management of Data*, pp. 160–172.

[Guttag 75] Guttag J.V. "The specification and application to programming of abstract data types." Ph.D. thesis, University of Toronto, Dept. of Computer Science, Technical Report CSRG-59.

[Hübel and Mitschang 88] Hübel C. and Mitschang B. "Object-Orientation within the PRIMA-NDBS." In *Advances in Object-Oriented Database Systems* (Dittrich,ed.), pp. 98–103, Springer-Verlag.

[Hull and Yoshikawa 90] Hull R. and Yoshikawa M. "ILOG: declarative creation and manipulation of object identifiers." In *Proc. 16th Int. Conf. on Very Large Databases*, 455–468.

[Jackson 90] Jackson M.S. "Beyond relational databases." In *Information and Software Technology* **32**(4), pp. 258–265.

[Jarke 84] Jarke M. "External semantic query simplification: a graph-theoretic approach and its implementation in Prolog." In *Proc. 1st Int. Workshop Expert Database Systems*, pp. 467-482.

[Jarke 91] Jarke M., ed. *ConceptBase V3.0 user manual*. Report MIP-9106, Universität Passau, Germany.

[Jarke and Koubarakis 89] Jarke M. and Koubarakis M. *Query optimization in KBMS: overview, research issues, and concepts for a Telos implementation*. Technical report KRR-TR-89-6, University of Toronto.

[Jeusfeld 91] Jeusfeld M. *Axioms of the Telos data model* (in German). Working paper, Universität Passau, Germany.

[Jeusfeld and Jarke 91] Jeusfeld M. and Jarke M. "From relational to object-oriented integrity simplification." In *Proc. 2nd Int. Conf. on Deductive and Object-Oriented Databases, LNCS 566*, Springer-Verlag, pp. 460–477.

[Jeusfeld and Krüger 90] Jeusfeld M. and Krüger E. *Deductive integrity maintenance in an object-oriented setting.* Report MIP-9013, Universität Passau, Germany.

[Kakas and Mancarella 90] Kakas A.C. and Mancarella P. "Database updates through abduction." In *Proc. 16th Int. Conf. on Very Large Databases*, pp. 650–661.

[Kemper and Moerkotte 90] Kemper A. and Moerkotte G. "Access support in object bases." In *Proc. ACM-SIGMOD Int. Conf. on Management of Data*, pp. 364–374.

[Klemann 91] Klemann A. *Schema integration of relational databases* (in German). Diploma thesis, Universität Passau, Germany.

[Kifer et al. 90] Kifer M., Lausen G., and Wu J. *Logical foundations of object-oriented and frame-based languages.* Report, *Reihe Informatik 3/1990*, Universität Mannheim, Germany.

[Koubarakis et al. 89] Koubarakis M., Mylopoulos J., Stanley M., and Borgida A. *Telos: features and formalization.* Technical Report KR-89-04, University of Toronto, Ontario.

[Lohmann et al. 91] Lohmann G.M., Lindsay B., Pirahesh H., and Schiefer K.B. "Extensions to Starburst: objects, types, functions, and rules." In *Comm. ACM* **34**(10), pp. 94–109.

[Lyngbæk et al. 90] Lyngbæk P., Wilkinson K., and Hasan W. "The Iris kernel architecture." *Proc. EDBT*, pp. 348–362.

[Maier 86] Maier,D. "Why object-oriented databases can succeed where others have failed." In *Proc. Int. Workshop on Object-Oriented Database Systems*, pp. 227–227.

[Moerkotte and Lockemann 90] Moerkotte G. and Lockemann P.C. *Reactive consistency control in deductive databases.* Internal Report No. 3/90, Universität Karlsruhe, Fakultät für Informatik.

[Mylopoulos et al. 90] Mylopoulos J., Borgida A., Jarke M., and Koubarakis M. "Telos: a language for representing knowledge about information systems." In *ACM Trans. Information Systems* **8**(4), pp. 325–362.

[Nicolas 82] Nicolas J.-M. "Logic for improving integrity checking in relational databases." In *Acta Informatika* **18**, pp. 227–253.

[Olivé 91] Olivé A. "Integrity constraints checking in deductive databases." In *Proc. 17th Int. Conf. on Very Large Databases*, pp. 513–524.

[Reiter 84] Reiter R. "Towards a logical reconstruction of relational database theory." In *On Conceptual Modeling*(Brodie et al., eds.), pp. 191–233, Springer-Verlag.

[Rose et al. 91] Rose T., Jarke M., Gocek M., Maltzahn C., and Nissen H. "A decision-based configuration process environment." In *Software Engineering Journal* **6**(5), Special Issue on Software Process and its Support, pp. 332–346.

[Sellis et al. 89] Sellis T., Lin C.-C., and Raschid L. "Data intensive production systems: the DIPS approach." In *SIGMOD Record* **18**(3), pp. 52–58.

[Shaw and Zdonik 90] Shaw G.M. and Zdonik S.B. "Object-oriented queries: equivalence and optimization." In *Deductive and Object-Oriented Databases* (Kim, Nicolas, and Nishio, eds.), pp. 281–296, North Holland.

[Staudt 90] Staudt M. *Query representation and evaluation in deductive object bases* (in German). Diploma thesis, Universität Passau, Germany.

7

Evaluation Aspects of an Object-oriented Deductive Database Language

Georg Lausen

Beate Marx

Abstract

Recently, F-logic [Kifer and Lausen 1989, Kifer, Lausen and Wu 1992] has been proposed as an attempt to extend deductive databases by typical concepts of object-oriented languages. Among these concepts are complex objects, (term-based) object identity, methods, classes, typing, inheritance and browsing. In [Kifer, Lausen and Wu 1992] syntax and model-theoretic semantics is discussed; however many algorithmic aspects which arise when computing the corresponding models are left open. In this paper we start to bridge this gap. Several topics in the context of the evaluation of programs are discussed in detail; among these are weak recursion, global stratification and dynamic type-checking.

7.1
Introduction

Over the past few years object-oriented database systems have been receiving a lot of attention from both experimental and theoretical views. Since pure object oriented systems suffer from a lack of formal semantics which traditionally was considered to be important for database languages, there have been several attempts to combine object orientation and deductive databases (e.g. [Abiteboul and Kanellakis 1989, Kifer and Wu 1989, Kifer and Lausen 1989, Kifer, Lausen and Wu 1992, Chen and Warren 1989, Maier 1986, Hull and Yoshikawa 1990, Abiteboul and Grumbach 1987, Beeri, Naqvi, Shmueli and Tsur 1987]).

In this paper we continue the research direction started by Maiers O-logic [Maier 1986] and later extended by O-logic [Kifer and Wu 1989], C-logic [Chen and Warren 1989] and F-logic [Kifer and Lausen 1989, Kifer, Lausen and Wu 1992]. Among these approaches F-logic is the most elaborated one. In contrast to [Abiteboul and Kanellakis 1989, Hull and Yoshikawa 1990, Abiteboul and Grumbach 1987, Beeri, Naqvi, Shmueli and Tsur 1987] F-logic is a logic with function symbols. This allows a flexible syntax which naturally supports the creation of new objects, the definition of user-defined data-types, the parametrization of classes, etc. As a distinctive feature, F-logic has a higher-order syntax with first-order semantics; querying and browsing of the database is integrated into the same language.

In [Kifer, Lausen and Wu 1992] syntax and model-theoretic semantics is discussed; however many algorithmic aspects which arise when computing the corresponding models are left open. In this paper we start to bridge this gap. We show how the definition of class-hierarchies, typing and monotonic inheritance may be incorporated into a bottom-up evaluation strategy. As F-logic allows function-symbols, even for safe programs infinite relations may be derived, if the program is recursive. Therefore, in addition to safety, programs must be weakly recursive. In case recursion involves functional methods in a certain way, we can show that previously introduced definitions for weak recursion can be weakened. We introduce a unification-based test for global stratification and discuss various concepts to achieve type correctness.

The structure of the paper is as follows: Section 7.2 gives a short overview of syntax and semantics of F-logic, Section 7.3 deals with the evaluation of programs and Section 7.4 discusses aspects of type checking; Section 7.5 concludes the paper.

7.2
Syntax and Semantics

In the following two subsections we introduce syntax and semantics of F-logic [Kifer, Lausen and Wu 1992]. Here we can simplify the presentation, because we are only interested in rule-programs under Herbrand-semantics. Further, we restrict our discussion to monotonic inheritance: the non-monotonic case is discussed in [Lausen and Uphoff 1992]. We assume some familiarity with first-order predicate logic and with Datalog^{neg} programs with function symbols (e.g., see [Lloyd 1987, Ullman 1988]).

7.2.1 Syntax

The alphabet of an F-logic language $\mathcal{L}$ consists of (1) a set of *object constructors* $\mathcal{F}$, (2) a set $\wp$ of *predicate symbols*, (3) an infinite set of *variables* $\mathcal{V}$ and (4) usual logical connectives and quantifiers $\wedge, \vee, \forall, \exists, \neg, \longleftarrow$ etc. [Kifer, Lausen and Wu 1992]. Object constructors are function symbols. Each function symbol has an arity; symbols of arity 0 play the role of constant symbols, symbols of arity ≥ 1 are used to construct new objects from simpler ones. An *id-term* is a term composed of function symbols and variables in the usual way. The set of all ground id-terms is denoted by $\mathcal{F}^*$. Conceptually, ground id-terms should be perceived as *object-denotations*. While id-terms correspond to terms in first-order predicate logic, F-terms and P-terms (as introduced below) are the atomic formulae. In contrast to [Kifer, Lausen and Wu 1992], we do not introduce molecular terms. Every F-logic object (represented by an id-term) can be viewed as an entity or a relationship, a class or a method, depending on the syntactic position in a formula. In its role as a method, an object can either be *single valued* (also called *functional*) or *set-valued*. The way it has to be considered is determined by the context. In the sequel we will use names starting with lower-case letters to denote ground terms, and names starting with capital letters to denote terms that may be non-ground.

An *F-term* is one of the following:

- An *is-a* F-term, $P : Q$, where P and Q are id-terms; is-a terms are used to define class hierarchies and class extensions. P represents an object, resp. a (sub-)class, Q represents a (super-)class.

- A *data* F-term,
  $P[FunM @ Q_1, \ldots, Q_k \rightarrow T]$ defining a functional method $FunM$, or
  $P[SetM @ Q_1, \ldots, Q_k \twoheadrightarrow \{S_1, \ldots, S_m\}]$ defining a set-valued method $SetM$ on object P. T and the S_i represent the results returned by the respective methods $FunM$ and $SetM$ when invoked in the context of the object P on the arguments $Q_1, \ldots, Q_k$. P, $FunM$ and $SetM$, $Q_1, \ldots, Q_k$, $S_1, \ldots, S_m$ and T are id-terms.

- A *signature* F-term,
  $P[FunM @ Q_1, \ldots, Q_k \Rightarrow \{A_1, \ldots, A_n\}]$, or $P[SetM @ Q_1, \ldots, Q_k \Rightarrow \{B_1, \ldots, B_m\}]$. The A_i and B_j represent classes which are the types of the results returned by the respective methods $FunM$ and $SetM$, when invoked in the context of an object of class P on arguments in classes $Q_1, \ldots, Q_k$. Here classes again are used as types. P, $FunM$ and $SetM$, $Q_1, \ldots, Q_k$, $A_1, \ldots, A_n$, and $B_1, \ldots, B_m$ are id-terms.

The following example illustrates these constructs. The first term defines a signature and states that *children* is a set-valued method that is applicable to objects belonging to class *person* resulting in a set of objects also belonging to class *person*. The second term respectively defines a signature for the method *age*. The third term states that *john* belongs to class *person* and the fourth and fifth term define actual values as results of methods *children* and *age* for the object *john*.

$$person[children \Rightarrow \{person\}]$$
$$person[age \Rightarrow \{integer\}]$$
$$john : person \qquad\qquad (7.1)$$
$$john[children \twoheadrightarrow \{sally, bob\}]$$
$$john[age \rightarrow 24]$$

Intuitively, a data F-term is a statement about an object asserting that it has properties specified by methods. A signature F-term specifies typing constraints on objects in the respective class. As types we allow standard classes, as *integer, string,* etc., and user-defined classes which may be defined by certain rules.

In addition to terms predicates are part of the language. If $p \in \wp$ is an n-ary predicate symbol and $T_1, \ldots, T_n$ are id-terms, then $p(T_1, \ldots, T_n)$ is a *predicate term* (abbrev. P-term). *Equality* of objects is expressed with the infix predicate $\doteq$, e.g., *john$\doteq$father(sally)*. The interpretation of the equality predicate is fixed in the usual way [Chang and Lee 1973].

An *F-rule* is a clause

$$H \longleftarrow B_1 \wedge \ldots \wedge B_k \wedge B_{k+1} \wedge \ldots \wedge B_{k+l},$$

where H and the B_i, $i = 1, \ldots, k+l$ are F-terms or P-terms; H is called the *head* of the rule and $B_1 \ldots B_{k+l}$ the *body*. $B_1, \ldots, B_k$ are not negated, $B_{k+1} \ldots B_{k+l}$ are negated terms; if $l = 0$ a rule is called *Horn*. A rule with an empty body is called a *fact*. An *F-logic program* is a finite set of (implicitly) $\forall$-quantified F-rules; in our simplified setting the equality-predicate is not allowed to occur in the head of a rule.

7.2.2   Semantics

For an F-logic language $\mathcal{L}$, its semantic structure, I, is a tuple $\langle U, \preceq_U, I_{\mathcal{F}}, I_{\wp}, I_{\rightarrow}, I_{\rightarrow\!\!\!\rightarrow}, I_{\Rightarrow}, I_{\Rightarrow\!\!\!\Rightarrow} \rangle$. Here U is the domain of the interpretation and $\preceq_U$ is a partial order on U. $I_{\mathcal{F}}$ interprets k-ary object constructors, i.e., the elements of $\mathcal{F}$, as functions from U^k to U. Predicate symbols are interpreted by $I_{\wp}$ as relations on U of the appropriate arities. Methods are interpreted by $I_{\rightarrow}, I_{\rightarrow\!\!\!\rightarrow}, I_{\Rightarrow}, I_{\Rightarrow\!\!\!\Rightarrow}$ as mappings from U to partial functions from U^{l+1} to U, where l is the arity of the corresponding method. Semantic aspects of methods are expressed by special properties of these partial functions. For a detailed description see [Kifer, Lausen and Wu 1992]; for the topics of this paper Herbrand semantics is sufficient which is introduced below.

A *variable assignment*, ν, is a mapping from the set of variables, $\mathcal{V}$, to the domain of U. Let I be a semantic structure and ν a variable assignment. Intuitively, an F-term T is *true* under a semantic structure I with respect to variable assignment ν, denoted $I \models_{\nu} T$, if and only if I contains an object $\nu(T)$ with properties specified in $\nu(T)$. We introduce the notion of truth with respect to Herbrand interpretations.

Herbrand Interpretations

Given an F-Logic language $\mathcal{L}$ with $\mathcal{F}$ as its set of function symbols and $\wp$ as its set of predicate symbols, its *Herbrand universe* is $\mathcal{F}^*$ - the set of all ground id-terms. The *Herbrand Base*, $\mathcal{HB}$, is the set of all ground atoms of the F-terms, equality and P-terms. *Atoms* are defined as follows. Every is-a F-term and data F-term of a functional method is also an atom. A data F-term of a set-valued method is an atom if it is either of the form $P[SetM @ Q_1, \ldots, Q_k \twoheadrightarrow \{S\}]$, or $P[SetM @ Q_1, \ldots, Q_k \twoheadrightarrow \{\}]$. The atoms of a set-valued F-term are those which can be derived from it, i.e., their result is a subset of the result of the given F-term. Signature terms are treated analogously.

Herbrand interpretations are subsets of the Herbrand base; truth in Herbrand interpretations is defined as follows:

- A ground term (an F-term or a P-term) t is *true* in an Herbrand interpretation H, if for all atoms t' of t it holds $t' \in H$,

- A ground negative term $\neg t$ is *true* in H, if for at least one atom t' of t it holds $t' \notin H$,

- A rule $r = A \longleftarrow B_1 \wedge \ldots \wedge B_{k+l}$ is *true* in H, if for all ground instances $r\nu$ of r, ν a variable assignment, either $A\nu$ is true in H or at least one of the $B_i\nu$ is not true in H.

Now, let H be a subset of $\mathcal{HB}$. Then H is an *F-Herbrand interpretation* of $\mathcal{L}$ if it satisfies the equality axioms [Chang and Lee 1973] w.r.t. $\doteq$ and in addition the following *closure properties* that reflect the properties of a semantic structure (cf. [Kifer, Lausen and Wu 1992]):

- ISA:
    ISA reflexivity: $p : p \in H$;
    ISA transitivity: If $p : q, q : r \in H$, then $p : r \in H$;
    ISA acyclicity: If $p : q, q : p \in H$, then $p \doteq q \in H$.

- Signature:
    Type inheritance:
    If $p[funM @ q_1, \ldots, q_k \Rightarrow \{s\}]$, $r : p \in H$, then
    $\qquad r[funM @ q_1, \ldots, q_k \Rightarrow \{s\}] \in H$;
    If $p[setM @ q_1, \ldots, q_k \Rrightarrow \{s\}]$, $r : p \in H$, then
    $\qquad r[setM @ q_1, \ldots, q_k \Rrightarrow \{s\}] \in H$.
    Argument subtyping:

If $p[funM @ q_1, \ldots, q_i, \ldots, q_k \Rightarrow \{s\}], q_i' : q_i \in H$ then
$$p[funM @ q_1, \ldots, q_i', \ldots, q_k \Rightarrow \{s\}] \in H;$$
If $p[setM @ q_1, \ldots, q_i, \ldots, q_k \twoheadrightarrow \{s\}], q_i' : q_i \in H$ then
$$p[setM @ q_1, \ldots, q_i', \ldots, q_k \twoheadrightarrow \{s\}] \in H.$$
Range supertyping:
If $p[funM @ q_1, \ldots, q_k \Rightarrow \{r\}], r : s \in H$ then
$$p[funM @ q_1, \ldots, q_k \Rightarrow \{s\}] \in H;$$
If $p[setM @ q_1, \ldots, q_k \twoheadrightarrow \{r\}], r : s \in H$ then
$$p[setM @ q_1, \ldots, q_k \twoheadrightarrow \{s\}] \in H.$$

- Data F-terms:
  functionality:
  If $p[funM @ q_1, \ldots, q_k \rightarrow r_1], p[funM @ q_1, \ldots, q_k \rightarrow r_2] \in H$, then
  $$r_1 \doteq r_2 \in H.$$

- Id-terms:
  For every id-term t, $t[\,] \in H$.

The notion of type correctness in F-logic is as follows. A program P is *well-typed* with respect to a Herbrand interpretation H, if, in addition, the following properties hold:

Signature:
   Well-typing:
If $p[funM @ q_1, \ldots, q_k \rightarrow q], \; p[funM @ q_1, \ldots, q_k \Rightarrow \{r\}] \in H$ then
$$q : r \in H;$$
if $p[setM @ q_1, \ldots, q_k \twoheadrightarrow \{q\}], \; p[setM @ q_1, \ldots, q_k \twoheadrightarrow \{r\}] \in H$ then
$$q : r \in H;$$
if $p[funM @ q_1, \ldots, q_k \rightarrow q] \in H$ then $p[funM @ q_1, \ldots, q_k \Rightarrow \{\}] \in H;$
if $p[setM @ q_1, \ldots, q_k \twoheadrightarrow \{q\}] \in H$ then $p[setM @ q_1, \ldots, q_k \twoheadrightarrow \{\}] \in H.$

Truth in F-Herbrand interpretations is analogous to the Herbrand case.

Given an F-logic program P, a Herbrand interpretation M is a *Herbrand model* for P, if all rules of P are true in M. M is an *F-Herbrand model* if, in addition, the closure properties hold. M is a minimal Herbrand model (resp. minimal F-Herbrand model) if, for all other models (F-models) N, whenever $N \subseteq M$ then $N = M$. If all rules in a program P are Horn, a unique minimal model exists. In the sequel we are interested in minimal F-models for general programs.

Closure and Inheritance Rules

For every F-logic program P the closure properties listed above may be restated as a finite set of Horn rules, which we call *closure rules*; they are denoted by the symbol $\overline{P}$. Thus, if P has a minimal model, $P \cup \overline{P}$ has a minimal model. Or in other terms: M is a minimal F-model of P if and only if M is a minimal model of $P \cup \overline{P}$. For example, the ISA properties are stated by the rules

$$
\begin{aligned}
P : P &\;\longleftarrow \\
P \doteq Q &\;\longleftarrow\quad P : Q \,\wedge\, Q : P \\
P : Q &\;\longleftarrow\quad P : R \,\wedge\, R : Q.
\end{aligned}
\qquad (7.2)
$$

Giving another example, type inheritance for functional methods may be stated as

$$
P[M @ X_1, \ldots, X_k \Rightarrow \{Y\}] \longleftarrow P : Q \,\wedge\, Q[M @ X_1, \ldots, X_k \Rightarrow \{Y\}] \quad (7.3)
$$

For every arity of a functional method occurring in P, such a rule is needed. The remaining closure properties are transformed to Horn rules in a similar way.

In the current paper we only consider monotonic inheritance. Monotonic inheritance may be stated as a set of Horn rules in a similar way as inheritance of signatures, i.e., for every arity of a functional (resp. set-valued) method a rule

$$
P[M @ X_1, \ldots, X_k \rightarrow Y] \longleftarrow P : Q \,\wedge\, Q[M @ X_1, \ldots, X_k \rightarrow Y] \quad (7.4)
$$

is needed. Throughout the following sections P^{inh} will denote the set of *inheritance rules* belonging to program P.

7.3
Evaluation of Programs

7.3.1 Extending the T-operator

We denote T_P the *immediate consequence operator* (which is defined as in [Apt, Blair and Walker 1989]). Intuitively, $T_P(I)$ is the set of immediate conclusions from an interpretation I, i.e., those which can be obtained by applying each rule from P exactly once. For Horn programs P, $T_P \uparrow \omega(\emptyset)$

(the least fixpoint of the operator T_P starting with the empty interpretation), and the minimal model of P, M_P, coincide.

For a Horn F-logic program P the minimal F-model, M_P, equals $T_{P \cup \overline{P} \cup P^{inh}} \uparrow \omega(\emptyset)$. Since the set of closure (resp. inheritance) rules is essentially the same for all F-logic programs (it only differs with respect to the arity of methods), we treat program and closure (resp. inheritance) rules separately and define the *F-completion* operator $\overline{T}$ as an abstraction of $T_{\overline{P} \cup P^{inh}}$; given any interpretation I for a program P, the operator $\overline{T}$ completes I to an F-interpretation of P. The minimal F-model of a Horn program P is thus computed as $(\overline{T}(T_P)) \uparrow \omega(\emptyset)$.

Note, that, in the general case, an F-interpretation of a program P may not satisfy the well-typing properties (see Section 7.2.2). The problem of type-checking will be discussed in Section 7.4.

After each application of the T_P-operator a functionality check should be performed. We believe, that equalities, that are introduced on account of the functionality or the ISA-antisymmetry property, are usually not intended by the user (cf. [Kifer, Lausen and Wu 1992]). In fact, if during program evaluation (after applying T_P and before applying the succeeding $\overline{T}$), an interpretation contains facts, say

$$obj[functional\_method \rightarrow a], \; obj[functional\_method \rightarrow b] \qquad (7.5)$$

but not

$$a \doteq b, \qquad (7.6)$$

the user has probably specified an inconsistent program and may find it helpful, if the system responds with a warning instead of producing an unintended equality.

To detect these inconsistencies during program evaluation we introduce a slightly modified completion operator: The derivation of equalities on account of the functionality and the ISA-antisymmetry property is blocked; we call the modified operator $\overline{T}^{block}$. The complementary operator, i.e., the operator that completes an interpretation with respect to functionality and ISA-antisymmetry, is called $\overline{T}^{unblock}$. In terms of the operators $\overline{T}^{block}$ and $\overline{T}^{unblock}$ the minimal F-model of a program P may be computed by evaluating $(\overline{T}^{unblock}(\overline{T}^{block}(T_P))) \uparrow \omega(\emptyset)$. If at any iteration step the operator $\overline{T}^{unblock}$ adds new terms to the interpretation computed thus far the system will notify these inconsistencies to the user.

7.3.2   Safety and Weak Recursive Programs

Informally, a logic program is called *safe*, if it is guaranteed that no rule creates an infinite relation from finite ones. Usually this is achieved by placing some syntactic restrictions on the rules. For Datalog programs the concept of *limited* variables is introduced (e.g., [Ullman 1988]). A rule is defined to be safe, if every variable occurring somewhere in this rule is limited. The notion of safety can be adopted to F-logic programs in an obvious way. Henceforth we only consider safe programs. However, even safe F-logic programs may have to be rejected because their bottom-up evaluation may not terminate due to an infinite creation of id-terms. The latter takes place, if there is recursion over rules containing object constructors (i.e. function symbols) in the head term. This problem is known from Datalog-like languages with function symbols (see e.g. [Hull and Yoshikawa 1990]), yet, on account of the syntax of F-logic (variables may occur at any position of an F-term) and because of the functionality of methods new aspects arise. Functional methods, when invoked on an object, have unique results. Thus infinite object-id creation may not be propagated over result positions of functional methods. This fact allows to weaken the safety restrictions concerning the use of object constructors with respect to other Datalog-like languages with function symbols, i.e., F-logic programs may be accepted in cases where corresponding Datalog programs would be rejected.

In analogy to Hull and Yoshikawa [Hull and Yoshikawa 1990] F-logic programs are called *weakly recursive* if there is no recursion through object constructors. The following examples show F-logic rules and programs respectively, that are not weakly recursive:

$$child(X)[address \rightarrow A] \longleftarrow X[address \rightarrow A] \qquad (7.7)$$

$$X[related \longrightarrow \{child(Y)\}] \longleftarrow X : person \wedge X[related \longrightarrow \{Y\}] \qquad (7.8)$$

$$\begin{aligned} f(X) : some\_class &\longleftarrow Y : some\_other\_class \wedge Y[method \longrightarrow \{X\}] \\ Y[method \longrightarrow \{X\}] &\longleftarrow X : some\_class \wedge Y : some\_other\_class \end{aligned} \qquad (7.9)$$

$$class[method \longrightarrow \{f(Z)\}] \longleftarrow object : class \wedge object[method \longrightarrow \{Z\}] \qquad (7.10)$$

Note, that the last rule, (7.10), shows object creation interleaving with monotonic inheritance of methods: it is an example for implicit recursion through object generation.

To detect recursion through object creation occurring within an F-logic program P we introduce the *safety graph* $\mathcal{S}(P)$ as follows: The nodes of the graph are the id-term positions[1] in terms occurring in $P \cup \overline{P} \cup P^{inh}$; the arcs of $\mathcal{S}(P)$ reflect the propagation of newly created objects during program evaluation. The closure rules and the inheritance rules, $\overline{P} \cup P^{inh}$, must be integrated into $\mathcal{S}(P)$ since recursion may be implicit as in Rule (7.10).

In the following we outline an informal specification of the procedure which, given a program P, constructs $\mathcal{S}(P)$. During an initializing step, only rules having a non-ground id-term t with at least one function symbol in the head (i.e., rules where an object creation takes place) must be considered. Considering just these rules during the first step ensures that all cycles, that may finally occur, are indeed cycles over object creation. Let $X_1, \ldots, X_k$ be the variables that occur in such t. To reflect the flow of the X_i into t, for each t'_j occurring somewhere in the body of that rule that contains at least one of the X_i an arc is introduced from t'_j to t. Consider Example (7.7): here an arc is drawn from the X at the object position in the F-term of the body to *child(X)* in the head.

For the remaining part of the procedure all rules of $P \cup \overline{P} \cup P^{inh}$ must be considered. Since we are interested in the propagation of object-ids (i.e., id-terms) that are built using function symbols we have to iteratively check nodes with ingoing arcs. Two cases must be distinguished:

(S1) The node is an id-term t in the head h of some rule.

For all terms b_i in the body of the same or any other rule that unify with h, draw an arc from t to the id-term at the corresponding position in b_i.

In Example (7.7) the head unifies with the body, thus an arc is drawn from *child(X)* to X in $X[address \rightarrow A]$.

(S2) The node is an id-term t in a term b in the body of some rule.

Let $X_1, \ldots, X_k$ be the variables of t, which also occur in the head h of the same rule. Let $t'_1, \ldots, t'_l$ be the id-terms containing at least one of the X_i's. Draw arcs from t to each of the t'_j, respectively.

In case the id-term t is part of an equality term, $t \doteq t'$, draw an additional arc from t to t'.

The procedure stops, when no more arcs can be entered into the graph (because of (S1) or (S2)).

In Figure 7.1 the safety graph of Example (7.9) is shown. The ellipses group together nodes which belong to the same term, they are labeled with

---

[1] An id-term position is any syntactical position within an F-term or a P-term, where an id-term (or a variable) may occur.

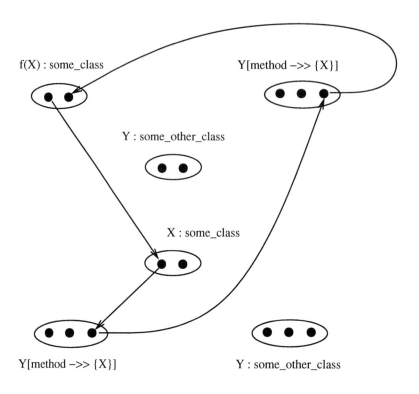

FIGURE 7.1
Safety graph

the F-term they correspond to. Nodes that are not connected to any other nodes do not contribute to the creation of new objects.

If, for a program P, $\mathcal{S}(P)$ does not contain any cycle, the program is free of recursion through object generation and thus weakly recursive. In the rest of this section we will show, that the functionality property of F-logic programs allows a weaker condition for weak recursion.

Consider the following example:

$$p(X, Y) \longleftarrow X : person \wedge X[best\_friend \rightarrow Y]$$
$$X[best\_friend \rightarrow child(Y)] \longleftarrow p(X, Y) \wedge q(\ldots) \qquad (7.11)$$

Here the method *best_friend* is functional, and thus the result of applying the method to any object of class *person* must be unique. The evaluation of these rules may or may not result in an infinite number of F-terms of the form $X[best\_friend \rightarrow child(child(...(Y)...))]$, depending on the predicate q. In our framework such a program will not be rejected. Since during program evaluation the functionality of methods must be checked anyway (see Section 7.3.1), the admission of this rule, independent of predicate q, will not lead to an infinite computation. Therefore, we can expect that a larger class of programs can be evaluated, because the syntactic safety check is replaced by a semantic one.

Consider one more example:

$$X[related \twoheadrightarrow \{child(Y)\}] \leftarrow X : person \wedge X[related \twoheadrightarrow \{Y\}] \wedge Y : person \tag{7.12}$$

Rule (7.12) is similar to Rule (7.8) belonging to the examples for rules, which are not weakly recursive. The former Rule (7.8) obviously is unsafe, since for every variable assignment for Y, a new id-term $child(Y)$ is created, which may be assigned to Y during the next evaluation step, and so on. Rule (7.12) differs from Rule (7.8): the variable Y also occurs in another positive term in the body of the rule. Here after one application of the rule, the newly created id-term $child(...)$ may only then be assigned to Y during the next step, if $child(...) : person$ holds. Provided the extension of class $person$ is finite, or in other terms, $person$ is a finite type, the evaluation of Rule (7.12) terminates.

To capture this intuition and the restrictions on cause of functionality, we extend the definition of the safety graph. Let $\mathcal{S}(P)$ be a safety graph according to (S1) and (S2). We now derive the *reduced* safety graph $\mathcal{S}^*(P)$ by applying the following two steps on $\mathcal{S}(P)$:

(S3) Let $X_1, \ldots, X_k$ be the variables of an id-term t, where t occurs in the body of some rule r. If each X_i is of a finite type, then any arc starting from t is removed.

(S4) Let t be an id-term which occurs in the result position of a functional method of an F-term f. Let $t \rightarrow t'$ be an arc in $\mathcal{S}(P)$ and let $t \rightarrow t' \rightarrow t_1 \rightarrow t_2 \rightarrow \ldots \rightarrow t_k \rightarrow t$, $k \geq 0$, be any cycle, where the t_i are id-terms ocurring in F-terms f_i, $i = 1, \ldots, k$. If for every f_i which unifies with f t_i occurs at the result position, then $t \rightarrow t'$ is removed.

Condition (S4) may seem unnecessarily restrictive. Yet, it is not sufficient to ignore cycles containing at least one node that corresponds to the result position of a functional method. As the following example shows, we must assure that the respective object (resp. the method or its arguments) does not change in such a way, that whenever a new result is created it is assigned a new object (resp. method or argument) in such a way, that there is a cyclic shift of object-ids:

$$f(Y)[method \rightarrow X] \longleftarrow X[method \rightarrow Y]. \tag{7.13}$$

Starting with a fact $a[method \rightarrow b]$ the following facts will be computed successively: $f(b)[method \rightarrow a]$, $f(a)[method \rightarrow f(b)]$, $f(f(b))[method \rightarrow f(a)]$, $f(f(a))[method \rightarrow f(f(b))]$ and so on. Although the cycle corresponding to Rule (7.13) contains a node which corresponds to the result position of a functional method, it is not weakly recursive; this special case is captured by extension (S4).

We now are in the position to redefine weak recursion; a program P is called *weak recursive*, if its extended safety graph $\mathcal{S}^*(P)$ does not contain a cycle.

7.3.3   Perfect Models of F-logic

Perfect model semantics for general logic programs [Przymusinski 1989] can be extended to F-logic programs. Consider the following examples:

$$X[wants \twoheadrightarrow \{Y\}] \longleftarrow \neg X[has \twoheadrightarrow \{Y\}] \tag{7.14}$$

and

$$peter[wants \twoheadrightarrow \{Y\}] \longleftarrow \neg john[wants \twoheadrightarrow \{Y\}] \tag{7.15}$$

Note, that both rules are recursive; in (7.14) we have recursion over the object-position - in (7.15) over the method-position of the respective F-terms. Moreover, in both cases recursion involves a negated F-term. However, both cases are compatible with stratification, because we either know, that the methods involved are different, or that the respective objects are different. Thus, stratification for F-logic programs should be ensured with respect to complete F-terms (resp. P-terms), not just with respect to objects or methods as the analogy to Datalog might suggest. The following example shows that techniques based on predicate names (respectively, their analogue) to derive a (global) stratification cannot be applied directly, because there might be F-terms, which have nonground id-terms in all positions:

$$married(sally, john)[shared\_methods \twoheadrightarrow \{address\}]$$

$$X[M \to V] \longleftarrow married(X, Y)[shared\_methods \twoheadrightarrow \{M\}] \wedge Y[M \to V]$$

$$X[owns \twoheadrightarrow \{car\}] \longleftarrow X[works \to T] \wedge \neg X[address \to T] \qquad (7.16)$$

To check whether an F-logic program P is globally stratified and to compute a global stratification (provided it exists), we introduce the *dependency graph* $\mathcal{D}(P)$ as follows: The nodes of $\mathcal{D}(P)$ are the terms of $P \cup \overline{P} \cup P^{inh}$.[2]

For every rule $r = A \longleftarrow B_1, \ldots B_n$ contained in $P \cup \overline{P} \cup P^{inh}$, we have arcs as follows:

(D1) From every term B_i occurring in the body of r, draw an arc to the head term A. If B_i occurs negated then the respective arc must be marked as negated.

(D2) For every term B in the body of a rule that unifies with A, draw an arc from A to B.

Note that in comparison to Datalog, we have to consider *unification arcs* (the second kind of arcs introduced above), since in F-logic variables may occur at any position of a term. Note further, that on account of closure and inheritance rules a lot of unification arcs are introduced to the graph. This may cause problems for the computation of the stratification of a program; we will consider this topic at the end of the section.

An F-logic program P is *globally stratified*, if $\mathcal{D}(P)$ has no cycle containing marked arcs.

Based on the concept of global stratification we now define an evaluation strategy for general programs as follows (see also [Apt, Blair and Walker 1989]):

Decompose the dependency graph $\mathcal{D}(P)$ into strongly connected components of maximum cardinality. Sort these components topologically; ambiguities may be solved in any way. Each component corresponds to a stratum of P (the assignment is done on account of the membership of a rule's head atom to a component), thus the ordering of the components induces an evaluation ordering on the rules of P. Evaluating the strata in this order yields the perfect model of P.

---

[2]For terms, that are textually equivalent modulo variable renamings, e.g., $X[M \to V]$ and $Y[M \to W]$, only one node may be introduced.

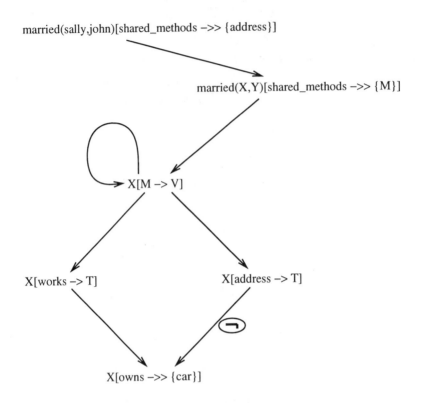

married(sally,john)[shared_methods ->> {address}]

married(X,Y)[shared_methods ->> {M}]

X[M -> V]

X[works -> T]

X[address -> T]

¬

X[owns ->> {car}]

FIGURE 7.2
Dependency graph

Consider once more Example (7.16). Figure 7.2 shows the relevant part of the corresponding dependency graph. The graph contains one negated arc that does not lie within a cycle, thus the program is globally stratified. The only cycle is enforced by the second rule; strata may thus be defined as follows:

$S_0 = \{married(sally, john)[shared\_methods \rightarrow\!\!\!\rightarrow \{address\}]\}$,

$S_1 = \{X[M \rightarrow V] \leftarrow married(X, Y)[shared\_methods \rightarrow\!\!\!\rightarrow \{M\}] \wedge Y[M \rightarrow V]\}$ and

$S_2 = \{X[owns \rightarrow\!\!\!\rightarrow \{car\}] \leftarrow X[works \rightarrow T \wedge \neg X[address \rightarrow T]\}$.

The evaluation of the perfect model of a general program P is then performed by computing the fixpoint (with respect to the combined operator $\overline{T}(T)$) of each stratum, beginning with stratum S_0 and the empty set as input and carrying on in such a way that the fixpoint of stratum S_i is the input for the computation of the fixpoint of stratum S_{i+1} (see [Ullman 1988, Apt, Blair and Walker 1989]).

7.3.4   Reducing the Dependency Graph

As mentioned before, including the closure and inheritance rules into the dependency graph leads to problems; the more arcs are introduced to the graph on behalf of unification (D2) the greater is the probability that cycles (and also negative cycles) may occur. The following example will show that unification arcs, introduced on behalf of closure (resp. inheritance) rules, very easily may cause unjustified cycles. Consider the following rule for monotonic inheritance:

$$P[M \rightarrow Y] \longleftarrow P : Q \wedge Q[M \rightarrow Y] \tag{7.17}$$

Any rule having terms with 0-ary functional methods in its body will cause an arc from the head of the inheritance rule to the respective term; any rule with head being of the respective form will cause an arc from its head to the respective term in the body of the closure rule. The impact on stratification may be demonstrated by the following program P.

$$john : empl$$
$$john[lives \rightarrow munich]$$
$$john[works \rightarrow mannheim] \tag{7.18}$$
$$[working\_address \rightarrow T] \longleftarrow X : empl \wedge X[works \rightarrow T]$$
$$[home\_address \rightarrow T] \longleftarrow X : empl \wedge X[lives \rightarrow T] \wedge \neg X[works \rightarrow T]$$

Figure 7.3 shows the dependency graph of Program (7.18); for the sake of simplicity we have omitted all closure and inheritance rules but Rule (7.17). According to the dependency graph P is not stratified since there is a cycle over a marked edge. P is rejected, although the intended meaning is quite clear and may be described as follows: *john* is an *employee*; thus he has 'Mannheim' as working_address and 'Munich' as home_address. A closer inspection of the dependency graph of Figure 7.3 shows that propagating the unifier computed at the unification arc ending in the inheritance rule along the cycle renders the unification arc starting at the inheritance rule invalid (since *home_address* does not unify with *works*). The cycle is thus not *stratification-relevant* and may be ignored. This example outlines a strategy that accepts a greater number of programs as being stratified than simply checking the dependency graph for cycles over marked edges and dismissing programs as suggested in the previous subsection: For each cycle containing a marked edge (only these cycles

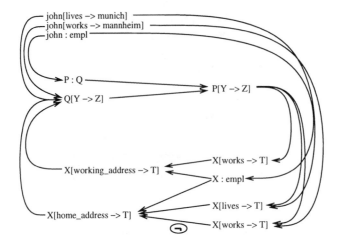

FIGURE 7.3
Dependency graph of Example 19

are relevant for stratification) check whether propagating unifiers along the cycle invalidates unification arcs. If one of the negative cycles is stratification-relevant (for a formal definition see below) reject the program; otherwise, if none of the cycles is stratification-relevant, break the cycles (e.g., by ignoring the body-head arc belonging to the closure (resp. inheritance) rule), compute the stratification and, depending on the stratification, the perfect model as outlined in the previous subsection.

Consider one final example sketched in Figure 7.4, where a cycle involving the inheritance rule

$$P[M \rightarrow X] \leftarrow P : Q \ \wedge \ Q[M \rightarrow X] \qquad (7.19)$$

is indicated. Here propagation of unifiers fails, since *person* does not unify with *empl*. Nevertheless, because of inheritance of methods, the *empl*-term depends on the *person*-term, i.e., the cycle is relevant for stratification.

To handle these cases correctly we define *isa-unification* of id-terms as follows: An id-term t isa↑-unifies with an id-term t' if either t unifies with t' or if for some t^* $t : t^*$ holds and t^* unifies with t'.[3] Accordingly, t isa↓-unifies with an id-term t' if either t unifies with t' or if for some t^* $t^* : t$ holds

---

[3] Here we assume, that before a stratification is computed the complete isa-relationships are known. In Section 7.4 we discuss corresponding evaluation frameworks.

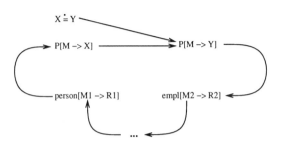

empl : person

$X \doteq Y$

$P[M \rightarrow X]$ $P[M \rightarrow Y]$

person[M1 $\rightarrow$ R1]   empl[M2 $\rightarrow$ R2]

...

FIGURE 7.4
An example for isa-unification

and $t^\star$ unifies with t'. For two data F-terms $t = P[M @ A_1, \ldots, A_k \rightarrow Q]$ and $t' = P'[M' @ A'_1, \ldots, A'_k \rightarrow Q']$ t *isa-unifies* with t' if P isa↑-unifies with P', M unifies with M', the A_i unify with the A'_i and Q unifies with Q'. For two signature F-terms $t = P[M @ A_1, \ldots, A_k \Rightarrow \{Q\}]$ and $t' = P'[M' @ A'_i, \ldots, A'_k \Rightarrow \{Q'\}]$ t *isa-unifies* with t' if P isa↑-unifies with P', M unifies with M', the A_i's isa↑-unify with the A''_i's and Q isa↓-unifies with Q' (note that isa-unification of F-terms is asymmetric); this definition is extended to terms over set-valued methods in the obvious way. Any cycle in the dependency graph is *stratification-relevant* if for all closure (resp. inheritance) rules, whose corresponding arcs occur in the cycle, any F-term, which is a direct successor, isa-unifies with the respective direct predecessor F-terms. For the sake of efficiency we do not propagate unifiers along the whole cycle but consider just the neighbourhood of closure rules.

We can now weaken the definition of global stratification: An F-logic program is *globally stratified* if it does not contain a stratification-relevant cycle over a negative (marked) edge.

7.4
Type Checking

Different to the treatment of types as it is done usually in object-oriented database systems, e.g., in [Albano, Cardelli and Orsini 1990], F-logic allows reasoning about data and meta-data (i.e., types) within an integrated framework. Thus type checking may in general not be done at compile time, i.e., static type checking in the strong sense may not be applied to F-logic programs.

In this section we will classify F-logic programs with respect to their type checking properties. We therefore characterize the rules of a program P as follows: a rule is a *signature rule*, if its head is a signature F-term, it is an *ISA rule*, if its head is an ISA F-term and it is a *data rule* otherwise. We further call a rule *data dependent*, if either any data F-term or P-term occurs in the body of the rule, or (recursively) if any term in the body of the rule unifies with the head of a data dependent rule. Given a Program P, the set of all signature (resp. ISA) rules belonging to P is called P^{sig} (resp. P^{isa}).

We distinguish three classes of programs:

- A program P is *partially statically typed*, if $P^{\text{sig}} \cup P^{\text{isa}}$ is *data independent*. Note that signature rules may depend on ISA-terms and vice versa.

- A program P is *dynamically typed*, if P^{isa} is data independent and if in addition P is *signature stratified* (as defined below).

- All other programs belong to the class of programs where type-checking may only be applied after evaluating the program.

Consider the class of partially statically typed programs. A partially statically typed program P may be split into P^{type}, the union of P^{sig} and P^{isa}, and P^{data}. After computing the fixpoint for P^{type} all type information concerning P is known and static type checking may be invoked on P^{data}. We do not further elaborate on this topic, since in the current paper we are mainly interested in dynamically typed programs.

Next consider programs belonging to the class of *dynamically typed* programs. Intuitively, a program P is dynamically typed, if, whenever a data term is computed during program evaluation[4], it may be immediately type-checked; particularly, information once established about type correctness of a data term should not be invalidated later. Since signature information is stated explicitly through signature rules and implicitly through inheritance (see Section 7.2.2), for dynamic type-checking it is necessary to know the complete hierarchy before computing the first data term, thus ISA rules must be data independent and they must be evaluated prior to all data rules. To check whether all relevant type information is available whenever a data-term is

---

[4]We assume that programs are evaluated bottom-up.

computed, we extend the dependency graph $\mathcal{D}(P)$ introduced in Section 7.3.3 to $\mathcal{D}^{\text{sig}}(P)$ by introducing *signature arcs* as follows:

(D3) For every pair consisting of a data- and a signature term both occurring either as a fact or in the head of a rule, check whether the latter may be *relevant* to the former. If this is the case insert a signature arc from the node corresponding to the signature term to the node corresponding to the data term.

A signature term having the form $obj[method @ \overrightarrow{args} \ldots]$ is *relevant* to a data term having the form $obj'[method' @ \overrightarrow{args'} \ldots]$, if there holds:

> obj unifies with an id-term t, obj' unifies with an id-term t, where $t' : t$, and *method* and *method'* may denote the same method, i.e., *method* and *method'* unify, the number of arguments is equal and both methods are either functional or set-valued.

A program P is *signature stratified*, if the extended dependency graph $\mathcal{D}^{\text{sig}}(P)$ has no cycles containing signature arcs. As stated before, signature stratified programs with data independent ISA-rules are dynamically typed. The evaluation strategy for general F-logic programs introduced in Section 7.3.3 may now be extended to integrate dynamic type checking by computing the strata of a program P with respect to $\mathcal{D}^{\text{sig}}(P)$. Then, while evaluating the rules in an order imposed by the ordering of the strata, each data term may be immediately type-checked; type checking may be integrated into the T-operator. Thus evaluating a program and type-checking of its results may be done within the same framework.

7.5
Conclusion

In this paper we discuss several aspects concerning the evaluation of F-logic programs when techniques are applied which are known from deductive databases. We discuss weak recursive programs and we are able to show, that the knowledge about functionality of methods can be used to weaken previous definitions. The stratification of general programs in F-logic is complicated by the fact that variables may occur anywhere in an F-term. Stratification for Datalog programs is defined with respect to predicate symbols. In general, F-terms do not embody something (syntactically) equivalent to predicate symbols; we thus define stratification with respect to the complete terms in the rules. To this end we have to base the definition of a dependency graph on unification arcs (which are not needed in Datalog).

Each program is extended by a set of closure and inheritance rules. Yet, building a dependency graph over an extended program may increase the number of negative cycles (because of the great number of unification arcs that are introduced on account of the closure rules). We distinguish between relevant and irrelevant cycles on behalf of the propagation of unifiers over closure rules. A stratification is then computed with respect to relevant cycles.

Finally, we discuss dynamic typing and type checking. We introduce various concepts of type correctness. Since we are interested in dynamic typing we define certain criteria which must be fulfilled such that dynamic type checking can be applied. We finally show how to integrate dynamic type checking into a bottom-up evaluation strategy.

Acknowledgements

We would like to thank Jürgen Frohn, Michael Kramer and Heinz Uphoff for helpful comments and discussions on the topics of this paper.

Bibliography

[Abiteboul and Grumbach 1987] Abiteboul S. and Grumbach S. "COL: A Logic-Based Language for Complex Objects." In *Proc. 1st Workshop on Database Programming Languages*, pp. 253–276.

[Abiteboul and Hull 1988] Abiteboul S. and Hull R. "Data Functions, Datalog and Negation." In *Proc. ACM SIGMOD Conference on Management of Data (SIGMOD)*, pp. 143–153.

[Abiteboul and Kanellakis 1989] Abiteboul S. and Kanellakis P. "Object Identity as a Query Language Primitive." In *Proc. ACM SIGMOD Conference on Management of Data (SIGMOD)*, pp. 159–173.

[Albano, Cardelli and Orsini 1990] Albano A., Cardelli C., and Orsini R. "Galileo: A Strongly Typed, Interactive Conceptual Language." In *Readings in Object-Oriented Database Systems* (Zdonik S.B. and Maier D., eds.), pp. 147–162. Morgan Kaufmann Publishers.

[Apt, Blair and Walker 1989] Apt K.R., Blair H., and Walker A. "Towards a Theory of Declarative Knowledge." In *Foundations of Deductive Databases and Logic Programming* (Minker J., ed.), pp. 1–77. Morgan Kaufmann Publishers.

[Beeri, Naqvi, Shmueli and Tsur 1987] Beeri C., Naqvi S., Shmueli O., and Tsur S. "Sets and Negation in a Logic Database Language (LDL)." (MCC Report).

[Chang and Lee 1973] Chang C.L. and Lee R.C.T. "Symbolic Logic and Mechanical Theorem Proving." Academic Press.

[Chen, Kifer and Warren 1989] Chen W., Kifer M., and Warren D.S. "HiLog: A First-Order Semantics for Higher-Order Logic Programming Constructs." In *Proc. of the North American Conference on Logic Programming.*

[Chen and Warren 1989] Chen W. and Warren D.S. "C-Logic of Complex Objects." In *Proc. ACM SIGMOD Conference on Management of Data (SIGMOD)*, pp. 369–378.

[Hull and Yoshikawa 1990] Hull R. and Yoshikawa M. "ILOG: Declarative Creation and Manipulation of Object Identifiers." In *Proc. 16th International Conference on Very Large Data Bases (VLDB)*, pp. 455–468.

[Kifer and Lausen 1989] Kifer M. and Lausen G. "F-Logic: A Higher-Order Language for Reasoning about Objects, Inheritance, and Scheme." In *Proc. ACM SIGMOD Conference on Management of Data (SIGMOD)*, pp. 134–146.

[Kifer and Wu 1989] Kifer M. and Wu J. "A Logic for Object-Oriented Programming (Maier's O-Logic Revisited)." In *Proceedings of the ACM SIGACT-SIGMOD-SIGART Symposium on Principles of Database Systems (PODS)*, pp. 379–393.

[Kifer, Lausen and Wu 1992] Kifer M., Lausen G. and Wu J. "Logical Foundations of Object Oriented and Frame-Based Languages." *Accepted for publication.*

[Lausen and Uphoff 1992] Lausen G. and Uphoff H. "Aspects of Inheritance in a Rule Language." *Manuscript.*

[Lloyd 1987] Lloyd J.W. "Foundations of Logic Programming." 2nd edition, Springer-Verlag.

[Maier 1986] Maier D. "A Logic for Objects." In *Proceedings of the Workshop on Foundations of Deductive Databases and Logic Programming*, pp. 6–26.

[Przymusinski 1989] Przymusinski T.C. "On the Declarative Semantics of Deductive Databases and Logic Programs." In *Foundations of Deductive Databases and Logic Programming* (Minker J., ed.), pp. 191–216. Morgan Kaufmann Publishers.

[Ullman 1988] Ullman J.D. "Principles of Database and Knowledgebase Systems." Computer Science Press.

8

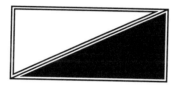

Tagging as an Alternative to Object Creation

Marc Gyssens
Lawrence V. Saxton
Dirk Van Gucht

Abstract

Based on the observation that graphs play an important role in the representation of databases, an algebra is presented for the manipulation of binary relations, i.e., of directed unlabeled graphs. This so-called *Tarski algebra* is based on early work by Tarski. The key notion that has been added to it here is *tagging*, which is needed for providing both enough modeling power and enough querying power. Moreover, tagging can also be seen as a value-based counterpart to object creation in object-oriented data models. We present tagging in a general formal framework that incorporates several specific tagging strategies as a special case. We show that each of these strategies allows for the simulation in the Tarski model of various other database models, in particular of the relational model. Finally, we discuss the genericity of tagging and show that the Tarski algebra augmented with multiple assignments and a while-construct is a computationally complete database language.

8.1
Introduction

The current trend in database research is towards systems that can support database applications that involve data objects with a complex external and internal organization. This trend is reflected by the emergence of systems supporting extendible databases [Carey 1987, Stonebraker 1988, Zdonik and Maier 1989] and object-oriented databases [Atkinson et al. 1989, Bancilhon 1988, Kim and Lochovsky 1989, Zdonik and Maier 1989]. The database theory community has followed this trend and has devised mathematical database models to both represent and manipulate complex-object databases. These database models can be categorized into two general classes: value-based models (the so-called *complex-object database models*) and object-identity-based models (the so-called *object-oriented database models*).

To illustrate the difference between these two classes, consider the persons relational database shown in Figure 8.1. This database could alternatively be represented as a complex-object database as shown in Figure 8.2. Although transforming a flat relational database into a complex-object database of course requires the creation of complex objects (i.e., the name-age pairs, the children sets, and the hobbies sets in our example), it is important to notice that *no* new atomic values are introduced.

Parent	Child
p_1	p_3
p_1	p_4
p_2	p_3
p_2	p_4
p_4	p_6
p_5	p_6

Person	Hobby
p_1	Soccer
p_1	Music
p_2	Dance
p_3	Soccer
p_4	Reading
p_4	Painting
p_5	Basketball
p_6	Music
p_6	Games

Person	Name	Age
p_1	Frank	50
p_2	Ellen	52
p_3	Eric	30
p_4	Lisa	28
p_5	Brad	31
p_6	Eric	6

FIGURE 8.1
A persons relational database

In contrast, an object-oriented representation requires the introduction of *new* atomic values in the form of object-identifiers of objects. For example, one possible way of representing the persons database in an object-oriented context is shown in Figure 8.3. (For simplicity, we used an untyped representation rather than a more traditional, i.e., class-oriented approach.) Each object carries its own value and identity, which in turn is allowed to occur in the value components of other objects. Consider for example the object with object-identifier s_1. This object-identifier uniquely represents a children set. Its value is the set of children of the parent objects identified by o_1 and o_2. Notice how s_1 is *shared* in the value components of the respective parents.

It would appear from this example that complex-object databases and object-oriented databases are fundamentally different, each offering its own advantages. The main advantage of the complex-object approach is that no new atomic values are introduced. This provides a clean framework in which to extend the theory of relational databases to that of databases with complex objects. On the other hand, the main advantage of the object-oriented approach is its economy of representation. For example, whereas in the object-oriented version of the person database, there is a unique representation for the children set of o_1 and o_2, this children set needs to be doubly represented in the complex-object persons database. This economy of representation, however, comes at the expense of being able to extend cleanly the theory of relational databases to that of object-oriented databases.

To bridge the gap between complex-object databases and object-oriented

Person	Personal-Data	Children	Hobbies
p_1	[name: Frank, age: 50]	Child / p_3 / p_4	Hobby / Soccer / Music
p_2	[name: Ellen, age: 52]	Child / p_3 / p_4	Hobby / Dance
p_3	[name: Eric, age: 30]	Child / p_6	Hobby / Soccer
p_4	[name: Lisa, age: 28]	Child / p_6	Hobby / Reading / Painting
p_5	[name: Brad, age: 31]	Child	Hobby / Basketball
p_6	[name: Eric, age: 6]	Child	Hobby / Music / Games

FIGURE 8.2

The persons database represented as a complex-object database

Object Identifier	Object Value
o_1	[id: p_1, info: i_1, children: s_1,] hobbies: {Soccer, Music}]
o_2	[id: p_2, info: i_2, children: s_1, hobbies: {Dance}]
o_3	[id: p_3, info: i_3, children: s_2, hobbies: {Soccer}]
o_4	[id: p_4, info: i_4, children: s_3, hobbies: {Reading, Painting }]
o_5	[id: p_5, info: i_5, children: s_3, hobbies: {Basketball}]
o_6	[id: p_6, info: i_6, children: s_2, hobbies: {Music, Games}]
i_1	[name: Frank, age: 50]
i_2	[name: Ellen, age: 52]
i_3	[name: Eric, age: 30]
i_4	[name: Lisa, age: 28]
i_5	[name: Brad, age: 31]
i_6	[name: Eric, age: 6]
s_1	$\{o_3, o_4\}$
s_2	$\emptyset$
s_3	$\{o_6\}$

FIGURE 8.3

The persons database represented as an object-oriented database

Parents	Children
τ_3	τ_1
τ_4	τ_2

Tag	Value
τ_1	$\{p_3, p_4\}$
τ_2	$\{p_6\}$
τ_3	$\{p_1, p_2\}$
τ_4	$\{p_4, p_5\}$

FIGURE 8.4

The parent-child relation using tags

databases, researchers have proposed database models and database languages in which new values can be introduced through object-creation. For example, returning to the persons database, assume that we have derived at some stage in a computation that the sets $\{p_3, p_4\}$ and $\{p_6\}$ are the children-sets of the (unordered) parent pairs $\{p_1, p_2\}$ and $\{p_4, p_5\}$, respectively. Instead of carrying the full representation of this derived information throughout the rest of the computation, we could decide to *create* four *new* values, say τ_1, τ_2, τ_3, and τ_4. These values uniquely represent the respective children sets and parent pairs. Using these values, the derived parent-child information can be represented as shown in Figure 8.4.

In this paper, we will call these new values *tags*. It must be emphasized that tags are *different* from object-identifiers. Tags can be thought of as succinct representations of complex objects, whereas object-identifiers are uniquely associated with objects whose value can be a complex object.

Indeed, turning back to our example, suppose that p_1 and p_2 have a new child, say p_7. In the complex-object database, this update would be reflected through the addition of p_7 to the children sets of the respective parents p_1 and p_2. In the object-oriented approach, however, p_7 would simply be added as a new object (say with object identifier o_7), and the value of the object s_1 would be updated to include o_7. In particular, s_1 does not have to be replaced throughout the database. In the tag-based approach, in contrast, the only reasonable strategy is to replace the tag τ_1 of the persons set $\{p_3, p_4\}$ by a new tag, say τ_5, representing the set $\{p_3, p_4, p_7\}$. In other words, after this update, τ_1 is *still* the representation of the "old" set $\{p_3, p_4\}$.

For this reason, the tagging technique is essentially value-based. However, at the same time, economy of representation and expression is obtained.

There exist essentially two classes of tag-based database models. The first class, which we call the class of *non-deterministic* tag-based database models, consists of database models that introduce tags non-deterministically. The non-determinism stems from the idea that it does not matter which new values are actually introduced to represent complex objects. Of course, the consequence of the non-deterministic approach is that there may be several tags, i.e., *copies*, representing the same complex object. The classic example of a non-deterministic tag-based database model is the the IQL model of [Abiteboul and Kanellakis 1989]. In the same class are also transactions-based database models of [Abiteboul and Vianu 1990] and the GOOD model of [Gyssens et al. 1990a, Gyssens et al. 1990b]. The second class, which we call the class of *deterministic* tag-based database models, consists of database models that introduce new tags deterministically through function evaluation of complex objects (this process is closely related to the notion of skolemization in logic). In this class, one finds LDM [Kuper and Vardi 1984], C-logic [Chen and Warren 1989] and F-logic [Kifer and Lausen 1989]. In the ILOG model of [Hull and Yoshikawa 1990], both the non-deterministic and the deterministic approach are combined. In the limit of course, any complex-object database model can be thought of as deterministic tag-based database model, simply because an object-value can always be thought of as its own tag (actually, such an approach has already been used for theoretical purposes by [Gyssens et al. 1989]).

Most tag-based database models have been proposed in a declarative, logic-based context, with the GOOD model and LDM being the exceptions. In contrast with the satisfactory status of declarative formulations of tag-based database models, we feel that there are currently few, if any, satisfactory algebraic formulations. This lack is unfortunate since algebraic formulations are better platforms from which to build real database systems. In this paper we offer such an algebraic formulation. We will introduce a tag-based database model, the *Tarski database model*. We called our model, based on binary relations, after the distinguished logician-mathematician Tarski who laid the set-theoretic foundations for our proposal.

Our model is an outgrowth of a mechanism to algebratize the GOOD model. To understand this, it is necessary to discuss briefly the GOOD database model and its associated data manipulation language. This will be the subject of Section 8.2. In Section 8.3, we then formally introduce the Tarski database model. Our main emphasis will be on the data manipulation language, which we call the *Tarski algebra*. In Section 8.4, we show how other database models (relational model, nested model, GOOD model) can be simulated using the essentially binary Tarski approach. In particular, we show that the Tarski algebra allows the expression of the relational algebra. In Section 8.5, we extend the Tarski algebra with a looping construct and show that this yields a computationally complete language. In this section, we also discuss the notion of genericity in the presence of tags. Finally in Section 8.6, we mention some ongoing and future research on the Tarski database model, including implementation issues.

8.2
Towards a Tag-based Database Model

8.2.1   The Graph-Oriented Object Database Model (GOOD)

The GOOD model of [Gyssens et al. 1990a, Gyssens et al. 1990b] was introduced as an attempt to construct an object-oriented database model in which both the data representation part and the data manipulation language are graph-based.

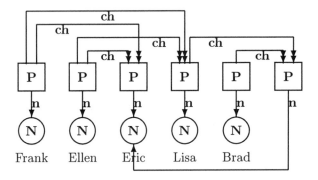

FIGURE 8.5
The persons database as a GOOD instance

In the GOOD model, a database is viewed as a labeled directed graph. For example, in Figure 8.5 we show a GOOD database for the persons database shown in Figure 8.1. For simplicity, we omitted the information about age and hobbies. Circle nodes represent printable information, while square nodes can easily be interpreted as tags for complex objects. Ordinary arrows represent functional properties whereas double arrows indicate multivalued properties.

Data manipulation operations in GOOD are specified in term of graph-transformations such as node additions, edge additions, node deletions and edge deletions. For example, in Figure 8.6 *(left)* we show a node addition operation the effect of which is to add new parent-pair nodes, i.e., one new such node for each pair of person nodes that have a common child. (In the context of our discussion of tags, think of these new nodes as tags for the respective parent-pairs.) In Figure 8.6 *(middle)* we show an edge addition operation. Its effect is to associate the children nodes directly with their

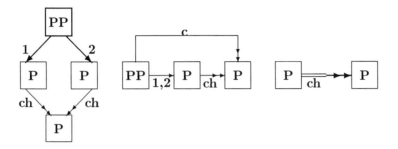

FIGURE 8.6
Some GOOD operations on the parents database

corresponding parent-pair nodes. Finally, in Figure 8.6 *(right)* we show an edge deletion that removes the original links between parents and children. The effect of the consecutive application of these three operations is displayed in Figure 8.7.

8.2.2   GOOD as Motivation for a Binary Tag-based Database Model

A natural way to represent a GOOD database algebraically is as a collection of mathematical (binary) relations [Ore 1962]. In one particular such representation there are two relations to represent the nodes in the GOOD database, i.e, one associating node labels to nodes and one associating print labels to printable nodes. Furthermore, there is a separate relation for each edge label occurring in the GOOD database. More concretely, an edge label e is represented by a relation consisting of all pairs of nodes (n_1, n_2) for which there is an e-labeled edge from n_1 to n_2 in the GOOD database. Figure 8.8 shows this representation for the portion of the persons database represented in GOOD in Figure 8.5.

Of course, one can easily think of other reasonable ways to represent GOOD databases in terms of mathematical relations.

Once a particular representation has been achieved, one can simulate GOOD graph transformations by set-theoretic operations on mathematical relations.

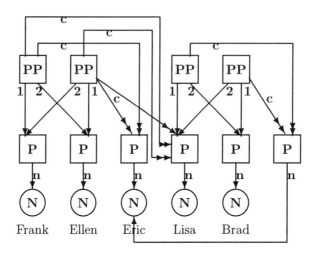

FIGURE 8.7

The effect of the operations in Figure 8.6 on the persons database

nodelabels			printlabels			ch			n	
p_1	P		n_1	Frank		p_1	p_3		p_1	n_1
p_2	P		n_2	Ellen		p_1	p_4		p_2	n_2
p_3	P		n_3	Eric		p_2	p_3		p_3	n_3
p_4	P		n_4	Lisa		p_2	p_4		p_4	n_4
p_5	P		n_5	Brad		p_4	p_6		p_5	n_5
p_6	P					p_5	p_6		p_6	n_3
n_1	N									
n_2	N									
n_3	N									
n_4	N									
n_5	N									

FIGURE 8.8

Using binary mathematical relations for representing GOOD instances

As it turns out, Tarski [Tarski 1941] had already specified an algebra to manipulate just such binary relations. In fact, Tarski called this algebra a *relation algebra* in later work. However, he did not use it to manipulate databases, but rather to study set-theoretical concepts. Tarski's algebra has (only) four fundamental and well-known operators: union, composition, complementation, and inversion. Furthermore, Tarski assumes that there is a special relation fixing the equality relation on the universe of discourse. In a very real sense, mathematicians and logicians were already doing relational algebra well before Codd introduced his relational algebra into the context of databases. Of course mathematicians almost invariantly dealt with infinite relations, while database theoreticians, and certainly database practitioners, worked with finite relations.

In this paper we approach database theory following Tarski's rather than Codd's formalism, as was already done by [Kraegeloh and Lockemann 1975]. The main difference between their proposal and ours, however, is that they do not consider the additions of new values to their database. As was demonstrated by [Tarski and Givant 1986], the expressive power of the data manipulation language then is very limited.

Here, we model a database by a set of mathematical relations and manipulate a database by performing Tarski algebraic operations on these relations. In order to study the notion of tagging, we add two new operators to Tarski's algebra. These so-called *tagging operators* allow the introduction of (new) tags. Each new tag represents a specific ordered pair in the database and is derived through a so-called *tagging function* evaluation. The power of the tagging technique stems from the fact that these new tag values can be used as values in other pairs, thus facilitating the succinct representation of complex objects. In combination with the other operators of the Tarski algebra, the tagging operators allow for complex database manipulations.

We will furthermore show that tagging can be achieved via tagging functions with special properties. These properties, we believe, are in fact effectively used in real-world database systems. So our contribution is two-fold: first, we give a simple algebraic formulation of tag-based database models, and second, our proposed tagging techniques correspond naturally to techniques already in use in database systems.

8.3
The Tarski Algebra

8.3.1   Codd Relations and Mathematical Relations

Throughout this paper, we assume infinitely enumerable sets U and V of *attributes* and *values*, respectively.

Using the formalism of [Gyssens et al. 1989], a *Codd scheme* is a finite subset of U. Let Ω be a Codd scheme. A tuple over Ω is a mapping of Ω into V; a *Codd instance* over Ω is a set of tuples over Ω. All Codd instances are considered to be finite unless explicitly stated otherwise. Finally, a *Codd relation* is a pair (Ω, ω) with Ω a Codd scheme and ω a Codd instance over Ω.

In contrast to Codd relations, which are the building blocks of the relational database model [Codd 1970, Codd 1972a, Codd 1972b], mathematical relations are sets of ordered pairs of values. For our purposes, a mathematical relation (or *relation*, for short) is a subset of $V \times V$. Of course, there is a close connection between a mathematical relation and a Codd relation with two attributes but, unlike the latter, the former does not have a scheme.

In what follows, we will develop tools to manipulate relations in the mathematical sense and show how these techniques apply to various database models. All relations are considered to be finite unless explicitly stated otherwise.

It is often important to know the values actually involved in a given relation r. We denote by $r\downarrow$ the smallest subset of V such that $r \subset r\downarrow \times r\downarrow$, i.e., $r\downarrow = \{v \in V \mid \exists w \in V : (v, w) \in r \vee (w, v) \in r\}$. The set $r\downarrow$ will be called the *active domain* of r. Similarly, if $r_1, \dots, r_m$ are relations, then $(r_1, \dots, r_m)\downarrow = r_1\downarrow \cup \dots \cup r_m\downarrow$ is the active domain of the database consisting of the mathematical relations $r_1, \dots, r_m$.

8.3.2   The Basic Algebra on Relations

Mathematical relations, because of their natural affinity with graphs, are very important and fundamental data structures in several areas of computer science and, therefore, it is important to have appropriate tools to manipulate them. Because of the close connection between mathematical relations and Codd relations with two attributes, it seems natural to borrow these tools from relational algebra. However, long before Codd devised his relational algebra in 1970 [Codd 1970], Tarski already had defined an algebra on mathematical relations [Tarski 1941]. The operators defined below are inspired by Tarski's algebra.

DEFINITION 8.1

Let r and s be relations. We define the following operations:

- *The* inverse *of r, denoted r^{-1}, is the relation $\{(v, w) \mid (w, v) \in r\}$.*

- *The* complement *of r, denoted $\bar{r}$, is the relation $\{(v, w) \mid (v, w) \in r\downarrow \times r\downarrow \wedge (v, w) \notin r\}$.*

- *The* union *of r and s, denoted $r \cup s$, is the relation $\{(v, w) \mid (v, w) \in r \vee (v, w) \in s\}$.*

- *The* composition *of r and s, denoted $r \cdot s$, is the relation $\{(u, w) \mid \exists v \in V : (u, v) \in r \wedge (v, w) \in s\}$.*

A major difference between the operators defined above and their counterparts in Tarski's algebra is that we define complementation relative to the active domain rather than to the set V of all values, as Tarski does. Our approach of course aims at avoiding generating infinite relations.

In order to introduce a *basic algebra expression (bae)* we assume an infinitely enumerable set of (relation) variables $x_1, x_2, x_3, \ldots$ Bae's are then recursively defined as follows:

1. $\emptyset$ is a bae;

2. each variable x_i is a bae; and

3. an expression obtained by applying the operators of Definition 8.1 to bae's is again a bae.

In writing down expressions, we assume that unary operators take precedence over binary operators; also, composition takes precedence over set-like operators. If $E(x_1, \ldots, x_m)$ is a bae and $r_1, \ldots, r_m$ are relations, then the interpretation of $E(r_1, \ldots, r_m)$ is defined in the customary way. The set of all bae's will be called the *basic algebra*.

8.3.3 Tagging

We will now formally introduce the concept of *tagging*. Intuitively, we view tagging as attaching new values (*tags*) to objects of the database with the purpose of identifying them. Tagging is a technique widely used in the field of databases, e.g., in order to manipulate nested relations or to introduce object identifiers in object-oriented databases. In this subsection, we will study the notion of tagging in the context of mathematical relations. Later on, we will discuss tagging in the context of relations, nested relations and object-oriented databases.

In order to introduce tagging, we have to assume that the set of values V consists of an infinite set D of *data values* and an infinite set T of *tag values*, i.e., $V = D \cup T$ with $D \cap T = \emptyset$. The set D consists of these values that actually represent "data" of our database, while T is a set of "auxiliary" values, needed to introduce tags.

In the context of mathematical relations, the "objects" we want to tag are, quite straightforwardly, the ordered pairs. Before we can proceed to a formal definition however, we first have to realize that several variations on the idea of tagging are conceivable, most of which are actually around in database practice. To illustrate our point, consider the relations shown in Figure 8.9.

r	
a	b
a	c
b	c
c	d
c	c

s	
c	a
b	a
a	b

FIGURE 8.9
Two mathematical relations

A first tagging strategy we wish to discuss will be called *tuple tagging*. In this strategy, a "generic" tag is associated to each ordered pair, e.g., by writing its components between square brackets, as shown in Figure 8.10. A non-operational variation on tuple tagging has already been considered by [Tarski and Givant 1986].

A consequence of this approach is that the same pair always gets the same tag, irrespective of the relation in which it occurs. In Figure 8.10, for instance, the ordered pair (a, b) obtains the same tag in both r and s. One could easily conceive situations in which the tag should not only depend on the ordered pair but also on the relation in which the ordered pair occurs. This latter tagging strategy will be called *relation tagging*. The assignment of tags in Figure 8.11 is consistent with a relation tagging strategy.

In the relation tagging strategy it is still possible that the same value is introduced multiple times, e.g., when the same relation needs to be tagged

$[a,b]$	a	b	
$[a,c]$	a	c	
$[b,c]$	b	c	
$[c,d]$	c	d	
$[c,c]$	c	c	

r

$[c,a]$	c	a
$[b,a]$	b	a
$[a,b]$	a	b

s

FIGURE 8.10
Tuple tagging

1	a	b
2	a	c
3	b	c
4	c	d
5	c	c

r

6	c	a
7	b	a
8	a	b

s

FIGURE 8.11
Relation tagging

twice in the course of solving a query. The tagging strategy in which no value is introduced more than once as a tag will be called *universal tagging*.

Rather than making a choice among these various alternatives, we preferred to introduce a more general notion of tagging that encompasses all three strategies outlined above as special cases.

To define this generalized tagging, let $\mathcal{V}$ be the set of all pairs (s, t) with s a relation (i.e., a finite subset of $V \times V$) and $t = (v, w)$ an ordered pair over V. (Relation s will be called a *context*). A *tagging function* τ is a bijection:

$$\tau : \mathcal{V} \longrightarrow T$$

(T being the set of tag values) such that for each pair $(s, t) \in \mathcal{V}$, $\tau(s, t)$ does *not* occur in $s \cup \{v, w\}$. Intuitively, τ associates a tag value to the ordered pair t that depends on the context s. Moreover, this tag must be "new", i.e., it cannot be a component of the pair t and it must not already occur in the context s.

The various tagging strategies discussed above can now easily be obtained by making a particular choice for the context.

If we systematically choose the empty relation $\emptyset$ as the tagging context, we achieve tuple tagging. If, alternatively, we take for the context the relation in which the pair under consideration occurs, we get relation tagging. Finally, if the context is a representation of the set of all values that up to then did occur at some point in the database under consideration, then we achieve universal tagging. Most of the results we prove in this paper hold independent of the particular tagging strategy chosen. This will become important in Section 8.5.3, where we discuss the expressive power of the language we are presently defining.

Given a tagging function, we now introduce two tagging operators:

DEFINITION 8.2

Let r and s be relations.

- *The* left-tagging *of r in the context of s, denoted $r_s^{\triangleleft}$, is the relation*

$$\{(\tau(s, (v, w)), v) | (v, w) \in r\}.$$

- *The* right-tagging *of r in the context s, denoted $r_s^{\triangleright}$, is the relation*

$$\{(\tau(s, (v, w)), w) | (v, w) \in r\}.$$

r	
a	b
a	c
b	c
c	d
c	c

$r^{\triangleleft}_r$	
1	a
2	a
3	b
4	c
5	c

$r^{\triangleright}_r$	
1	b
2	c
3	c
4	d
5	c

FIGURE 8.12
Example of tagging

Observe that the relation r can always be reconstructed from its left- and right-tagging whatever context was used, provided it was the same for both operations. Indeed, left- and right-tagging always satisfy the property:

$$r = (r^{\triangleleft}_s)^{-1} \cdot r^{\triangleright}_s.$$

As data values and tag values are disjoint ($D \cap T = \emptyset$), the actual values of the tags are immaterial; only their equality or difference is of relevance. Therefore, in concrete examples, rather than specifying a tag function, which would be quite cumbersome a job, we shall use (consecutive) integers to represent tag values; data values will be represented by lower case letters.

EXAMPLE 8.1
In Figure 8.12, we show the result of left and right tagging a relation in its own context.

The algebra obtained by augmenting the basic algebra with the left- and right-tagging operators will be called the *Tarski algebra*. An expression of the Tarski algebra will be called a *Tarski algebra expression (tae)* and defined in analogy to a bae.

The Tarski algebra is considerably more powerful than the basic algebra. To illustrate this, we show the following:

PROPOSITION 8.1

Let r be a relation over V. The identity operator

$$r^{\mathrm{id}} = \{(v, w) \in r\!\downarrow \times\, r\!\downarrow \mid v = w\}$$

can be expressed in the Tarski algebra.

PROOF

Let s be an arbitrary relation. The proposition follows from the equality:

$$r^{\mathrm{id}} = (r_s^{\triangleleft})^{-1} \cdot r_s^{\triangleleft} \cup (r_s^{\triangleright})^{-1} \cdot r_s^{\triangleright}.$$

∎

Clearly, the identity operator is not expressible in the basic algebra. Several auxiliary operators can be expressed using the identity operator:

PROPOSITION 8.2

Let r and s be relations. The following operations can be expressed in the basic algebra plus the identity operator:

- *the diversity operator $r^{\mathrm{di}} = \{(v, w) \in r{\downarrow} \times r{\downarrow} \mid v \neq w\}$;*
- *the relative universe $r^{\mathrm{un}} = r{\downarrow} \times r{\downarrow}$;*

PROOF

The proposition follows from the equalities:

$$r^{\mathrm{di}} = \overline{r^{\mathrm{id}}},$$
$$r^{\mathrm{un}} = r^{\mathrm{id}} \cup r^{\mathrm{di}}.$$

∎

Another useful operator is the intersection operator. We show that intersection can also be expressed in the Tarski algebra. While the proof is based on the well-known set-theoretic property relating intersection, union, and complementation, some care is needed since, unlike in set theory, our notion of complementation is relative to the set of values occurring in the relation under consideration.

PROPOSITION 8.3

Let r and s be relations over V. The intersection operator $r \cap s = \{(v, w) \mid (v, w) \in r \wedge (v, w) \in s\}$ can be expressed in the Tarski algebra.

PROOF

Let $(r \cap s)^{=}$ and $(r \cap s)^{\neq}$ be the identical and the non-identical tuples of $r \cap s$, respectively. The reader is invited to verify that

$$(r \cap s)^{\neq} = \overline{r \cup (r \cup s)^{\mathrm{id}} \cup \overline{s \cup (r \cup s)^{\mathrm{id}}} \cup (r \cup s)^{\mathrm{id}}}. \tag{1}$$

Now let q be an arbitrary relation and let $p = (r \cup s)^{\triangleright}_q \cdot \left((r \cup s)^{\triangleright}_q\right)^{-1}$. Then

$$(r \cap s)^= = \overline{\overline{r \cup (r \cup s \cup p)^{\mathrm{di}}} \cup \overline{s \cup (r \cup s \cup p)^{\mathrm{di}}} \cup (r \cup s \cup p)^{\mathrm{di}}}. \quad (2)$$

An expression for $r \cap s$ is now obtained by taking the union of the expressions displayed in (1) and (2).   ∎

In order to understand better the previous proof it should be noted that whenever $(r \cup s){\downarrow}$ is a singleton, $(r \cup s)^{\mathrm{di}} = \emptyset$ due to the relative complementation. Hence $(r \cup s)^{\mathrm{di}}$, contrary to $(r \cup s)^{\mathrm{id}}$, does not always contain all values present in r or s, and for that reason the equality

$$(r \cap s)^= = \overline{\overline{r \cup (r \cup s)^{\mathrm{di}}} \cup \overline{s \cup (r \cup s)^{\mathrm{di}}} \cup (r \cup s)^{\mathrm{di}}}$$

does *not* always hold. If r and s are both the same singleton relations consisting of an identical pair, then the above expression yields the empty relation rather than the singleton relation. Since a tag to a pair by definition cannot be a value of that pair, $(r \cup s \cup p{\downarrow})$ contains *two* values whenever $(r \cup s){\downarrow}$ is a singleton. Hence $(r \cup s \cup p)^{\mathrm{di}}$ *always* contains all values present in r, s or p, whence equality (2) in the proof holds.

An alternative and much shorter proof follows from the equality

$$r \cap s = (r^{\triangleleft}_q)^{-1} \cdot s^{\triangleright}_q, \quad (3)$$

with q an arbitrary relation. The simplicity of the latter equality is due to the fact that associating a tag to the *same* tuple in the *same* context, yields the *same* tag value. We preferred, however, to exhibit an expression that is not "context-sensitive", proving that all tagging strategies presented thus far allow the expression of the intersection operator. Notice that although equality (3) can be used to show that intersection is expressible using the tuple tagging strategy (put $q = \emptyset$), it does not show that intersection is also expressible using the relation tagging strategy.

As a corollary to Proposition 8.3, we have:

PROPOSITION 8.4

Let r and s be relations. The following operations can be expressed in the Tarski algebra:

- *the* identity selection $r^= = \{(v, w) \in r \mid v = w\}$;
- *the* diversity selection $r^{\neq} = \{(v, w) \in r \mid v \neq w\}$; *and*

- *the* difference $r - s = \{(v, w) \mid (v, w) \in r \wedge (v, w) \notin s\}$.

PROOF

The proposition follows from the equalities:

$$r^{=} = r^{\mathrm{id}} \cap r,$$
$$r^{\neq} = r^{\mathrm{di}} \cap r,$$
$$r - s = r \cap \left(\overline{s \cup r^{\mathrm{id}}} \cup \overline{s \cup r^{\mathrm{di}}}\right).$$

∎

As a final example illustrating the power of the Tarski algebra, we formally introduce conditional queries:

DEFINITION 8.3

A conditional query is an expression of the form

$$\textbf{if } E_1(\vec{x}_1) = \emptyset$$
$$\textbf{then}$$
$$E_2(\vec{x}_2)$$
$$\textbf{else}$$
$$E_3(\vec{x}_3),$$

with $E_1(\vec{x}_1)$, $E_2(\vec{x}_2)$ and $E_3(\vec{x}_3)$ arbitrary Tarski algebra expressions. (The variables $\vec{x}_1$, $\vec{x}_2$ and $\vec{x}_3$ denote finite sequences of (mathematical) relation variables.)

We can show:

PROPOSITION 8.5

The conditional expression Q can be expressed in the Tarski algebra.

PROOF

Consider the following expression:

$$
\begin{aligned}
E_4(\vec{x}_1, \vec{x}_2, \vec{x}_3) \quad = \quad & E_3(\vec{x}_3) \cdot \left(E_1(\vec{x}_1) \cdot (E_1(\vec{x}_1) \cup E_3(\vec{x}_3))^{\mathrm{un}}\right)^{\mathrm{id}} \\
& \cup E_2(\vec{x}_2) \\
& - E_2(\vec{x}_2) \cdot \left(E_1(\vec{x}_1) \cdot (E_1(\vec{x}_1) \cup E_2(\vec{x}_2))^{\mathrm{un}}\right)^{\mathrm{id}}.
\end{aligned}
$$

Clearly, for any three relation r_1, r_2, r_3, $Q(r_1, r_2, r_3) = E_4(r_1, r_2, r_3)$. ∎

8.4
Simulating Other Database Models

In this section, we intend to show that binary relations equipped with the Tarski algebra suffice to simulate many other languages. In particular, we shall show that the relational model, the nested model and the GOOD model, together with their respective basic languages, can be expressed in the Tarski model.

The Tarski algebra turns out to be too weak however to express more complete extensions of these languages. Therefore a possible extension of the Tarski algebra dealing with this problem will be discussed in Section 8.5.

8.4.1   Relational Model

We first turn to the classical relational model [Codd 1970, Codd 1972a, Codd 1972b], in which a database consists of a set of *Codd relations* (see Subsection 8.3.1).

Of course, there is a major difference between Codd relations and (even binary) mathematical relations in that the components of Codd relations are marked with attribute names. In order to be able to reconstruct A Codd relation from a set of mathematical binary relations, one needs names for these relations to preserve the links with the attributes. In order to be able to simulate attribute renaming in Codd's relational algebra, the Tarski algebra then needs to be extended with an operator allowing the renaming of relations.

For simplicity's sake, however, we shall deliberately ignore this minor problem. Thus, a Codd relation can be represented by a set of mathematical binary relations as follows:

DEFINITION 8.4

Let (Ω, ω) be a *Codd relation over* V *with* $\Omega = \{A_1, \ldots, A_n\}$. *A set of mathematical relations* $\{r_{A_1}, \ldots, r_{A_n}\}$ *is called a* representation *of* (Ω, ω) *if there exists a one-to-one mapping* ρ *from* ω *into* T, *called a* representation function, *such that for all* $i = 1, \ldots, n$, $r_{A_i} = \{(\rho(t), t(A_i)) \mid t \in \omega\}$.

EXAMPLE 8.2
In Figure 8.13, $\{r_A, r_B, r_C\}$ is a representation of (Ω, ω)

Using this encoding of Codd relations into mathematical relations, we can now give a natural meaning to simulating a relational query in the Tarski algebra:

$$(\Omega, \omega)$$

A	B	C
a	b	c
a	b	d
a	c	d
b	c	c

r_A	
1	a
2	a
3	a
4	b

r_B	
1	b
2	b
3	c
4	c

r_C	
1	c
2	d
3	d
4	d

FIGURE 8.13

Representation of a Codd relation

DEFINITION 8.5

Let $E(x_1, \ldots, x_m)$ be an expression in the relational algebra in which x_i, $1 \le i \le m$, is a variable representing a Codd-relation of arity n_i. We say that $E(x_1, \ldots, x_m)$ can be simulated in the Tarski algebra if there exists a tae $E'(y_{11}, \ldots, y_{1n_1}, \ldots, y_{m1}, \ldots, y_{mn_m})$ such that for all Codd relations $(\Omega_1, \omega_1), \ldots, (\Omega_m, \omega_m)$ for which $E((\Omega_1, \omega_1), \ldots, (\Omega_m, \omega_m))$ exists, and for all mathematical relations $r_{11}, \ldots, r_{1n_1}, \ldots, r_{m1}, \ldots, r_{mn_m}$ for which the set $\{r_{i1}, \ldots, r_{in_i}\}$ is a representation of (Ω_i, ω_i) for all i, $1 \le i \le m$, $E'(r_{11}, \ldots, r_{1n_1}, \ldots, r_{m1}, \ldots, r_{mn_i})$ is a representation of $E((\Omega_1, \omega_1), \ldots, (\Omega_n, \omega_m))$.

We have:

THEOREM 8.1

The relational algebra can be simulated in the Tarski algebra.

PROOF

We show how each of the relational algebra operators can be simulated in the Tarski algebra. We shall develop the proof in such a way that it will become obvious that each of the tagging strategies discussed in

Subsection 8.3.3 suffices to achieve the simulations. To this end, p and q will denote arbitrary mathematical relations throughout this proof.

In order not to obscure the argument with heavy notation, we shall limit the number of attributes in the relations under consideration. The generalization of our argument, however, will be obvious.

Projection

Let (Ω, ω) be a relation with $\Omega = \{A, B, C\}$ and let $\{r_A, r_B, r_C\}$ be a representation of (Ω, ω). Consider the projection $\pi_{\{A,B\}}(\Omega, \omega)$ of $\{\Omega, \omega\}$ onto $\{A, B\}$. Unfortunately $\{r_A, r_B\}$ in general is *not* a representation of $\pi_{\{A,B\}}(\Omega, \omega)$, simply because some tuples of this projection may be multiply represented. In order to overcome this problem, we "retag" r_A and r_B as follows.

First, consider the relation $r'_A = r_A^{-1} \cdot r_A$. This relation consists of all identical pairs of A-values occurring in ω. Now let

$$s_A = (r'_A)^{\triangleright}_p \cdot r_A^{-1}.$$

Each tag in s_A corresponds to *precisely one* tuple of $\pi_{\{A\}}(\Omega, \omega)$. Moreover, the relation s_A gives the relationship between the "new" and the "old" tags.

Now, let $r'_B = s_A \cdot r_B$ and let

$$s_B = (r'_B)^{\triangleright}_q \cdot r_B^{-1} \cap (r'_B)^{\triangleleft}_q \cdot s_A.$$

Each tag in s_B corresponds to *precisely one* tuple of $\pi_{\{A,B\}}(\Omega, \omega)$. Moreover, the relation s_B gives the relationship between the newly created tags and the original ones. Hence $\{s_B \cdot r_A, s_B \cdot r_B\}$ is a representation of $\pi_{\{A,B\}}(\Omega, \omega)$.

Selection

Let (Ω, ω) be a relation with $\Omega = \{A, B, C\}$ and let $\{r_A, r_B, r_C\}$ be a representation of (Ω, ω). Consider the selection $\sigma_{A=B}(\Omega, \omega)$ of $\{\Omega, \omega\}$.

Let $r = (r_A \cdot r_A^{-1})^{\mathrm{id}}$ be the set of all identical pairs of "tags" used in the representation of (Ω, ω). Let $r_{A,B} = r_A \cdot r_B^{-1} \cap r$. The relation $r_{A,B}$ is the set of all identical pairs of tags corresponding to tuples t of ω with $t(A) = t(B)$. Hence, $\{r_{A,B} \cdot r_A, \ r_{A,B} \cdot r_B, \ r_{A,B} \cdot r_C\}$ is a representation of $\sigma_{A=B}(\Omega, \omega)$.

Union

Let (Ω, ω_1) and (Ω, ω_2) be relations with $\Omega = \{A, B\}$. Let $\{r_{1,A}, r_{1,B}\}$ and $\{r_{2,A}, r_{2,B}\}$ be representations of (Ω, ω_1) and (Ω, ω_2), respectively.

The proof for this case is quite similar to the proof for the case of projection.

First, consider the relation $r'_A = r_{1,A}^{-1} \cdot r_{1,A} \cup r_{2,A}^{-1} \cdot r_{2,A}$ consisting of all identical pairs of A-values occurring in ω_1 or ω_2. Let

$$s_{1,A} = (r'_A)_p^\triangleright \cdot r_{1,A}^{-1},$$
$$s_{2,A} = (r'_A)_p^\triangleright \cdot r_{2,A}^{-1}.$$

Each tag value introduced above corresponds to *precisely one* tuple of $\pi_{\{A\}}(\Omega, \omega_1 \cup \omega_2)$. Moreover, $s_{1,A}$ and $s_{2,A}$ give the relationship between the "new" and the "old" tags.

Now, let $r'_B = s_{1,A} \cdot r_{1,B} \cup s_{2,A} \cdot r_{2,B}$ and let

$$s_{1,B} = (r'_B)_q^\triangleright \cdot r_{1,B}^{-1} \cap (r'_B)_q^\triangleleft \cdot s_{1,A},$$
$$s_{2,B} = (r'_B)_q^\triangleright \cdot r_{2,B}^{-1} \cap (r'_B)_q^\triangleleft \cdot s_{2,A}.$$

Each tag value introduced above corresponds to *precisely one* tuple of $(\Omega, \omega_1 \cup \omega_2)$. Moreover, $s_{1,A}$ and $s_{2,A}$ give the relationship between the newly created tags and the original ones. Hence $\{s_{1,B} \cdot r_{1,A} \cup s_{2,B} \cdot r_{2,A}, \ s_{1,B} \cdot r_{1,B} \cup s_{2,B} \cdot r_{2,B}\}$ is a representation of $(\Omega, \omega_1 \cup \omega_2)$.

Difference

Let (Ω, ω_1) and (Ω, ω_2) be relations with $\Omega = \{A, B, C\}$. Let $\{r_{1,A}, r_{1,B}, r_{1,C}\}$ and $\{r_{2,A}, r_{2_B}, r_{2,C}\}$ be representations of (Ω, ω_1) and (Ω, ω_2), respectively. Let

$$r = r_{1,A} \cdot r_{2,A}^{-1} \cap r_{1,B} \cdot r_{2,B}^{-1} \cap r_{1,C} \cdot r_{2,C}^{-1}.$$

Let ρ_1 and ρ_2 be the representation function used for representing (Ω, ω_1) respectively (Ω, ω_2). Then $r = \{(\rho_1(t), \rho_2(t)) | t \in \omega_1 \cap \omega_2\}$. Now let $s = (r_{1,A} \cdot r_{1,A}^{-1})^{\mathrm{id}} - (r \cdot r^{-1})^{\mathrm{id}}$. Then $s = \{(\rho_1(t), \rho_1(t)) | t \in \omega_1 - \omega_2\}$. Hence $\{s \cdot r_A, \ s \cdot r_B, \ s \cdot r_C\}$ is a representation of $(\Omega_1, \omega_1 - \omega_2)$.

Cartesian product

Finally, let us consider the Cartesian product $(\Omega_1 \cup \Omega_2, \omega_1 \times \omega_2)$ of two relations (Ω_1, ω_1) and (Ω_2, ω_2), $\Omega_1 \cap \Omega_2 = \emptyset$, with $\Omega_1 = \{A, B, C\}$

r'_A	
a	a
b	b

s_A	
5	1
5	2
5	3
6	4

r'_B	
5	b
5	c
6	c

s_B	
7	1
7	2
8	3
9	4

FIGURE 8.14

Computing a representation of a projection

and $\Omega_2 = \{D, E\}$. Let $\{r_A, r_B, r_C\}$ be a representation of (Ω_1, ω_1) and let $\{r_D, r_E\}$ be a representation of (Ω_2, ω_2). Let $r_1 = (r_A \cdot r_A^{-1})^{\mathrm{id}}$, $r_2 = (r_D \cdot r_D^{-1})^{\mathrm{id}}$ and $r = (r_1 \cup r_2)^{\mathrm{un}}$. Let $s = r_1 \cdot r \cdot r_2$. Then $s = \{(\rho_1(t_1), \rho_2(t_2)) \mid t_1 \in \omega_1 \wedge t_2 \in \omega_2\}$. Hence $\{s_p^{\triangleleft} \cdot r_A,\ s_p^{\triangleleft} \cdot r_B,\ s_p^{\triangleleft} \cdot r_C,\ s_p^{\triangleright} \cdot r_D,\ s_p^{\triangleright} \cdot r_E\}$ is a representation of $(\Omega_1 \cup \Omega_2, \omega_1 \times \omega_2)$. ∎

EXAMPLE 8.3

To illustrate some of the constructions in the proof of Theorem 8.1, consider the Codd relation (Ω, ω) and its representation $\{r_A, r_B, r_C\}$ shown in Figure 8.13 and consider the projection $\pi_{\{A,B\}}(\Omega, \omega)$. The corresponding auxiliary relations r'_A, s_A, r'_B and s_B defined in the proof are shown in Figure 8.14.

The set of relations $\{s_B \cdot r_A, s_B \cdot r_B\}$ shown in Figure 8.15 is a representation of $\pi_{\{A,B\}}(\Omega, \omega)$.

$s_B \cdot r_A$	
7	a
8	a
9	b

$s_B \cdot r_B$	
7	b
8	c
9	c

FIGURE 8.15

Representation of a projection

8.4.2   Nested Model

In this subsection, we discuss the simulation of the nested model (e.g., [Schek and Scholl 1986, Thomas and Fischer 1986]) in the Tarski approach.

We use the formalism of [Gyssens et al. 1989, Gyssens and Van Gucht 1991] here.

$$\nu_{\{A\}}(\Omega, \omega)$$

A	$\{B\}$

	B
a	b
	c

	B
d	b
	c

	B
c	a

$$(\Omega, \omega)$$

A	B
a	b
a	c
d	b
d	c
c	a

$$\nu_{\{B\}}\nu_{\{A\}}(\Omega, \omega)$$

$\{A\}$	$\{B\}$

A	B
a	b
d	c

A	B
c	a

FIGURE 8.16

Nesting a relation

For the sake of concreteness and clarity, we shall use the very simple Codd relation (Ω, ω) shown in Figure 8.16 *(left)* as a running example. Figure 8.16 *(middle)* shows $\nu_{\{A\}}(\Omega, \omega)$, the result of nesting (Ω, ω) over $\{A\}$ and Figure 8.16 *(right)* shows $\nu_{\{B\}}\nu_{\{A\}}(\Omega, \omega)$, the result of nesting $\nu_{\{A\}}(\Omega, \omega)$ over $\{B\}$.

Ways of representing nested relations have already been discussed in the Introduction. We shall therefore concentrate on how these representations can be obtained in the Tarski algebra, starting for instance from the representation of a flat relation.

Therefore, let $\{r_A, r_B\}$ be some representation of (Ω, ω) in the Tarski model. By Theorem 8.1, we know that there exists a representation r'_{AB} of $\pi_{\{A\}}(\Omega, \omega)$, as shown in Figure 8.17 *(left)*. Figure 8.17 *(middle)* shows the relation $r'_B = r'_{AB} \cdot (r_A)^{-1} \cdot r_B$.

r'_{AB}		r'_B		r'	
1	a	1	b	1	1
2	d	1	c	1	2
3	c	2	b	2	1
		2	c	2	2
		3	a	3	3

FIGURE 8.17
A representation of $\nu_{\{A\}}(\Omega, \omega)$

Alternatively, the tags in Figure 8.17 can be interpreted as representing the sets of B-values occurring in $\nu_{\{A\}}(\Omega, \omega)$. From this standpoint, the relation in Figure 8.17 *(left)* can be seen as associating A-values with tags representing sets of B-values while the relation in Figure 8.17 *(middle)* identifies these sets.

Unfortunately, and contrary to the representation proposed in the Introduction, the same set of B-values can have more than one tag, as is the case in our example. Although we cannot do away with multiply represented sets in the Tarski algebra, we can compute all pairs of tags representing the same set. Turning to our example, let

$$\tilde{r}'_B = r'_B \cdot (r'_B)^{\mathrm{un}} \cdot r'_B - r'_B$$

In $\tilde{r}'_B$, each tag value is associated to all values *not* belonging to the set of B-values identified by that tag. Using the set-theoretical property that two sets are different if and only if the first set and the complement of the second have a nonempty intersection, it follows that $r'_B \cdot (\tilde{r}'_B)^{-1}$ is the set of all pairs of tags representing different sets of B-values and that

$$r' = r'_B \cdot (r'_B)^{\mathrm{un}} \cdot (r'_B)^{-1} - r'_B \cdot (\tilde{r}'_B)^{-1}$$

shown in Figure 8.17 *(right)* is the set of all pairs of tags representing the same set of B-values.

Hence $\{r'_{AB}, r'_B, r'\}$ can be seen as a representation of $\nu_{\{A\}}(\Omega, \omega)$.

Figure 8.18 shows a possible representation of $\nu_{\{B\}}\nu_{\{A\}}(\Omega, \omega)$. The tags in $r''_A = r' \cdot r'_{AB}$ can also be seen as representing the sets of A-values occurring in $\nu_{\{B\}}\nu_{\{A\}}(\Omega, \omega)$. $r''_B = r'_B$ still shows the set of B-values in $\nu_{\{B\}}\nu_{\{A\}}(\Omega, \omega)$.

r''_{AB}	
1	1
2	2
3	3

r''_A	
1	a
1	d
2	a
2	d
3	c

r''_B	
1	b
1	c
2	b
2	c
3	a

r''	
1	1
1	2
2	1
2	2
3	3

FIGURE 8.18
A representation of $\nu_{\{B\}}\nu_{\{A\}}(\Omega, \omega)$

$r''_{AB} = r'_A \cdot (r'_A)^{-1}$ associates sets of A-values and sets of B-values and, finally, $r'' = r'$ indicates which pairs of tags identify the same set of B-values (and hence also the same set of A-values).

To some extent, it is remarkable that the nested model can be simulated in the Tarski model without having to add complex constructs to the latter. However, this fact is not so surprising when seen in the perspective of the main result of [Paredaens and Van Gucht 1988]. There it has been shown that all nested algebra queries on flat relations returning a flat relation can be expressed in the flat relational algebra as well. In other words, the nest operator and its counterpart, the unnest operator, do not add anything essential to the language in terms of expressive power and only affect the way in which the data are grouped. In the Tarski algebra, this grouping is achieved using tagging.

8.4.3   GOOD model

In Section 8.2, we already explained how to represent a GOOD instance in the Tarski model. In particular, Figure 8.8 represents the GOOD instance shown in Figure 8.5. In this subsection, we shall discuss how the three queries dealt with in Subsection 8.2.1 and shown in Figure 8.6 can be solved in the Tarski algebra. Due to space limitations, this discussion will be held rather informal. We trust the reader by now has acquired sufficient familiarity with the Tarski algebra to fill in the technical details.

The first query, shown in Figure 8.6 *(left)*, was a node addition adding a new node for each pair of parents having a common child. Using the representation in Figure 8.8, this query can be solved as follows in the Tarski algebra. First, the relation $ch \cdot ch^{-1}$ contains the set of all pairs of parent nodes having a common child. For these, new nodes can be "created" by tagging $ch \cdot ch^{-1}$. The left and right tagging automatically provide representations for the newly introduced edge labels "1" and "2", respectively. A suitable node label for the newly created nodes could be obtained from tagging the relation $(nodelabels^{-1} \cdot nodelabels)^{\mathrm{id}}$ as the tag associated to the pair (P, P).

The second query, shown in Figure 8.6 *(middle)*, was an edge addition associating children directly to parent pairs. In the Tarski representation, a relation representing the edge label c must then be added. This can easily be achieved by composing the relations representing the edge labels "1" and "2" with ch, and taking their intersection.

Finally, the third query, shown in Figure 8.6 *(right)*, was an edge deletion removing all the original parent-children links. This operation can be simulated straightforwardly by "removing" the relation ch.

At this point, it should be emphasized that more elaborate GOOD queries, involving unbounded iteration, *cannot* be expressed in the Tarski algebra. In order to overcome this problem, we shall discuss ways in the next section to extend the Tarski algebra to a computationally complete language.

8.5
The Extended Tarski Algebra

From Theorem 8.1, in which we showed that the Tarski algebra can emulate Codd-relational queries, it follows that the Tarski algebra is at least as expressive as the standard (Codd-) relational algebra. It should be clear however that, as already alluded to at the end of the previous section, there remain queries that cannot be expressed in the Tarski algebra. The classical example of such a query is the *transitive closure* of a binary relation. (If r is a binary relation, then its transitive closure is defined as the smallest relation s containing r, such that whenever (u, v) and (v, w) are in s, (u, w) is also in s.) The usual solution to this problem is to add a looping construct to the language. This will be done in Subsection 8.5.1. To examine the expressiveness of this *extended Tarski algebra*, we need to re-investigate the notion of "generic query". This will be the subject of Subsection 8.5.2. In Section 8.5.3 we will then show that the extended algebra is computationally complete for the class of generic queries defined in Section 8.5.2, thus emphasizing the combined power of tagging and unbounded looping in the context of mathematical relations.

8.5.1   While-expressions

In this subsection, we will introduce the extended Tarski algebra obtained by augmenting the Tarski algebra with assignment statements and while-loops. These additional constructs will be written in a program-like fashion so as to make their semantics obvious.

In the previous section, we saw that in order to simulate a relation or a database in another model, several binary relations are needed. Therefore we shall introduce assignment queries in which several binary relations can be computed in one expression. These assignment queries will then turn out to be key constructs in the definition of an iterative query.

DEFINITION 8.6

Let $\vec{u}_1, \ldots, \vec{u}_l$ be finite sequences of relation variables. An assignment query $E(x_1, \ldots, x_m)$ is an expression of the form:

$$\textbf{query } E(x_1, \ldots, x_m);$$
$$\textbf{begin}$$
$$z_1 := E_1(\vec{u}_1);$$
$$z_2 := E_2(\vec{u}_2);$$
$$\vdots$$
$$z_l := E_l(\vec{u}_l);$$
$$\textbf{return } (y_1, \ldots, y_n)$$
$$\textbf{end},$$

where, for $j = 1, \ldots, l$,

1. *the variables in $\vec{u}_j$ belong to $\{x_1, \ldots, x_m, z_1, \ldots, z_{j-1}\}$;*

2. *z_j may belong to $\{x_1, \ldots, x_m, z_1, \ldots, z_{j-1}\}$; and*

3. *$E_j(\vec{u}_j)$ is an (extended) Tarski algebra expression returning a single relation,*

and $y_1, \ldots, y_n$ belong to $\{x_1, \ldots, x_m, z_1, \ldots, z_l\}$.

Given a relation r, we shall make no distinction between r and the 1-tuple (r). In this way, an assignment query remains meaningful if, for instance, the right-hand side of one of the assignments is in turn an assignment query returning one relation. Conversely, this assumption also allows us to interpret ordinary Tarski algebra expressions as special cases of assignment queries.

Using assignment queries, we can define iterative queries:

DEFINITION 8.7

Let $\vec{u}$ and $\vec{v}$ be finite sequences of variables, and let u_k be the last element of $\vec{u}$. An iterative query $E(x_1, \ldots, x_m)$ is an expression of the form:

> **query** $E(x_1, \ldots, x_m)$;
> > **begin**
> > > $\vec{u} := F(x_1, \ldots, x_m)$;
> > > **while** $u_k \neq \emptyset$
> > > > **do**
> > > > > $\vec{u} := G(\vec{v})$
> > > > **od**;
> > > **return** $(y_1, \ldots, y_n)$
> > **end**,

where $y_1, \ldots, y_m$, and the variables in $\vec{v}$ are in $\vec{u}$ or in $\{x_1, \ldots, x_m\}$, and F and G are assignment queries.

EXAMPLE 8.4

The following is an iterative query for the transitive closure query mentioned in the introduction to this section:

> **query** $E(x)$;
> > **begin**
> > > $y := x$;
> > > $z := y \cdot y - y$;
> > > **while** $z \neq \emptyset$
> > > > **do**
> > > > > $y := y \cup x \cdot y$;
> > > > > $z := y \cdot y - y$;
> > > > **od**;
> > > **return** y
> > **end**.

The smallest set of expressions containing the taes and closed under assignment and iteration will be called the *extended Tarski algebra*; we will denote its expressions as *etae*'s.

We observe that etaes may also contain *conditional statements*. These can indeed be replaced by a number of ordinary assignments as can be easily seen using an argument analogous to the proof of Proposition 8.5.

We claim that adding assignment and iteration to the Tarski algebra makes this query language computationally complete. In order to substantiate this claim, however, we need to review the notion of genericity in the presence of tags.

8.5.2   Generic Queries

In this subsection we will discuss the notion of genericity in query environments wherein tags can be introduced. We would like to emphasize that the contents of this section are completely independent of any specific query language. For us, a *query* is merely a (partial) mapping from $\mathcal{R}^m$ to $\mathcal{R}^n$ for some m and n, where $\mathcal{R}$ is the set of all (mathematical) relations over $V = D \cup T$.

The notion of genericity was introduced by [Aho and Ullman 1979] and [Chandra and Harel 1980] in the relational model and has become a subject of frequent study in other environments (e.g., [Abiteboul and Kanellakis 1989, Abiteboul and Vianu 1990, Hull and Su 1989]). The principle of all notions of genericity that are around is that a generic query should commute with all permutations on the set of data values. While this principle can immediately be applied to, e.g., the relational model, this is not the case for more elaborate database models where the result of a query may contain objects or values not present in one of the arguments. In these cases, the original permutation must first be extended in some "natural" way to the newly introduced objects or values.

Therefore we shall first discuss how a permutation ψ on the set of data values can naturally be extended to a permutation ψ^e on V. This will be done in an iterative way. Let $D_0 = D$, and let for all $i \geq 0$, V_i be the largest subset of V (cfr. Subsection 8.3.3) in which only values from D_i are used. Finally, let, for all $i \geq 1$, $D_i = D \cup \tau(V_{i-1})$. (All mappings under consideration are assumed to be extended to sets, ordered pairs and relations in the natural way.) We then define ψ^e recursively: if $v \in D_0 = D$ then $\psi^e(v) = \psi(v)$, otherwise, if $v \in D_i$, $i \geq 1$, and $\tau^{-1}(v) = (s, t)$, then $\psi^e(v) = \tau\big(\psi^e(s), \psi^e(t)\big)$. Let $D_\infty = \bigcup_{i \geq 0} D_i$. Clearly D_∞ is a subset of V. We will make the assumption that D_∞ is equal to V, i.e., that all tag values in T are effectively used.

LEMMA 8.1

The function ψ^e has the following properties:

1. *the restriction of ψ^e to D equals ψ,*

2. *the restriction of ψ^e to T equals $\tau \psi^e \tau^{-1}$, and*

3. *ψ^e is a permutation on V.*

PROOF

Since Properties 1 and 2 follow directly from the definition of ψ^e, we immediately turn to Property 3. Since $V = \bigcup_{i \geq 0} D_i$ and $D_{i-1} \subseteq D_i$ for $i \geq 0$, it suffices to establish by induction that for each i, $i \geq 0$, the restriction of ψ^e to D_i is a permutation on D_i. Since $D_0 = D$, it follows from Property 1 that ψ^e is permutation on D_0. Assume that ψ^e is a permutation on D_i, $i \geq 0$. We need to prove that ψ^e is also a permutation on D_{i+1}.

First, we show that ψ^e is an injection. Therefore, let x_1, $x_2 \in D_{i+1}$ be such that $\psi^e(x_1) = \psi^e(x_2)$. If x_1 and x_2 are both in D_i, then $x_1 = x_2$, by the induction hypothesis. So assume that one of these two values, say x_1, is an element of $D_{i+1} - D_i$. Let $(s_1, t_1) \in \mathcal{V}_i$ be such that $\tau(s_1, t_1) = x_1$. Then by Property 2, $\psi^e(x_1) = \tau(\psi^e(s_1), \psi(t_1))$. If x_2 would be in D_0 then $\psi^e(x_2) = \psi(x_2) = \tau(\psi^e(s_1), \psi(t_1)) = \psi^e(x_1)$, a contradiction, because $\psi(x_2)$ is in D. Hence for some k, $0 \leq k \leq i$, there exists (s_2, t_2) in $\mathcal{V}_k$ (and hence also in $\mathcal{V}_i$) such that $\tau(s_2, t_2) = x_2$. Then by Property 2, $\psi^e(x_2) = \tau(\psi^e(s_2), \psi(t_2))$. Now, because $\psi^e(x_1) = \psi^e(x_2)$ and τ is a bijection, it follows that $(\psi^e(s_1), \psi^e(t_1)) = (\psi^e(s_2), \psi^e(t_1))$. Since s_1, s_2, t_1 and t_2 take all their values in D_i, it follows by induction that $(s_1, t_1) = (s_2, t_2)$ and therefore $x_1 = x_2$. Thus we have established that ψ^e is an injection on D_{i+1}.

Let us now finally prove that ψ^e is also a surjection. Let $x \in D_{i+1}$. If $x \in D_i$, it follows from the induction hypothesis that x is in the range of ψ^e restricted to D_i and we are done. Therefore assume that $x \in D_{i+1} - D_i$ and let $(s, t) \in \mathcal{V}_i$ be such that $\tau(s, t) = x$. Since s and t take all their values in D_i, it follows from the induction hypothesis that there exist an s' and a t', which take their values in D_i, such that $\psi^e(s') = s$ and $\psi^e(t') = t$. By Property 2 it now easily follows that $x = \psi^e(\tau(\gamma', t'))$. Thus ψ^e is also a surjection on D_{i+1}, completing the proof.

■

In Lemma 8.1 we established that any permutation ψ on D can be extended to a permutation ψ^e on V such that this extension *permutes* with the tagging function τ on T. In the next theorem we will establish that ψ^e is the *only* extension with this property.

THEOREM 8.2

Let ψ be a permutation on D. Then there exists a unique permutation ϕ on V that is an extension of ψ such that the restriction of ϕ to T equals $\tau\phi\tau^{-1}$.

PROOF

The existence of the permutation ϕ follows from Lemma 8.1. We now show that there is only one such permutation.

Let ϕ_1 and ϕ_2 be permutations on V that are both extensions of ψ and that both permute with τ on T. Reconsider the sets D_i ($i \geq 0$). We will prove by induction that ϕ_1 and ϕ_2 agree on D_i for each $i \geq 0$. Since $V = \bigcup_{i \geq 0} D_i$ it will then follow that $\phi_1 = \phi_2$.

Since $D_0 = D$, it follows immediately that ϕ_1 and ϕ_2 agree on D_0. Assume by induction that ϕ_1 and ϕ_2 agree on D_i ($i \geq 0$). We need to prove that ϕ_1 and ϕ_2 also agree on D_{i+1}. Let therefore $x \in D_{i+1} - D_i$. Then there exists $(s,t) \in V_i$ be such that $\tau(s,t) = x$. Since s and t take all their values in D_i, it follows from the induction hypothesis that $\phi_1(s,t) = \phi_2(s,t)$ and therefore also that $\tau\big(\phi_1(s,t)\big) = \tau\big(\phi_2(s,t)\big)$. Because both ϕ_1 and ϕ_2 permute with τ and because $x = \tau(s,t)$, it follows that $\phi_1(x) = \phi_2(x)$. Hence, ϕ_1 and ϕ_2 also agree on D_{i+1}. ∎

Let us denote by $\mathcal{S}_\tau$ the set of all permutations on V that permute with τ on T. Theorem 8.2 establishes that there is an injective mapping from the set of permutations over D into $\mathcal{S}_\tau$. This mapping sends a permutation ψ on D to its unique extension ψ^e on V that permutes with τ. In the next theorem, we will establish that this mapping is actually a bijection.

THEOREM 8.3

Let ϕ be a permutation over V that permutes with τ on T. Then there exists a permutation ψ over D such that $\psi^e = \phi$, where ψ^e is the unique extension of ψ the restriction of which to T permutes with τ.

PROOF

First we show that the restriction of ϕ to D must be a permutation on D.

Let $x \in D$ and consider $\phi(x)$. We need to show that $\phi(x)$ is in D. Assume that $\phi(x) \in T$ Since $T = \bigcup_{i \geq 0} D_i - D_0$, it follows that there exists a context s and a pair t taking their values in V such that $\phi(x) = \tau(s,t)$. Thus $x = \phi^{-1}\big(\tau(s,t)\big)$. Because the restriction of ϕ to T permutes with

τ, it follows that also $x = \tau\big(\phi^{-1}(s), \phi^{-1}(t)\big)$ implying that $x \in T$, a contradiction.

Next we need to show that if $x \in T$ then $\phi(x)$ is also in T. Since $x \in T$, we can again find a context s' and a pair t' taking their values in V such that $x = \tau(s', t')$. Thus $\phi(x) = \phi\big(\tau(s', t')\big) = \tau\big(\phi(s'), \phi(t')\big)$ is also in T.

Having established that the restriction to D of ϕ is a permutation on D, let ψ be this restriction. The theorem then immediately follows from Theorem 8.2. ∎

Theorem 8.3 states that there is natural bijection between the set of permutations over D and the set $\mathcal{S}_\tau$ of permutations over V that permute with τ on T. This allows us to finally define in a natural way the concept of a τ-generic query in the context of tagging.

DEFINITION 8.8

A query $Q : \mathcal{R}^m \to \mathcal{R}^n$ is τ-generic if for each $\phi \in \mathcal{S}_\tau$ and for each sequence of relations $r_1, \ldots, r_m$ in $\mathcal{R}$ such that $Q(r_1, \ldots, r_m)$ is defined, one has that

$$\phi\big(Q(r_1, \ldots, r_m)\big) = Q\big(\phi(r_1, \ldots, r_m)\big).$$

In the following proposition we establish that all the operators of the Tarski algebra define τ-generic queries.

PROPOSITION 8.6

The union, composition, inverse, complement, left-tagging, and right-tagging operators define τ-generic queries.

PROOF

We will only prove this proposition for the left-tagging operator. Let r and s be relations and let $\phi \in \mathcal{S}_\tau$. We have to establish that $\phi(r_s^\triangleleft) = \phi(r)_{\phi(s)}^\triangleleft$. Let $t \in \phi(r_s^\triangleleft)$. Then there exists a pair $(v, w) \in r$ such that

$$t = \Big(\phi\big(\tau(s, (v, w))\big), \phi(v)\Big).$$

Since the restriction of ϕ to T permutes with τ,

$$t = \Big(\tau\big(\phi(s), \phi(v, w)\big), \phi(v)\Big).$$

Thus $t \in \phi(r)^q_{\phi(s)}$. A similar argument can be made to show the converse.

■

We can now state our first main result.

THEOREM 8.4

If E is an extended Tarski expression then E defines a τ-generic query.

PROOF

This theorem follows by induction from Proposition 8.6.   ■

8.5.3   Computational Completeness of the Extended Tarski Algebra

In this section we will establish that the extended Tarski algebra (relative to a fixed computable tagging function τ) is a computationally complete language for a large class of τ-generic queries.

In the previous subsection, we "decomposed" the set V of all values into a hierarchy of layers D_i. In order to define the class of τ-generic queries for which we will show the completeness of the extended Tarski algebra, we need to elaborate a little further on this decomposition into layers.

DEFINITION 8.9

Let τ be a tagging function. Let $W \subseteq V$. We define recursively:

1. *$W_0 = W$,*

2. *$\mathcal{W}_i$, $i \geq 0$, is the largest subset of $\mathcal{V}$ in which only values from W_i are used; and*

3. *for $i > 0$, $W_i = W \cup \tau(\mathcal{W}_{i-1})$.*

The set $W_\infty = \bigcup_{i \geq 0} W_i$ is called the natural extension of W (with respect to τ).

DEFINITION 8.10

Let τ be a tagging function. A query $Q : \mathcal{R}^m \to \mathcal{R}^n$ is called τ-domain-preserving if for all relations $r_1, \ldots, r_m$,

$$Q(r_1, \ldots, r_m)\!\downarrow \; \subseteq (r_1\!\downarrow \; \cup \ldots \cup \; r_m\!\downarrow)_\infty,$$

with $(r_1\!\downarrow \; \cup \ldots \cup \; r_m\!\downarrow)_\infty$ the natural extension of $r_1\!\downarrow \; \cup \ldots \cup \; r_m\!\downarrow$ with respect to τ.

The notion of *domain-preserving* originates from the fact that the (extended) Tarski algebra only allows for tagging, and not for "de-tagging." A query such as "find the minimal set of data values necessary to generate all values of a given input relation" is clearly beyond the power of the Tarski operators and must therefore be excluded.

The second main result of this section is the following theorem:

THEOREM 8.5

Let τ be a computable tagging function. The extended Tarski algebra with tagging function τ is complete for the class of computable, τ-domain-preserving, τ-generic queries.

By Theorem 8.4, each extended Tarski expression defines a τ-generic query, which is obviously τ-domain-preserving and computable. The proof of the converse follows that of a theorem by [Abiteboul and Vianu 1990 (Theorem 3.2.2, p. 212)]. Due to space limitations, it is not explicited here. We just mention that from the proof it follows that each of three tagging strategies discussed in Subsection 8.3.3 (tuple tagging, relation tagging and universal tagging) already suffices to guarantee completeness.

8.6
Directions for Future Research

We conclude this article with a (non-exhaustive) list of topics not addressed in this paper, but clearly relevant for tagged-based database models in general and for the Tarski database model in particular. Specifically, we will discuss:

- *tagging of complex objects* other than ordered pairs;

- *constraints* such as functional dependencies in the Tarski database model; and

- *implementation considerations* for the Tarski database model and the Tarski algebra.

Turning to the first item, it should be emphasized that in this article, we limited ourselves (deliberately) to the use of tagging functions that associate tag values to *ordered pairs*. In Subsection 8.4.2 we showed that, even within this limited setting, it is possible to interpret certain tags as representations for finite sets. We also indicated, however, that, unlike for ordered pairs, we cannot guarantee that a finite set of objects is represented by a *unique* tag. Thus we are confronted with the problem of multiple tags (copies) for the same complex object. A simple way to overcome this problem is to admit tagging functions defined over domains of *complex objects other than ordered pairs*. We could, for example, consider a tagging function associating a unique tag to each finite set of values (i.e., data values or tag values). Such a tagging function would allow the definition of *finite-set tagging operators* in addition to the (ordered-pair) tagging operators already considered in this paper. This approach would of course overcome the multiple-copies problem and would yield a cleaner language to simulate the nested relational algebra. It should however be emphasized that we would still remain within the realm of binary (flat) relations.

An important database design tool for relational database we would like to discuss here in the context of tagging is the theory of *constraints*. The best-known examples of such constraints for Codd-relational databases are functional dependencies. Clearly, it is reasonable to assume that such constraints play as pivotal a role in Tarski-relational databases. The fact we wish to elicit here is that it is possible to use Tarski algebra expressions to formulate such constraints, as was already pointed out by Tarski himself in his original paper on the calculus of (binary) relations [Tarski 1941].

The underlying idea is quite simple. Suppose that we have a binary relation f. In general f will not define a function. However, if we postulate that f satisfies the constraint

$$f^{-1} \cdot f \subseteq f^{id},$$

then f clearly defines a function. This observation is the key to the problem of formulating (general) functional dependencies.

Of course, other types of constraints can equally well be expressed in this way. Suppose for example that we wish to state that r is a transitively closed binary relation. This can be formulated with the constraint $r \cdot r \subseteq r$.

We wish to conclude this article with some observations concerning the (possible) implementation of the Tarski database model and the Tarski algebra. As it turns out, various researchers have proposed storage architectures to facilitate such implementations. We are thinking in particular about the so called *decomposed storage model* [Copeland and Khoshafian 1986, Khoshafian et al. 1987]. In the decomposed storage model, the database is internally stored as a collection of binary relations. So-called *surrogates* (our tags) are used to conceptually connect arbitrary relations. Thus, in a strong sense, the data is highly partitioned.

As discussed convincingly in [Copeland and Khoshafian 1986], however, this storage model offers many advantages. The most striking characteristic is the simplicity and uniformity of the data structures needed to store and access data. This leads in turn to simpler data access methods. In particular, the set of access operations is small and straightforward to implement. On the other hand, due to the fragmentation of the data, access methods typically translate to complex sequences of access operations. The developers of the decomposed storage model justifiably make the analogy to RISC technology for computer hardware. It is in such a sense that we think Tarski algebra expressions can best be viewed. Although each individual operation in such an expression is simple, the complexity resides in the entire expression.

The authors of [Khoshafian et al. 1987] also hint at the potential to support the decomposed storage structure on parallel machines. In summary, there appears evidence in the literature of database systems that the Tarski database model can be effectively and efficiently supported. In an age wherein it is believed that the majority of improvements in performance will come through parallel computation, the Tarski database model presents itself as a serious competitor to the relational database model as a conceptual model to improve the performance of general purpose database management systems.

Acknowledgments

The authors would like to express their gratitude to the following persons: Ed Robertson for discussions about the Tarski approach; Vijay Sarathy and Ed for discussions on the GOOD→Tarski mapping; George Springer for letting us use his "Scheme" programs to manipulate binary relations, which helped us in finding several counterexamples and allowed us to test certain Tarski programs; and Jan Van den Bussche for discussions about the genericity concept. All these persons greatly helped us in clarifying several issues discussed in this paper.

The first author also wishes to acknowledge the financial support of the Belgian National Fund for Scientific Research (NFWO), which enabled him to visit Indiana University, where most of this work was carried out.

Bibliography

[Abiteboul and Kanellakis 1989] Abiteboul S. and Kanellakis P. "Object identity as a query language primitive." In *Proc. ACM SIGMOD Int'l Conf. on Management of Data*, Portland, OR, pp. 159–173.

[Abiteboul and Vianu 1990] Abiteboul S. and Vianu V. "Procedural languages for database queries and updates." *Journal of Computer and System Sciences*, **41**, pp. 181–229.

[Aho and Ullman 1979] Aho A.V. and Ullman J.D. "Universality of data retrieval languages." In *Proc. 6th ACM SIGPLAN-SIGACT Symp. on Princ. Programming Languages*, San Antonio, TX, pp. 110–117.

[Atkinson et al. 1989] Atkinson M., Bancilhon F., DeWitt D., Dittrich K., Maier D., and Zdonik S. "The object-oriented database system manifesto." In *Proc. 1st Int'l Conf. on Deductive and Object-Oriented Databases*, Kyoto, Japan, pp. 40–57.

[Bancilhon 1988] Bancilhon F. "Object-oriented database systems." In *Proc. 7th ACM SIGACT-SIGMOD-SIGART Symp. on Princ. Database Systems*, Austin, TX, pp. 152–162.

[Carey 1987] Carey M.J., ed. Special issue on extensible database systems. *Database Engineering*, **9**, 2, June 1987.

[Chandra and Harel 1980] Chandra A.K. and Harel D. "Computable queries for relational databases." *Journal of Computer and System Sciences*, **21**, pp. 156–178.

[Chen and Warren 1989] Chen W. and Warren D. "C-Logic of complex objects." In *Proc. 8th ACM SIGACT-SIGMOD-SIGART Symp. on Princ. Database Systems*, Portland, OR, pp. 369–378.

[Codd 1970] Codd E.F. "A relational model for large shared data banks." *Communications of the ACM*, **13**, pp. 377–387.

[Codd 1972a] Codd E.F. "Further normalizations of the relational data base model." In *Data Base Systems* (Rustin R., ed.), pp. 33-64. Englewood Cliffs, NJ: Prentice Hall.

[Codd 1972b] Codd E.F. "Relational completeness of database sublanguages." In *Data Base Systems* (Rustin R., ed.), pp. 65-98. Englewood Cliffs, NJ: Prentice Hall.

[Copeland and Khoshafian 1986] Copeland G. and Khoshafian S. "A decomposition storage model." In *Proc. ACM SIGMOD Int'l Conf. on Management of Data*, Austin, TX, pp. 268–279.

[Gyssens et al. 1989] Gyssens M., Paredaens J. and Van Gucht D. "A uniform approach towards handling atomic and structured information in the nested relational database model." *Journal of the ACM*, **36**, pp. 790–825.

[Gyssens et al. 1990a] Gyssens M., Paredaens J. and Van Gucht D. "A graph-oriented object database model." In *Proc. 9th ACM SIGACT-SIGMOD-SIGART Symp. on Princ. Database Systems*, Nashville, TN, pp. 417–424.

[Gyssens et al. 1990b] Gyssens M., Paredaens J. and Van Gucht D. "A graph-oriented object model for database end-user interfaces." In *Proc. ACM SIGMOD Int'l Conf. on Management of Data*, Atlantic City, NJ, pp. 24–33.

[Gyssens and Van Gucht 1991] Gyssens M. and Van Gucht D. "A comparison between algebraic query languages for flat and nested databases." *Theoretical Computer Science*, **87**, pp. 263–286.

[Hull and Su 1989] Hull R. and Su J. "Untyped sets, invention, and computable queries." In *Proc. 8th ACM SIGACT-SIGMOD-SIGART Symp. on Princ. database Systems*, Philadelphia, PA, pp. 347–359.

[Hull and Yoshikawa 1990] Hull R. and Yoshikawa M. "ILOG: Declarative creation and manipulation of object identifiers." In *Proc. 16th Int'l Conf. on Very Large databases* (McLeod D., Sacks-Davis R. and Schek H.-J., eds.), Brisbane, Australia.

[Kifer and Lausen 1989] Kifer M. and Lausen G. "F-logic, a higher-order language for reasoning about objects, inheritance, and scheme." In *Proc. ACM SIGMOD Int'l Conf. on Management of Data*, Portland, OR, pp. 134–146.

[Kim and Lochovsky 1989] Kim W. and Lochovsky F.H., eds. *Object-oriented concepts, databases, and applications*. Reading, MA: Addison-Wesley (ACM Press Frontier Series).

[Khoshafian et al. 1987] Khoshafian S., Copeland G., Jagodits T., Boral H. and Valduriez P. "A query processing strategy for the decomposed storage model." In *Proc. 3rd IEEE Int'l Conf. on Data Engineering*, Los Angeles, CA, pp. 636–643.

[Kraegeloh and Lockemann 1975] Kraegeloh K.-D. and Lockemann P.C. "Hierarchies of data base languages: an example." *Information Systems*, **1**, pp. 79–90.

[Kuper and Vardi 1984] Kuper G.M. and Vardi M.Y. "A new approach to database logic." In *Proc. 3rd ACM SIGACT-SIGMOD Symp. on Princ. Database Systems*, Waterloo, Ont., Canada, pp. 86–96.

[Ore 1962] O. Ore. *Theory of graphs.* Providence, RI: American Mathematical Society.

[Paredaens and Van Gucht 1988] Paredaens J. and Van Gucht D. "Possibilities and limitations of using flat operators in nested algebra expressions." In *Proc. 7th ACM SIGACT-SIGMOD-SIGART Symp. on Princ. database Systems*, Austin, TX, pp. 29–38.

[Schek and Scholl 1986] Schek H.-J. and Scholl M.H. "The relational model with relation-valued attributes." *Information Systems*, **11**, pp. 137–147.

[Stonebraker 1988] Stonebraker M., ed. *Readings in database systems.* San Mateo, CA: Morgan Kaufmann Publishers.

[Tarski 1941] Tarski A. On the calculus of relations. *Journal of Symbolic Logic*, **6**, 1941, pp. 73–89.

[Tarski and Givant 1986] Tarski A. and Givant S. *A formalization of set theory without variables.* Providence, RI: American Mathematical Society.

[Thomas and Fischer 1986] Thomas S.J. and Fischer P.C. "Nested relational structures." In *Advances in Computing Research* Vol. 3: *The Theory of databases* (Kanellakis P.C. and Preparata F.P., eds.), pp. 269–307. Greenwich, CT: JAI Press.

[Zdonik and Maier 1989] Zdonik S.B. and Maier D., eds. *Readings in object-oriented database systems.* San Mateo, CA: Morgan Kaufmann Publishers.

PART III

Object-Oriented and Complex Object Approaches

9

Towards a Unification of Rewrite-Based Optimization Techniques for Object-Oriented Queries

Sophie Cluet
Claude Delobel

9.1
Introduction

Current studies of object-oriented query optimization can be divided into three distinct approaches. The first stems from research on the ORION system [Jenq et al. 90] and has been extended by Kemper and Moerkotte [Kemper and Moerkotte 90]. They consider the various class extensions involved in a query and evaluate what could be a simple selection in an object algebra through joins on these extensions. The second is based on algebraic query rewriting and has a number of followers   including   [Shaw and Zdonik 89a, Beeri and Kornatzky 90, Straube and Özsu 90]. The last approach focuses on method code optimization [Graefe and Maier 89].

In this paper, we propose a formalism that unifies the first two groups, optimization based on classes extensions and algebraic query rewritings.

The approach is simple. It consists of introducing types in algebraic expressions and of reducing complex expressions representing selection, projection or join criterias.

When these different techniques are combined, the number of possible expressions of a simple query is so large that it is fundamental to investigate heuristics to reduce the search space for an equivalent expression, thereby reducing the rewriting phase. The heuristics we advocate rely on the knowledge of indices [Bertino and Kim 89] and object placement policies [Benzaken and Delobel 90]. These two kinds of information can be represented by paths of length equal to or greater than one and by trees, respectively. Accordingly, we have chosen a DAG representation for algebraic expressions into which it is easy to map indices and placement trees.

The information that we use to reduce query rewriting will be useful to the physical level of the optimizer in charge of finding the best implementation of a given algebraic expression and of evaluating its cost.

There exists another technique of optimization that we have not mentioned and that has not been considered much yet in the object-oriented domain: the factorization of common query subexpressions. This technique is definitely important in an environment that involves complex structures and methods. There are two kinds of factorization. Local factorization consists of factorizing subexpressions common to one algebraic operation. Global factorization consists of factorizing subexpressions common to a sequence of algebraic operations that are liable to be evaluated by a single algorithm (e.g., the nested loop algorithm that may evaluate a sequence of join, selection, projection operations). The formalism presented in [Kemper and Moerkotte 90] provides local factorization but does not consider global factorization.

We extended our formalism in a simple manner to provide global factorization. To each sequence of algebraic expressions that may be evaluated as a whole, we associate a unique representation in which the boundaries between subexpressions belonging to distinct algebraic operations are invisible.

Besides the formalization, our contribution is threefold. First, we expand algebraic expressions to introduce precise typing and intermediary variables. This results in a formalism that has the combined power of the algebraic and ORION approaches and provides local factorization. Also, we represent our algebraic expressions using DAG's which allows highlighting information on physical accesses such as indices or object placement policies. Such information is crucial if one wants to limit the number of equivalent candidate query expressions to be considered. Last, we group some chosen sequences of algebraic operations in one unique representation. This grouping provides the factorization of subexpressions common to distinct algebraic operators.

In the next section, we briefly describe the data model and languages that we will use throughout the paper. We explain our motivations and goals in Section 9.3. Sections 9.4, 9.5, and 9.6 introduce our formalism in three stages. We conclude in Section 9.7.

9.2
Preliminaries

We assume the reader to be familiar with object-oriented models and systems [Atkinson et al. 89].

The Data Model

Here we consider a model that is close to the O_2 data model [Deux et al. 90]. The ideas also apply to the optimization of query languages in other data models as well.

The model has classes and concrete types. Each class has a name, defines a structure and a behavior. Classes obey the inheritance principle, and each has an extension, i.e., the set of all their instances. Their instances are called **objects** and respect the encapsulation and identity principles. A concrete type only defines a structure. It may be named or not. Its instances are called **values** and provide neither encapsulation nor identity. A concrete type does not have an extension. Concrete type can also be found in the Exodus data model [Carey et al. 88].

We next present a travel agency database that we will use in the sequel.

The Classes		
Country:	tuple(	name: string, capital: Capital inverse of Capital::country, continent: string ....)
City:	tuple(	name: string, country: Country, brochure: Brochure, info: Information)
Capital is a City	tuple(	country: Country inverse of Country::capital)
Brochure:	tuple(	map: Bitmap, text: Text)
Information:	tuple(	hotels: Set(Hotel), restaurants: Set(Restaurant), day: activities, night: activities)
Destination:	tuple(	city: City, hotel: Hotel)
....		
Employee:	tuple(	cv: CV, sales: set(Sale) inverse of Sale::employee, ...)
CV:	tuple(	name: name, birthplace: birthplace ....)
Sale:	tuple(	dest: Destination, number: integer, amount: float employee: Employee, inverse of Employee::sales, ...)

For instance, an object of class "Country" has two atomic attributes "name" and "continent" and an object attribute "capital". The class "Capital" is a subclass of "City". The attribute "country" has been redefined to be the inverse of attribute "capital" in class "Country". Set-valued attributes are found in class "Information".

The Named Types		
activities:	set(	string)
name:	tuple(	first_name: string,
		last_name: string)
birthplace:	tuple(	city: string,
		country: string)

Concrete type names are in lowercase while class names are capitalized. Class extensions are set **values** that are named after their class.

We will consider *path indices* as defined in [Bertino and Kim 89] but the way we are using them can easily be extended to others. A path index is a data structure which provides a direct backward link.

Indices are defined on a class and a path.

```
create index Country in continent
create index Sale in dest.city.name
```

Objects Placement Policies

The default object storage consists of a single file which objects are stored in the order of their creation. There is one physical record per complex value, string value or object. Each record has an address by which it can be referenced. Records corresponding to complex or string values can only be referenced once while those corresponding to objects may be referenced several times. This is due to the identity principle respected by the latter and that allows sharing of objects.

The database administrator may define other storage policies. For instance, to have all the instances of class "Employee" stored together in one file, one uses the instruction:

```
create group on Employee[1]
```

---

[1]In [Benzaken and Delobel 90], a group of objects stored together is called a cluster. We do not use this word here because it is used for other purposes in other systems.

This kind of policy is the default in most object-oriented systems.

The administrator may also want objects of one class to be stored along with one or more of their components. The following instruction notifies the system that objects of class "Brochure" must be stored in one single file and that each object record must be followed in the file by the records of its two components.

```
create group on Brochure:  (map, text)
```

This last policy is the default one for value components of objects in the Exodus system. It is important to note that, due to the sharing of objects, it is not always possible for the system to follow the placement policies exactly.

In the O_2 system, placement policies are represented by trees. We will present other placement policies on the schema when needed.

Languages

Queries will be expressed in the O_2Query language [Bancilhon et al. 89]. This language does not respect encapsulation in its *ad hoc* mode. An object may be considered as an object or as the value it encapsulates. In the first case, it will be queried through the methods it knows and in the latter by directly accessing its components.

The queries we present, do not use methods. This is why we have not defined any on the sample schema. We assume that a method invoked in a query has no side effects and thus that, as far as rewriting is concerned, a method call is comparable to a field selection. The difference between the two operations would lay in their arity but we will see that our formalism is able to treat n-ary as well as unary operations. The information on a method's possible side effects can be obtained during method code compile time.

We will use algebraic operators that are similar to those defined in the ENCORE data model [Shaw and Zdonik 89a]. They are the following:

- Select(A, λ a (p(a))) selects the elements "a" of set "A" such that "p(a)" holds. Predicate "p" is a combination of the O_2 query language basic Boolean functions.

- Project(A, λ a (f(a))) applies function "f" to the elements of set "A". Function "f" is a combination of the O_2 query language basic functions (e.g., field selection, message sending, tuple construction). This operator is a combination of the ENCORE "Image" and "Project" operators.

- Join(A, B, λ a,b (p(a,b))) joins sets "A" and "B" according to predicate "p". If no predicate is given, the join operation is equivalent to a Cartesian product. In the relational algebra, the join operation takes two sets of tuples and returns a set of tuples. Because of their data model, object algebras work differently. The join operation takes two sets of anything and returns a set of tuples. Thus, each join operation adds a level of tuple nesting. This unfortunately means the loss of the join associativity property as known in the relational model. It is a real handicap. Therefore, we propose the following *ad hoc* variation.

    - If the elements of set "A" are tuple **values** of type $<a_1:e_{a_1}, a_2:e_{a_2}, ..., a_n:e_{a_n}>$ and the elements of set "B" are not, then the result of the join operation is a set of tuple **values** $<a_1:e_{a_1}, a_2:e_{a_2}, ..., a_n:e_{a_n}, b:e_b >$ where e_b represents an element of set "B".

    - If the elements of set "A" and "B" are tuple **values** of type $<a_1:e_{a_1}, a_2:e_{a_2}, ..., a_n:e_{a_n}>$ and $<b_1:e_{b_1}, b_2:e_{b_2}, ..., b_m:e_{b_m}>$, then the result of the join operation is a set of tuple **values** $<a_1:e_{a_1}, a_2:e_{a_2}, ..., a_n:e_{a_n}, b_1:e_{b_1}, b_2:e_{b_2}, ..., b_m:e_{b_m} >$.

    - If the elements of set "A" and "B" are not tuple **values**, then the result of the join operation is a set of tuple **values** $<a:e_a, b:e_b >$ where e_a and e_b represent elements of set "A" and set "B" respectively.

- Union(A, B) performs a union operation between sets "A" and "B".

- Difference(A, B) performs a difference operation between sets "A" and "B".

This set of operators can support the O_2 queries. Higher level operators such as "Nest" and "Unnest" can be defined using these lower-level ones.

The operators are defined on and return set values in contrast with the ENCORE operators that are defined on and return set objects. Thus, the algebra we consider can be compared to complex object algebras (e.g., [Abiteboul and Beeri 87, Schek and Scholl 86, Vandenberg and DeWitt 90]). The fact that we do not generate object identifiers eliminates the distinction that is made in the ENCORE algebra between identity and structural equivalences.

9.3
Motivation and Goals

We intend to give a formal logical layer for an object-oriented query optimizer. We consider three distinct and interesting techniques and we propose a formalism that covers them all. The combination of these different techniques will make it possible to generate a large number of expressions equivalent to a single query. Accordingly, we are also interested in finding heuristics to reduce the search space for an equivalent expression.

The first technique we consider, and that we will call the type-based rewriting technique, was developed for the ORION system [Jenq et al. 90] and extended in [Kemper and Moerkotte 90]. It works on the types involved in a query. In most object-oriented models, to a type corresponds an extension, i.e., the set of all its instances. The technique consists of performing joins between these different extensions to evaluate what could be expressed as a simple algebraic selection operation.

The second technique, which has also been used in relational systems, is algebraic query rewriting based on equivalence of operators (e.g., [Shaw and Zdonik 89a, Beeri and Kornatzky 90, Straube and Özsu 90]).

The last technique concerns common subexpressions factorization. A query in an object-oriented environment may invoke complex methods or follow long paths to access a given component. It would be a great gain not to evaluate the same method or follow the same path twice.

We first study these three approaches separately. Then, we summarize the desired features of our optimization model.

Three Different Approaches

In [Jenq et al. 90], Jenq, et. al. propose a graph-oriented representation of ORION queries and tree traversal algorithms that allows rewritings based on types. This optimization concerns a distributed system but is also relevant in a centralized one. The queries are those of the ORION language first release [Banerjee et al. 1987, Kim 89] that can be translated to a selection operation in an object algebra. This is its main drawback, the ORION technique does not concern other algebraic operations. We will see later that this drawback has been overcome in [Kemper and Moerkotte 90].

Consider the following query:

Query Q1

What are the African capitals where one can scuba dive by day

and swim at midnight?

select c

from c in Capital

where c.country.continent = "Africa" and

"scuba diving" in c.info.day and

"midnight bathing" in c.info.night

□

Its corresponding ORION representation is given in Figure 9.1.

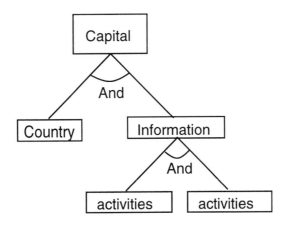

FIGURE 9.1
ORION representation of the query

The tree describes the complex types of the selection criteria. In the ORION data model, an extension is associated to each complex type. Accordingly, to a node we may associate a set.

The tree is first reduced through decomposition into *clusters*. A cluster is a subtree whose root is an attribute node. The tree on Figure 9.1 may be reduced in two ways. We may consider the tree as a whole or build a cluster whose root is the "info" node. Figure 9.2 illustrates this second possibility.

There are three methods for evaluating a cluster.

- The forward traversal starts at the root node of a cluster. It consists of a projection on the children attributes, an evaluation of the qualified

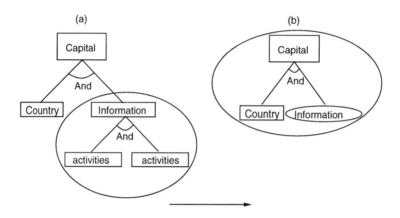

FIGURE 9.2
A reduction of the ORION query tree

children that, then, allows the qualification of their parent. This can
be done algebraically (projection, selection, semi-join) or instance by
instance.

- The backward traversal starts at the cluster leaves. The qualified attributes are evaluated through a selection. Then, a semi join returns
  the qualified parents.

- The mixed traversal combines the two previous methods. Some links are
  evaluated in forward traversals and others in backward traversals. For
  instance, in Figure 9.2 the query may be evaluated through a backward
  traversal from node "Country" to node "Capital" and then through
  a forward traversal toward the node representing the "Informations"
  cluster.

These three kinds of traversals lead to a great number of possible evaluations of the simple Query Q1. They goes from a naïve instance by instance
forward traversal to more complex evaluations involving joins. However, this
approach lacks a formalism that would make it possible to draw a line between
logical and physical optimizations.

In [Kemper and Moerkotte 90], a query expressed in a QUEL-like language is transformed into a procedural language corresponding to a query evaluation plan. The language is composed of low level algebraic operators such as *retrieve* (ordered nested loops), *getasr* (index access), etc. Then, rewriting rules are applied to the new expression. The rewriting rules are defined on the selective part of a query plan and provide a good formalism of the ORION technique. This technique also allows the factorization of the subexpressions common to a selection operation. It seems that expressions common to two distinct operations cannot be factorized.

We next consider the algebra-based rewriting technique. In algebraic terms, the query is the following selection:

Query Expression E1

select (Capital, λ c (c.country.continent = "Africa" and
                     "scuba diving" in c.info.day and
                     "midnight bathing" in c.info.night))

☐

On such a simple query, the only possible transformation is a partitioning of the selection operation. For instance, we can rewrite the query in the following manner:

Query Expression E2

Select (Select (Capital, λ c (c.country.continent = "Africa"))
               λ c2 ("scuba diving" in c2.info.day and
                     "midnight bathing" in c2.info.night))

☐

Assuming that there is an index on the path "country.continent" of the capitals, this rewriting would emphasize the use of that index.

However, there seems to be no way to generate, from this algebraic expression, the join operations that were detected by the ORION technique. Neither is it possible to emphasize the possible use of an index we may have on the path "continent" of the "Country" extension and the inverse property on the attribute "country" of class Capital. In other words, it seems that we cannot transform Expression E1 into the following expression, that first selects the African countries and work from then on to find the appropriate capitals:

Query Expression E3

Project (Select (Select (Country, λ c (c.continent = "Africa"))
                λ c2 ("scuba diving" in c2.capital.info.day and
                        "midnight bathing" in c2.capital.info.night))
            λ c (c.capital))

□

This use of a partial index and of an inverse function is possible with the type-based rewriting technique. It corresponds in ORION to a backward traversal from node "Country" to node "Capital."

On the other hand, the algebraic approach is not limited to the rewriting of selection operations whereas the type-based rewriting technique is. We will illustrate this with an example that features a join operation that is transformed into a selection operation. This kind of transformation, although converse to the ORION ones, is not considered in the type-based rewriting technique.

Consider the following example:

Query Q2

Find the employees who have sold travel to their city of birth.
select e from e in Employee, s in e.sales where e.cv.birthplace.city = s.dest.city.name
□

The algebraic query translation is the following:

Query Expression E4

Project (Select (Join (Employee, Sale, λ e, λ s (s in e.sales))
                λ t (t.e.cv.birthplace.city = t.s.dest.city.name))
            λ t (t.e))

□

Now, let us consider the two following equivalences that we find in [Shaw and Zdonik 89a] and [Shaw and Zdonik 89b].

Equivalence Eq1

Select (Join (A, B, λ a, b (p(a,b))) λ t (p_s(t.a,t.b))) $\equiv$
Join (A, B, λ a, b (p(a,b) and p_s(a,b)))
□

Equivalence Eq2

Project (Join(A, B, λ a, b (p(a, b))) λ t (t.a)) $\equiv$
Select(A, λ a, $\exists$ b (b in Bs and p(a, b)))
$\square$

Equivalence Eq2 only applies if we do not consider duplicates in the resulting set. Using these two equivalences, we can eliminate the query join operation and consider instead the following simple selection:

Query Expression E5

Select(Employee, λ e, $\exists$ s
           (s in e.sales[2] and
               e.cv.birthplace.city = s.dest.city.name))
$\square$

The gain of this transformation is not to consider all the sales of a given employee but, instead, we stop at the first sale that validates the predicate.

Before we go further, we would like to point out a problem one has to consider when studying query optimization in a object-oriented data model where some types do not have an extension. In Query Q2, the definition of variable "s" depends on variable "e." In the corresponding join operation, variable "s" is defined on its membership in the "Sale" extension and the variables dependence is translated with the predicate "(s in e.sales)." Now, supposing that the type associated with variable "s" did not have an extension, this would appear to forbid an algebraic translation. A solution to this problem is to consider two kinds of extensions. Extensions of the first kind are maintained by the database system while extensions of the second are not, but could be evaluated at a huge cost by scanning the database. We call the extensions belonging to the second category "virtual extensions." In the data model we are considering, concrete type extensions are virtual extensions. The rules that manage these unordinary sets are simple enough. Select, projection, union and difference operations are not defined on virtual sets. Join operations between two virtual sets are not considered. One virtual set is accepted in a join operation if the join condition contains a membership test on the variable associated to the virtual set. For instance, the following join expression is acceptable:

Query Expression E6

Join (Informations, activities, λ i, a, (a in i.day))
$\square$

---

[2]Since "s in e.sales" is more specific, "s in Sale" has been omitted.

This join can be evaluated in the following manner:

```
for each i in Informations
    for each a in i.day
        . . .
```

The type-based rewriting technique combined with the algebraic formalism will make it possible to return a large number of expressions equivalent to a single query. In the environment we are considering, the knowledge of placement policies makes it possible to eliminate some of them as irrelevant. For instance, let us consider again the query represented on Figure 9.1 and let us suppose that the database administrator has specified the following storage policy:

```
create group on Capital: (info (day, night))
```

This means that all objects of class "Capital" should be stored along with their "info" component and followed by these component's attribute values. In that case, and in the absence of appropriate indices, we know that it will be more appropriate to evaluate the right part of the tree instance by instance in a forward manner rather than performing a join between the "Capital" and "Informations" extension. For the same reasons, partitioning the two selection conditions concerning the info attribute should not be considered.

Now, we will study the third technique, the factorization of common query subexpressions.

Consider the following query:

Query Q3

Find the employees who have sold travel to their city of birth. Give their names and cities of birth. The travel must be a special offer or have prices greater than $2,000.
select tuple(name: e.cv.name, city: e.cv.birthplace.city)
from e in Employee, s in e.sales
where e.cv.birthplace.city = s.dest.city.name and
        (s.dest = special_offer or s.amount > 2000)
□

This query can be translated into the following algebraic expression:

Query Expression E7

Project (Select (Join (Employee, Sale, λ e, s (s in e.sales))
$$\lambda \text{ t (t.e.cv.birthplace.city} = \text{t.s.dest.city.name and}$$
$$(\text{t.s.dest} = \text{special\_offer or t.s.amount} > 2000)))$$
$$\lambda \text{ t (tuple(name: t.e.cv.name, city: t.e.cv.birthplace.city)))}$$

$\square$

At this point we emphasize the problems that the two approaches studied, so far cannot solve. The operation "e.cv.birthplace.city" is performed twice on the qualified employees, once to test a selection condition and the second time to perform the projection operation. Another point is that this operation is evaluated for every pair (employee, sale) while it only concerns employees. One must remember that in an object-oriented environment, a simple field selection may cause a page fault. Thus, it might be a gain to factorize all possible operations especially if this can be done at reduced cost. However, it seems that none of the two approaches we previously studied can provide an appropriate treatment of these anomalies.

We plan to overcome this drawback.

To Summarize

We consider a formalism for the logical layer of an optimizer. We want it

- *to subsume the type-based rewriting technique and the algebraic approach,*

- *to support information on object placement policies and indices to limit the rewriting phase,*

- *to allow easy and exhaustive factorization of common subexpressions and to detect subexpressions depending on one variable in a multi-variables query.*

We will present our formalism in three stages, each one corresponding to one of our three goals.

9.4
A Simple Idea: a Typed Algebra

With each possible traversal of the ORION tree representing a query, one may associate an algebraic expression. If we consider the query represented in Figure 9.1, a forward instance per instance traversal corresponds to

Expression E1, a mixed traversal starting from node "Country" going backward to node "Capital" and then forward, instance by instance, from node "Capital" to the nodes "activities" corresponds to Expression E3.

However, we have seen that, using algebraic equivalences, it seemed impossible to go from the first algebraic expression to the second. Neither was it possible to generate join operations from a simple selection. These limitations are due to the lack of a good typing information.

To overcome this shortcoming, a simple idea is to consider all the elementary operations involved in an algebraic expression and typae them.

We illustrate this on Expression E1 that is appropriately expanded to incorporate the necessary typing:

Query Expression E8

Select (Capital, $\lambda\ c_a$, $\exists\ c_{ou}$, c_{ont}, i, a_d, a_n,
$\qquad$ (c_{ou} in Country and c_{ont} in string and i in Informations and
$\qquad\qquad a_d$ in activities and a_n in activities and
$\qquad\qquad c_{ou} = c_a$.country and $c_{ont} = c_{ou}$.continent and $i = c_a$.info
$\qquad\qquad$ and $a_d = i$.day and $a_n = i$.night and
$\qquad\qquad c_{ont} = $ "Africa" and "scuba diving" in a_d and
$\qquad\qquad$ "midnight bathing" in a_n))

$\square$

On the first line, we associated a variable with each elementary operation. On the second and third lines, we specified the variable types by their membership in virtual or real extensions. The next two lines define the links between variables and the last line expresses the initial selection condition.

In more formal terms, the selection operation has been expanded in the following manner:

Select(A, λ a, $\exists\ v_1$, v_2, ..., v_n
$\qquad$ ($p_{type}(v_1, v_2, ..., v_n)$
$\qquad\quad$ and $p_{def}(a, v_1, v_2, ..., v_n)$
$\qquad\quad$ and $p_{sel}(a, v_1, v_2, ..., v_n)$))

Predicate p_{type} specifies the variable types and predicate p_{def} defines the links between the different variables. It is important to note that these links express all the elementary operations one has to perform. Predicate p_{sel} is the initial selection condition.

We note that every variable represents a different operation. The expression "c.info" that shows up twice in the original selection has been factorized and appears only once in this new translation. However, this factorization does not satisfy us entirely since it is just local to an operation. We will come back later to this problem.

Now, let us consider a new algebraic equivalence.

Equivalence Eq3

Select(S1, λ s (s.a in S2)) $\equiv$ Project(S2, λ a (inverse(a)))

$\square$

If we apply this equivalence to Expression E8, we may generate a typed version of Expression E3. We previously used equivalence Eq2 to transform a join operation into a selection. It can also be used the other way round and allows us to generate as many joins as possible between the various extensions. For instance, we may generate the following expression:

Query Expression E9

$S_{join} \leftarrow$ (Join (Capital, Informations, λ c_a, i, $\exists$ c_{ou}, c_{ont}, a_d, a_n ,

$(c_{ou}$ in Country and c_{ont} in string and

a_d in activities and a_n in activities

$c_{ou} = c_a$.country and $c_{ont} = c_{ou}$.continent and

$i = c_a$.info and $a_d = i$.day and $a_n = i$.night and

$c_{ont} =$ "Africa" and "scuba diving" in a_d and

"midnight bathing" in a_n)))

Result $\leftarrow$ Project(S_{join}, λ t, $\exists$ c_a,

$(c_a$ in Capital and

$c_a = t.c_a$),

c_a)

$\square$

This expression consists of a join operation, whose condition is the initial selection condition, and of a projection. Other equivalences can be applied to this expression to introduce new selection or join operations.

We notice that the typing we performed on the selection operation has also been performed on the join and projection operations.

The ENCORE algebraic equivalences are adapted to this new formalism in a straightforward manner. Details on this formalism can be found in [Cluet 91].

At this stage we have reached our first goal. By introducing typing and intermediary variables into the algebraic expressions, we made it possible to use equivalences that could not be applied otherwise (e.g., equivalences Eq2 and Eq3 on expression E1) and that generate expressions equivalent to the ORION tree traversals. It is obvious that all the other algebraic equivalences are still applicable. Accordingly, we have a formalism that subsumes the ORION technique and the traditional algebraic formalism.

Another major goal was to support information on object placement policies and indices in order to reduce the rewriting phase. Since this information is represented by trees and paths, we chose a DAG representation for the algebra.

<h1 style="text-align:center">9.5
Graphical Representation of a Typed Algebra</h1>

Let us study the graphical representation of Expression E8 given in Figure 9.3.

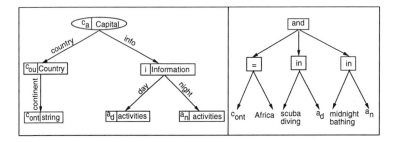

FIGURE 9.3
A Graphical Representation of Expression E8

The selection operation consists of (i) a graph holding the selection variables, their types, the way they are linked and (ii) a tree representing the selection condition.

The graph has two different kinds of nodes. The oval node represents the set on which the selection is made and its associated variable (here c_a:

Capital). Each rectangular node represents an intermediary variable (c_{ou}, c_{ont}, i, a_d, a_n) and its type (p_{type} in the textual representation).

The edges represent the operations that link the variables (p_{def} in the textual representation). There cannot be two edges representing the same operation starting from the same node. This guarantees an exhaustive local factorization and at a lesser cost since the number of edges starting from one node is limited by the type of the node. The operations of the example are unary. However, as we will see later, we can also represent n-ary operations (method calls, tuple construction, ...). An n-ary operation is represented by "n" numbered edges having the same destination.

The initial selection predicate (p_{sel}) is represented by a tree whose leaves are the variables or the constants on which the predicate is defined.

Now, let us map the necessary information on this representation. The result is in Figure 9.4.

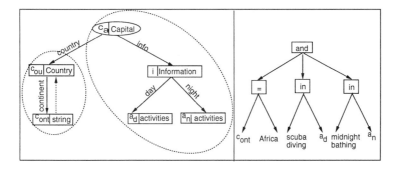

FIGURE 9.4
An Adorned Graphical Representation of Expression E8

In this figure, areas bordered by a dashed line indicate placement trees and the dotted edge represents an index. This information, as we will illustrate it now, is used to limit the rewriting phase.

The first rule to limit rewriting is given below.

Rule R1

In the absence of appropriate indices, it is preferable not to introduce joins on nodes that are in the same dotted area.
□

For instance, nodes c_a, i, a_d and a_n are in the common area that does not contain any index edge. Thus, it is better not to introduce a join between the "Capital" extension of node c_a and the "Informations" extension of node i. Accordingly, Expression E9 would not be generated from this DAG representation. This restriction can easily be understood by the fact that, according to the placement algorithm, the values corresponding to the nodes occurring in the same area are stored in sequential order in the same file.

Another rule concerning placement policies is the following:

Rule R2

In the absence of appropriate indices, it is better not to partition a selection into two if the corresponding nodes are in the same dotted area.

□

For instance, we do not allow a partitioning of the selection operation that would cut the tree formed by nodes i, a_d and a_n into two.

If we do not consider the ordering of the conditions expressed in a selection, rules R1 and R2 leave us with four possible expressions of the query. The one represented on the graph, Expression E3, the following one that we do not type for clarity, and another one that is pretty much the same except for the use of an inverse function:

Query Expression E10

Project (Join (Select (Country, λ c_{ou} (c_{ou}.continent $=$ "Africa")),
           Select (Capital, λ c_a ("scuba diving" in c_a.info.day and
                   "midnight bathing" in c_a.info.night))
       λ c_a, c_{ou} (c_a.country $=$ c_{ou}))
   λ t ($t.c_a$))

□

We have seen some ways to use placement policies to reduce rewriting. This can also be achieved by simply using index information. First, one has to specify the notion of "compulsory index". For instance, one may decide that an index whose path is longer than two and that is not covered by a placement policy area is a "compulsory index".

Rule R3

The branch corresponding to a compulsory index cannot be cut into two by a transformation.

□

Consider the following query:

Query Q4

What are the sales whose amount is greater or equal to $2,000 and whose destination is "Paris"

select s
from s in Sale
where s.dest.city.name = "Paris" and s.amount >= 2000

□

We will suppose that we have the placement policy and index represented in Figure 9.5.

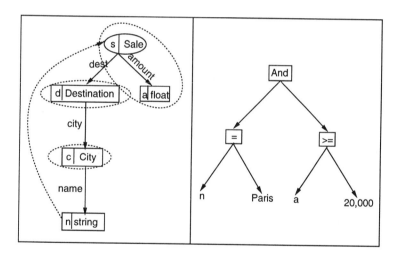

FIGURE 9.5

A Graphical Representation of Query Q4

The index from node n to node s is a compulsory index. Thus, the left branch of the graph cannot be cut by an algebraic transformation.

We now summarize what has been achieved. User queries are transformed into typed algebraic operations that are represented as graphs and that support information on object placement policies and indices. The transformations we perform are based on algebraic equivalences and limited by rules concerning object placement policies and indices. In other words, our optimizer rewriting rules are of the following form:

algebraic condition, system condition → algebraic transformation

The *algebraic condition* specifies the structure of the expression before its transformation, the *system condition* prohibits transformation when the object placement policy and indices context is not right and the *algebraic transformation* specifies the resulting algebraic expression.

At this stage we have reached two out of three goals. We will now see how to achieve global factorization.

9.6
A Global Representation for a Global Factorization

Sequences of join, selection and projection operations can be evaluated by a single algorithm. For instance, Expression E7 can be evaluated by the single nested loop algorithm we gave in Section 9.3. In these sequences, one may find subexpressions common to distinct algebraic operations (e.g., "e.cv.birthplace.city" common to the selection and projection operations of Expression E7). The type-based and algebra-based rewriting techniques cannot detect and factorize these expressions because they consider each algebraic operation separately.

To solve this problem, a simple idea consists of having a global representation for each sequence of algebraic expressions that may be evaluated as a whole. In this global representation, the boundaries between subexpressions belonging to distinct algebraic operations are invisible. This allows exhaustive factorization whereas the previous approaches only considered local factorization. Currently, we only consider sequences of join-selection-projection operations.

We illustrate our meaning by considering the global representation of Expression E7 given in Figure 9.6.

For clarity, we have not adorned the representation. It shows the three

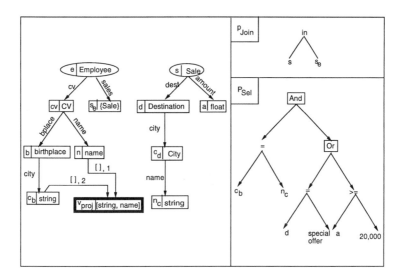

FIGURE 9.6
A graphical representation of Expression E7

algebraic operations of join, selection and projection. It consists of (i) two sub-graphs whose roots represent the sets on which the join operation is performed and whose other nodes indicate intermediary variables representing elementary operations, their types, the way they are linked, (ii) a tree representing the join condition and (iii) a tree representing the selection condition. The variable representing the projection operation is in a bold rectangle (v_{proj}). In this example, the two subgraphs rooted at nodes "Employee" and "Sale" are disjoint. However, this is not always the case.

The graph has two different kinds of nodes. The oval nodes represent the sets on which the operations are defined and their associated variables (e, s) and the rectangular nodes represent the intermediary variables and their types $(cv, b, c_b, n, v_{proj}, s_e, d, c_d, n_c, a)$. The edges represent the operations that link the variables. One may notice the representation of an n-ary operation. The function that constructs a tuple having two attributes is represented by two labeled edges into variable v_{proj}.

This grouped representation of three sequential algebraic operations allows an exhaustive factorization of the common query subexpressions that would not have been possible by considering each operation separately. For instance, the subexpression "e.cv.birthplace.city," that is represented by the intermediary variable c_b, is common to the selection and projection operations and has been factorized. One can also notice two disjoint subgraphs. The first that includes nodes e, cv, b, c_b, n and v_{proj} concerns the operations on the "Employee" objects. The second, that includes nodes s, d, c_d, n_c and a concerns the operations on the "Sale" objects. These disjoint subgraphs indicate that these operations do not have to be evaluated for every pair (Employee, Sale) resulting from the join operation and that it would be a gain to push them out of the join operation.

It is important to understand that this factorization serves as an indication to the physical layer of the optimizer that may ignore it to implement an algorithm that better serves its purpose.

So, once again, we summarize what has been achieved.

User queries are transformed into typed algebraic expressions that are represented as graphs. The typed algebra is now limited to three operators: union, intersection and an operator representing three ordered and sequential operations of join-selection-projection that we call JSP.

The textual expression of this operator is as follows:

$$JSP\ (A,\ B,\ \lambda\ a,\ b,\ \exists\ v_{proj},\ v_1,\ v_2,\ ...,\ v_n$$
$$(p_{type}(v_{proj},\ v_1,\ v_2,\ ...,\ v_n)\ \text{and}\ p_{def}(a,\ b,\ v_{proj},\ v_1,\ v_2,\ ...,\ v_n)\ \text{and}$$
$$p_{join}(a,\ b,\ v_{proj},\ v_1,\ v_2,\ ...,\ v_n))\ \text{and}$$
$$p_{sel}(a,\ b,\ v_{proj},\ v_1,\ v_2,\ ...,\ v_n),$$
$$v_{proj}))$$

Variables a and b are defined on the two sets we are considering. Variables v_{proj}, v_1, v_2, ..., v_n are intermediary variables representing the join, selection and projection elementary operations. Predicate p_{type} defines the intermediary variables types. Predicate p_{join} is the join predicate and predicate p_{sel} is the selection predicate. Variable v_{proj} represents the projection operation.

We note that this operator is also able to represent single selection (B $= \emptyset$, $p_{join} =$ true and $v_{proj} = \epsilon$), projection (B $= \emptyset$, $p_{join} =$ true and $p_{sel} =$ true), and join ($p_{sel} =$ true and $v_{proj} = \epsilon$) or any of the following combinations: join-selection, join-projection and selection-projection.

The transformation from a select-from-where user query to a graphical typed algebra expression is straightforward. Once this transformation is made we have succeeded in a *global factorization* that we will keep through the rewriting process.

As we specified it, rewriting rules consist of three parts: two that are traditional (*algebraic condition* and *algebraic transformation*) plus one that concerns system information and that will be used to *limit the rewriting phase*.

The ENCORE algebraic equivalences are easily adapted to the new formalism. For instance Equivalence Eq1 is translated as follows:

Equivalence Eq4

JSP (A, B, λ a, b, $\exists$ v_{proj}, v_1, v_2, ..., v_n
    (p_{type} and p_{def} and
        p_{join} and
        p_{sel},
        v_{proj}))

$\equiv$

JSP (A, B, λ a, b, $\exists$ v_{proj}, v_1, v_2, ..., v_n
    (p_{type} and p_{def} and
        p_{join} and p_{sel} and
        true,
        v_{proj}))

$\square$

Translations of more complex equivalences can be found in [Cluet 91].

As we have seen, the intermediary variables we included in the algebraic expressions and the appropriate type information give us *the combined power of algebra-based and type-based rewriting techniques*.

So, finally, we have reached the three goals we defined in Section 9.3.

9.7
Conclusion

In this paper, we have presented a formalism that covers the rewriting phase of a query optimizer for an object-oriented database system. It consists of a DAG typed algebra that subsumes the ORION optimization technique [Jenq et al. 90] and the traditional algebraic formalism.

This formalism supports information on object placement policies and indices that are used to considerably reduce the rewriting phase. This information is also useful to the physical level of the optimizer in charge of finding the best implementation of a given algebraic expression and of evaluating its cost.

The formalism we proposed also allows a simple and exhaustive factorization of the common subexpressions of a query and emphasizes the expressions that only depend on one variable in a multi-variables query.

We are now working on extending our formalism to treat nested queries in an appropriate manner. For this, we consider adapting relational techniques as found in [Kim 82, Dayal 87, Muralikrishna 89, Lohman 84].

We also work on a functional optimization technique called memoization [Michie 68] which consists of recording the arguments applied to a given function together with the corresponding results. This technique can advantageously be applied to methods that are called several times in the same query.

Acknowledgements

We wish to express our everlasting gratitude to Serge Abiteboul for his support and enlightened advice. We are also very grateful to Jean-Claude Mamou, Shaun Marsh and Dominique Steve for their great patience in putting up with one of the authors.

Bibliography

[Abiteboul and Beeri 87] Abiteboul S. and Beeri C. "On the Power of Languages for the Manipulation of Complex Objects." *Technical Report*, INRIA, Le Chesnay, France.

[Atkinson et al. 89] Atkinson M., Bancilhon F., DeWitt D., Dittrich K., Maier D., and Zdonik S. "The Object-Oriented System Manifesto." In *Proc. International Conference on Deductive and Object-Oriented Database (DOOD)*. Kyoto: ACM.

[Bancilhon et al. 89] Bancilhon F. and Cluet S. and Delobel C. "Query Languages for Object-Oriented Database Systems: the O2 Proposal." In

Proc. Workshop on Database Programming Languages(DBPL). Salishan Lodge, Oregon.

[Banerjee et al. 1987] Banerjee J. and Kim W. and Kim K. "Queries in Object-Oriented Databases." *Technical Report DB 188-87*, MCC Austin, Texas.

[Beeri and Kornatzky 90] Beeri C. and Kornatzky Y. "Algebraic Optimization of Object-Oriented Query Languages." In *Proc. International Conference on Database Theory (ICDT).* Paris: Springer-Verlag.

[Benzaken and Delobel 90] Benzaken V. and Delobel C. "Enhancing Performance in a Persistent Object Store: Clustering Strategies in O_2." In *Proc. Workshop on Persistent Object Management Stores (POMS).* Martha's Vineyard, Massachusetts.

[Bertino and Kim 89] Bertino E. and Kim W. "Indexing Techniques for Queries on Nested Objects." *IEEE Transaction Knowledge and Date Engineering.*

[Carey et al. 88] Carey M., DeWitt D., and Vandenberg S. "A Data Model and Query Language for EXODUS." In *Proc. SIGMOD.* Chicago: ACM.

[Cluet 91] Cluet S. "Languages et Optimisation de requêtes pour Systèmes de Gestion de Base de données orienté-objet." *PhD Thesis.* Université de Paris-Sud, France.

[Dayal 87] Dayal U. "Of Nests and Trees: A Unified Approach to Processing Queries that Contain Nested Subqueries, Aggregates and Quantifiers." In *Proc. International Conference on Very Large Databases (VLDB).* Brighton.

[Deux et al. 90] Deux O. et al. "The Story of O2." *IEEE Transaction on Knowledge and Date Engineering* **2(1)**.

[Graefe and Maier 89] Graefe G. and Maier D. "Query Optimization in Object-Oriented Database Management Systems with Encapsulated Behavior." *Technical Report*, Oregon Graduate Center, Portland, Oregon.

[Jenq et al. 90] Jenq P., Woelk D., and Kim W., and Lee W. "Query Processing in Distributed ORION." In *Proc. Extending Database Technology (EDBT).* Venice: Springer-Verlag.

[Kemper and Moerkotte 90] Kemper A. and Moerkotte G. "Advanced Query Processing in Object Bases Using Access Support Relations." In *Proc. International Conference on Very Large Databases (VLDB)*. Brisbane.

[Kim 82] Kim W. "On Optimizing SQL-Like Nested Query." *ACM Transaction on Database Systems*. **7(33)**, pp. 443–469.

[Kim 89] Kim W. "A Model of Queries for Object-Oriented Databases." In *Proc. International Conference on Very Large Databases (VLDB)*. Amsterdam.

[Lohman 84] Lohman G. et al. "Optimization of Nested Queries in a Distributed Relational Database." In *Proc. International Conference on Very Large Databases (VLDB)*. Singapore.

[Michie 68] Michie D. "Memo Functions and Machine Learning." *Journal Nature*. **268**, pp. 19–22.

[Muralikrishna 89] Muralikrishna M. "Optimization and Dataflow Algorithms for Nested Tree Queries." In *Proc. International Conference on Very Large Databases (VLDB)*. Amsterdam.

[Schek and Scholl 86] Schek H. J. and Scholl M. H. "The Relational Model with Relation-Valued Attributes." *Journal on Information Systems*. **11(2)**.

[Shaw and Zdonik 89a] Shaw G. and Zdonik S. "An Object-Oriented Query Algebra." In *Proc. Workshop on Database Programming Languages (DBPL)*. Salishan Lodge, Oregon.

[Shaw and Zdonik 89b] Shaw G. and Zdonik S. "Object-Oriented Queries: Equivalence and Optimization." In *Proc. International Conference on Deductive and Object-Oriented Databases (DOOD)*. Kyoto: ACM.

[Straube and Özsu 90] Straube D. and Özsu T. "Queries and Query Processing in Object-Oriented Database Systems." *Technical Report*, University of Alberta, Canada.

[Vandenberg and DeWitt 90] Vanderberg S. and DeWitt D. "An Algebra for Complex Objects with Arrays Identity." *Technical Report*, University of Wisconsin, Madison, USA.

10

Implementation
of the Object-Oriented
Data Model TM

Hennie J. Steenhagen
Peter M.G. Apers

Abstract

Generally, one expects to find the solution to the growing need for database support in non-traditional application domains in object-oriented data models. Currently, at the University of Twente, work is being done on the high-level object-oriented data model **TM**. **TM** is an object-oriented data model, based on an extension of the type theory of Cardelli. **TM** includes a logical formalism for constraint specification, which is an important aspect of the data model, and the notion of predicative sets. Predicative set expressions provide for a high-level, descriptive specification mechanism. Topics of research are the theoretical foundations of **TM**, as well as implementation aspects. Just as in case of relational database systems, algebraic optimization is expected to be an important aspect of efficient implementation of the data model. With this expectation in mind, we have defined the language ADL, an algebraic database language based on the functional programming language FP, designed by Backus. Like FP, ADL is a language in which programs are functions, built up from primitive operators and functionals (higher order functions). In this paper, the main topic is the translation of **TM** to ADL. An algorithm is presented to translate (safe) **TM** expressions into ADL expressions. Furthermore, optimization in ADL is briefly discussed, and some equivalence rules are given.

10.1
Introduction

Nowadays, it has been widely accepted that the relational data model lacks certain modeling capabilities. The strength of the relational model, its simplicity, may at the same time be considered its weakness: in many new application domains, such as CAD/CAM and carthography, and even in the traditional business application domain, the requirement to store all sorts of data in tables causes inconvenience, as well as inefficiency.

Generally, one expects to find the solution to the growing need for database support in non-traditional application domains in object-oriented data models. Object-oriented data models provide for advanced modeling concepts with regard to the structure of the data, as well as the operations on it.

Though object-oriented database systems have been on the market for several years, there still seems to be no general consensus about what constitutes an object-oriented data model. Several lists with 'necessary features,' 'desired features,' 'optional features,' and the like have been published [Atkinson et al. 89, Zdonik and Maier 90]. Moreover, little is known about the theoretical foundations of object-oriented data models and database management systems.

Currently, at the University of Twente, work is being done on the object-oriented data model **TM** [Balsters et al. 90b, Balsters and de Vreeze 91]. Foci of research are the theoretical foundations of **TM** as well as implementation aspects. **TM** is a strongly-typed, object-oriented data model supporting object-oriented concepts such as classes, object identity, complex objects, and multiple inheritance of data, methods, and constraints. As in O_2 [Lécluse and Richard 89], a distinction is made between objects (classes) and values (auxiliary classes). Constraint specification is an important aspect of the data model. In **TM**, it is possible to specify methods as well as constraints on three different levels: on the object, the class extension, and the database state level.

TM is based on the language **FM**, a strongly-typed, functional language, which, in turn, is based on the type system of Cardelli [Cardelli 84]. **FM**, supporting subtyping and inheritance, extends the Cardelli type theory by introducing set constructs and a logical formalism [Balsters et al. 90b]. Moreover, **FM** has been given a simple set-theoretical semantics [Balsters and Fokkinga 91, Balsters and de Vreeze 91, de Vreeze 91].

Refinement of the data model **TM**, still based on well-defined semantics, will take place guided by further study of user requirements in non-traditional application domains (cartography by name). To be able to judge functionality in an early stage, **TM** is implemented using ONTOSindexONTOS, the object-oriented database management system of Ontologic [ONTOS 90]. At the same time, research directed towards efficient implementation of **TM** is progressing. Because **TM** is a language with highly declarative language constructs, and also because **TM** is to be provided with a logical query language, algebraic optimization is expected to be an important aspect of efficient implementation of **TM**, just as in the case of the relational model.

In this paper, the main topic is the translation of **TM** to the language ADL (Algebraic Database Language). ADL is an algebraic language, based on the functional programming language FP, which was designed by Backus, and described in his famous Turing Award paper [Backus 78]. An important feature of FP is the emphasis on function-level programming. In FP, programming consists of nothing but the construction of functions from others by means of functionals, which are higher-order functions. An important advantage of FP is the fact that, because FP is a variable-free language, it is possible to state clear, concise algebraic laws concerning program equivalence. Clearly, equivalence rules form the basis of program transformation and optimization.

The rest of the paper is organized as follows. In Section 10.2, we introduce the data model **TM** by means of an example. In Section 10.3, we informally present the language ADL, and in Section 10.4 the translation of **TM** to ADL is discussed. An algorithm for the translation of (a subset of) **TM** expressions is given. In Section 10.5 we present some equivalence rules, and finally, in Section 10.6, we outline future directions.

10.2
Introduction to TM

This section presents the data model **TM** by means of an example. It is not the intent to treat **TM** in full detail, but only to present those features that are interesting with regard to the translation of **TM** to ADL. For a more detailed overview of **TM** we refer to [Balsters et al. 90b], or the reference manual [Balsters et al. 90a].

In a nutshell, **TM** is a high-level, object-oriented data model, and as such it has the characteristic features of object-oriented data models: classes, object identity, complex objects, and (multiple) inheritance of data, methods, and constraints. Besides classes (objects), **TM** has auxiliary classes (values). The method specification language is essentially of a functional nature, but **TM** also has a general set notion. An important new feature of **TM** is the predicative set construct. **TM** includes a comprehensive constraint definition facility, and for constraint specification, a logical sublanguage based on first order predicate logic has been included.

Below we present the classical example to illustrate the main features of the model.

10.2.1   Example

Consider the following **TM** specification, modeling a database of persons, employees, managers, secretaries, and departments. (Explanation will follow in subsequent sections.)

begin specification

Class Person **with extension** Persons
  attributes
      name   : string
      address : Address
      birthdate : Date
      sex   : string
      spouse   : Person
  object constraints
     p_1 : sex = "M" or sex = "F"
  object methods
    update
    move (in newaddress:Address) =
       self except (address = newaddress)
    retrieval
    age (out int) =
       system_date.year - birthdate.year
end Class Person

Class Employee **ISA** Person **with extension** Employees
  attributes
      salary : int
  object methods
    update
    raise_salary (in amount:int) =
       self except (salary = salary + amount)
  object constraints
     e_1 : salary $> 30,000$ and salary $< 80,000$
end Class Employee

Class Manager **ISA** Employee **with extension** Managers
  object constraints
     m_1 : salary $> 60,000$
end Class Manager

Class Secretary **ISA** Employee **with extension** Secretaries
  end Class Secretary

Class Department **with extension** Departments
  attributes
      name   : string

```
        address    :  Address
        employees :  PEmployee
  object methods
     retrieval
     manager (out Manager) =
        unique  in {m:Manager | m sin self.employees}
  class methods
     retrieval
     emps_living_elsewhere (out PEmployee) =
        unnest (collect {e in d.employees | e.address.city ≠
        d.address.city} for d in self)
  object constraints
```
de_1 :   sum (collect e.salary for e in self.employees) $<$ 800,000

de_2 :   count {m:Manager | m sin self.employees} = 1

end **Class** Department

AuxClass Date
  type
     $\langle$day:int,month:int,year:int$\rangle$
  object constraints
da_1 : $1 \leq$ day **and** day $\leq$ 31

da_2 : $1 \leq$ month **and** month $\leq$ 12

da_3 :   month in {2,4,6,9,11} **implies** day $\neq$ 31

da_4 :   month = 2 **implies** day $\leq$ 29

da_5 :   month = 2 **implies**
        (year **mod** 4 $\neq$ 0 **or**
        (year **mod** 100 = 0 **and** year **mod** 400 $\neq$ 0) **implies** day $\neq$ 29)

end **AuxClass** Date

AuxClass Address
  type
     $\langle$street:string,zipcode:string,city:string$\rangle$
end **AuxClass** Address

Database specification
        system_date :   Date
  database constraints
db_1 :   **forall** m:Manager (**forall** s:Secretary
        (**not exists** e:Employee (m **isa** e **and** s **isa** e)))

end **specification**

10.2.2 Conceptual Schema

A conceptual schema in **TM** consists of a collection of class and auxiliary class definitions and a database specification. In the *class definitions*, the structure of, the constraints holding for, and the operations on the entities of the universe of discourse are specified. In our example, entities of interest are persons, employees (which of course are persons), managers, secretaries (being employees), and departments. *Auxiliary class definitions* are useful to specify complex, dependent entity types. Dependent entities do not exist on their own, but are part of other entities. Dates and addresses are examples of dependent entities.

In the *database specification*, database attributes, database constraints, and database methods are specified. Database attributes are useful to store general database state information, such as the system date, or date of last change. Database constraints are useful to express constraints holding between classes. An example of a database constraint is constraint db_1, stating that a manager cannot be a secretary, and vice versa, i.e., the classes `Manager` and `Secretary` are disjoint. Database methods operate on the database as a whole, regarding the database as a record of classes, and are in fact transactions.

10.2.3 Classes

A class is denoted by its class name. Classes may have several superclasses, specified by the **ISA** clause, and the attributes, object constraints, and methods of the superclasses are inherited by the subclass. Inheritance in **TM** is based on an extension of Cardelli's subtyping relation. Class extensions are explicitly named (though there cannot be more than one).

Structurally class extensions are sets of records, and the names and domains of the record fields (*attributes*) are specified in the **attributes** clause. The **attributes** clause may be omitted in case one or more superclasses are defined. Notice the class `Secretary`, for which no attributes (nor methods nor constraints) are defined.

In **TM** *domains* are either basic domains or composite domains. Basic domains are basic types such as `int`, `real`, `bool`, `string` (and possibly others), class names, and auxiliary class names. Composite domains are record ($\langle \cdot \rangle$) and variant (or union) ($[\cdot]$) domains, and set ($\mathbf{P}\cdot$) and list ($\mathbf{L}\cdot$) domains. The following are examples of domains.

```
int
Employee
```

⟨str_nr:string, zipcode:string, city:string⟩
[home_address:⟨str_nr:string, city:string⟩, pobox:string]
PEmployee
⟨dept:Dept, emps:LEmployee⟩

The domain

[home_address:⟨str_nr:string, city:string⟩, pobox:string]

is an example of a variant domain: a mail address may be either a home address or a post office box.

The domains of the attributes of classes may be arbitrarily complex. Also recursive attribute domain specifications are allowed.

In **TM**, it is possible to specify *constraints* on three different levels: on the level of objects, on the level of class extensions, and on the level of database states [Balsters et al. 90b]. Constraints are labeled predicates. Object constraints should hold for each individual object in a class, class constraints should hold for each class extension, and database constraints (specified in the database specification) should hold for each database extension. Unlike object constraints, class constraints are *not* inherited by subclasses. In general, class constraints do not necessarily hold for subclasses. Consider for example a constraint on the class **Person**, stating that the percentage of female persons must lie between 40 and 60. Certainly in the Netherlands, this constraint does not hold for the subclass **Employee**.

The *methods* specified in a class definition are update or retrieval methods. A further distinction has been made between object and class methods. Subject of object methods are the individual members of a class, whereas in class methods sets of class members are the subject. Method definitions are of the form:

<method name> (**in** <variable-domain list> **out** <domain>) =
    <method body>

The variable-domain list determines the names and domains of the formal input parameters. For retrieval methods the domain of the result of the method has to be specified. For update methods the domain of the result is known (the domain of **self**), so it may be omitted. The method body of a retrieval method and a class update method may be an arbitrary **TM** expression (to be described below); in object update methods, the **self except** construct is used to update attribute values. In the example some update and retrieval methods have been specified.

Besides classes, **TM** has auxiliary classes. Auxiliary classes differ from classes in that auxiliary classes do not have an extension, and instead of an attribute list a *type* is specified. Unlike auxiliary class names, class names may not occur in type specifications, and type specifications may not be recursive. As mentioned already, auxiliary classes are useful to specify complex dependent values (such as addresses and dates) with accompanying constraints and methods.

10.2.4   Expressions

TM expressions include the following: the special expression **self**, constants, variables, parenthesized expressions, and expressions having local definitions, defined with a **where** clause. For each composite domain there exists a collection of domain-specific language constructs to build up expressions of that domain (record, variant, set, and list expressions). Furthermore, **TM** has an if-then-else construct, arithmetical expressions, and aggregate expressions. Important types of expressions are the iteration expressions, for iterating over sets and lists, and predicates. And of course method calls belong to the expression language. Some of these expressions will be described in more detail below.

Self. When used in object constraints or object methods, **self** denotes the object at hand, when used in class constraints or class methods, **self** denotes the class extension.

Record expressions. A record expression is either an explicit record construction (such as ⟨name="Jones",age=37,salary=50,000⟩), a field selection (dot notation), or a record overwriting (used in object update methods). An example of a record overwriting is the expression **self except** (address = newaddress) (the body of the object update method move of the class Person), and the result is a record with the address field modified.

Set expressions. Set expressions are either enumerated set expressions, set expressions obtained through set operators (**union**, **intersect**, **minus**), or predicative set expressions. An example of a predicative set expression is the following expression, delivering the set of employees not living in the city where the department d is located:

$$\{\text{e in d.employees} \mid \text{e.address.city} \neq \text{d.address.city}\}$$

In fact, this expression is an abbreviation of the expression:

```
{e:Employee|e in d.employees and
              e.address.city ≠ d.address.city}
```

Note that predicative set expressions, when evaluated, have set values as a result, so predicative set expressions may, as any other expression, be used as part of other expressions.

List expressions. List expressions are either enumerated list expressions, or expressions built up by the operators **head**, **tail**, and **concat**.

Iteration expressions. Iteration expressions include expressions for selectively collecting or replacing elements of sets or lists, and for nesting and unnesting sets. Nesting is comparable to SQL's GROUP BY operation; unnesting a set of sets results in the union of those sets. We take the following collect expression, which contains a nested collect expression, as an example of an iteration expression:

> **collect** (**collect** e
> > **for** e **in** d.employees
> > **iff** e.address.city ≠ d.address.city)
>
> **for** d **in self**

This expression determines, for each department d, the set of employees not living in the city where d is located. The general format of a collect expression is:

> **collect** <result expression>
> **for** <variable> **in** <operand expression>
> **iff** <predicate>

The meaning of the collect expression is as follows. The operand expression is evaluated, a variable is iterated over the resulting set or list, for each value of the variable it is determined whether the predicate holds, if so, the result expression is evaluated, and this value is included into the resulting set or list. The result expression and the predicate are optional. If the result expression is missing, the set or list elements are included in the result unaltered; if the predicate is missing, the result expression is evaluated for each element of the operand.

Predicates. Predicates, always of type `bool`, are expressions built up by comparison operators, connectives **and**, **or**, **implies**, and **equiv**, negation **not**, and quantifiers **forall** and **exists**. An example of a predicate is the database constraint concerning secretaries and managers:

> **forall** m:Manager (**forall** s:Secretary
>   (**not exists** e:Employee (m **isa** e **and** s **isa** e)))

stating that the classes Manager and Secretary are disjoint.

Some special comparison operators are **isa**, comparing objects of distinct types, such that one is a subtype of the other (equality modulo the subtype relation), $\simeq$ for shallow equality (where = denotes deep equality), **in** and **subset** for element of and subset, and **sin** and **ssubset** for element of and subset modulo the subtype relation.

10.3
Introduction to ADL

ADL is an algebraic language for complex objects. The language is based on the functional programming language FP, designed by Backus [Backus 78]. Independently, Beeri and Kornatzky took a similar approach [Beeri and Kornatzky 90]. ADL and the language defined Beeri and Kornatzky have very much in common. The main difference is that in [Beeri and Kornatzky 90] an abstract definition of the notion of data collection is used. Instead of having, for example, set, list, and array constructors, an abstract type 'constructor' is defined. However, a distinction is made between constructors that are permutable (e.g., the set constructor), constructors that eliminate duplicates (e.g., the set constructor), and constructors that eliminate nulls.

ADL is a typed language consisting of three layers:

- data objects — basic data objects (basic constants or persistent object names) and composite data objects (built up from other data objects by applying data constructors),

- operators — functions operating on data objects, delivering data objects, and

- functionals — higher order functions, having functions or data objects as parameters and delivering functions.

At present, ADL does not have subtyping nor parametric polymorphism.

10.3.1   Data objects

The data types of ADL are basic types or composite types. Basic types are int, real, bool, string, and oid, composite types are set types ($\{\cdot\}$), list types ($[\cdot]$), labeled tuple types ($<\cdot>$) and ordered tuple types ($(\cdot)$), and variant types ($<|\cdot|>$). Types can be arbitrarily nested. The data objects of ADL are either:

- basic data objects: basic constants and persistent object names
- composite data objects: data objects built up from other data objects by applying data constructors.

Let c denote basic constants, let v denote persistent variable names, and let a denote labels, then data objects o are given by the following syntax rule:

$$o ::= c\,|\,v\,|\,\{o,\ldots,o\}\,|\,[o,\ldots,o]\,|\,<a=o,\ldots,a=o>\,|\,(o,\ldots,o)\,|\,<|a=o|>$$

Examples of data objects are the following.

3, true, $\{1,2,3\}$, $\emptyset$, ("Doe", 25), <name="Doe", age=25>, Employees

We often refer to data objects as objects. Notice, however, that in ADL the term 'object' does not have the usual object-oriented connotation 'member of a class,' but instead stands for a value.

10.3.2   Operators

In the FP style of programming operators have only one argument. Multiple arguments are collected in sequences (the sequence constructor is the only data type constructor in FP). In ADL, we use ordered tuples for this purpose.

Operators are functions from data objects to data objects. For each data type a collection of useful operators is defined. Overloading is applied as much as possible, but we do not allow mixing of set and list type operands (e.g. appending a list to a set) for reasons of clarity.

ADL supports the following constructors as operators: the (unary) set constructor $\{\cdot\}$, the (unary) list constructor $[\cdot]$, the labeled tuple constructor $< a_1,\ldots,a_n >$ (where $a_1,\ldots,a_n$ are labels), and the variant constructor $<|\,a\,|>$ (a a label).

Important operators are selectors a (a a label), to select labeled tuple fields, and $s1, s2,\ldots$ (si for $i \in I\!N^+$), to select ordered tuple fields.

Furthermore, we have operators id (identity operator), : (prefix an element to a list or insert an element into a set), + (set union, list append and tuple concatenation), - (set difference and list subtraction), int (set and list intersection), `prod` (Cartesian product of sets or lists), `hd` and `tl` (list head and tail), `flat` (union of set of sets and append of list of lists), `el` (taking the element from a singleton set), `mkset` (converting a list to a set) and `uniq` (removing duplicates from a list). In case of list operators, the order of the operands is preserved in obvious ways.

Aggregate operators supported are `min`, `max`, `cnt`, `sum`, and `avg`. Other operators included in the language are `sort`, for sorting a set or list, and `nest` and `unnest`, for both sets and lists of tuples, defined as in the nested relational model. Some of these operators have an extra parameter indicating the (possibly nested) attribute on which the operation has to take place.

Furthermore, we have arithmetical operators, comparison operators `<`, `<=`, `=`, `=>`, `>` (= also defined for objects of type `oid`), Boolean connectives `or` and `and`, and negation `not`.

10.3.3 Functionals

A functional is a higher order function: a function having functions and objects as parameters and delivering a function as result. Unlike operators, functionals have various arities. Roughly, functionals can be divided into two groups: the non-iteration functionals, and the iteration functionals.

Non-iteration functionals are functionals employed for control or construction. Iteration functionals are functionals mapping functions to elements of aggregate objects such as sets and lists. Iteration functionals correspond to the loop constructs from imperative programming languages.

Definitions are given below. In the definitions, : denotes function application. Notice, however, that : may also denote the prefix operator.

Non-iteration Functionals

Constant. If o is an object, then $\mathtt{C}[\![o]\!] : x = o$. For example, $\mathtt{C}[\![1]\!] : x = 1$, where x is an arbitrary object. This functional is useful to replace constants by functions.

Composition. Sequencing of functions is accomplished by function composition:

$$(f \circ g) : x = f : (g : x)$$

Condition. The condition functional is a ternary functional:

$$(p \to f; g) : x = \begin{cases} f : x & \text{if } p : x \\ g : x & \text{otherwise} \end{cases}$$

Construction. By means of construction it is possible to apply several functions to one object:

$$(f_1, \ldots, f_n) : x = (f_1 : x, \ldots, f_n : x)$$
$$\{f_1, \ldots, f_n\} : x = \{f_1 : x, \ldots, f_n : x\}$$
$$[f_1, \ldots, f_n] : x = [f_1 : x, \ldots, f_n : x]$$

Product. The product functional is used to distribute functions over a tuple of objects:

$$(f_1 \times \cdots \times f_n) : (x_1, \ldots, x_n) = (f_1 : x_1, \ldots, f_n : x_n)$$

The product functional can be expressed by means of construction and selector functions:

$$(f_1 \times \cdots \times f_n) = (f_1 \circ s1, \ldots, f_n \circ sn)$$

and is included in the language to avoid excessive use of selector functions.

Iteration Functionals

Map. The functional `map` applies a function to every element of a set or list. For example, for a list:

$$\mathtt{map}[\![f]\!] : [\,] = [\,]$$
$$\mathtt{map}[\![f]\!] : [x_1, \ldots, x_n] = [f : x_1, \ldots, f : x_n]$$

Restrict. The functional `res` applies a predicate (a function having a Boolean result) to every element of a set or list and includes into the result those elements for which the predicate holds. For example, for a list:

$$\mathtt{res}[\![p]\!] : [\,] = [\,]$$
$$\mathtt{res}[\![p]\!] : [x_1, \ldots, x_n] = \begin{cases} x_1 : {}^1(\mathtt{res}[\![p]\!] : [x_2, \ldots, x_n]) & \text{if } p : x_1 \\ \mathtt{res}[\![p]\!] : [x_2, \ldots, x_n] & \text{otherwise} \end{cases}$$

Generate. The functional `gen` is a combination of the functionals `res` and `map`. The parameters of the functional `gen` are a predicate and a function. To each element of the operand set or list the function is applied, and then it is checked whether the predicate holds for the result of the function application. If so, the result of the function application is included in the result. The functional adds no power to the language, but it is included to be able to apply a function and a predicate to a set or list in succession, without having to create intermediate results (pipelining of operations [Beeri and Kornatzky 90]). For example, for a list:

---

[1]Note this : denotes the prefix operator, prefixing an element to a list (used in infix notation).

$$\texttt{gen}[\![p, f]\!] : [\,] = [\,]$$
$$\texttt{gen}[\![p, f]\!] : [x_1, \ldots, x_n] = \begin{cases} (f:x_1):{}^1(\texttt{gen}[\![p, f]\!]:[x_2, \ldots, x_n]) & \text{if } p:(f:x_1) \\ \texttt{gen}[\![p, f]\!]:[x_2, \ldots, x_n] & \text{otherwise} \end{cases}$$

Accumulate. The functional accumulate is a very powerful functional, which is also known as fold [Turner 85], or insert [Backus 78]. For lists, two different versions of the functional (right and left associative) exist:

$$\texttt{accr}[\![op, z]\!] : [x_1, \ldots, x_n] = x_1 \ op \ (x_2 \ op \ (\cdots (x_n \ op \ z) \cdots))$$
$$\texttt{accl}[\![op, z]\!] : [x_1, \ldots, x_n] = ((\cdots ((z \ op \ x_1) \ op \ x_2) \cdots) op \ x_n)$$

and, if applied to the empty list:

$$\texttt{accr}[\![op, z]\!] : [\,] = z$$
$$\texttt{accl}[\![op, z]\!] : [\,] = z$$

Note *op* is used in infix notation. The functional accumulate is also defined for sets, but then is it required, for the semantics to be well-defined, that the operator *op* is commutative and associative, because sets are unordered. The two versions of accumulate for lists then coincide (`acc`).

Forall and forsome. The forall functional tests whether a predicate holds for all elements of a set or list. For example, for a list:

$$\texttt{all}[\![p]\!] : [\,] = \texttt{true}$$
$$\texttt{all}[\![p]\!] : [x_1, \ldots, x_n] = \begin{cases} \texttt{all}[\![p]\!] : [x_2, \ldots, x_n] & \text{if } p:x_1 \\ \texttt{false} & \text{otherwise} \end{cases}$$

The forsome functional tests whether a predicate holds for at least one element of a set or list. For example, for a list:

$$\texttt{some}[\![p]\!] : [\,] = \texttt{false}$$
$$\texttt{some}[\![p]\!] : [x_1, \ldots, x_n] = \begin{cases} \texttt{true} & \text{if } p:x_1 \\ \texttt{some}[\![p]\!] : [x_2, \ldots, x_n] & \text{otherwise} \end{cases}$$

As is well-known from functional programming, many operators, and all other iteration functionals can be expressed in terms of `acc(1/r)`. This fact may be useful in generalizing equivalence rules and proofs. For lists, some examples using `accr` are given below.

$$\texttt{flat} = \texttt{accr}[\![+, [\,]]\!]$$
$$\texttt{cnt} = \texttt{accr}[\![+ \circ (1 \times \texttt{id}), 0]\!]$$
$$\texttt{sum} = \texttt{accr}[\![+, 0]\!]$$

$$\texttt{map}[\![f]\!] = \texttt{accr}[\![\,: \circ(f \times \texttt{id}), [\,]\,]\!]$$
$$\texttt{res}[\![p]\!] = \texttt{accr}[\![\,+\circ((p \to [\,]; \texttt{C}[\![\,[\,]\,]\!]) \times \texttt{id}), [\,]\,]\!]$$
$$\texttt{all}[\![p]\!] = \texttt{accr}[\![(p \circ s1 \to s2; \texttt{C}[\![\texttt{false}]\!]), \texttt{true}]\!]$$

10.3.4   Expressions

ADL expressions are of the form $f : o$, where f is a function, composed of functionals and operators, and o is an object.

10.4
Translation of TM to ADL

Mapping one typed language to another involves a mapping of types (or classes) and a mapping of expressions. In Section 10.4.1 we discuss the mapping of **TM** class definitions to ADL, in Section 10.4.2 we discuss the mapping of expressions. An example translation will be given in Section 10.4.3.

10.4.1   Translation of Classes

Before we are in the position to discuss translation of **TM** expressions into ADL expressions, we have to decide how to translate the following (related) issues.

- Classes.

- Auxiliary classes.

- Object identity.

- Domains.

- Transparent references (see below).

- Inheritance of data, constraints, and methods.

- Constraints and methods.

Classes may be mapped to ADL object types in many different ways (possibly depending on performance characteristics). Class attributes may be distributed over several ADL object types, different classes may be brought together into one ADL object type, etc. Being the most obvious choice, in this paper we decide to map each **TM** class to one persistent object type in ADL. As a class extension structurally is a set of records, the corresponding persistent object in ADL is a set of labeled tuples.

Auxiliary classes have no extension; when used in object attribute definitions, an auxiliary class name is replaced by its (translated) type specification.

Object identity is implemented by means of object identifiers of type `oid`. Occurrences of class names in object attribute definitions are replaced by the type `oid`.

Mapping of basic or composite *domains* is straightforward: the collection of basic types of **TM** is a subset of the collection of basic types of ADL, and the collection of type (domain) constructors of both languages is identical. As an example we translate the following **TM** specification.

begin specification

AuxClass Date
  type
      ⟨day:int,month:int,year:int⟩
end AuxClass Date

Class Person **with extension** Persons
  attributes
        name   :   string
        birthdate :   Date
        spouse   :   Person
end Class Person

end specification

In ADL this is:

```
type Date = <day:int, month:int, year:int>
type Person = <name:string,
               birthdate:<day:int, month:int, year:int>,
               spouse:oid>
object Persons :   {Person} = ∅
```

In **TM**, relationships between classes are modeled by the use of class names in attribute domain specifications. By means of the dot notation we have direct access to objects being 'referenced' in attribute domain specifications, i.e. *references* are *transparent*. For example, in the **TM** specification above the name of the spouse of some person p is obtained with the expression p.spouse.name. Because class names are replaced by the type `oid`, 'dereferencing' must take place whenever attributes, of which the domain specification contains a class name (one or more), are accessed. In ADL this operation implies a 'join' between the two objects representing the class extensions.

Also *inheritance of data* can be mapped in many different ways. The mapping of inheritance of data in **TM** to ADL is comparable to the mapping of the EER concept of generalization to the relational model. The same options, as for example described in [Elmasri and Navathe 89], are applicable in this case. For example, one way to model inheritance of data on the ADL level is to include the attribute set of the superclass in the attribute set of the subclass(es), meaning that objects belonging to the superclass are distributed over several ADL persistent objects. Another way to model inheritance of data is to leave the attribute sets of sub- and superclasses as they are, and to use oid equality to implement the sub-superclass relationship. This means that attribute values of objects belonging to the superclass are distributed over several ADL persistent objects.

The specific choice of translation of inheritance of data of course influences the translation of constraints and methods. Translation of constraints and methods results in expressions $f:t$, where t, besides objects, also contains formal parameter names (the expression **self** is treated as a formal parameter name). When a method call or a constraint evaluation takes place, the actual parameters are substituted for the formal parameter names.

10.4.2   Translation of TM expressions

In this section we will give the outline of an algorithm to translate a subset of (safe) **TM** expressions to ADL expressions. In doing so, we assume there is no inheritance, and no class names occur in attribute specifications. Translation of inheritance and transparent references presents no fundamental problems, but this way we can concentrate on the translation algorithm itself, without having to take into consideration unnecessary details. Before giving the translation algorithm, we first discuss some general issues concerning safety and the translation of predicative set expressions.

General Considerations

Safety

TM is a language with highly declarative language constructs. Predicative set expressions for instance are in general descriptive, not constructive: it is stated what the result of a query is, not how it should be obtained. In contrast, ADL is essentially a procedural language. ADL expressions represent a specific algorithm to find the answer to a query.

The declarative nature of **TM** causes problems with respect to termination, and even computability. For example, evaluation of the simple expression {x:int |x > 0} will be non-terminating (if it even will get started computing). The expression {x:real|0 < x < 1} not only represents an infinite set, but also a set containing non-computable numbers. On the other hand, ADL expressions always represent finite and computable sets or lists.

To solve this problem we need a notion of safety: **TM** variables are allowed to range over finite sets only. A variable is safe if it ranges over a finite set; an expression is safe if the variables occurring in it are safe. Some examples of safe expressions are the following. Let c be a constant, e a safe set expression, and p a safe predicate.

1. {x:int |x = c }
2. {x:int |x in e and p(x)}
3. {x:int |exists v in e (x = v.a)}
4. {x:int |exists v in e (x = v.a and p(v))}
5. {x:int |exists v in e (x = v.a and p(x))}
6. {x:int |0 < x < 10}
7. {x:int |0 < x < 10 and x mod 2 = 0 }

The notion of safety is needed whenever in **TM** a clause of the form <variable>:<domain> is allowed, i.e. in predicative set expressions and quantified predicates. In [de By 91] a formal notion of safety is defined for a similar language. In the sequel, we assume all **TM** expressions to be translated are safe.

Predicative Set Expressions

Translation of most **TM** constructs and operators in itself is rather simple, because many **TM** constructs have ADL counterparts. Translation of the predicative set construct, however, is not so obvious, due to its possible highly descriptive nature. (Above all, predicative set expressions must be safe, as explained before.)

Considering the expressions listed above, each set is constructed differently. Evaluation of a predicative set expression almost always implies iterating over some set (the first expression being an exception to this rule). The set over which the iteration takes place either has already been constructed (the set e in expressions 2, 3, 4, and 5), or yet has to be constructed (expressions 6 and 7). For expression 6, the evaluation strategy may be to draw consecutive values from the domain of the positive integers, while the predicate holds. For expression 7, the strategy might be to do the same, but to stop when both literals are false, and only to include those integers for which the conjunction is true. For the expressions 2, 3, 4, and 5, evaluation may come down to filtering an existing set (2), applying a function to an existing set (3), or both: filtering before application (4), or application before filtering (5).

There seems to be no general evaluation strategy for predicative sets; the choice of a specific strategy strongly depends on the form of the predicate. It is not clear yet, how, *in general*, predicative set expressions should be translated.

A restricted form of a predicative set expression which is easily translated is $\{v : D \,|\, v \textbf{ in } e \textbf{ and } p\}$, where D is a domain, e a set expression, and p a predicate. This may be abbreviated to $\{v \textbf{ in } e \,|\, p\}$; its translation in ADL is an expression involving the restrict functional. Translation of predicative set expressions in general is a topic of further research.

Algorithm

We present the following simplified syntax for a subset of **TM** expressions. Among other things, variant and list expressions are not included for simplicity. Let v denote variables, c constants, a labels, and e expressions.

$$e ::= \quad be \mid ie$$

$$
\begin{aligned}
be ::= \quad & v \mid c \mid \textbf{self} \mid \\
& \langle a = e, \ldots a = e \rangle \mid e.a \mid \\
& \{e, \ldots, e\} \mid \\
& \textbf{if } e \textbf{ then } e \textbf{ else } e \mid \\
& unop(e) \mid e \; binop \; e
\end{aligned}
$$

$$
\begin{aligned}
ie ::= \quad & \textbf{collect } [e] \textbf{ for } v \textbf{ in } e \; [\textbf{iff } e] \mid \\
& \{v \textbf{ in } e \mid e\}
\end{aligned}
$$

$$unop ::= \textbf{not} \mid \textbf{count} \mid \ldots$$

$$binop ::= \; = \mid + \mid - \mid / \mid * \mid \textbf{and} \mid \textbf{or} \mid \textbf{union} \mid \ldots$$

Translation of a **TM** expression e (which is a constraint specification or a method body) proceeds bottom-up: subexpressions are translated first. Each subexpression of e is translated into an applicative expression $f : t$, where

f is a function and t contains formal parameter names, class extension names, and iteration variables. Iteration variables are the bound variable names used in iteration expressions, predicative set expressions, and quantified predicates. The expression **self**, which denotes an object (in object constraints or object method bodies), or a class extension (in class constraints or class method bodies), is treated as a formal parameter name. In the translation algorithm, formal parameter names, class extension names, and iteration variables are just called variables, or variable names. Ultimately, the expression e is translated into an applicative expression $f:t$, where t no longer contains iteration variables. Iteration variables are eliminated in the translation process.

We have the following translation for the expressions given in the syntax above.

Variables. Assuming identical name spaces, variables v (formal parameter names, class extension names, and iteration variables) are replaced by $\text{id}:v$. The function id is necessary because, as explained above, every subexpression is translated in an applicative expression $f:t$.

Constants. If a constant c occurs in a collect or predicative set expression iterating over variable v then c is replaced by $C[\![c]\!]:v$; if not, then c is replaced by $C[\![c]\!]:self$. Because every subexpression is translated in an applicative expression, the constant functional is given an artificial argument (the most obvious one in the context).

Self. The expression **self** is treated as a formal parameter name (a variable), so it is translated as $\text{id}:self$.

Record construction. Let $e = \langle a_1 = e_1, \ldots a_n = e_n \rangle$ be a record construction, and let $f_i : o_i$ be the translation of the expressions e_i for i within the range. The translation of e is then

$$< a_1, \ldots, a_n > \circ (f_1 \times \cdots \times f_n):(o_1, \ldots, o_n)$$

Field selection. If $f:o$ is the translation of the expression e, then the translation of a field selection $e.a$, where a is an attribute name, is $(a \circ f):o$.

Set enumeration. Let $e = \{e_1, \ldots, e_n\}$ be an enumerated set expression, and let $f_i : o_i$ be the translation of the expressions e_i for i within the range.

The translation of e is then

$$\{f_1 \circ s1, \ldots, f_n \circ sn\} : (o_1, \ldots, o_n)$$

The conditional. Let $f_i : o_i$ be the translation of the expression e_i for $1 \leq i \leq 3$, then the translation of the expression **if** e_1 **then** e_2 **else** e_3 is

$$(f_1 \circ s1 \to f_2 \circ s2; f_3 \circ s3) : (o_1, o_2, o_3)$$

Unary operations. If u is some unary operator, and $f : o$ is the translation of the expression e, then the translation of the expression $u(e)$ is $u' \circ f : o$, where u' is the ADL version of the operator u.

Binary operations. If b is some binary operator, and $f_i : o_i$ is the translation of the expression e_i for $1 \leq i \leq 2$, then the translation of the expression $e_1 \, b \, e_2$ is $b' \circ (f_1 \times f_2) : (o_1, o_2)$, where b' is the ADL version of the operator b.

The collect expression. Let e be the expression **collect** e_1 **for** v **in** e_2 **iff** e_3, where e_2 is a set expression, and let

$f_1 : o_1$ be the translation of the result expression e_1,
$f_2 : o_2$ be the translation of the operand expression e_2,
$f_3 : o_3$ be the translation of the predicate e_3.

Now, whenever a free variable name w occurs in o_1 or o_3, this variable is used in every step of the evaluation of the collect expression. By forming the product of the set $\{w\}$ and the operand object (tuples (w, v) for each v in the operand object), and applying the translated collect function f_1 and predicate f_3 to this product, using appropriate selector functions, we achieve a 'materialization' of iteration over a set or list with a free variable w. Of course o_1 or o_3 may contain several free variables.

So, let V be the set of variable names occurring in o_1 or in o_3. Let FV be the set $V \setminus \{v\}$, the set of free variable names occurring in o_1 or in o_3. Now two cases are distinguished: FV is not empty (free variables in o_1 or o_3, so a product has to be formed) or FV is empty (no free variables in o_1 or o_3; no product has to be formed).

1. $FV \neq \emptyset$. Let n be the cardinality of FV. Define a function $sel :$ $FV \to \{s1, \ldots, s(n+1)\}$, with $sel(x) \in \{s1, \ldots, sn\}$, if $x \in FV$, and $sel(v) = s(n+1)$. The function sel binds each variable to a unique selector. Let o be the ordered tuple $(x_1, \ldots, x_n, o_2)$, where $x_i = x$ if

$sel(x) = si$ for $1 \leq i \leq n$. The tuple o collects all variable names used in the expressions o_1, o_2, and o_3. Replace each $x \in V$ by $sel(x)$ in the expressions o_1 and o_3, and let the results be g_1 and g_3. In the expressions o_1 and o_3, the variable names are replaced by selector functions, so that, instead of objects, we now have functions. Finally, the result of the translation of e is:

$$\texttt{map}[\![f_1 \circ g_1]\!] \circ \texttt{res}[\![f_3 \circ g_3]\!] \circ \texttt{prod} \circ (\underbrace{\{\} \times \cdots \times \{\}}_{n \ times} \times f_2) : o$$

As explained, first tuples $(w_1, \ldots, w_n, v)$ are formed for each free variable w_i and each element v of the operand object, then a restriction on the product takes place, and finally the result is delivered by mapping $f_1 \circ g_1$ to the restricted product.

2. $FV = \emptyset$. Replace each $x \in V$ ($V = \{v\}$) by $\texttt{id}$ in the expressions o_1 and o_3, resulting in g_1 and g_3. The expressions o_1 and o_3 cannot simply be omitted, because they may contain multiple occurrences of v. The result of translation of e is:

$$\texttt{map}[\![f_1 \circ g_1]\!] \circ \texttt{res}[\![f_3 \circ g_3]\!] \circ f_2 : o_2$$

If the result expression e_1 or the **iff** clause are missing, the translation can be easily adapted. If the result expression is missing, i.e., $e = $ **collect for** v **in** e_2 **iff** e_3, we omit the map functional; if the **iff** clause is missing, we omit the restrict functional. If both optional clauses are missing, then the collect expression is equivalent to the operand expression.

Predicative set expressions. Let e be the expression $\{v \textbf{ in } e_1 \mid e_2\}$, and let

$f_1 : o_1$ be the translation of the operand expression e_1,
$f_2 : o_2$ be the translation of the predicate e_2.

Let V be the set of variable names occurring in o_2. Let FV be the set $V \setminus \{v\}$, the set of free variable names occurring in o_2. Again, two cases are distinguished.

1. $FV \neq \emptyset$. Let n be the cardinality of FV. Define the function sel as above. Replace each $x \in V$ by $sel(x)$ in the expression o_2. Let the result be g_2. Let o be the ordered tuple $(x_1, \ldots, x_n, o_1)$, where $x_i = x$ if

$sel(x) = si$ for $1 \leq i \leq n$. The result of the translation now is:

$$\texttt{map}[\![s(n+1)]\!] \circ \texttt{res}[\![f_2 \circ g_2]\!] \circ \texttt{prod} \circ \underbrace{(\{\} \times \cdots \times \{\}}_{n\ times} \times f_1):o$$

Whenever a predicative set expression is a subexpression, and its translation involves a product (that is, free variables occur), then the final result is achieved by a 'projection' on the product.

2. $FV = \emptyset$. Replace in the expression o_2 each $x \in V$ ($V = \{v\}$) by $\texttt{id}$, resulting in g_2. The result is:

$$\texttt{res}[\![f_2 \circ g_2]\!] \circ f_1 : o_1$$

As mentioned before, this form of predicative set expressions is a severely restricted form.

10.4.3   Example translation

To illustrate the algorithm we present the translation of the body of the class retrieval method `emps_living_elsewhere`, which was defined in the example specification given in Section 10.2.1. The result of the method is the set of employees who do not live in the same city as they work in.

In this example, the field selection `d.employees` occurs. Because each class is mapped to one persistent object type, and class names in attribute domain definitions are replaced by oid's, in the translation to ADL a dereference, or 'join,' should be inserted. However, for reasons of simplicity, in this case we translate the expression `d.employees` to the expression `employees ∘ id:d`, without dereferencing, and we assume the selector `employees` delivers the desired result immediately.

In the translation below, translated subexpressions of intermediate forms have been underlined.

The initial expression is:

unnest (
  collect {e **in** d.employees |
           e.address.city $\neq$ d.address.city}
  for d **in self**)

The subexpressions of the nested predicative set expression are translated first. Before translating the entire predicate, the subexpressions of the binary operation are translated.

unnest (
  collect {e **in** employees ∘ id:d |
                address ∘ city ∘ id:e ≠ address ∘ city ∘ id:d }
  for d **in** self)

Translation of the binary operation is easy:

unnest (
  collect {e **in** employees ∘ id:d |
                ≠ ∘(address ∘ city ∘ id × address ∘ city ∘ id):(e, d) }
  for d **in** self)

We see that the expression $o_2 = (e, d)$ has a free variable d, so the first of the two options given above applies. We define $sel(d) = s1, sel(e) = s2$, and substitute:

unnest (
  collect map⟦$s2$⟧∘
    res⟦≠ ∘(address ∘ city ∘ id × address ∘ city ∘ id) ∘ $(s2, s1)$⟧∘
    prod ∘ ({} × employees ∘ id):(d, d)
  for d **in** id:$self$)

For each department, the product is formed of the singleton set containing the department, and the set of employees working for the department. A projection on the desired employee-field follows the restriction on the product. Translation of the collect expression is simple: no free variables occur in $o_1 = (d, d)$, so the second option applies. The ADL version of the **unnest** operator is flat.

flat ∘ map⟦map⟦$s2$⟧∘
  res⟦≠ ∘(address ∘ city ∘ id × address ∘ city ∘ id) ∘ $(s2, s1)$⟧∘
  prod ∘ ({} × employees ∘ id) ∘ (id, id)⟧ ∘ id:$self$

The expression above can, by using algebraic rewrite rules (see Section 10.5), be simplified to:

flat ∘ map⟦map⟦$s2$⟧ ∘ res⟦≠ ∘(address ∘ city × address ∘ city)⟧∘
  prod ∘ ({}, employees)⟧:$self$

The meaning of the result expression is as follows. For each department, the product is formed of the set of employees working for the department, and the singleton set containing the department. Then, for each tuple in the product (for each employee-department pair), it is checked whether the city the employee lives in is different from the city where the department is located. If so, the tuple is included in the result. After that, a field selection has to take place: we are not interested in the product tuples generated, but we only want the employee part (the second field). The final step consists of flattening the result (for each department a set of employees is delivered).

10.5
Optimization in ADL

Algebraic optimization involves the rewriting of an algebraic expression into a semantically equivalent (but syntactically different) expression, which can be evaluated at lower (or even minimal) cost. The rewrite process, being a difficult search problem, must be guided by a set of powerful heuristic rules. In this section, we will present some ADL equivalence rules, which may be useful in the rewriting process.

In [Backus 78] and [Beeri and Kornatzky 90] many examples of useful equivalence rules have been given already. However, in [Beeri and Kornatzky 90] rules are classified by the kinds of operators or functionals occurring in the rule. Here we will try to classify some rules by their intended purpose.

Heuristic optimization rules well-known from relational algebra optimization, such as:

- perform selections and projections as soon as possible,
- perform as many operations as possible during one access (grouping of operations),
- of a cascade of projections perform only the last one,

are just 'instantiations' of the more general optimization goals:

- reduce sizes of intermediate results,
- generate as few intermediate results as possible,
- avoid useless computations.

For these three optimization goals, which are generally valid, and possibly others, we have to find ADL analogues. In addition, we need a collection of equivalence rules that do not so much serve some specific optimization goal, but that are needed in the rewrite process.

Reduce sizes of intermediate results

Pushing restriction. The following equivalence rules are examples of the well-known selection rule, prescribing to perform selections as soon as possible. (Notice that, in general, equivalence rules must be read from left to right to achieve the desired effect.)

- Distributing restriction over binary operators is one example of the selection rule. For $op \in \{\texttt{+},\texttt{-},\texttt{int}\}$, we have:

$$\textbf{res}[\![p]\!] \circ op \equiv op \circ (\textbf{res}[\![p]\!] \times \textbf{res}[\![p]\!])$$

- For pushing a restriction beyond a product we have several rules:

$$\textbf{res}[\![p \circ q]\!] \circ \textbf{prod} \circ (h_1, h_2) \equiv \textbf{prod} \circ (\textbf{res}[\![p]\!] \circ h_1, h_2)$$
$$\text{if } q \circ (h_1, h_2) \equiv h_1$$
$$\textbf{res}[\![p \circ q]\!] \circ \textbf{prod} \circ (h_1, h_2) \equiv \textbf{prod} \circ (h_1, \textbf{res}[\![p]\!] \circ h_2)$$
$$\text{if } q \circ (h_1, h_2) \equiv h_2$$

  If a restriction follows a product operation, and the restriction predicate only involves one product field, then the restriction can be performed before the product is taken. Typically this is the case when the function q is a selector function.

  In the following rule the restriction predicate involves both fields of the product:

$$\textbf{res}[\![\texttt{and} \circ (p_1 \times p_2)]\!] \circ \textbf{prod} \equiv \textbf{prod} \circ (\textbf{res}[\![p_1]\!] \times \textbf{res}[\![p_2]\!])$$

- Pushing a restriction beyond an application is possible if the application does not affect the predicate domain, for instance when a projection is applied to some set of tuples, and this projection is followed by a restriction involving one of the tuple fields preserved.

$$\textbf{res}[\![p \circ q]\!] \circ \texttt{map}[\![f]\!] \equiv \texttt{map}[\![f]\!] \circ \textbf{res}[\![p \circ q]\!] \text{ if } q \circ f \equiv q$$

Pushing application. Pushing a `map` down the operator tree (or graph) is especially profitable when selector functions are mapped (projections) or when `map` is pushed beyond a product.

$$\mathrm{map}[\![f \circ h]\!] \circ \mathrm{prod} \circ (g_1, g_2) \equiv \mathrm{map}[\![f]\!] \circ g_1$$
$$\quad \text{if } h \circ (g_1, g_2) \equiv g_1 \text{ and } g_1, g_2 \text{ deliver sets and}$$
$$\quad g_2 \text{ delivers a non-empty set}$$
$$\mathrm{map}[\![f \circ h]\!] \circ \mathrm{prod} \circ (g_1, g_2) \equiv \mathrm{map}[\![f]\!] \circ g_2$$
$$\quad \text{if } h \circ (g_1, g_2) \equiv g_2 \text{ and } g_1, g_2 \text{ deliver sets and}$$
$$\quad g_1 \text{ delivers a non-empty set}$$
$$\mathrm{map}[\![(f_1 \times f_2)]\!] \circ \mathrm{prod} \equiv \mathrm{prod} \circ (\mathrm{map}[\![f_1]\!] \times \mathrm{map}[\![f_2]\!])$$

Generate as Few Intermediate Results as Possible

Grouping (or pipelining, [Beeri and Kornatzky 90]) avoids the generation of intermediate results by applying several operations during one access. The following rules express grouping:

$$\mathrm{map}[\![f]\!] \circ \mathrm{map}[\![g]\!] \equiv \mathrm{map}[\![f \circ g]\!]$$
$$\mathrm{res}[\![p]\!] \circ \mathrm{res}[\![q]\!] \equiv \mathrm{res}[\![\mathrm{and}\circ(p, q)]\!]$$
$$\mathrm{res}[\![p]\!] \circ \mathrm{map}[\![f]\!] \equiv \mathrm{gen}[\![p, f]\!]$$
$$\mathrm{map}[\![f]\!] \circ \mathrm{res}[\![p]\!] \equiv \mathrm{accr}[\![+\circ(p \to [\,] \circ f; \mathtt{C}[\![[\,]\!]), [\,]]\!]$$

In the last expression the parameter function of the functional **accr** appends the singleton list $[f\!:\!x]$ to the result if $p\!:\!x$ is true, otherwise the empty list is appended.

Avoid Useless Computations

Some rather simple examples of this rule are the following:

$$f \circ \mathrm{id} \equiv \mathrm{id} \circ f \equiv f$$
$$\mathrm{el} \circ \{\} \equiv \mathrm{id}$$
$$\mathrm{map}[\![f]\!] \circ \{\} \equiv \{\} \circ f$$
$$\mathrm{map}[\![(s1, s2)]\!] \circ \mathrm{prod} \equiv \mathrm{prod}$$
$$h \circ (s2, s1) \circ (f, g) \equiv h \circ (g, f) \text{ if } h \text{ is commutative}$$
$$(f_1 \times \cdots \times f_n) \circ \underbrace{(g, \ldots, g)}_{n \ times} \equiv (f_1, \cdots, f_n) \circ g$$
$$si \circ (f_1, \cdots, f_n) \equiv f_i$$

10.6
Future Work

With respect to the translation of **TM** to ADL, one of the problems to be addressed in the future concerns the formalization of the notion of safety in

TM. Another problem is the translation of predicative set expressions. The work done in [Partsch 90] concerning the development of (efficient) programs from formal problem specifications may be of help in solving this problem.

The actual optimization by rewriting in ADL is a major topic of research. The following subproblems may be distinguished.

- Definition of a cost model, possibly incorporating different access routines.

- Definition of a suitable set of rewrite rules. Because ADL has many operators and functionals, a large set of equivalence rules can be written down. The task is to define a minimal set of useful equivalence, or rewrite rules.

- Definition of a rewrite algorithm (algebraic optimizer). As is well-known, even for the relational model algebraic optimization represents a difficult search problem, and construction of an algebraic optimizer is a hard task [Freytag 87, Graefe and DeWitt 87]. Because ADL is a rich language, the problem even gets harder.

Bibliography

[Atkinson et al. 89] Atkinson, M., Bancilhon F., DeWitt D., Dittrich K., Maier D., and Zdonik S. "The Object-Oriented Database System Manifesto." In *Proc. 1st DOOD*, 1989.

[Backus 78] Backus, J. "Can Programming Be Liberated from the von Neuman Style? A Functional Style and its Algebra of Programs." *Communications of the ACM*, 21 (8), 1978, pp. 613-641.

[Balsters et al. 90a] Balsters, H., de By R.A., and de Vreeze C.C. "The **TM** Manual version 1.2." Manuscript, University of Twente, Enschede, 1990.

[Balsters et al. 90b] Balsters, H., de By R.A., and Zicari R. "Sets and Constraints in an Object-Oriented Data Model." Memoranda Informatica 90-75, University of Twente, Enschede, 1990.

[Balsters and Fokkinga 91] Balsters, H. and Fokkinga M.M. "Subtyping Can Have a Simple Semantics." To appear in TCS 87, 1991.

[Balsters and de Vreeze 91] Balsters, H. and de Vreeze C.C. "A Semantics of Object-Oriented Sets." In *Proc. 3rd International Workshop on Database Programming Languages,"* Nafplion, Greece, 1991.

[Beeri and Kornatzky 90] Beeri, C. and Kornatzky Y. "Algebraic Optimization of Object-Oriented Query Languages." In *Proc. 3rd ICDT*, LNCS 470, Springer-Verlag, 1990.

[de By 91] de By, R.A. "The Integration of Specification Aspects in Database Design." Ph.D. Thesis, University of Twente, Enschede, 1991.

[Cardelli 84] Cardelli, L. "A Semantics of Multiple Inheritance." In *Semantics of Data Types*, (Kahn G., MacQueen D.B., and Plotkin G. eds.), LNCS 173, Springer-Verlag, 1984, pp. 51-67.

[Elmasri and Navathe 89] Elmasri, R. and Navathe S.B. *Fundamentals of Database Systems*. Benjamin/Cummings Publishing Company Inc., 1989.

[Freytag 87] Freytag, J.C. "A Rule-Based View of Query Optimization." In *Proc. ACM SIGMOD*, 1987, pp. 173-180.

[Graefe and DeWitt 87] Graefe, G. and DeWitt D.J. "The EXODUS Optimizer Generator." In *Proc. ACM SIGMOD Conference*, May 1987, San Francisco, pp. 160-172

[Lécluse and Richard 89] Lécluse, C. and Richard P. "The O_2 Database Programming Language." In *Proc. 15th VLDB*, Amsterdam, 1989.

[ONTOS 90] "ONTOS Object Database Developer's Guide." Ontologic Inc., Burlington, 1990.

[Partsch 90] Partsch, H.A. *Specification and Transformation of Programs – A Formal Approach to Software Development*. Springer-Verlag, 1990.

[Turner 85] Turner, D.A. "Miranda: A Non-Strict Functional Language with Polymorphic Types." In *Proc. IFIP International Conference on Functional Programming Languages and Computer Architecture*, LNCS 201, Springer-Verlag 201, 1985.

[de Vreeze 91] de Vreeze, C.C. "Formalization of Inheritance of Methods in an Object-Oriented Data Model." Memoranda Informatica 90-76, University of Twente, Enschede, 1991.

[Zdonik and Maier 90] Zdonik, S.B. and Maier D., eds. *Readings in Object-Oriented Database Systems.* Morgan Kaufmann Publishers, 1990.

11

Extensible Query Optimization and Parallel Execution in Volcano

Goetz Graefe
Richard L. Cole
Diane L. Davison
William J. McKenna
Richard H. Wolniewicz

Abstract

The goal of the Volcano project is to provide efficient, extensible tools for algebraic query and request processing in novel application domains, in particular for object-oriented and scientific database systems. At this point, the Volcano project provides data model-independent and architecture-independent tools for optimized parallel query processing over large data sets using multiple operators or data processing steps. This overview describes the new rule-based Volcano Optimizer Generator and Volcano's architecture-independent parallel processing capabilities.

11.1
Introduction

Among the numerous current research projects in the areas of extensible and object-oriented database management, none attempts to combine extensibility and data model-independence with efficient, optimized, parallel request execution. Considering that efficient execution of requests and queries specified in high-level languages has contributed significantly to the success of relational systems, we feel it is very important to combine extensibility, query optimization, and parallelism in powerful next-generation database management systems. The dominant direction in current database research is object-oriented database management, and many researchers are working on complex objects, their representation, storage, retrieval, maintenance, or clustering. While managing complex objects and their behavior, i.e., moving data structures and logic from the application program into the database management system, are important and interesting research topics, we feel that ignoring manipulation of large data volumes and derivation of new information from large data sets could cost object-oriented systems their well-deserved success in real applications.

The Volcano project explores query processing techniques, both query optimization and query execution, that can support modern data models and, at the same time, exploit modern and forthcoming parallel hardware architectures. We do not propose to reintroduce relational query processing into next-generation database systems; instead, we work on a new kind of query processing engine that is independent of any data model. The basic assumption is that high-level languages are and will continue to be based on sets (and other bulk data types), predicates, and operators (on instances and collections). Therefore, the only assumption we make in our research is that the fundamental building blocks of next-generation query and request processing systems are operators consuming and producing sets or sequences of items. In other words, we assume that some algebra of collections is the basis of query processing, and our research tries to support any algebra of sets. Fortunately, algebras and algebraic equivalence rules are a very suitable basis for database query optimization. Moreover, sets (permitting definition and exploitation of subsets) and operators with data passed (or pipelined) between them are also the foundations for parallel algorithms for database query execution.

To investigate query and request processing in next-generation database management systems, we have built an extensible and parallel query processing prototype called Volcano [Graefe 1992a]. The important differences to all other extensible database projects are that (1) Volcano does not rely on the relational model (although it would be perfectly reasonable to implement a relational query processing system based on Volcano) and that (2) it is more than yet another storage server for efficient storage and retrieval of records and objects. Instead, we strictly maintain model-independence and focus on manipulation of large sets of items, using as the only assumption that query and request processing is based on sets and sequences of objects. Volcano consists of an optimizer generator, an extensible set of operators, and a file system.

The optimizer generator is based on experiences building and using the EXODUS optimizer generator and uses a similar general architecture and paradigm but employs a more efficient search algorithm and provides significantly better support for physical properties such as sort order, compression status, and location/partitioning.

The execution engine already includes sort- and hash-based matching functions such as join, semi-join, division, intersection, union, etc., but the collection of operators is also extensible, both at the algorithm level with new algorithms and at the instance level with new data types and functions on them. Operators can be designed and implemented in a single- process system and later parallelized by a novel "exchange" operator. This operator encapsulates all information about parallelism, process and flow control, and even the underlying architecture.

Database query processing can be divided into query optimization and query execution. The former is based on techniques of dynamic programming, numerical optimization, artificial intelligence (planning and search),

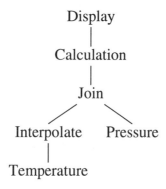

FIGURE 11.1
Simple Scientific Computation

and statistics (selectivity and cost estimation). The latter is most closely related to data and storage structures, algorithm design, operating systems, and computer architecture. Our research in the Volcano project follows this division between optimization and execution, and we will discuss each of them in turn after introducing a running example.

11.2
An Example

One of the goals of the Volcano project is to push the limits of extensibility in database query processing in order to make the advantages of database systems available to new application domains. The Volcano software is being used for several projects, including the REVELATION object-oriented query processing project [Daniels et al. 1991, Graefe and Maier 1988], Texas Instruments' Open OODB project [Wells et al. 1992], and a request processing system for scientific applications [Wolniewicz and Graefe 1992]. Our example in this paper is a simple scientific computation.

The core of our research into scientific database systems is to specify not only data management but also numerical computations in an extensible framework supporting a many-sorted algebra in order to facilitate automatic optimization and parallelization. Figure 11.1 shows a simple computation that combines temperature and pressure data for some further calculation such as digital filtering and display. Since pressure data are collected more frequently than temperature data, additional temperature values must be interpolated before the two data sets can be combined. The Volcano execution software includes operators for interpolation, extrapolation, digital filtering, and random sampling.

In traditional scientific processing, the data sets are stored in files and the entire computation is specified as an application program. Thus, database query optimization techniques cannot be exploited. In more recent systems, in which data storage and retrieval is provided by relational database systems, optimization of relational queries can be applied to the portion of the computation dealing with data retrieval. However, scan and join processing cannot be optimized in our example, because the temperature data must be interpolated and thus leave the scope of the database management before the join is computed. Our goal is to include as many operations as possible in an extensible query processing system in order to increase the part of a computation that can be optimized and parallelized.

In the next section, we discuss the Volcano optimizer generator, which has been used (among other projects) to build an optimizer that explores alternative processing plans for integrated numerical and non-numerical processing plans. In Section 11.4, we discuss mechanisms to execute plans on a wide variety of parallel computer architectures.

11.3
Query Optimization

We consider query optimization to be a planning problem similar to many other planning problems in artificial intelligence (AI). However, there is no standard formulation or solution to the query optimization problem in AI, because query optimization and AI researchers have traditionally not interacted very much - if at all, mostly to consider database techniques to support knowledge bases rather than AI techniques for database problems. Furthermore, the separation of logical algebra (e.g., relational algebra with operators such as join) and executable algebra (with operators such as nested loops, hybrid hash join, merge-join, and sort) makes this planning problem unique[1]. A second reason is that there is no standard formulation of "the"

---

[1]We draw many of our examples from the relational algebra and from relational query execution techniques; however, the Volcano optimizer generator is not limited to relational systems, and we are using it for object-oriented query optimizers in the REVELATION

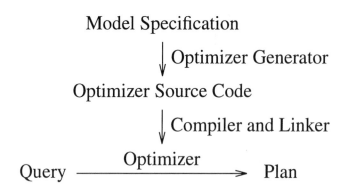

FIGURE 11.2
The Optimizer Generator Paradigm

query optimization problem among database researchers, because data models and query languages differ as well as query execution engines, their facilities and execution costs.

Query optimization in Volcano is based on a new optimizer generator. There are five fundamental design decision embodied in the Volcano optimizer generator design, which are only mentioned here because they are discussed and justified in more detail elsewhere [Graefe and McKenna 1992]. First, query processing, including both optimization and execution, is presumed to be based on algebraic techniques. Second, rules are used to specify the data model and its properties. Third, all rules specify as algebraic equivalences. This excludes a grammar-like multi-level expansion of expressions as used in Starburst's cost-based optimizer [Lee et al. 1988, Lohman 1988]. Fourth, rules are transformed by an optimizer generator into source code in a standard programming language (C) to be compiled and linked with the other DBMS modules. Fifth, the search algorithm is based on dynamic programming, which until now has been used only for relational select-project-join optimization, augmented with a very goal-oriented control strategy.

The basic idea of an optimizer generator, shown in Figure 11.2, is taken

project [Daniels et al. 1991, Graefe and Maier 1988] and the Open OODB project at Texas Instruments [Wells et al. 1992]. The application of the optimizer generator is limited only by its fundamental design decisions.

in principal from the EXODUS project [Carey et al. 1990]. When the DBMS software is built using an extensible toolkit, the optimizer source code is generated from a data model description, i.e., an algebra and its rule set are translated into pattern matching code and integrated with the search engine. After the DBMS software has been built, it can be used efficiently for all queries and requests without further code generation and compilation.

The core of the data model description are the query algebra's transformation rules and the implementation rules, which specify possible mappings of logical algebra expressions to query processing algorithms. The correctness of these rules as well as their soundness and completeness[2] cannot be verified by the optimizer generator, because these rules are the optimizer generator's only source of knowledge about the data model, its operations, and its equivalence criteria. However, we plan on complementing the Volcano optimizer generator with an "advisor" that scans the rule set and suggests modifications to the optimizer implementor, e.g., rules that seem redundant, missing implementation algorithms for logical operators, etc. Other important concepts used in the design of the Volcano optimizer generator and throughout this paper are summarized in the table of figure 11.3. At this point, we are prototyping a small recursive search algorithm that determines what knowledge about expressions and subexpressions is interesting and useful, derives this knowledge as efficiently as possible, and then stores it in a look-up table. For example, in order to use merge-join in the earlier example of a computation in a scientific database system, it is interesting to know the costs of the left and right inputs sorted appropriately. Therefore, the search algorithm will optimize each input sorted. Execution plans with unsorted output will not be considered, unless there is a sort algorithm to create the required sort order from the optimal plan with unsorted output.

The look-up table is organized into equivalence classes, i.e., groups of logical and physical expressions that are equivalent to one another. The most important components of an equivalence class are the logical properties such as the intermediate result schema, system properties that are logical properties presumably used in any database query optimizer such set cardinality, a set of logical expressions, and a set of plans. Figure 11.4 shows a simplified diagram of an equivalence class. The look-up table is basically a network of equivalence classes that contains all optimization results, augmented by a hashing scheme to determine for any newly transformed expression whether

---

[2]Sound - only correct expressions and plans, i.e., equivalent to the original user query, can be derived. Complete - all correct expressions and plans can be derived.

Query	Logical algebra expression.
Logical algebra, operator	High-level operators that specify data transformations without specifying the algorithm to be used; for example, relational algebra.
Plan	Physical algebra expression.
Physical algebra, algorithm	Algorithms for data transformations that can be combined into complex query evaluation plans.
Transformation rules	Rules that govern rewriting logical algebra expressions; e.g., join commutativity.
Implementation rules	Rules that specify the relationships between logical operators and physical operators; e.g., (logical operator) join and (physical algorithm) hybrid hash join.
Condition code	Determines, after a rule pattern match has succeeded, whether or not a transformation rule or an algorithm are applicable to a logical algebra expression.
Property	Description of results of (sub-) queries and (sub-) plans; divided into logical, system, and physical properties.
Property vector	Indicates which physical properties must be enforced during optimization of a logical algebra expression, e.g., sortedness.
Enforcer	Part of the physical algebra that enforces physical properties such as sort order, location in a network, or decompression.
Applicability function	Decides whether an algorithm or enforcer can deliver a logical expression conforming to a physical property vector, and determines what physical properties its inputs must satisfy.
Cost, Cost function	An abstract data type that captures an algorithm's or a plan's cost; typically a number or a record. A cost function estimates the cost of a algorithm or enforcer.
Property function	One for each operator and algorithm, they determine logical, system, and physical properties.

FIGURE 11.3

Optimizer Generator Concepts

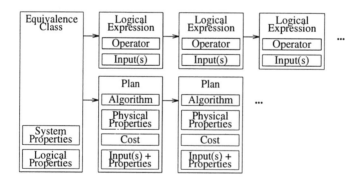

FIGURE 11.4

Data Structure of an Equivalence Class (Simplified)

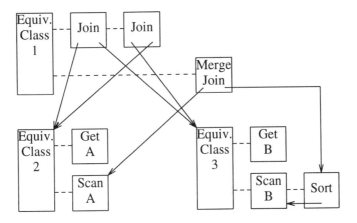

FIGURE 11.5
Equivalence Classes for 'A join B' (Simplified)

or not this expression has been created before.

A simple example of the network of equivalence classes (without the hash directory) is shown in Figure 11.5. The arrows indicate inputs of logical operators and algorithms; note the case that an enforcer (sort) points to a plan in its own equivalence class.

The search algorithm is controlled by a logical algebra and its transformation rules (e.g., join is commutative), the set of algorithms available in the query execution engine and the associations of logical algebra operators with algorithms (e.g., merge-join and hybrid hash join implement join), required physical properties such as sort order, selectivity functions, cost functions, etc. The input into the optimizer and its search algorithm is an expression over the logical algebra, i.e., the query to be optimized, plus specific requirements for physical properties such as sort order or partitioning in parallel and distributed systems. Sort order and interesting orderings have been used effectively in the System R optimizer [Selinger et al. 1979], and we have generalized them into physical properties, which are supported explicitly in the optimization model realized in the Volcano optimizer generator. The output of optimizing a query is a query evaluation plan, i.e., a tree whose nodes are query processing algorithms.

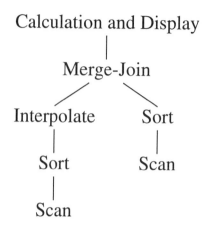

FIGURE 11.6
A Possible Execution Plan

A possible execution plan for our example computation is shown in Figure 11.6. A comparison of the original scientific computation specified on the logical level (Figure 11.1) with the plan shown in Figure 11.6 shows some of the capabilities of the Volcano optimizer generator. First, multiple logical operations can be mapped to a single physical algorithm. Another example for the need of this feature is a relational join followed by a projection (without duplicate removal). Second, generated optimizers choose among multiple alternative implementations for a logical operator, such as merge-join and hybrid hash join. This choice is based on cost estimates determined with the help of cost functions provided by the optimizer implementor. Third, physical properties useful for subsequent consumer algorithms are considered when optimizing subexpressions. In the example, the optimization goal for the left subtree is not to find the cheapest plan for interpolation and scan but to find the cheapest such plan with sorted output. An optimization goal is always a pair consisting of a logical algebra expression and a set of physical properties.

The search strategy, i.e., heuristic guidance of the search algorithm, is much more directed, controllable, and efficient than the one used in EXODUS, and it is modularized such that the Volcano optimizer generator can be used as a highly extensible experimental vehicle. Furthermore, a second class of algorithms used in query processing is introduced, called enforcers in Volcano, that enforce physical properties. Typical enforcers are sort (for sort order), exchange (for partitioning) [Graefe 1990a, Graefe and Davison 1991], compression and decompression (for database systems that can store and process compressed data [Graefe and Shapiro 1991]), and chooseplan (for plan robustness under estimation errors during query optimization [Graefe and Ward 1989]). Volcano's enforcers are similar to the "glue" operators in Starburst [Haas et al. 1989], but their optimization is handled very differently in Volcano.

Figure 11.7 shows an outline of the search algorithm included by the Volcano optimizer generator in each generated optimizer. The original invocation of the FindBestPlan procedure indicates the logical expression passed to the optimizer as the query to be optimized, physical properties as requested by the user (for example, sort order as requested with a SORT BY clause of SQL), and a cost limit. This limit is typically infinity for a user query, but the user interface may permit users to set their own limits to "catch" unreasonable queries, e.g., ones requiring a Cartesian product due to a missing join predicate. The set of possible physical properties is encoded in the physical property vector, which is an abstract data type defined by the optimizer implementor; the optimizer inspects and manipulates physical property vectors only via functions provided by the optimizer implementor as part of the abstract data type. The cost limit can be given in any unit, since cost is also an abstract data type defined by the optimizer implementor and all cost computations, including comparisons and additions, are performed in functions provided by the optimizer implementor. An abstract data type for costs permits experimentation with new cost measures such as the combination of latency and bandwidth proposed by Ganguly et al. for response time optimization in parallel systems [Gangulu et al. 1992].

The FindBestPlan procedure is broken into two parts. First, if a plan for the expression satisfying the physical property vector can be found in the look-up table, either a plan and its cost or a failure indication are returned, depending on whether or not the found plan satisfies the given cost limit. If the expression cannot be found in the look-up table, or if the expression has been optimized before but not for the currently required physical properties, actual optimization is begun.

There are three sets of possible "moves" the optimizer can explore at any point. First, the expression can be transformed using a transformation rule. Second, there might be some algorithms that can deliver the logical expression with the desired physical properties, e.g., hybrid hash join for unsorted output

FindBestPlan (LogExpr, PhysProp, Limit)
if the pair LogExpr and PhysProp is in the look-up table
    if the cost in the look-up table < Limit
        return Plan and Cost
    else
        return failure
else /* optimization required */
    create the set of possible "moves" from
        applicable transformations
        algorithms that give the required PhysProp
        enforcers for required PhysProp
    order the set of moves by promise
    for the most promising moves
        if the move uses a transformation
            apply the transformation creating NewLogExpr
            call FindBestPlan (NewLogExpr, PhysProp, Limit)
        else if the move uses an algorithm
            TotalCost := cost of the algorithm
            for each input I of the algorithm while TotalCost ≤ Limit
                determine required physical properties PP for I
                find Cost using FindBestPlan (I, PP, Limit − TotalCost)
                add Cost to TotalCost
        else /* move uses an enforcer */
            TotalCost := cost of the enforcer
            modify PhysProp for enforced property
            call FindBestPlan for LogExpr with modified PhysProp
    /* maintain the look-up table of explored facts */
    if LogExpr is not in the look-up table
        insert LogExpr into the look-up table
    insert PhysProp and best plan found into the look-up table

---

FIGURE 11.7
Outline of the Search Algorithm

and merge-join for join output sorted on the join attribute. Third, an enforcer can be useful to permit additional algorithm choices, e.g., a sort operator to permit using hybrid hash join even if the final output must be sorted.

After generating all possible moves, the optimizer assesses their promise of leading to the optimal plan. Clearly, good estimations of a move's promise are useful for finding the best plan fast. Considering that we are building an optimizer generator with as few assumptions as possible with respect to the logical algebra and the set of query execution algorithms, it is not possible to estimate a move's promise without assistance by the optimizer implementor. Thus, the optimizer implementor must provide estimation functions. Their accurary will have a significant impact on an optimizer's search efficiency, although not on the optimizer's correctness.

The most promising moves are then pursued. For an exhaustive search, these will be all moves. Otherwise, a subset of the moves is selected determined by another function provided by the optimizer implementor. Pursuing all moves or only a selected few is the second major heuristic placed into the hands of the optimizer implementor. Using this control function, an optimizer implementor can choose to transform a logical expression without any algorithm selection and cost analysis, which covers the optimizations that in Starburst are separated into the QGM (Query Graph Model) level [Haas et al. 1990, Hasan and Pirahesh 1988]. The difference between Starburst's two-level approach and Volcano's design is that this separation is mandatory in Starburst whereas it is a choice left to the optimizer implementor in Volcano[3].

The cost limit is used to improve the search algorithm using branch-and-bound pruning. Once a complete plan is known for a logical expression and a physical property vector, no plan or partial plan with higher cost can be part of the optimal query evaluation plan. Therefore, it is important (for optimization speed, not for correctness) that a relatively good plan be found fast, even if the optimizer uses exhaustive search. Furthermore, cost limits are passed down in the optimization of subexpressions, and tight upper bounds also speed the optimization of subexpressions.

Branch-and-bound search exploits knowledge of an upper cost bound.

---

[3]Actually, the organization of the Starburst optimization subsystem forces the optimizer implementor to use a three-level approach, namely the query rewrite level for heuristics optimiza- tion of all operators except select, project and join; the cost- based level designed primarily to perform join transformations implemented as rules encoded in compiled C procedures; and the level of low-level plan operators using strategy alternative rules (STARs) that can be manipulated as catalog data at DBMS run-time.

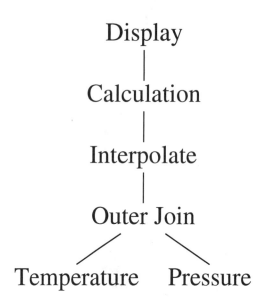

FIGURE 11.8
The Scientific Database Query After a Transformation

If a lower cost bound is known, it can also be exploited. An example for a lower bound in database query optimization is the cost of an optimal plan for an expression with fewer constraints in the physical property vector. If the optimal cost for an expression with unsorted output is known to be L, the optimal cost for the same expression with sorted output must be at least L. If a known plan for the expression with sorted output has a cost only 10plan for sorted output might not be worthwhile, because the improvement over the known plan cannot exceed 10.

If a move to be pursued is a transformation, the new, transformed expression is created and optimized using FindBestPlan. In order to detect the case that two (or more) rules are inverses of each other, the current expression and physical property vector is marked as "in progress." If a newly formed expression already exists in the look-up table and is marked as "in progress," the new expression is ignored, because its optimal plan will be considered when it is finished.

Figure 11.8 shows the computation of Figure 11.1 after a transformation. Not only the order but also the nature of some of the operations have been changed. In this particular case, the reason for changing the operation is that there are no temperature data for some of the original pressure data. Thus, in order to retain these pressure data in the join output, the join must be changed into an outer join.

If a move to be pursued is the consideration of a normal query processing algorithm such as merge-join, its cost is calculated by a cost function provided by the optimizer implementor. All its input (logical) expressions and their required physical property vectors (such as sort order for the inputs of merge-join) are determined by another function provided by the optimizer implementor, and their costs are found using FindBestPlan. Finally, all costs are added up. In this process, the Limit passed to FindBestPlan is the original Limit minus costs already computed. For example, if the total cost limit for the merge-join and its inputs in Figure 11.6 is 10 cost units, the merge-join algorithm itself takes 1 cost unit, and the left input (scan, sort, and interpolate) takes 6 cost units, the limit for the right input (scan and sort) is 3 cost units. If the sort in the right input takes more than 3 cost units, the right scan in not even optimized, because the merge-join and its input cannot possibly be cheaper than the limit of 10 cost units. (Recall that cost arithmetic is performed using the cost ADT provided by the optimizer implementor; this example presumes a very simple cost model.)

If the move to be pursued is consideration of an enforcer such as sort, its cost is estimated by a cost function provided by the optimizer implementor and the original logical expression with a suitably modified physical property vector is optimized using FindBestPlan. When optimizing the logical expression with the modified (i.e., relaxed) physical property vector, algorithms that already applied before relaxing the physical properties must not be explored again. For example, if a join result must be sorted on the join column, merge-join (an algorithm) and sort (an enforcer) will apply but hybrid hash join will not. When optimizing the input to the sort enforcer, i.e., the join expression without the sort condition, hybrid hash join applies but merge-join should not. To ensure correct consideration of merge-join and hybrid hash join (or similar interactions of algorithms and physical properties), FindBestPlan uses an additional parameter not shown in Figure 11.8, called the excluding physical property vector, that is used only when inputs to enforcers are optimized. In the example, the excluding physical property vector for the sort enforcer's input would contain the sort condition, and since merge-join is able to satisfy the excluding properties, it would not be considered a suitable algorithm for the sort input.

At the end of (or actually already during) the optimization procedure FindBestPlan, newly derived interesting facts are captured in the look-up table. "Interesting" is defined with respect to possible future use. This can include both plans optimal for given physical properties as well as failures that can preempt future attempts to optimize a logical expression and physical properties again with the same or even lower cost limits.

This description of the search algorithm used in Volcano does not cover all details for two reasons. First, further details would make the algorithm description even harder to follow, while the present level of detail presents the basic structure. Second, the algorithm implementation has only recently become operational, and we are still experimenting with it and tuning it to make more effective use of the look-up table of explored expressions and optimized plans.

The algorithm used in the Volcano optimizer generator differs significantly from the one designed for the EXODUS project in a number of important aspect. First, Volcano makes a distinction between logical expressions and physical expressions. In EXODUS, only one type of node exists in the look-up table, called MESH, which contains both a logical operator such as join and a physical algorithm such as hybrid hash join. To retain equivalent plans using merge-join and hybrid hash join, the logical expression (or at least one node) has to be kept twice, resulting in a large number of nodes in MESH.

Second, the Volcano algorithm is driven top-down; subexpressions are optimized only if warranted. In the extreme case, it is possible to optimize a logical expression without ever optimizing its subexpressions by selecting only one move, a transformation. For example, the transformation shown in Figure 11.8 might be the only move considered from the algebra expression in Figure 11.1; in other words, if the optimizer implementor knows that this transformation will always lead to better plans and specifies this knowledge, the plan shown in Figure 11.6 would never be considered. In EXODUS, a transformation is always followed immediately by algorithm selection and cost analysis. Moreover, transformations are explored whether or not they are part of the currently most promising logical expression and physical plan for the overall query. Worst of all for optimizer performance, however, is the decision to perform transformations with the highest expected cost improvement first. Since the cost improvement is calculated as product of a factor associated with the transformation rule and the current cost before transformation, nodes at the top of the expression (with high total cost) are preferred over lower expressions. When the lower expression are finally transformed, all consumer nodes above (of which there are many at this time) have to be reanalyzed, creating even more MESH nodes. A comparison of efficiency and effectiveness of the EXODUS and Volcano search algorithms for a simple relation model has indicated that the Volcano search engine can easily be an order of magnitude faster than the earlier EXODUS prototype and use an order of magnitude less main memory.

Third, physical properties are handled only very haphazardly in EXO-DUS. If the algorithm with the lowest cost happens to deliver results with useful physical properties, this fact is recorded in MESH. Otherwise, the cost of enforcers (although this is a Volcano term) has to be included in the cost function of other algorithms such as merge-join. In other words, the ability to specify required physical properties and let them, together with the logical expression, drive the optimization process (as it is done in Volcano) is entirely absent in EXODUS.

Fourth, cost is defined in much more general terms in Volcano than in the EXODUS optimizer generator. In Volcano, cost is an abstract data type that is handled only by invoking functions provided by the optimizer implementor. It can be a simple number, e.g., estimated elapsed seconds, a structure, e.g., a record consisting of CPU cost and I/O cost similar to the cost measures in System R [Selinger et al. 1979], or a function. A function offers entirely new possibilities for query optimization. For example, it can be a function of the size of the available memory. This function would allow optimizing plans for any run-time situation with respect to available memory and memory contention. Of course, it is not always possible to compare functions, i.e., to determine which of two functions is "less" than the other. In some situations, it might be possible, e.g., if one plan dominates another one independently of memory availability. If two functions cannot be compared because neither dominates the other in all situations, we propose using the choose-plan operator we had suggested earlier [Graefe and Ward 1989], which permits including several equivalent sub-plans in a single plan and delaying an optimization decision until query execution time.

Finally, we believe that the Volcano optimizer generator is more readily extensible than the EXODUS one, in particular with respect to the search strategy. The look-up table that holds logical expressions and physical plans and operations on this look-up table are quite general, and would support a variety of search strategies, not only the procedure outlined in Figure 11.8. We are still modifying (extending and refining) the search strategy, and plan on modifying it further in subsequent years and on using the Volcano optimizer generator for further research.

Algebraic transformation systems always include the possibility and danger of deriving the same expression in several different ways. Detecting duplicate expressions and preventing redundant optimization effort is a major concern in algebraic query optimization. The Volcano optimization system uses a look-up table of explored expressions to identify such duplicates. For global or multi-query optimization, duplicate expression detection is the major concern. We plan on extending this duplicate detection scheme from equivalent to subsumed expressions, which will significantly increase the power of the optimizer generator for global query optimization.

Since query optimization can be a very time-consuming task, as shown many times for "simple" relational join optimization [Kooi 1980, Ono and Lohman 1990], all means that can speed up the process should be explored. Beyond traditional methods, we will explore storing logical expressions and their optimal plans for later reuse when re-optimizing the same query or when optimizing a different query. While a plan optimized for an expression in one context (query) may not be optimal for the same expression in a different context, stored subplans hold promise for two reasons. First, they provide an upper bound; equivalent plans explored while optimizing the larger query can be safely abandoned if their cost surpasses that of the known plan. Second, since the optimizer is based on algebraic transformations, the stored optimal plan can be used as a basis from which to search for an optimal plan within the new context. Both reasons allow us to speculate that storing optimized plans may be a very useful concept, and we feel it can be explored most effectively in an extensible context such as the Volcano optimizer generator.

While dynamic query evaluation plans, global query optimization, and storage and reuse of optimized subplans are interesting and challenging research topics in the context of relational systems, we plan on pursuing them within an extensible system. There are two reasons for our approach. First, an extensible query optimization environment modularizes the various components of query optimizers [Graefe 1987], e.g., selectivity estimation, cost calculation, query transformation, search heuristics, etc. Modularization facilitates change, modification, and experimentation, and may indeed be a requirement for successful pursuit of our research goals. Second, none of these research problems is restricted to the relational domain, and we hope that our results will benefit relational, extensible, and object-oriented systems alike.

11.4
Query Execution

Volcano's query execution research is complementary to the optimizer work. It provides a wide variety of mechanisms for query execution parameterized and implemented in such a way that policies can be set by an optimizer or a human experimenter. Like the optimizer generator, the execution module was designed for extensibility. Another important design goal was high performance, including the effective use of parallel execution on a variety of computer architectures.

Volcano's execution module is fairly complete - it already includes operators for file and B+-tree scan and maintenance [Graefe 1992a], sorting [Graefe 1990b], sort- and hash-based versions of a "one-to- one match" operator for matching operations such as join, semi- join, outer joins, intersection, union, difference, aggregation, and duplicate elimination [Graefe 1992a], universal quantification [Graefe 1989], interpolation, extrapolation, digital filtering, and random sampling [Wolniewicz and Graefe 1992]. Moreover, extension of the Volcano execution module is a continuing process.

Each operator is designed as an iterator implemented with three functions, called the open, next, and close procedures in Volcano. Their names as well as their semantics are taken from conventional file scans. The open procedure prepares an operator to deliver data items; the next procedure delivers one data item and can be called repeatedly; and the close procedure performs final house-keeping. Complex queries are evaluated by composing trees of Volcano operator in which a consumer operator invokes the open, next, and close procedures of its producers. For example, the sort operator does not scan an input file but invokes the iterator procedures of its input operator, which in the simplest case may be a file scan operator.

All operations on instances are imported into the operators as function entry points, e.g., for predicate evaluation. Such strict separation of set iteration and instance interpretation enables all Volcano operators to manipulate records and tuples as well as complex objects consisting of multiple, shared components. Furthermore, a simple and uniform interface between operators allows easy addition of new operations if required. In other words, the execution module is extensible both on the instance level (through imported functions on items) and on the operator level (through a uniform operator interface).

The most recent extensions were those required for distributed-memory and hierarchical machines (multiple shared- memory nodes) [Graefe and Davison 1991], for fast assembly of sets of complex objects in memory [Keller et al. 1991], and for scientific, numerical operations on time series [Wolniewicz and Graefe 1992]. Furthermore, we are currently redesigning the hash-based one-to-one match operator, which is based on hybrid hash join [DeWitt et al. 1990], to exploit hash value skew in its input data for better performance rather than being handicapped by skew and uneven partitioning.

The hybrid hash join algorithm partitions both inputs, called the build and probe inputs by their use of the hash table, into multiple pairs of partition files using a hash function on the join attributes. If the build input is small enough that it does not require the entire available memory as output buffers for the partitioning files, a hash table is kept in memory during the partitioning process and a part of the join is performed immediately. However, if the inputs are large and the fan-out is small (which it should be to permit fast, large-chunk I/O [Bratbergsengen, 1984, Graefe et al. 1992]), recursive partitioning is required. In Volcano's new, skew-resistant one-to-one match operator, statistics about hash value distributions are gathered in one recursion level for use in the next level. These statistics are used to assign hash buckets to the in-memory hash table or to partition files. Moreover, they are used to decide when switching to nested loops join is required due to excessive duplication of an individual join key. In detailed simulation experiments, we found that not only can the detrimental effects of skew be completely avoided but skew can also, with proper handling, improve the performance over hybrid hash join with uniformly distributed input data [Graefe 1992b].

Volcano's execution module includes two novel "meta- operators" that control query execution without directly contributing to data manipulation. First, the choose-plan operator implements dynamic query evaluation plans for embedded queries optimized at compile time with incomplete knowledge (e.g., predicate constants, current system load) [Graefe and Ward 1989]. Second, the exchange operator allows parallelizing Volcano operators that were designed and implemented in single-process environments [Graefe 1990a]. We are considering additional meta-operators for common subexpressions, control flow reversal for real-time database systems (data- vs. demand-driven data flow), and extensions to the choose-plan operator to be used in very complex queries that do not permit complete optimization before run-time because of selectivity estimation errors.

The module responsible for parallel execution and synchronization is called the exchange iterator in Volcano. Notice that it is an iterator with open, next, and close procedures; therefore, it can be inserted at any one place or at

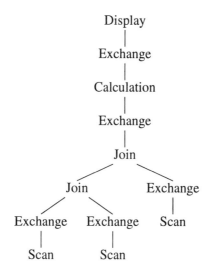

FIGURE 11.9
Operator Model of Parallelization

multiple places in a complex query tree. Figure 11.9 shows a query execution plan, which is slightly more complex than our earlier scientific computation and includes database operators, i.e., file scans and joins, scientific operators, and exchange operators.

Figure 11.10 shows the processes created when this plan is executed, including both vertical parallelism (pipelining) and horizontal parallelism (partitioning) by the exchange operators in the query plan of Figure 11.9. The graphical display is performed within the root process, the calculation prior to display is shared by two processes, the join operators are executed by three processes, and the file scan operators are executed by one or two processes each. Parallel file scans typically scan file partitions on different devices. To obtain this grouping of processes, the "degree of parallelism" arguments to the exchange operators have to be set to 2 or 3, and a partitioning function must be provided for each exchange operator that transfers file scan output to the join processes.

There are two "modes" in which the calculation operator in Figure 11.10 can be parallelized. First, the set of data items may be horizontally partitioned, and any one data item is sent to one of the two calculation processes.

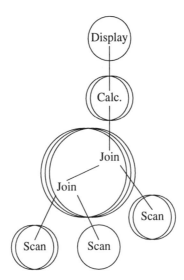

FIGURE 11.10
Processes Created by Exchange Operators

This mode is very common is database systems, because the defitions of relation and set naturally lead to processing based on disjunct subsets. Second, each data item may be vertically partitioned, such that some values (fields) from each data item are passed to the left and the others to the right calculation process. This mode is not used in traditional database query processing, but this form of data parallelism has been used successfully in some scientific, numerical computations and will therefore be supported soon in Volcano's exchange operator for experimental evaluation in scientific database processing.

All file scan processes in Figure 11.10 can transfer data to all join processes; however, data transfer from the lower to the upper join operators occurs only within each of the join processes. Unfortunately, this restriction renders this parallelization infeasible if the two joins are on different attributes (and partitioning-based parallel join methods are used). For this case, a variant of exchange, called "interchange," is supported in Volcano's exchange operator. This and other variants of Volcano's exchange operator have been described earlier [Graefe 1992a].

The original version of Volcano's exchange operator supported only shared memory. When extending Volcano and its exchange operator to sup-

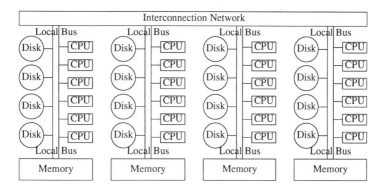

FIGURE 11.11
A Hierarchical-Memory Architecture

port query processing on distributed- memory machines, we did not want to give up the advantages of shared memory, namely efficient communication, synchronization, and load balancing. A recent investigation demonstrated that shared-memory architectures can deliver near-linear speed-up for modest degrees of parallelism; we observed a speed-up of 14.9 with 16 CPUs and disks for parallel sorting in Volcano [Graefe and Thakkar 1992]. To combine the best of both worlds, Volcano now runs on an interconnected group, e.g., a hypercube or mesh architecture, of shared-memory parallel machines. Within each shared-memory machine, shared-memory mechanisms are used for synchronization and communication, while message-passing is used between machines. We can now investigate query processing on hierarchical architectures and heuristics of how CPU and I/O power as well as memory can best be placed and exploited in such machines.

Figure 11.11 shows a general hierarchical architecture consisting of three shared-memory nodes, which we believe should be the target architecture for any parallel query processing software. The important point in Figure 11.11 is the combination of local busses within shared-memory parallel machines and a global interconnection network between machines. The diagram is only a very general outline of such an architecture; many details are deliberately left out and unspecified. The network could be implemented using a bus such as an ethernet, a ring, a hypercube, a mesh, or a set of point-to-point connections. The local busses may or may not be split into code and data or by address range to obtain less contention and higher bus bandwidth and hence higher scalability limits for the use of shared memory. Design and placement of caches, disk controllers, terminal connections, and local- and wide-area network connections are also left open. Tertiary storage devices such as optical juke-boxes and robot- operated tape archives as well as tape drives and other backup devices would probably be connected to local busses.

Beyond the effect of faster communication and synchronization, this architecture can also have a significant effect on control overhead, load balancing, and therefore response time. Investigations in the Bubba project at MCC demonstrated that large degrees of parallelism may reduce performance unless startup overhead (e.g., synchronization and communication) and load imbalance can be kept relatively low [Copeland et al. 1988]. Consider placing 100 nodes with one CPU each either in 100 nodes or in 10 nodes with 10 CPUs each. It is much faster to distribute query plans to all CPUs and much easier to achieve reasonably balanced loads in the second case than in the first case. Load balancing within a shared-memory machine can be accomplished by exchanging data (relatively cheaply) or by allocating resources such as CPUs, disk drives, and memory to reflect an uneven load and to attempt to achieve similar processing times among parallel processes.

Most of today's parallel machines are built as one of the two extreme cases of this hierarchical design: a distributed- memory machine uses single-CPU nodes, while a shared-memory machine consists of a single node. Software designed for this hierarchical architecture runs on conventional designs as well as genuinely hierarchical machines, and allows exploring tradeoffs in the range of alternatives in between. Thus, the operator model of parallelization also offers the advantage of architecture- and topology-independent parallel query evaluation. In other words, the parallelism operator is the only operator that needs to "understand" the underlying architecture, while all "work" operators can be implemented without any concern for parallelism, data distribution, flow control, etc. As current shared-memory and distributed-memory machines are subsumed by this architecture, the model of parallel query processing in Volcano subsumes those of Bubba [Boral 1988, Boral et al. 1990, Khoshafian and Valduriez 1987], Gamma [DeWitt et al. 1986, DeWitt et al. 1990], and the Teradata database machine [Neches 1984, Neches 1988, Teradata 1983] (distributed memory) as well as those of XPRS [Hong and Stonebraker 1991, Hong 1992, Stonebraker et al. 1989, Stonebraker et al. 1988] (shared memory). The versatility of the Volcano software to run on shared-memory, distributed-memory, and hierarchical architectures makes the Volcano project unique among experimental parallel database platforms.

Using the Volcano engine as an experimental testbed, we are now exploring tradeoffs in extensible parallel query processing, e.g., vertical parallelism (pipelining) versus horizontal parallelism (partitioning), left-deep versus right-deep versus bushy plans, shared-everything (single bus) versus shared-disks (e.g., VAX cluster) versus shared-nothing (distributed memory) versus hierarchical-memory architectures, data- versus demand- driven dataflow in database systems, self-scheduling operators versus central scheduling, extensibility versus performance, granularity of data exchange between processes, etc. None of these issues can be answered trivially; for example, the granularity of data exchange was found to have some influence on system performance even in a shared-memory system due to operating system semaphore and scheduling overhead [Graefe and Thakkar 1992]; however, reducing such overhead and choosing the granules too large can create unnecessary waiting, in particular at the beginning and the end of a data stream.

We have completed the design and implementation of the experimental Volcano parallel request processing testbed. We are now exploring some of the tradeoffs listed earlier. Future research will analyze current trends in computer architecture, operating systems, and database systems, and determine where matches, overlaps, and inconsistencies enable, further, hamper, or prevent the development of next-generation high-performance database management systems.

11.5
Summary

Research into extensible, parallel query processing is one of the central challenges in building high-performance next-generation, object-oriented database management systems. Performance in query and request processing can be achieved through effective optimization, suitable physical database design, efficient processing algorithms, and parallel execution.

The work on the Volcano optimizer generator focuses on strategies and mechanisms to derive important facts and subplans for a query or request in a data model-independent yet efficient way. After an appropriate number of possible query evaluation plans have been explored, the optimal plan is one of the facts derived. Future work will include deriving dynamic query execution plans, a knowledge base of logical expressions and suitable plans to speed other optimizations and facilitate global query optimization, and the foundations of an expert system for physical database design that interacts with the query optimizer.

The work on parallel query processing in the Volcano extensible database system has already provided mechanisms for parallelizing existing and new operators on various architectures, including hierarchical architectures based on a closely tied group of shared-memory parallel nodes. Current work includes research into performance tradeoffs in extensible, parallel database systems, into understanding current trends in computer architecture, operating systems, and database systems and into identifying their concepts that are complementary to or inconsistent with the needs of an extensible DBMS.

The Volcano research is unique as it combines architecture- independent parallelism with extensibility and data model- independence. Data model-independence is pursued far enough in both modules, the optimizer generator and the execution engine, to allow integration and optimization of non-traditional operations such as interpolation and digital filtering in scientific databases [Wolniewicz and Graefe 1992]. Our test cases will be the integration of numerical operations in scientific database systems and the use of the Volcano concepts and software as one main component of the request processing engine in an object-oriented database management system [Daniels et al. 1991, Graefe and Maier 1988, Graefe et. al. 1990].

11.6
Acknowledgements

We appreciate the thorough comments by the book editors, which have improved the presentation of this paper considerably. This manuscript is based on research partially supported by the National Science Foundation with grants IRI-8996270, IRI-8912618, IRI-9006348, and IRI-9116547, ADP, Intel Supercomputer Systems Division, Sequent Computer Systems, the Oregon Advanced Computing Institute (OACIS), and a DARPA Research Assistantship in Parallel Processing administered by the Institute for Advanced Computer Studies, University of Maryland.

Bibliography

[Alexander and Copland 1988] Alexander W. and Copeland G. "Process and Dataflow Control in Distributed Data-Intensive Systems." In *Proc. ACM*

SIGMOD Conference, Chicago, IL, June 1988, p. 90.

[Boral 1988] Boral H. "Parallelism in Bubba." In *Proc. International Symp. on Databases in Parallel and Distributed Systems*, Austin, TX, December 1988.

[Boral et al. 1990] Boral H, Alexander H., Clay L., Copeland G., Danforth S., Franklin M., Hart B., Smith M. and Valduriez P. "Prototyping Bubba, A Highly Parallel Database System." In *IEEE Transactions on Knowledge and Data Engineering*, **2, 1** (March 1990), p. 4.

[Bratbergsengen, 1984] Bratbergsengen K. "Hashing Methods and Relational Algebra Operations." In *Proc. International Conference on Very Large Data Bases (VLDB)*, Singapore, August 1984, p. 323.

[Carey et al. 1990] Carey M. J., DeWitt D. J., Graefe G., Haight D. M., Richardson J. E., Schuh D. T., Shekita E. J. and S. Vandenberg. "The EXODUS Extensible DBMS Project: An Overview." In *Readings on Object-Oriented Database Systems* (Maier D. and Zdonik S., eds.), Morgan Kaufmann, San Mateo, CA, 1990.

[Copeland et al. 1988] Copeland G., Alexander W., Boughter E. and Keller T. "Data Placement in Bubba." In *Proc. ACM SIGMOD Conference*, Chicago, IL, June 1988, p. 99.

[Daniels et al. 1991] Daniels S., Graefe G., Keller T., Maier D., Schmidt D. and Vance B. "Query Optimization in Revelation, an Overview." *IEEE Database Engineering* **14, 2** (June 1991).

[DeWitt et al. 1984] DeWitt D. J., Katz R., Olken F., Shapiro L., Stonebraker M. and Wood D. "Implementation Techniques for Main Memory Database Systems." In *Proc. ACM SIGMOD Conference*, Boston, MA, June 1984, p. 1.

[DeWitt et al. 1986] DeWitt D. J., Gerber R. H., Graefe G., Heytens M. L., Kumar K. B. and Muralikrishna M. "GAMMA - A High Performance Dataflow Database Machine." In *Proc. International Conference on Very Large Data Bases(VLDB)*, Kyoto, Japan, August 1986, p. 228.

[DeWitt et al. 1990] DeWitt D. J., Ghandeharizadeh S., Schneider D., Bricker A., Hsiao H. I. and Rasmussen R. "The Gamma Database Machine Project." *IEEE Transactions on Knowledge and Data Engineering* **2, 1** (March 1990), p. 44.

[Gangulu et al. 1992] Ganguly S., Hasan W. and Krishnamurthy R. "Query Optimization for Parallel Execution." In *Proc. ACM SIGMOD Conference*, San Diego, CA, June 1992, p. 9.

[Graefe 1987] Graefe G. "Software Modularization with the EXODUS Optimizer Generator." *IEEE Database Engineering* **10, 4** (December 1987).

[Graefe and Maier 1988] Graefe G. and Maier D. "Query Optimization in Object- Oriented Database Systems: A Prospectus." In *Advances in Object-Oriented Database Systems* Vol. 334: (Dittrich K. R. eds.), Springer-Verlag, September 1988, p. 358.

[Graefe 1989] Graefe G. "Relational Division: Four Algorithms and Their Performance." In *Proc. IEEE Conference on Data Engineering*, Los Angelos, CA, February 1989, p. 94.

[Graefe and Ward 1989] Graefe G. and Ward K. "Dynamic Query Evaluation Plans." In *Proc. ACM SIGMOD Conference*, Portland, OR, May-June 1989, p. 358.

[Graefe 1990a] Graefe G. "Encapsulation of Parallelism in the Volcano Query Processing System." In *Proc. ACM SIGMOD Conference*, Atlantic City, NJ, May 1990, p. 102.

[Graefe 1990b] Graefe G. *Parallel External Sorting in Volcano*. CU Boulder Computer Science Technical Report 459, 1990.

[Graefe et. al. 1990] Graefe G., Maier D., Daniels S. and Keller T. "A Software Architecture for Efficient Query Processing in Object-Oriented Database Systems with Encapsulated Behavior." *Unpublished manuscript*, April 1990.

[Graefe and Davison 1991] Graefe G. and Davison D. L. "Encapsulation of Parallelism and Architecture-Independence in Extensible Database Query Processing." *Submitted for publication*, 1991.

[Graefe and Shapiro 1991] Graefe G. and Shapiro L. D. "Data Compression and Database Performance." In *Proc. ACM/IEEE-CS Symp. on Applied Computing*, Kansas City, MO, April 1991.

[Graefe 1992a] Graefe G. "Volcano, An Extensible and Parallel Dataflow Query Processing System." To appear in *IEEE Transactions on Knowledge and Data Eng.*, 1993.

[Graefe 1992b] Graefe G. "Five Performance Enhancements for Hybrid Hash Join." *In preparation, 1992.*

[Graefe and McKenna 1992] Graefe G. and McKenna W. J. "Extensibility and Search Efficiency in the Volcano Optimizer Generator." *Submitted for publication, 1992.*

[Graefe and Thakkar 1992] Graefe G. and Thakkar S. S. "Tuning a Parallel Database Algorithm on a Shared-Memory Multiprocessor." *Software-Practice and Experience*, **22, 7** (July 1992), pp. 495-517.

[Graefe et al. 1992] Graefe G., Linville A. and Shapiro L. D. *Sort versus Hash Revisited.* CU Boulder Computer Science Technical Report 534, July 1991, 1992.

[Haas et al. 1989] Haas L. M., Freytag J. C., Lohman G. and Pirahesh H. "Extensible Query Processing in Starburst." In *Proc. ACM SIGMOD Conference*, Portland, OR, May-June 1989, p. 377.

[Haas et al. 1990] Haas L., Chang W., Lohman G., McPherson J., Wilms P.F., Lapis G., Lindsay B., Pirahesh H., Carey M. J.and Shekita E. "Starburst Mid-Flight: As the Dust Clears." *IEEE Transactions on Knowledge and Data Eng.* **2, 1** (March 1990), p. 143.

[Hasan and Pirahesh 1988] Hasan W. and Pirahesh H. *Query Rewrite Optimization in Starburst.* Computer Science Research Report, San Jose, CA, August 1988.

[Hong and Stonebraker 1991] Hong W. and Stonebraker M. "Optimization of Parallel Query Execution Plans in XPRS." In *Proc. International Conference on Parallel and Distributed Information Systems*, Miami Beach, Fl, December 1991.

[Hong 1992] Hong W. "Exploiting Inter-Operation Parallelism in XPRS." In *Proc. ACM SIGMOD Conference*, San Diego, CA, June 1992, p. 19.

[Keller et al. 1991] Keller T., Graefe G. and Maier D. "Efficient Assembly of Complex Objects." In *Proc. ACM SIGMOD Conferences*, Denver, CO, May 1991, p. 148.

[Khoshafian and Valduriez 1987] Khoshafian S. and Valduriez P. "Parallel Execution Strategies for Declustered Databases." In *Proc. 5th International Workshop on Database Machines*, Karuizawa, Japan, October 1987.

[Kooi 1980] Kooi R. P. "The Optimization of Queries in Relational Databases." *Ph.D. Thesis, Case Western Reserve University, September 1980.*

[Lee et al. 1988] Lee M. K., Freytag J. C. and Lohman G. "Implementing an Interpreter for Functional Rules in a Query Optimizer." In *Proc. International Conference on Very Large Data Bases*, Long Beach, CA, August 1988, p. 218.

[Lohman 1988] Lohman G. M. "Grammar-Like Functional Rules for Representing Query Optimization Alternatives." In *Proc. ACM SIGMOD Conference*, Chicago, IL, June 1988, p 18.

[Neches 1984] Neches P. M. "Hardware Support for Advanced Data Management Systems." *IEEE Computer* **17, 11** (November 1984), p. 29.

[Neches 1988] Neches P. M. "The Ynet: An Interconnect Structure for a Highly Concurrent Data Base Computer System." In *Proc. 2nd Symposium on the Frontiers of Massively Parallel Computation*, Fairfax, October 1988.

[Ono and Lohman 1990] Ono K. and Lohman G. M. "Measuring the Complexity of Join Enumeration in Query Optimization" In *Proc. International Conference on Very Large Data Bases (VLDB)*, Brisbane, Australia, 1990, p. 314.

[Selinger et al. 1979] Selinger P. G., Astrahan M., Chamberlin D. D., Lorie R. A. and Price T. G. "Access Path Selection in a Relational Database Management System." In *Proc. ACM SIGMOD Conference*, Boston, MA, May-June 1979, p. 23.

[Stonebraker et al. 1989] Stonebraker M., Aoki P. and Seltzer M. "Parallelism in XPRS." *UCB/Electronics Research Lab. Memorandum M89/16*, Berkeley, February 1989.

[Stonebraker et al. 1988] Stonebraker M., Katz R., Patterson D. and Ousterhout J. "The Design of XPRS." In *Proc. International Conference on Very Large Data Bases (VLDB)*, Long Beach, CA, August 1988, p. 318.

[Teradata 1983] Teradata, DBC/1012. "Data Base Computer, Concepts and Facilities." *Teradata Corporation*, Los Angeles, CA, 1983.

[Wells et al. 1992] Wells D., Blakeley J. A. and Thompson C. W. "Architecture of an Open Object-Oriented Database Management System." Submitted to *IEEE Computer*, Dallas, TX, January 1992.

[Wolniewicz and Graefe 1992] Wolniewicz R. H. and Graefe G. "Automatic Optimization and Parallelization of Computations in Scientific Databases." *In preparation, 1992.*

12

Challenges for Query Processing in Object-Oriented Databases

David Maier
Scott Daniels
Thomas Keller
Bennet Vance
Goetz Graefe
William McKenna

Abstract

Object-oriented databases (OODBs) have now appeared in the commercial marketplace. Their support of user-defined types to model complex structures and behaviors has brought about initial acceptance in some applications, such as electronic, mechanical and software CAD, where more traditional record-oriented databases have been found wanting in modeling power. To branch out into related areas of engineering and manufacturing, as well as address applications in science and office automation, OODBs will have to provide query processing facilities of the power and efficiency available in relational systems. These query languages must allow database clients to fully exploit user-defined types.

This paper enumerates features useful for defining database types, and also discusses the challenges they introduce for query processing. We then consider approaches being advocated and explored for query processing in OODBs and other next-generation database systems. The last part of the paper outlines the approach the REVELATION project is taking towards the challenges listed, in the context of object-oriented databases with encapsulated behavior.

12.1
Motivation

Many new database systems are being designed to support applications with advanced data management requirements, such as computer-aided design, engineering and manufacturing, document and multimedia preparation, office automation and scientific computing. Prototypes and early commercial versions are beginning to appear for many of these next-generation approaches, based on, for example, semantic models, relational extensions, persistent programming languages, structural and behavioral object-oriented databases and deductive databases. While these systems are clearly more powerful than conventional DBMSs so far as **expressiveness** is concerned they must become more powerful **performers** as well if they are to succeed. Some of these systems are seeing performance success in particular applications. An example is in design-tool support for electronic, mechanical and software CAD. A major need in this area is for interactive manipulation of complex design artifacts. Record-oriented databases typically have not been tuned to the access pattern of navigation of a single compound object. In this domain, OODBs are typically supplanting a storage manager implemented on a file system, rather than replacing a record-oriented database management system.

However, these new systems have yet to prove their capabilities for query processing. We think that fast associative access to data will remain the dominating factor in some of the application areas listed above, such as document retrieval in office automation, and will be essential for at least some applications in each area, such as design evaluation and simulation in the computer-aided engineering area. The problem, as we see it, is that these new database systems introduce many new data model features that are not handled by current query processing technology (i.e., the query processing subsystems of relational DBMSs). Examples of these features are heterogeneous collections, complex objects, constructors for parameterized types, procedural attachment, object identity, versions, derived fields, class hierarchies, ordered bulk data types, user-defined types and recursion. The overall problem, then, is to expand query optimization and query evaluation to address and exploit these new modeling and query extensions. This paper views this problem in the context of behavioral object-oriented databases, and concentrates in particular on those features that aid in producing user-defined database types. Even though our focus is on OODBs, we believe that much of the discussion applies to other next-generation databases systems, such as extended relational models and logic databases.

Our understanding from early users of object database prototypes and products is that the feature they value most is type extensibility the ability for database programmers to define their own data types beyond what the DBMS provides. Such type definition capability allows customizing a DBMS to a particular application domain, giving larger or more natural building blocks for modeling domain entities. It also provides data independence at a logical level, allowing data reorganization or reimplementation of behavior while providing a constant interface of operations to applications. Further, user-defined data types are well suited to reusability, combining both data structure and operations in logical units unlike record-based systems where the routines to manipulate a particular data item are likely to be dispersed throughout the application code.

Some commercial relational products are already supporting user-defined data types as extensions to the set of base types in the system. For example, one can add a *Date* or *Time* data type if it does not already exist. We believe that users want a more potent type extensibility than just new basic types.

We have chosen the name manifest types to describe the desired capabilities. Manifest types are first-class, immediate and abstract.

First-class means that user-defined types have equal footing with system-supplied types. Thus, instances of these types can appear anywhere an instance of a system-supplied type can, not just as a field in a record. For example, a single instance of a user-defined type could be the value of a database variable, and persist independently of membership in any collection.

Immediate means that type definition facilities are available to any database programmer at any time. Thus, the system for defining new types should be the Data Definition Language (DDL) and Data Manipulation Language (DML) of the database system, rather than the implementation language of the DBMS. Further, new types should be definable whenever schema definition can happen, and not just at database system generation or installation time. This requirement does not preclude other mechanisms for adding new types.

Abstract means that the implementation of a type can be hidden from its clients; that data and function can be encapsulated from clients of the type. However, it is desirable that the functions associated with a type be understandable by the database system, and not just black-box routines to be linked in. We leave open for the time being whether the ability to define new types should imply the ability to define new type constructors or parameterized types. However, we do believe that type constructors, whether system supplied or user defined, should be freely composable.

Having recognized the importance of user-defined types in next-generation database systems, we have concentrated our efforts in the REVELATION project on features that we see as most useful for manifest user-defined data types, while trying to recast as much as we can of set-processing technology from relational databases. Among the features we think most important for type definition are encapsulation, complex state, object identity, polymorphism, ordered data structures (such as sequences and multidimensional arrays), and specification and implementation hierarchies. Some of the technology we want from relational query processing is query optimization, index selection, set-oriented processing and parallel evaluation.

In the next section, we explain why we think those features are useful for type definition, mostly by means of example. We then point out what complication each feature introduces, and indicate how we plan to handle these challenges. Following that is an initial view of the REVELATION approach to meeting these challenges, and also some discussion of related work addressing similar issues. We then cover in turn some of the major components of the REVELATION approach: the Revealer and Annotator, the query algebra, issues in query optimizer generation (in particular extensibility of physical property calculation and cost estimation) and the runtime system, including a special operation for object assembly.

12.2
Utility and Drawbacks of Modeling Features

12.2.1   Usefulness of New Data Model Features

For discussing some of the features below, we introduce a simple example on which to draw for illustrations. We imagine a database for scene description, as might be used for rendering images or motion planning. The two principal types are *Polygon* and *Prop* Polygons will be the basic building blocks for scenes. The behavior of a polygon includes returning an ordered list of its vertices (points in 3-space), computing its intersection with a given line or plane, and updating its vertices subject to the constraint that they remain co-planar and the polygon remain convex. A *Prop* is like a stage property in a theater it is a logical unit in a scene, composed of polygons. The behavior of a *Prop* includes returning a sequence of the polygons in it, saying which polygons in it intersect a given plane or polygon, and returning a translation of itself. Either type may have subtypes. We also allow that instances of these types can exist in `value` and `object` forms. The distinction is that the object instances possess identity and can be multiply referenced, whereas a value represents just an abstract state.

Encapsulation allows multiple implementations of a type to exist in the same database. Consider some possible implementations of *Prop*:

- as an explicit list of *Polygon* values

- as a list of references to *Polygon* objects

- as a collection of sub-props. Here the *allPolygons* message could be implemented by sending *allPolygons* to the sub-props and concatenating the results. Such an implementation captures the hierarchical structure of certain *Props*.

- as a reference to a sub-prop and a list of translations of that sub-prop. For example, a torus might be modeled as one *Prop* representing a 15-degree slice of the torus, plus 23 translations of that slice.

- computationally. A sphere might just store a center, radius and granularity, and compute the component polygons as requested.

- as a reference to another *Prop* and a transformation matrix specifying translation, reflection and scaling.

To illustrate the use of different implementations, Figure 12.1 depicts three *Props* for tree objects. *Tree1* is implemented as an explicit list of *Polygon*, perhaps generated with fractal surface techniques. *Tree2* is implemented using reference to *Tree1* and a transform matrix representing a reflection. The implementation of *Tree3* holds a reference to *Tree2* with scaling and translation. Naturally, the methods that implement behavior in different implementations of *Prop* will be different, in general. For example, the *allPolygons* message sent to *Tree1* can just access the internal list of polygons. The same message sent to *Tree2* could send the *allPolygons* message to the *Prop* it references *Tree1* (in this case) and then iterate over that list, applying the transform matrix to each polygon.

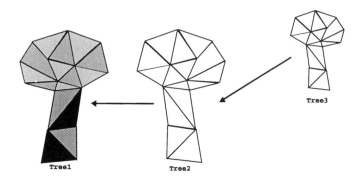

FIGURE 12.1
Different implementations of Prop

It is easy to imagine cases where any one of these implementations is the most appropriate. Encapsulation says the particular choice can be hidden from clients of the type (applications or other types), because each supports the same group of operations. Encapsulation also gives control over enforcing semantic invariants during update. If a *Polygon* is represented as a list of points and applications can modify that list directly, it is difficult to ensure that invariants such as co-planarity and convexity hold. If the basic update operations for a *Polygon* are encapsulated with its representation, then those operators can check the invariants, and the checks need not be in the application code.

Complex State means a rich set of data structuring mechanisms is available for specifying the internal representation of a type, and these constructors can be freely composed. Thus, one representation of a *Prop* might be *set of list of* $(X, Y, Z : Int)$. The lists capture the data to specify polygons and the XYZ-tuple the information for their vertex points. Note the nesting of the tuple constructor inside the list constructor inside the set constructor. Another representation could be *set of Polygon*. For the first representation, the method for the *allPolygons* message would have to construct a *Polygon* instance from each *list of* $(X, Y, Z : Int)$. With the second representation, the *Polygon* instances already exist.

Object Identity allows shared references to subcomponents of an object irrespective of their values. We might want an implementation of *Polygon* that uses *list of ThreeDimPoint* as a representation, where a *ThreeDimPoint* is an object, and two polygons can share points in their representations, in order, for example, to keep a side in common. Update to the position of a *ThreeDimPoint* from either containing polygon would be available in both places. Figure 12.2 shows a pair of polygons that share two *Point* objects, $P1$ and $P2$, and how the two polygons remain connected when the state of $P2$ is updated.

Type Hierarchies exploit similarities among classes of entities, for type specification or type implementation. An example on the specification side is if *ColoredPoly* is a subtype of *Polygon* that can respond to a *color* message, and *PatternedPoly* as a subtype of *ColoredPoly* with additional behavior to provide texturing in addition to color. If a *Polygon* responds to a message as to whether it intersects a certain plane, then *ColoredPoly* and *PatternedPoly* also respond to that message. Thus, a heterogeneous set of *Polygon*, *ColoredPoly*, and *PatternedPoly* can be queried uniformly to select those that intersect a plane P, since that is common behavior to all three types. Similarly, a collection of *ColoredPoly* and *PatternedPoly* can be queried for *color* equal to red, although *Polygon*'s cannot be included in the collection for correct typing of the query. An example of implementation inheritance is if we have an implementation **I1** for type *InsertableList*, and

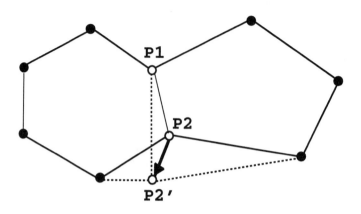

FIGURE 12.2
Two Polygons sharing common Point objects

want to use this implementation, with possible additions or modifications, to generate implementation **I2** for *Polygon*. Note that while **I2** inherits representation and methods from **I1**, it may be the case that *Polygon* is not below *InsertableList* in the specification hierarchy.

In investigating needs for scientific data management, we have seen that **ordered data structures** are valuable for the representation of scientific data types. Examples of ordered structures are lists, time series and multidimensional arrays. Here we draw an example from protein structure analysis. Proteins themselves are sequences of amino acids. For describing tertiary protein structure (how the molecule twists and folds in 3-space), the atoms in the amino acids need to be represented, in order to associate spatial coordinates with certain carbon atoms along the backbone, among others. To deduce the spatial patterns from this positioning information, it is useful to form a threshold matrix. The threshold matrix is derived from a matrix of atom-to-atom distances of the backbone carbon atoms in the protein, by setting all entries above a certain threshold value to 1 and the rest to 0. Diagonal bands of 1's in the threshold matrix represent locations where the protein strand parallels itself. In implementing types to represent such protein structures and threshold matrices, it is certainly useful to have ordered data structures available. Although a list or matrix can be represented as a set of records (a relation) by explicitly coding order or array index in a field, updating and accessing such a representation is inefficient.

Many of the new data models provide more general **persistent name spaces** than conventional data models possess. These name spaces resemble those of programming languages, with variables declared of arbitrary types, and arbitrary numbers of variables that can be declared of a given type. Moreover, the variables can have their values reassigned arbitrarily. Contrast this situation with that in relational databases, where the only persistent variables have type relation (as opposed to a tuple or scalar type). Also, type definition is directly coupled with variable declaration. Typically, a relational DDL defines a relation type at the same time it creates a variable of that type. Moreover, there is also a relation instance created that is permanently bound to the relation name (although the state of that relation instance may be updated).

12.2.2 Complications Introduced by New Features

While all these features make for powerful data definition facilities, they create new challenges for query processing. Query processing has traditionally had a structural orientation data models did not attach behavior to data items beyond that dictated by their data structure. Hence encapsulation, since it bundles behavior with structure, is a new wrinkle. Encapsulation makes it difficult for the optimizer to get the **"big picture."** Current query optimization assumes that a complete description of the query is available, in terms of structural operators. In an object-oriented database, a query may be as simple as a single message to a single object. With just a small expression to optimize, the range of transformations the optimizer can apply is limited. Moreover, since a message can represent an arbitrary amount of computing, it is hard to estimate its cost or the cost of alternative evaluation plans even if they are available. Another problem with encapsulation comes when there are multiple implementations of a type. Current set processing depends a great deal on homogeneity of structure as in, for example, allocating temporary storage space to records in intermediate results, or in computing offsets for fields in records. However, a collection of elements of type T could have heterogeneous structure because of multiple representations in various implementations of T. For instance, consider a collection C of $Prop$, where $Prop$'s in C use a variety of the implementations given in Section 12.2.1

A problem with complex state is that only a small part of that state may be needed for a particular query. Reading in the entire state of the object (especially if **entire** includes other objects that are referenced) can fill memory with irrelevant information. Consider an instance PP of $PatternedPoly$ that has a texture bitmap as part of its representation. Suppose PP is in a set S of $Polygon$ that we query for intersection with a given plane. To answer the query, there is no need to retrieve the bitmap for PP. Bringing the needed pieces of an object from disk only as they are demanded for computation may not be efficient for I/O, however. There are similar problems with object identity. If object identifiers are dereferenced only on demand, secondary storage management degenerates to pointer chasing on disk.

We noted how type hierarchies allow heterogeneous collections of objects to be queried on their common protocol. The same complications arise with the multiple implementations of objects in such a collection as do with multiple implementations of a single type, mentioned above. Encapsulation and hierarchies also introduce problems with defining, maintaining, and determining the applicability of auxiliary access structures such as indexes [Bertino and Kim 1989, Kim et al. 1989, Maier and Stein 1986].

In looking at ordered data structures, we see that the **iteration idioms** that are supported by operators in record-processing systems (such as select and join) are not necessarily suited to the common manipulations on scientific data types. Returning to the protein structure example, biochemists are interested in correlating patterns of amino acids with structural features. Supporting pattern searching efficiently at the physical level means running a scan over the underlying list structure that keeps a window of elements in memory. Typical physical scans in relational implementations are oriented towards operating on a single data item at a time, such as iterating over the members of a set.

Having persistent names (that semantically resemble variables in a programming language) presents a problem with where to attach statistics that an optimizer would use in cost estimation. In a relational system, there is not much distinction between associating statistics with a relation name or a relation instance. However, with a collection-valued variable that can be reassigned during a transaction, it seems that statistics should be associated with collection instances. However, it may be that only the variable name is known during query optimization, and not the identity of the particular instance that will occupy it at run time. Thus there is a conflict in that one wants to associate statistics with instances for maintenance, but needs statistics with names for optimization.

12.3
REVELATION Overview

In the REVELATION project we are looking at ways to deal with each of the problems described above. We will state briefly some solutions we are pursuing, and then survey approaches to some of the same problems taken by other projects. We will later return to REVELATION, discussing the principal components in a prototype query processor we are building.

To deal with encapsulation, we have introduced a **Revealer**, a trusted system component that is allowed to break encapsulation in order to provide the optimizer with more choices for transformations and to provide a larger scope for planning the query. To deal with hierarchies and polymorphism we plan to employ at least two approaches. One is to look across multiple types and implementations for a **coincidences** : commonalities over several definitions. Another is an algebra operator that logically partitions a collection into multiple data streams based on type [Vandenberg and DeWitt 1991]. For ordered structures, we want our object algebra to contain operators that can represent the most common iterators over those structures. We are looking at scientific codes and statistical analysis packages such as newS [Becker et al. 1988] for insights here. Among the main challenges in formulating such an algebra is including multiple bulk types without making the algebra unwieldy for optimization or implementation. To avoid inefficiencies with object-at-a-time access associated with naive handling of complex objects and on-demand dereferencing of object identifiers, we have added an **assembly** operator to the query evaluation routines [Keller et al. 1991]. Finally, in dealing with a more general naming scheme for persistent data items, we are tracking the stability of bindings in our name space. The query optimizer can incorporate more or less of this information based on the expected lifetime of a query (one transaction, one execution of an application program, multiple executions of an application program).

An underlying concern in all these areas is **extensibility**: producing an architecture in which the effects of change are non-catastrophic. As we have already discussed, we want it to be quite easy for database users to extend the collection of types a database supports. We also want to provide for extensions made by the implementors of the query processor. In our own work, we do not by any means expect to make all the **right** choices the first time through, and so want to construct the system so we can change our minds later without having to do a complete rewrite. Possible extensions include new data structures and operators in the object algebra, new physical formats for those data structures, new query optimizer rules and heuristics, new physical properties of interest, different kinds of statistics, additional types of auxiliary access paths, and new runtime evaluation algorithms.

12.4
Related Work

In this section we first consider briefly the query facilities of some current OODB products and prototypes. We then look more carefully at the query processing mechanisms in some extensible database systems and at proposals for query algebras in object-oriented and functional languages.

12.4.1   Query Processing in Current Object-Oriented Database Systems

Query processing capabilities in most current OODB products and advanced prototypes are limited in their expressivity or the sophistication of their query optimization and processing techniques. In the current crop of commercial systems, queries are generally limited to selecting a subset from a set of existing objects with conditions that are given as a conjunction of path comparisons. There is seldom post-processing of selected elements as part of the query, nor is the combination of elements from different collections generally supported. Query optimization consists largely of detecting opportunities to apply indexes. Often methods are excluded from consideration during query processing, or limited to those procedures that can themselves be expressed as queries. Dynamic binding of operations to methods is generally inefficient or lacking, thus limiting query processing abilities on heterogeneous collections. Only O_2 and Exodus, to our knowledge, support querying against bulk types other than sets. Even in O_2, where queries can be posed against ordered collections, there is no facility for constructing auxiliary access paths on such data structures. The query processing facilities of these systems tend to be hardwired into a particular language at the top end. The OQL[X] approach at Texas Instruments [Blakeley et al. 1990] is a notable exception to this single-language dependence. Extended relational systems, such as POSTGRES and Starburst, have more mature query processing technology. However, they do not support all aspects of manifest types. Their type extension facilities are currently aimed at providing new base types, with the extension done in the database implementation language. Hence, they have not addressed all the ramifications of user-defined database types upon query processing.

We mention some of the characteristics of specific products and proto-types vis-a-vis query processing.

The EXODUS project [Carey et al. 1990a] focuses on a structural data model and query processing algebra, bypassing some of the difficulties for query optimization and execution introduced by data abstraction and encapsulation envelopes. (Methods are allowed if they are expressible as queries, and overriding of methods in subtypes is allowed.) The EXTRA data model does include support for bulk data types other than set, for example, one-dimensional array. However, the algebraic operators on these types in the EXODUS algebra are limited to what is expressible in the EXCESS query language [Vandenberg and DeWitt 1991]. We will say more about EXODUS in the section on query algebras.

The ZEITGEIST project at Texas Instruments [Ford at al. 1988] and the Open OODB project [Wells et al. 1992] aim at defining and implementing a general, portable object-oriented database platform based on a consensus of what mechanisms and services such a DBMS should provide. The main contribution of this design will be the modularization of the OODBMS with well-defined interfaces to allow future extension. One of the modules iden-tified is the query processor. That group is devoting considerable effort to determining the interaction of the query processor with other system com-ponents, such as the storage manager, the schema and the object manager. They are also concerned with how to specify an object query language that can be bound to more than one language environment.

Hewlett-Packard has developed the IRIS prototype [Wilkinson et al. 1990] into a product (Open ODB). The IRIS system makes extensive use of functions to implement the capabilities of extensible and object-oriented systems. In fact, the external data model and query language for IRIS look much like those for functional data models. However, the internal physical structures and query processing make extensive use of relational technology. An interesting point regarding IRIS and function inheritance is that in IRIS the method for a function is bound statically based on the declared types of the arguments, whereas we are supporting dynamic binding of messages to methods based on the immediate (runtime) type of the object receiving the message.

The O_2 project [Deux 1990, Deux et al. 1991] at Altair pursued an object-oriented product based on a client-server architecture. This project made innovative contributions on object clustering, language interaction and formal methods. The O_2 query language is one of the most flexible and expressive among OODB products. The O_2 approach to query optimization does not currently include use of an object algebra for optimization, but an internal representation of queries has been proposed that is claimed to support currently known query optimization transformations [Cluet and Delobel 1993].

The ORION project [Kim et al. 1990] at MCC investigated a variety of object-oriented concepts including clustering, versioning (including schema versioning), and some issues in query processing. The ORION model assumes that type extents are always the base collections for queries. This approach to naming is close to what the relational approach supports, and avoids some of the problems of where to attach statistics. ORION provides method definitions, but these methods are not expanded for query optimization. However, ORION has dealt extensively with queries over complex object structures defined by reference links and a part-of hierarchy.

There are also projects concerned with structural object-oriented databases, which have contributed generalized algebraic operator definitions and implementation algorithms for them. We will be looking towards that work for inspiration these areas. The DASDBS project [Schek, Paul, and Weikum 1990] aims at defining an extensible kernel of services that are useful in implementing next-generation database management. DASDBS query processing facilities are based on a single hierarchical scan over a nested relation. It is up to the particular semantic model implemented on top of this kernel to utilize such scans for efficient query evaluation. The DAMOKLES prototype [Dittrich et al. 1987] is a structural object model with a more expressive query facility, but without an abstract type definition system. Its query model is interesting in that the result of a query is a subdatabase, rather than just a single collection of objects. While we do not cover that topic in this paper, we think database-to-database queries will be quite important in the context of imposing object models on record-oriented data models [Mitschang and Pirahesh 1993].

The GemStone [Butterworth et al. 1991] and ObjectStore [Lamb et al. 1991] database systems are typical of commercial OODB products in their query capabilities. Both base queries on selection from instances of system-supplied collection types, and both integrate this query facility into the syntax of the method-definition language. The ObjectStore notation can distinguish between requesting a subset of the queried collection that meets the selection condition, or just a single element of the collection. In neither system are the queriable collections limited to type extents, so when the result of a query is a collection, that result itself can be further queried. For both systems, the range of selection conditions (at least those that can be optimized) is less than the full set of Boolean expressions in the method language.

12.4.2   Query Processing in Extended Relational Systems

In the following subsections we consider in more detail two advanced database system prototypes, POSTGRES and Starburst. While neither completely supports manifest types, both projects have given serious attention to extensibility, including user-defined database types.

POSTGRES

The POSTGRES project at UC Berkeley [Stonebraker and Rowe 1986, Stonebraker, Rowe, and Hirohama 1990, Stonebraker and Kemnitz 1991] approaches the needs of modern applications by providing support for data, object and knowledge management with an extended and extensible relational model. Data management support addresses database topics such as concurrency and transaction support. Knowledge management support deals with the addition of rules to a database management system [Stonebraker et al. 1986, Stonebraker et. al 1990]. It is support for object management that is of most interest here. The POSTGRES data model [Rowe and Stonebraker 1987] builds upon the relational data model while trying to maintain the simplicity of that model. Features of the POSTGRES data model include object identity, an abstract data type facility for adding base types, constructed types with inheritance, user-defined functions, user-defined query operators and POSTQUEL functions.

User-defined type extensions in POSTGRES are made through the ADT facility. That facility was adapted from extensions made to INGRES [Stonebraker 1986]. Adding a new data type involves specifying the amount of space an instance of it will require and providing input and output functions to convert between a literal string and instances. When defining the new type, only the number of bytes needed are specified. The interpretation of what those bytes represent is left to functions on the new type. Defining a function entails providing a signature specification and the location of the code implementing the function. Other additions needed for query optimization are discussed below. ADT functions are typically used in query predicates. Note that ADTs provide for new scalar operations, but not new iterators on bulk types.

Complex objects were introduced in INGRES originally [Stonebraker et al. 1984] and later POSTGRES [Stonebraker et al. 1987] by allowing data fields to contain procedures. When accessing a data field containing a procedure, the query represented by the procedure is executed. Logically it appears that the field takes on the value of the result of the query. For data fields that logically may contain several items of different types, such as *Circle*, *Line* and *Box*, this representation reduces the number of joins needed for evaluation. Instead of an arbitrary number of joins, only those explicitly mentioned in the **query field** are performed. For example, suppose a *Shape* object can contain *Circle*'s, *Line*'s and *Box*'es (Here we are assuming that there is a separate relation for each of *Circle*, *Line* and *Box*.). If procedures are not allowed in data fields, a general query will require three joins to materialize all *Circle*'s, *Line*'s and *Box*'es for a given *Shape*. When a *Shape* does not contain all three components some unnecessary joins will be executed. Note that object-to-object links require one join per navigation step. Thus navigational queries are still expensive in this model.

Increased performance for queries involving new data types is accomplished either extending the current access methods or writing completely new access methods. Extending POSTGRES access methods requires the data type implementor to define a number of additional operations on that data type. For example, the use of a B-Tree access method for a new data type requires a companion operation to determine ordering. If current POSTGRES access methods are unsuitable, it is possible to create a new access method. However, the creation of new access methods was determined, in retrospect, to be impossible for ordinary database users. The ability to optimize queries involving new data types is directly determined by the availability of access methods.

Functions on new data types are not currently addressed in the query optimization process. The assumption appears to be that such a functions is a simple expression that only affects the local state of its arguments. (However, the POSTGRES project is now starting to consider costs of function evaluation [Stonebraker 1991].) In this respect, functions are not equivalent to general methods found in object-oriented database systems. Also, functions are currently restricted to one or two arguments that must be instances of the data type for which the function is defined.

Optimization of stored procedures is limited to those written in POST-QUEL. General C functions, although allowed, cannot be optimized and must be blindly executed at query evaluation time. POSTQUEL procedures are expanded within the query optimizer by recursive calls to the planner. The results of nested queries are assumed to be small [Fong 1986] and thus their cost may not be accurately accounted for. POSTGRES only supports encapsulation for its ADT mechanism, and the query optimizer does not attempt to understand function implementations. Instead, functions on ADTs, in combination with access methods, must be used to create indexes on fields containing ADTs. Generation information vital to query optimization, such as selectivity estimates, for ADTs is an even greater problem.

Starburst

The goal of IBM's Starburst project [Haas et al. 1990, Lohman et al. 1991] is to develop a completely extensible relational database management system without sacrificing performance. This approach is motivated by a desire to preserve support for traditional applications and, at the same time, develop a means of extending the system for more advanced applications. Starburst has been designed to support extensions including new data types, new operations and support for efficient access to data. Starburst has also considered extensibility in other dimensions, such as rules and integrity constraints. Here we concentrate on those related to query processing.

The two major components of Starburst are the language processor, Corona [Haas et al. 1989], and the data manager, Core. At the front-end of Starburst is an extensible DML and DDL. This extension of SQL allows the addition of table expressions, functions on table columns, data types in table columns, and table functions. These additions are supported by an extensible internal representation of queries, the Query Graph Model (QGM). The QGM is primarily extended by adding new operations and quantifiers on tables. Such additions require an execution routine in Core, also called a Low-Level Plan Operator (LOLEPOP), and a Strategy Alternative Rule (STAR) to replace a logical operator with the the physical LOLEPOP when the QGM is transformed into a Query Execution Plan (QEP). The LOLEPOP is an extension to Core while the STAR is an extension to the plan optimization phase of Corona.

Starburst's approach to query optimization and performance may be separated into the extensibility of the cost-insensitive **query rewrite** and cos-sensitive **plan optimization** phases of Corona and the ability to define new storage methods and attachments in Core. Query optimization extensions are facilitated by a rule-driven query-rewrite phase. The rule-based approach to query rewrite allows the database customizer to add new rewrite rules without modifications to the rule engine and search facility. We note that the intermediate forms that STARs produce implicitly encode context and strategy information, so the interaction of a new rule with an existing ones must be understood.

QEPs are generated from QGMs by applying STARs. A STAR is represented by a grammar-like set of parameterized production rules. The generality of the specification allows a STAR to express strategies for many extensions, including new access methods, join methods or new operations. Plan optimization, the last step before executing the query, requires each LOLE-POP to produce a set of properties for its output from the properties attached to its inputs. Properties include columns accessed, predicates applied, sort order of tuples, estimated cardinality and estimated cost. When adding new operations, and new LOLEPOPs to implement them, the database customizer must also develop property functions. We see extensibility of property sets as an important capability for an object query processor. Not only do we see the need to supply property functions along with new physical operators, but also the need to define new properties. We can foresee many properties that will be useful for query planning in object queries, such as clustering and information on the portion of an object currently in memory.

New storage methods allow a customizer to provide alternative storage and access for tables. This facility has been used to create table implementations that use a heap, a B-Tree and hashing to store records. Attachments provide the capability to add new access paths (indices), integrity constraints and triggers. Further information on the addition of external data types (EDTs) and the approach adopted by Starburst can be found in Wilms, et al. [Wilms et al. 1988]. We note that EDTs are similar to ADTs in POSTGRES in supporting base type extension; they do not give full support for manifest types.

Complex object support through extensions has also been considered by the Starburst group [Schwarz et al. 1986]. Their initial proposals rely on a combination of primary database enhancements and external extensions. The extensions necessary to implement complex objects include extending records with **component identifiers**, access methods recognizing component identifiers and a query form to materialize complex objects. This particular method of adding complex objects relies on using an attachment. The attachment serves as an index on the tables that hold the components of the complex object. When combined with functions at the language level that use this attachment, a complex object structure can be imposed across multiple tables. Other means of adding complex object support to Starburst are possible. More recently, complex object support through complex views has been proposed [Mitschang and Pirahesh 1993].

12.4.3   Object Algebras

The other area we consider carefully is object algebras. We view finding an appropriate object algebra as central to a successful architecture for object query processing. Clearly, the relational algebra has been a keystone for much of relational query processing technology. However, that algebra is tied closely to one bulk type, relation, which is essentially a set of records. We want an algebra that can deal with other bulk-type constructors (sequences, arrays) and with free compositions of type constructors (such as array of record of set). In that connection, we are interested in operators that work over multiple bulk types (or, more accurately, an operator with versions having similar properties over different bulk types). One such operator we will use in the following discussion is $fold$, which applies a function over elements of a collection, then combines the results using a specified binary operator. It exists in versions for lists, multisets, arrays and trees (but not multidimensional arrays). We describe it here in the context of lists. We will use ++ for the list concatenation operator and [ ] for the empty list. We start with a few examples of its use, writing $fold$ as a three-argument message sent to a list.

$$
\begin{aligned}
[2,3,4] \, fold \, (0, square, +) \;\; &= \;\; square(2) + square(3) + square(4) \\
&= \;\; 4 + 9 + 16 \\
&= \;\; 29 \\
[2,3,4] \, fold \, (1, id, *) \;\; &= \;\; 2 * 3 * 4 = 24 \\
[\,] \, fold \, (1, id, *) \;\; &= \;\; 1
\end{aligned}
$$

Schematically, if $f : \alpha \rightarrow \beta$ is a function on the elements of an α-list, $op : \beta \times \beta \rightarrow \beta$ is any associative binary operator, and $u : \beta$ is the algebraic identity for op, then we have

$$
\begin{aligned}
[X1, X2, \ldots, Xn] \, fold \, (u, f, op) \;\; &= \;\; f(X1) \; op \; f(X2) \; op \ldots op \; f(Xn) \\
[\,] \, fold \, (u, f, op) \;\; &= \;\; u
\end{aligned}
$$

At first glance it is surprising that from $fold$ one can derive all the traditional relational operators and more, but in fact one can. In our examples above, the list elements are integers, and op is bound to arithmetic operators. However, the following uses of $fold$ are also legitimate:

$$
\begin{aligned}
[[u, v, w,], [x], [y, z]] \, fold \, ([\,], id, ++) \;\; &= \;\; [u, v, w] + +[x] + +[y, z] \\
&= \;\; [u, v, w, x, y, z] \\
[one, five, two] \, fold \, ([\,], p, ++) \;\; &= \;\; [one] + +[\,] + +[two] \\
&= \;\; [one, two]
\end{aligned}
$$

where $p(X)$ is a function on strings where $p(X) = [X]$ if X is greater or equal to **one** lexicographically and $p(X) = [\,]$ otherwise. Note that $fold$ used with $++$ preserves list order. These examples generalize to the following operators derived from $fold$.

$$
\begin{aligned}
Xs\ flattenmap\ (f) &= Xs\ fold\ ([\,], f, ++) \\
Xs\ flatten &= Xs\ flattenmap\ (id) \\
Xs\ filtermap\ (p, f) &= Xs\ flattenmap\ (\lambda X.if\ p(X)\ \ then\ [f(X)] \\
&\qquad\qquad\qquad\qquad\qquad else\ [\,]) \\
\\
Xs\ select(p) &= Xs\ filtermap\ (p, id) \\
Xs\ map\ (f) &= Xs\ filtermap\ ((\lambda X.true), f) \\
Xs\ project\ (A_1, \ldots, A_n) &= Xs\ map\ (\lambda X.A_1 = X[A_1], ..., A_n = X[A_n])
\end{aligned}
$$

The operator $flattenmap$ assumes that f yields lists when applied to the elements of a collection, and concatenates those lists. The $flatten$ operator assumes its argument is a list of lists. The operator $filtermap$ applies a selection predicate p as well as mapping a function f across list elements. The $select$ shown is relational selection applied to lists, and $project$ is relational projection applied to lists of records. The map operator, also known as $mapcar$, $apply\_to\_all$ and $collect$, appears in functional languages, and in other object-oriented query algebras.

EXCESS/EXTRA

Vandenberg and DeWitt [Vandenberg and DeWitt 1991] describe a complex-object algebra, which we will refer to as the EXCESS/EXTRA algebra. This algebra was designed to be equivalent the EXTRA language in expressive power. The EXTRA/EXCESS algebra assumes a data model in which several general type constructors are provided, and data structures are built through free composition of those constructors. The EXCESS/EXTRA algebra defines a small number of powerful bulk operators that allow multisets and arrays to be processed in analogous ways. Multidimensional arrays are not directly supported by EXTRA/EXCESS. Users may construct them as arrays of arrays or using other representations, but we see the absence of primitive support for them as a potential barrier to efficient implementation of dense arrays. Note in the arrays of arrays implementation one must ensure that the inner arrays have the same length. One problem with $fold$ or similar operators is that its output can be of a length different from its input. Hence, applying it over a multidimensional array in this representation can give a result of non-uniform structure.

The EXTRA/EXCESS algebra is many-sorted, but base types are all grouped together in the same sort. Thus, integers, Booleans, and so forth are all treated simply as **values**, and are not further distinguished; nor are operators provided on **values**. As in the relational algebra, Boolean expressions appear in the algebra, but only as subscripts to operators over some other sort. Consequently, a Boolean expression at the top level of a query cannot be optimized using identities of the algebra. The same applies to Boolean subexpressions of a query if they are not attached to other operators, as well as to integer subexpressions, string subexpressions and so on. The lack of operators and identities for base types concerns us because a complex query, especially after methods are revealed, may contain many subexpressions of many sorts. Whenever possible, we would like to be able to optimize these queries in their entireties.

In the EXTRA/EXCESS algebra there are general operators called *set_apply* and *array_apply* that are equivalent to *map* above. In fact, they are made more powerful through a sleight of hand. The function that is applied to each element of a collection may, for some of those elements, return the special value *dne* for **does not exist**. These result values are discarded from the result collection using a builtin facility, so *set_apply* or *array_apply* need not preserve the cardinality of a collection. This modification makes it possible to implement *filtermap* and *select* with *set_apply*, but still does not give *set_apply* the generality of *fold*. One important reduction, flattening a multiset of multisets, or an array of arrays, is addressed with special operators *set_collapse* and *array_collapse*. However, other reductions, such as summing the elements of an array, are apparently not provided. It is unclear whether a user could write a general, type-safe *fold* operation in the data manipulation language.

ENCORE

Shaw and Zdonik [Shaw and Zdonik 1989a] describe an algebra for the ENCORE object-oriented database system. They characterize all types as abstract data types whose implementations are hidden from the algebra. Axioms on the abstract data types assist the optimizer without revealing implementations. At the same time, they allow for the possibility of making use of **optimization strategies for encapsulated behavior** similarly to the REVELATION approach.

ENCORE's data model provides only two built-in parameterized types, *Tuple* and *Set*. Consequently, bulk data cannot be constructed without sets.

Given this limitation, processing of multisets, lists, and arrays is likely to be costly.

ENCORE has an interesting treatment of object identity. In the tradition of pure object-oriented languages, ENCORE views everything as an object with an identity. An opposing viewpoint is that there is a distinction between **objects** (which possess identity) and **values** (which do not, as in O_2). For atomic types such as Boolean and integer, the distinction is only a matter of terminology. For compound types the distinction is important. If an ENCORE user creates two separate tuples $x = \langle A : 2, B : true \rangle$ and $y = \langle A : 2, B : true \rangle$ then x and y, though equal, will be distinguishable by an identity test. However, in systems that treat tuples as values, x and y would be indistinguishable. The ability to generate values without identity is a great asset in query optimization. For example, it is the indistinguishability of multiple instances of the same value that makes it possible to optimize $g(f(a), f(a))$ to

$$(\lambda z.g(z, z))(f(a))$$

assuming f has no side-effects. In ENCORE, these two expressions could not be guaranteed to yield the same result in general. In fact, given ENCORE's object semantics, very few algebraic transformations can be applied to a query without changing its meaning.

To deal with this difficulty, Shaw and Zdonik have introduced new notions of equivalence of queries [Shaw and Zdonik 1989b]. The roughest form of equivalence they define is **weak equivalence**; it holds on any pair of queries whose results contain the same database objects, glued together in any manner. Thus, if o_1 and o_2 are database objects, then queries returning $\{o_2, \{\{o_1\}, o_2\}\}$ and $\{o_1, o_2\}$ are weakly equivalent. Under this liberal definition of equivalence it again becomes relatively easy to transform a query into a different but equivalent query. However, if the user frames a query so as to structure the result in a particular way, a result with an entirely different structure will hardly do. Thus, one needs somewhat stronger notions of equivalence that still admit query transformations.

Accordingly, Shaw and Zdonik define a family of relations called **i-equality** or **equality at depth i**. This family of equalities generalizes the familiar object-oriented concepts of identity, shallow equality, and deep equality: Identity is equality at depth 0, shallow equality is equality at depth 1 and deep equality may be thought of as equality at infinite depth. Two queries are **i-equivalent** if their results are always i-equal; they are **equivalent at depth i** if, in addition, their results have isomorphic graph structures.

Shaw and Zdonik present a number of query transformations that preserve id-equivalence at depth 2. Using such transformations, one can optimize a query without losing much structural information from its result.

One objection to ENCORE's complicated approach to equivalence is that it could be difficult for users to master. A second, more technical, objection concerns composition of equivalences. Suppose we have a transformation rule that says query Q is k-equivalent to query R for some $k > 0$, and let f be some function. What can we say about the relationship between $f(Q)$ and $f(R)$? In general, we cannot even assure weak equivalence on these two expressions, since f may perform computations sensitive to the structure of its argument. In other words, we may not freely substitute equivalents for equivalents in subqueries. Similarly, if the result of one query may be referred to in subsequent queries, then the initial query may safely be transformed only in ways that preserve equivalence at depth 1.

The most interesting contribution of ENCORE is its provision of query transformations that involve inverse relationships between database collections. These transformations make it clear that vast improvements can be achieved on some queries by exploiting inverse relationships. Such transformations differ from other algebraic transformations in that they rely not only on the properties of the algebraic operators, but also on integrity constraints on the underlying database.

An Algebra Based on FP

A general and abstract approach to algebraic manipulations on bulk types is suggested by Beeri and Kornatzky [Beeri and Kornatzky 90]. Asserting that **functional languages such as Lisp with higher-order functions do not possess a useful algebra of programs due to the unrestrained use of these higher-order function**, they base their algebra on Backus's FP. To FP's tuple constructor they add constructors for sets, multisets, lists, arrays and trees, but they treat all these constructors in a uniform way at least as far as the bulk operators are concerned. The distinctions they make between the constructors are expressed through axioms. For example, a **permutability** axiom on sets says that

$$o_1, o_2, \ldots, o_n = \rho(o_1, o_2, \ldots, o_n)$$

where ρ is any permutation. In this way their model neatly relieves the bulk operator definitions of the need to distinguish between constructor types. On the other hand, it is not clear how such a model might be implemented efficiently.

The bulk operators themselves are familiar: $apply_toa ll$ map, product (a kind of generalized Cartesian product) and pump (similar to fold). Beeri and Kornatzky achieve selection or filtering by using $apply_toa ll$ with a function that yields null for items to be discarded. A constructor axiom for **null elimination** has the effect of removing the unwanted items. The concept here is of course the same as the use of **does not exist** in EXTRA/EXCESS.

The null values are also used to distinguish internal nodes of a tree from its leaves. If a node's subtrees are null, then it is a leaf. The lack of explicit discriminated unions to distinguish different node types restricts the kinds of trees that can be described conveniently. This limitation also leads to cumbersome implementations of simple operations, despite the power of the pump operator. For example, to sum the leaf values of a binary tree, ignoring internal node values, entails passing pump an argument function of surprising messiness.

Maps

Atkinson et al. [Atkinson et al. 1991, Atkinson et al. 1992] take a very different approach to combining minimality with generality. They define a single bulk data type, called a **map**, that can be specialized to any other bulk type one might be interested in: finite functions, arrays, relations, other kinds of sets and so on. Although the authors describe relations as just one of many bulk types that maps can represent, one can also turn this view upside down and take relations as a starting point. Then maps can be characterized as relations whose unique-key constraints are enforced, and whose attribute types are arbitrary. For example, a relation can be used as a finite **function** from its key to its other attributes. If the key is an integer, the function represents an **array** of sorts. A **set** is simply a relation whose key includes all its attributes. For efficiency reasons, these relations implementing maps of different kinds are maintained in key-sorted order, and in some operations this order affects semantics.

Maps come with both imperative and algebraic operations. Among the latter are union, intersection and difference, which are almost the same as their relational counterparts. However, union and intersection are not commutative if the operand maps, viewed as relations, have keys in common. There is a generation construct that achieves selection, projection, and so forth, using a syntax akin to that of list comprehensions. We comment briefly on comprehensions in the next subsection.

Abstract Bulk Types

List comprehension notation, found in several functional languages, allows lists to be generated in a concise, declarative manner that resembles mathematical set-former notation. Wadler [Wadler 1990] has given an algebraic characterization of comprehensions that can be motivated by category theory. Trinder and others have explored the use of comprehensions as a database query notation refmai:Heyt91,mai:Nik91,mai:Trin92. Trinder emphasizes the possibilities for query optimization offered by the algebraic structure underlying comprehensions.

In Trinder's treatment, the possible manipulations on a bulk data type are distilled to a quadruple of functions. Such a quadruple, provided it is associated with a type constructor and that its components satisfy certain algebraic laws, is called a **quad**. As an example, the four functions for the list constructor would be map, $\lambda X.[X]$, $flatten$, and $\lambda X.[\ ]$. Evaluation of a list comprehension involves translating the comprehension into an algebraic expression built from these four functions.

Quadric descriptions also exist for sets, multisets, and some trees. Each such description includes four functions, which we refer to generically as map, $single$, $flatten$ and $empty$. A comprehension for a given bulk type can always be translated into a quadric expression; thus, comprehensions provide nothing in expressiveness that cannot be obtained by other means. (What comprehensions do provide is notational convenience an important consideration in the design of user languages, but less important to the construction of an algebra.)

Of concern to us is the expressiveness of the quads themselves. Clearly they can express map and $flatten$, since these functions are built into the quad definition. Selection can be expressed in a straightforward manner using the four quad operators, but they cannot express general reductions or conversions. More fundamentally, there is no way, using the quad functions, to express ++; indeed, there is no way to create any bulk type instance with cardinality greater than 1. For the quadric description of a bulk type to be useful, one needs some mechanism external to the quad to build up instances of that bulk type. Trinder assumes the existence of ++ but does not relate it to the quad components by any algebraic laws. One has no assurance that the ++ operators for different bulk types will have similar algebraic properties. Thus, the quad structure by itself is inadequate to characterize bulk types in an abstract, encapsulated way.

In recent work of Watt and Trinder [Watt and Trinder 1991], the quad is supplanted by a richer algebraic structure, the **ringad**. The components of a ringad for a bulk type are *single*, *flattenmap*, ++ and [ ]. A rich set of laws relates these components and assures that they interact in a way that most would consider reasonable. Note, though, that *fold* is not included in the ringad, nor can it be constructed from the functions that are. Just as ++ operated externally to the quad abstraction, *fold* operates externally to the ringad abstraction. Thus, the ringad, while a step forward, still falls short of providing a complete abstract model of bulk types.

Other Algebras and Systems

FAD [Bancilhon et al. 1987] introduced the *pump* operator, which is essentially the same as the *fold* operator applied to non-empty binary trees. The cited paper points out the usefulness of *pump* for parallel reduction, but does not take full advantage of its generality: a *filter* function (our *filtermap*) is defined separately rather than being derived from *pump*.

Straube and Ozsu [Straube and Ozsu 1990] have developed a set-based object-oriented query algebra, and have presented transformation rules for it. However, their algebra is less expressive than others we have examined. They have also studied the problem of type unions in some detail. An important application for type unions arises in the typing of elements of a heterogeneous set. Naive approaches force the elements of such sets to be given a general type such as *Object*, or some other type high up in the type hierarchy. This restriction can result in a loss of type information. With union types, the element type of the set union can be taken to be the union of the element types of the two sets. The authors apply analogous thinking to other operators, and develop a set of type inference rules to determine the most informative type for any expression.

VBase [Andrew and Harris 1987] deserves mention in connection with discriminated unions. Atypically for an object-oriented system, VBase provided discriminated unions as a data structuring facility, and, as a separate feature, also allowed variable definitions to be unions of different types supporting the same messages. (These type unions are not discriminated from the user's point of view.)

12.5
The REVELATION Query Processing Architecture

In order to validate our research ideas and to assess their practical value for future database systems, we are complementing our conceptual research with the development of a software prototype. The REVELATION software architecture has four levels, depicted in Figure 12.3. The top level consists of the **Interpreter** and **Schema Manager**. The schema language allows definition of type interfaces (protocols) and their implementations, consisting of representations and methods. It also provides a persistent name space. The Interpreter can naively evaluate expressions formed from persistent variables and type operations. As an alternative to naive evaluation, the interpreter can pass an expression to the next level down, the **Revealer**. The Revealer attempts to expand an expression into a tree in the object algebra, through replacement of operations by their methods, and obtaining information about bindings and statistics from the name space. The resulting algebra tree, with possible annotations, is passed to the third level, the **Optimizer**. The REVELATION query optimizer will be produced with the VOLCANO optimizer generator [Graefe 1993] developed based on experiences with the EXODUS Optimizer Generator [Graefe and DeWitt 87]. The Optimizer will produce a query plan, which in essence is a program for the REVELATION **Query Evaluator**, the fourth level. This level is based on the VOLCANO extensible query evaluation software [Graefe 1992a]. We describe these levels in more detail in the subsections to follow. First we give some of our philosophical viewpoint on query processing.

At the most basic level, query optimization embraces two activities creating choices and making choices. Given an expression to optimize, we want to generate other expressions that are semantically equivalent to the given one, but that might differ in computational or I/O requirements. We then choose from among those expressions one we expect to have minimum evaluation cost. The feasibility of such a process generally depends on a declarative query language with an interesting set of equivalence-preserving transforms, and a data model that supports physical data independence.

Much of our approach in the REVELATION project can be seen as helping to create or make choices. The Revealer expands query expressions to give a large scope in which to optimize, in addition to annotating them with other information that can indicate if certain optimizations are allowed or advisable. The object algebra provides the formal framework in which query transformations that generate the alternatives can be expressed and shown correct. The Optimizer guides the generation of alternative expressions and must estimate their costs to intelligently select one. In order to make these estimates, the optimizer must also plan the evaluation of the alternative expressions, which includes selection of algorithms for the logical operators and their order of evaluation. Planning a particular expression again involves creating and making choices. In choosing a plan, physical properties of inputs and intermediate results, such as size, sort order, striping and clustering, affect the cost of the various operator algorithms and determine buffering and I/O requirements for different evaluation orders. Hence we believe careful modeling of these properties is necessary for reasonable cost estimation. Furthermore, capabilities of the underlying computing platform also need to be incorporated in the planning process, such as available main memory, temp space on disk and the number of processors and disks.

In some cases we can create choices during query planning but put off making a choice until runtime. Such is the case with the runtime assembly algorithm. The query optimizer produces an order-independent template of the pieces of an object that need to be assembled in memory. At runtime the assembly operator can choose what pieces of an object to add next, based on such things as buffer contents and physical address on disk.

A secondary theme in our work is making the REVELATION architecture easily extensible. Obviously, we support extensions by users in the form of new type definitions, but here we mean mainly ease of extension by the query processor developers. We do not expect to come up with the ideal algebra and logical operators on the first try we will likely be adding new data structures and operators on them. Nor do we expect to know a priori the best query transformation heuristics. At the physical level, we expect new algorithms for the logical operators to be invented and implemented, and we might change our minds as to the best format of each of the system-supplied data structures. Also, we do not know yet what physical properties and system capabilities will be most useful for cost estimation and query planning.

There are two main strategies we have for supporting extensibility. The first is the use of a query-optimizer generator to produce the query optimizer and planner. The generator takes as input logical transformation rules, mappings from logical operators to physical algorithms and definitions of cost functions and physical properties. From those it produces an optimizer tailored to that information. It also provides a means for a developer to provide guidance in plan selection to achieve certain physical properties. The second is the use of the Volcano extensible query execution software, which performs the plan execution. This software is constructed to be extensible in the set of algorithms it employs, and is also easily adapted to new physical formats of data structures.

12.5.1   Interpreter and Schema Manager

A REVELATION schema has three parts: protocols, implementations, and the name space. Protocols describe the interfaces to database elements and correspond to the idea of type as specification. These protocols list the permitted operations on instances and give signatures for those operations. Protocols do not describe data structures or layout of instances. Protocols are related in a hierarchy by conformance, meaning that, if protocol P conforms to protocol Q, an instance of P can be substituted where an instance of Q is expected. For example, if protocol *ColoredPoly* conforms to protocol *Polygon*, then a *ColoredPoly* instance can be used as an argument to an operator declared as taking a *Polygon* as input. An implementation consists of a representation and method definitions. Representations for instances are constructed by free composition of pre-supplied data structures, such as set, array, and tuple over a collection of base types, such as Boolean, integer and character. Methods are defined in a language that extends the object algebra with more general control structures and assignment. A given implementation may inherit parts of its representation or some of its methods from another implementation, but the implementation hierarchy is not constrained to follow the conformance relationship. We allow that one implementation may satisfy several protocols, and one protocol may have multiple implementations.

The name space contains persistent variables that may be typed by any of the defined protocols. These variables may have other properties than types statically bound to them, such as implementation, object identity, auxiliary access paths, statistics or even state. The name space is also the place where constraints are defined, such as referential dependencies and subset relationships. The Schema Manager keeps track of protocol and implementation definitions, and declarations in the name space, supplying information as requested by the Interpreter and the Revealer.

The Interpreter can execute expressions (queries and other requests) involving the persistent variables in **immediate mode**. Each object carries a reference to its implementation. When the Interpreter encounters an operation on an object, it looks up the method for that operation in the appropriate implementation and evaluates the expressions in it (which may invoke other operations). The Interpreter relies on the lower levels of the storage manager

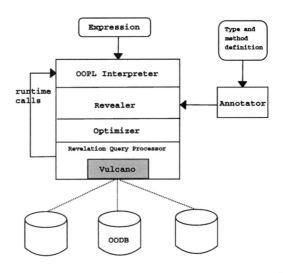

FIGURE 12.3
Levels in the REVELATION Architecture

to fetch objects or fragments of objects on demand when executing in this mode.

The Interpreter serves two conceptual functions. First, it is a backstop that ensures computational completeness, that is, complex queries and requests can be executed naively but correctly even if the request cannot be revealed into an algebra expression. Second, in some cases we may only be able to or choose to reveal a portion of an expression. We allow that algebra expressions contain embedded message sends. These embedded messages are then evaluated by the Interpreter at runtime at the request of the query evaluation layer.

12.5.2   The Revealer

If the Interpreter passes an expression to the Revealer, the Revealer attempts to expand that expression by incorporating information from the schema and name space. The reason for the expansion is to gain more foreknowledge of what the computation steps and data elements used in a query actually are. The expression as given may contain operations whose methods are encapsulated from the issuer of the expression. Leaving those operations encapsulated severely limits the choices for transformations available to the query optimizer. Therefore, the Revealer is allowed to break encapsulation on operations, expanding them to their methods, where possible. The goal of the Revealer is to recursively expand these methods until a tree in the object algebra results. Complete expansion may not be possible, because of multiple implementations per protocol or because general control constructs such as recursion prevent it. In that case, expressions can be passed down to the algebra level as unexpanded subtrees, to be evaluated by the Interpreter at run time. In some cases, even when the method for a message cannot be determined, the Revealer may be able to provide partial information about such a subtree. Examples of such information are the portion of the object representation accessed by the method, or whether the method is read only.

As an example of how revealing might proceed, recall $Tree2$ from Figure 12.1. Assume in its implementation it has a representation that is a tuple with two fields: $refProp$, which points to another prop (in this case $Tree1$) and $tMat$, which contains a translation matrix. Certain hidden surface elimination algorithms for sets of polygons use a plane to split the set, recursively rendering polygons behind the plane, then in front of the plane. Polygons that intersect the plane are split in two. One might be interested in looking for a plane that splits a small number of polygons. Suppose $Plane5$ is a splitting plane under consideration. Then an application might want to evaluate the expression

$$count(touch(Tree2, Plane5))$$

where $touch$ is a message on $Prop$ that returns the set of $Polygon$ in the receiver intersecting the plane, and $count$ is a cardinality operation on set structures. (The first argument is assumed to the the receiver of the message in this notation.) Here $Tree2$ is a variable in the persistent name space, hence the Revealer can look at the implementation of the object to which it is bound. Doing so, it discovers that the $touch$ message expands to

$$select(polygons(Tree2), X : intersect(X, Plane5))$$

Here $polygons$ is a message to $Prop$ requesting the set of its polygons, and the $select$ expression returns members of that set for which the Boolean function given returns true. Knowing the implementation of $Tree2$, we can reveal the $polygons$ message to

$$map(polygons(Tree2.refProp), Y : trans(Y, Tree2.tMat))$$

Here we are starting to expose the structural access to the internal state of $Tree2$. We see that to get the polygons of $Tree2$, we send the *polygons* message to the $Prop$ that $Tree2$ references, and map them all using the translation matrix $tMat$. Suppose the revealer chooses to stop at this point (say, because it does not want to assume that the value of $Tree2.refProp$ is static). With this much information revealed, the optimizer might choose to transform the expanded expression to

$$count(select \quad (polygons(Tree2.refProp),$$
$$Z: intersect(Z, trans(Plane5, inv(Tree2.tMat)))$$
$$))$$

Instead of doing the translation on **each** $Polygon$ in $Tree2.refProp$ before intersecting it with $Plane5$, the query applies the inverse translation to $Plane5$ **once**, before intersecting with the untranslated polygons in $Tree2.refProp$. Note that this transformation is correct only because of the enclosing *count* message. Without that message, there would need to be a final translation of the selected polygons.

While the Revealer is primarily concerned with revealing method bodies, there are other kinds of information it can insert into an expression. This information may enable further revealing or provide information on the suitability of certain transformations in the optimizer. The Revealer may find out from the name space that an identifier is statically bound to a particular implementation of a protocol or even a particular object. The name space might also yield useful integrity constraints. Another kind of information is the extent for the representation of an object relative to a method: the fragment of object state needed for a particular operator or method.

The conversation between the Revealer and the Schema Manager during expression expansion takes place by means of the **Annotator**. A certain collection of annotation kinds and possible values for each kind are defined for nodes in an expression tree. Examples of annotation kinds are protocol, implementation and representation extent. The Revealer makes requests of the Annotator to derive a particular annotation for a specific expression node. The Annotator deduces the value of the annotation and fills it in for the node. The Annotator might return a collection of values, because of ambiguity arising from multiple implementations of a single protocol, for example. Note that expansion of an operation to its implementing method is a particular kind of annotation. The Revealer can specify the level of stability the Annotator should assume when deriving annotations, such as whether or not to assume the set of implementations is fixed. The Annotator operates on a single expression node at a time it is up to the Revealer to select which nodes to consider next for expansion and when to stop expanding. In the revealing example above, the Revealer might have requested a level of stability that assumes namespace bindings are static, but that database state is changeable (which is why the implementation of $Tree2$ is revealed, but not that of $Tree1$). This decision might be based on the expression being executed multiple times in a loop with intervening update expressions. In that case, the Annotator can provide an implementation for $Tree2$, because it depends on a namespace binding, but not for $Tree2.refProp$, which happens to be equal to $Tree1$ initially, but which might change with a database update.

A few remarks on annotation are appropriate. We choose to reveal method implementations by attaching annotations to the original expression tree rather than by directly replacing the revealed message for several reasons. One is that the annotation might be a set of methods. Another is that we want to leave the original message expression in place, should the optimizer decide it is likely more efficient just to interpret a message at runtime. For example, suppose a selection message to a set is revealed as having three possible methods. For a large set, one might consider splitting the set by implementation at runtime, and providing a subquery for each partition. However, if the optimizer estimated the set has 10 elements in it, we might forget the expansion and have the Interpreter evaluate the message at runtime. Another capability of the Annotator we hope to explore is to let it make deductions over the namespace and schema rather than simply looking up information. It might reason with integrity constraints or discover that all methods for a message use the same fragment of object structure.

12.5.3 The Optimizer

The annotated expression tree is handed off to the Query Optimizer for optimization and transformation to a query plan. The expression tree hopefully is mostly in terms of operators from the REVELATION object algebra, with possibly embedded invocations on schema-level types. The object algebra is structural, operating on values formed by free composition of a fixed set of constructors. While the exact set of constructors is still being determined, it will be the same as the constructors for object representations, containing at the least base types, tuples, multidimensional arrays, multisets and object references. It may contain term or tree structures as well. As we mentioned before, we are designing the system so we can extend the algebra without great pain.

Many of the operators in the algebra will be analogous to those in relational algebra, such as selection and join. However, in examining scientific and engineering applications we have found the existing sets of algebraic operators inadequate for capturing the **iteration idioms** for data manipulations on ordered data types. Hence we are concentrating on operators that will capture some of the common control patterns in scientific data manipulation, such as matrix algebra operations, time-series filtering and multidimensional aggregates. In talking to scientific programmers, we have seen other classes of operations on bulk types we should support. One is conversions between bulk types. An example is a relation with attributes *(Altitude, Temperature, Pressure)*. What is desired is to sort on *Altitude*, and then project *Temperature* and *Pressure* into two parallel one-dimensional arrays to provide as input for statistical operations. Relational query languages do not work on this query since, although most can express sort orderings, they do not guarantee order preservation after the sort key is projected away. Another common manipulation is structural selection, such as taking a **slab** or **pencil** from a multidimensional array. We are seeking a small set of operations on ordered structures that expresses a large variety of the desired manipulations. A related issue in the design of the algebra is dealing with multiple bulk types. Existing data models and algebras typically employ a single bulk type, while we intend to have several [Vance 1992].

The Optimizer itself will be produced by an optimizer generator, as mentioned before. Providing rules for algebraic identities on algebra operators should be straightforward. However, developing rules for translation of algebra trees into query plans and estimating costs of alternative plans will require more work, as they must take account of physical properties of the database and capabilities of the underlying hardware platform.

To discover common iteration patterns on ordered data types, and to identify useful identities on operations, we have been examining the newS system [Becker et al. 1988]. While newS is aimed at exploratory data analysis, it is an interesting language in this context as most of its computational values are instances of ordered types, such as vector, matrix and time series. Moreover, most computations are expressed with operations that operate directly on objects of these bulk types, rather than as explicit iteration through the elements in the aggregate. As an example, in S, if Y is a time-series object, a running average over a window of 3 elements can be expressed as

$$(lag(Y, -1) + Y + lag(Y, 1))/3$$

where *lag* shifts a time series ahead or back in time, and the arithmetic operators work with respect to elements on values with the same time index. If this expression is evaluated naively, Y will have to be scanned multiple times. If it is too large to fit in main memory, that evaluation will involve much I/O. However, if the algebra has a **windowed** scan operation over a sequence, then there will be an equivalent expression that can be evaluated with one pass over Y.

While we have identified some operations, such as *fold*, that can be adapted to most bulk types, we are actively considering operations that are specific to ordered structures. Examples are **stenciling** a function over all elements of an array, extracting subslabs of a multidimensional array, and pattern matching on sequences.

A **query plan** is a directive as to what physical operators to execute, where and in what order to run them and how to transfer results between them. The physical operators correspond largely to the operators in the logical object algebra in terms of the functions they compute. However, the physical operators use different algorithms to realize those functions and their execution costs typically exhibit differing dependencies on dataset sizes and layouts. For example, for the logical join operator there are physical join operators using merge-join, nested-loop-join and hash-join algorithms. The optimal choice in a particular situation depends on the size of the arguments and their sort orderings, among other factors. There are also some physical operators that are the identity function at the logical level (such as sort in relational systems, and the assembly operator described in the next section), but serve to change the physical characteristics of a dataset. Other physical operators are concerned with matching query evaluation to machine architecture, such as mapping onto parallel processors [Graefe 1990a, Graefe and Davison 1991].

The optimizer for the REVELATION prototype will be constructed using the VOLCANO optimizer generator, a new optimizer generator based on experiences with the EXODUS optimizer generator prototype. As part of the REVELATION project we are undertaking a methodical examination of physical properties of data and their interaction with different physical operators in an OODBMS. Examples of physical properties are sort order, clustering, size, compression, partitioning, distribution, presence of duplicates, robustness under estimation errors, density, existence of auxiliary access paths, and location in the memory hierarchy. We are categorizing physical operators relative to these properties by whether they *require, preserve, enforce* or *destroy* a particular property. For example, a nested-loop join preserves the sort order of the outer input, while hash join may destroy it. Optimizers generated with the VOLCANO generator will have explicit support for physical properties, which is one of the main improvements of the VOLCANO generator over the earlier EXODUS prototype. We are further looking at how to construct cost functions that incorporate information on these data properties, as well as factoring processor capabilities, such as number of processing nodes or amount of main memory. This knowledge should guide us in constructing input specifications for the optimizer generator that deal with physical properties [Maier 1991].

12.5.4 The Query Evaluator

The Query Evaluator for the REVELATION project is a runtime system that executes query plans provided by the optimizer. It is based on the VOLCANO extensible query execution software, which provides implementation of the physical operators and handles data flow between these operators [Graefe 1992a]. It also provides low-level file, index, and buffer management routines. VOLCANO can execute plans efficiently in both single-processor and shared-memory-multiprocessor environments, and has recently been extended to operate on distributed-memory and hierarchical hybrid architectures. The current physical operator set of VOLCANO contains file and index scans, sort- and hash-based binary matching (for join, semi-join, intersection, difference, etc.), division (for universal quantification [Graefe 1989], sort, exchange (for parallel query execution) [Graefe and Davison 1990], and choose-plan (for plans optimized with incomplete information [Graefe and Ward 1989], among others. Thus, we believe that we already have a fairly complete operator set that we can exploit in the development of the REVELATION prototype.

VOLCANO is extensible in at least two dimensions. Its physical operator implementations are parameterized by the actual data structure elements and accessors they operate upon. This flexibility is accomplished by moving the data-dependent portion of these operators into *support functions*, allowing the VOLCANO operators to be extended to operate on new kinds of data structures without changing the core code (or having a new version of the operator for each element data type). This capability also permits combining interpretation of instance operators with compiled set processing and control. The other dimension of extensibility is in adding new physical operators. Such extensions are readily made because all VOLCANO physical operators conform to a fairly general **open, next, close** interface.

For REVELATION, we are taking advantage of both kinds of extensibility. The support-function mechanism lets us have more than one **realization** of a given data structure. For example, an array might be realized as a single record at the physical level, or as a tree of records. The VOLCANO physical operators can accommodate this variability by using different accessor routines in their support functions. We are also adding operators that deal explicitly with the kinds of processing that occurs in complex object manipulations. The **assembly** operator [Keller et al. 1991] is one that we have added. It takes a template describing some fragment of an object's state and a set of object references. It then assembles the required pieces of each referenced object in main memory. However, unlike the naive access of the interpreter that uses a fixed order for accessing the pieces, the assembly operator is free to reorder the accesses to take advantage of clustering information or optimize disk-arm movement. The assembly operator is an example of a physical operator that exists mainly to affect physical characteristics of data, namely its presence in main-memory buffers. We point out that the assembly operator is an example of moving the choice-making in query processing to runtime. While assembly might look like a pointer-based join [Carey et al. 1990b], in fact it can produce access orders for objects that do not correspond to any fixed join ordering and can assemble recursive structures. Another place we extend the operators is in having an operator to invoke the interpreter at runtime, to handle unrevealed subtrees passed down from the optimizer.

12.6
Status and Conclusion

We have nearly completed the architectural design of the query processor and have made some significant progress towards a first prototype to validate our research. Our hope is to integrate a first (zero-level) prototype with all important components shortly. The initial design of the data definition facility and namespace is nearly complete [Daniels 1992]. The specification of the interface between the revealer and annotator is underway. By including a **value** annotation kind for expressions, the annotator will actually serve as our initial interpreter. We also have the first draft of the structures and operators for the complex object algebra [Vance 1991].

We have also been constructing working prototypes of several parts of the system. A **throw-away** prototype of the Revealer was implemented in C++ and taught us several valuable lessons. First, C++ does not provide or use type-defining objects (unlike Smalltalk, for example). Thus, it was not clear where to inquire for type information. We ended up placing the burden on the type definer to provide additional messages for use by the Revealer. Clearly, we want to be able to extract such information automatically from the type definition in the future. Second, the interface between type and schema information and the Revealer needs to be very extensible, which led to the definition of the Annotator described earlier. The VOLCANO query execution engine was extended with a novel operator for complex object assembly. This operator was implemented in VOLCANO for use in the REVELATION project, but its techniques are easily more widely applicable. We also have a schema and name space parser running, an in-memory version of the object algebra, and an early release of the VOLCANO query-optimizer generator.

We hope this paper has conveyed some of the challenges present in query processing for object-oriented databases. We have presented the approach of the REVELATION project to the problem; our contributions will need to be combined with those of other research groups to meet the needs of commercial systems. There are still many problems in the area that we have not faced, but hope to address in the future or see solutions from other groups. One is the proper integration of updates into our query algebra. Much of the work we are doing at the physical implementation level is to provide such a mechanism. We still need to experiment with what we have to discover reasonable policies to govern the mechanisms. We also need selectivity estimation techniques to build good cost functions for our optimizer. Another large area, which we will consider in the future, is applying parallelism and distribution to query processing.

Acknowledgement

We would like to thank Duri Schmidt and Len Shapiro for their interaction and discussion on this work. This research was supported in part by National Science Foundation grants IRI-89-20642 and IRI-89-12618.

Bibliography

[Andrew and Harris 1987] Andrews, T. and Harris, C. Combining language and database advances in an object-oriented development environment.

Proc. of the Second Int. Conference on Object-Oriented Programming Systems, Languages, and Applications, Orlando (Florida), Oct. 1987.

[Atkinson et al. 1991] Atkinson M., Lecluse C., Richard P. "Bulk Types for Data Programming Languages, a Proposal." Altair Technical Report 67-91, February 1991.

[Atkinson et al. 1992] Atkinson M., Lecluse C., Philbrow P., Richard P. "Design Issues in a Map Language." *Database Programming Languages: Bulk Types and Persistent Data,* J.W. Schmidt, ed., Morgan Kaufmann, 1992.

[Bancilhon et al. 1987] F. Bancilhon et al. FAD, A Simple and Powerful Database Language. *Proc. of VLDB Conf.,* pp. 97-105, 1987.

[Becker et al. 1988] Becker R.A., Chambers J.M., Wilks A.R. *The New S Language: A Programming Environment for Data Analysis and Graphics,* Wadsworth & Brooks/Cole, Pacific Grove, CA, 1988.

[Beeri and Kornatzky 90] Beeri, C. and Kornatzky Y. "Algebraic Optimization of Object-Oriented Query Languages." In *Proc. 3rd ICDT,* LNCS 470, Springer-Verlag, 1990.

[Bertino and Kim 1989] Bertino, E. and Kim, W. "Indexing Techniques for Queries on Nested Objects." *IEEE Trans. on Knowledge and Data Engineering,* **1, 2** (1989), 196-214.

[Blakeley et al. 1990] Blakeley J.A., Thompson C.W., Alashqur A.M. "Strawman Reference Model of Object Query Languages." In *Proc. First OODB Standardization Workshop X3/SPARC/DBSSG/OODBTG,* Atlantic City, NJ, 1990.

[Butterworth et al. 1991] Butterworth P., Otis A., Stein J. "The GemStone Object Database Management System." *Communications of the ACM, Special Section on Next-Generation Database Systems* **34, 10** (October 1991), pp. 64.

[Carey et al. 1990b] Carey J., Shekita E., Lapis G., Lindsay B., McPherson J. "Advanced Query Processing in Object Bases Using Access Support Relations." In *Proc. Int. Conf. on Very Large Databases,* pp. 662–673, Brisbane, August 1990. Morgan Kaufmann, San Mateo, Ca.

[Carey et al. 1990a] Carey M.J., DeWitt D.J., Graefe G., Haight D.M., Richardson J.E., Schuh D.T., Shekita E.J., Vandenberg S. "The EX-ODUS Extensible DBMS Project: An Overview." In Zdonik S. and Maier D., editors, *Readings in Object-Oriented Databases*, pp. 474–499. Morgan Kaufmann Publ. Co.

[Cluet and Delobel 1993] Cluet S., Delobel C. "Towards a Unification of Rewrite-Based Optimization Techniques for Object-Oriented Queries." In *this volume*.

[Daniels 1992] Daniels S. "Speaking in Tongues: The Language of Revelation." Research Report Oregon Graduate Center, Beaverton, OR. CS Tech. Rep., revised 1992.

[Deux 1990] Deux, O. "The story of O_2." *IEEE Trans. on Knowledge and Data Engineering*, **2, 1** (1990), pp. 91-108.

[Deux et al. 1991] Deux Q.O., et al. "The O_2 System." *Communications of the ACM, Special Section on Next-Generation Database Systems* **34, 10** (October 1991), p. 34.

[Dittrich et al. 1987] Dittrich K., Gotthard W., Lockemann P.C. "DAMOK-LES - The Database System for the UNIBASE Software Engineering Environment." *IEEE Database Eng.* **10, 1** (March 1987), p. 37.

[Fong 1986] Fong Z. "The Design and Implementation of the POSTGRES Query Optimizer." Master's Thesis, University of California, Berkeley, CA, August 1986.

[Ford at al. 1988] Ford S., Joseph J., Langworthy D.E., Lively D.F., Pathak G., Perez E.R., Peterson R.W., Sparacin D.M., Thatte S.M., Wells D.L., Agarwala S. "ZEITGEIST: Database Support for Object-Oriented Programming." In Dittrich K. R., editor, *Advances in Object-Oriented Database Systems*, Lecture Notes in CS, Springer-Verlag, September 1988, p. 334.

[Graefe and DeWitt 87] Graefe, G. and DeWitt D.J. "The EXODUS Optimizer Generator." In *Proc. ACM SIGMOD Conference*, May 1987, San Francisco, pp. 160-172.

[Graefe and Ward 1989] Graefe G. and Ward K. "Dynamic Query Evaluation Plans." In *Proc. ACM SIGMOD Conference*, Portland, OR, May-June 1989, p. 358.

[Graefe 1989] Graefe G. "Relational Division: Four Algorithms and Their Performance." In *Proc. IEEE Conference on Data Engineering*, Los Angelos, CA, February 1989, p. 94.

[Graefe 1990a] Graefe G. "Encapsulation of Parallelism in the Volcano Query Processing System." In *Proc. ACM SIGMOD Conference*, Atlantic City, NJ, May 1990, p. 102.

[Graefe and Davison 1990] Graefe G., Davison D.L. "Architecture-Independent Parallel Query Evaluation in Volcano." Research Report CU Boulder CS Tech. Rep. 500, University of Colorado, Boulder, CO, December 1990.

[Graefe and Davison 1991] Graefe G. and Davison D.L. "Encapsulation of Parallelism and Architecture-Independence in Extensible Database Query Processing." *Submitted for publication*, November 1991.

[Graefe 1992a] Graefe G. "Volcano, An Extensible and Parallel Dataflow Query Processing System." To appear in *IEEE Transactions on Knowledge and Data Eng.*, 1993.

[Graefe 1993] Graefe G. "Extensible Query Optimization and Parallel Execution in Volcano." In *this volume*.

[Haas et al. 1989] Haas L.M., Freytag J.C., Lohman G. and Pirahesh H. "Extensible Query Processing in Starburst." In *Proc. ACM SIGMOD Conference*, Portland, OR, May-June 1989, p. 377.

[Haas et al. 1990] Haas L., Chang W., Lohman G., McPherson J., Wilms P.F., Lapis G., Lindsay B., Pirahesh H., Carey M.J. and Shekita E. "Starburst Mid-Flight: As the Dust Clears." *IEEE Transactions on Knowledge and Data Eng.* **2, 1** (March 1990), p. 143.

[Heytens and Nikhil 1991] Heytens M.L., Nikhil R.S. "List Comprehensions in AGNA, a Parallel Persistent Object System." Computation Structures Group Memo 326, MIT, Cambridge, MA, March 1991.

[Keller et al. 1991] Keller T., Graefe G. and Maier D. "Efficient Assembly of Complex Objects." In *Proc. ACM SIGMOD Conferences*, Denver, CO, May 1991, p. 148.

[Kim et al. 1989] Kim, W., Kim, K.C., Dale, A. Indexing techniques for object-oriented databases. *Object-Oriented Concepts, Databases, and Applications*, W. Kim, and F. Lochovsky, eds., Addison-Wesley, 1989.

[Kim et al. 1990] Kim, W., Garza. J., Ballou N., Woelk D. "Architecture of the ORION Next-Generation Database System." *IEEE Transactions on Knowledge and Data Eng.* **2, 1** (March 1990), p. 109.

[Lamb et al. 1991] Lamb C., Landis G., Orenstein J., Weinreb D. "The ObjectStore Database System." *Communications of the ACM, Special Section on Next-Generation Database Systems* **34, 10** (October 1991), p. 50.

[Lohman et al. 1991] Lohman G., Lindsay B., Pirahesh H., Schiefer K.B. "Extensions to Starburst: Objects, Types, Functions, and Rules." *Communications of the ACM, Special Section on Next-Generation Database Systems* **34, 10** (October 1991), p. 94.

[Maier and Stein 1986] Maier D. and Stein J. "Indexing in an Object-oriented DBMS." In Dittrich K. R. and Dayal U., editors, *Proc. IEEE Int'l. Workshop on Object-Oriented Database Systems*, Asilomar, Pacific Grove, CA, pp. 171–182. IEEE Computer Society Press.

[Maier 1991] Maier D. "Specifying a Database to Itself." In Harper D.J. and Norrie M.C., editors, *Proc. Proc. Int'l. Workshop on Specifications of Database Systems*, Glasgow, Scotland, July 1991, Springer-Verlag 1992.

[Mitschang and Pirahesh 1993] Mitschang B. and Pirahesh H. "Integration of Composite Objects into Relational Query Processing: The SQL/XNF Approach." In *this volume*.

[Nikhil and Heytens 1991] Nikhil R.S. and Heytens M.L. "Exploiting Parallelism in the Implementation of AGNA, a Persistent Programming System." In *Proc. IEEE Conference on Data Engineering*, Kobe, Japan, April 1991, p. 660.

[Rowe and Stonebraker 1987] Rowe L. and Stonebraker M. "The POSTGRES Data Model." In *Proc. Int. Conf. on Very Large Databases*, Brighton, (September 1987), MK, p. 83.

[Schek, Paul, and Weikum 1990] Schek J., Paul B., Weikum G. "The DASDBS Project: Objectives, Experiences, and Future Prospects." *IEEE Transactions on Knowledge and Data Eng.* **2, 1** (March 1990), p. 25.

[Schwarz et al. 1986] Schwarz P., Chang W., Freytag J.C., Lohman G.M., McPherson J., Mohan C., Pirahesh H. "Extensibility in the Starburst Database System." In Dittrich K. R. and Dayal U., editors, *Proc. IEEE Int'l. Workshop on Object-Oriented Database Systems*, Asilomar, Pacific Grove, CA, p. 85. IEEE Computer Society Press.

[Shaw and Zdonik 1989a] Shaw, G.B., Zdonik S.B. "An Object Oriented Query Algebra." *Proc. of the Second Int. Workshop on Database Programming Languages*, Portland (Oreg.), June 1989, Morgan Kaufmann, p. 103.

[Shaw and Zdonik 1989b] Shaw, G.B., Zdonik S.B. "Object-Oriented Queries: Equivalence and Optimization." In *Proc. First Int'l. Conf. on Deductive and Object-Oriented Databases*. Kyoto, Japan, December 4-6, 1989.

[Stonebraker et al. 1984] Stonebraker M., Anderson E., Hanson E., Rubenstein B. "QUEL as a Data Type." In *Proc. of the ACM SIGMOD Conf.*, Boston, MA, June 1984, p. 208.

[Stonebraker et al. 1986] Stonebraker M., Sellis T., Hanson E. "An Analysis of Rule Indexing Implementations in Data Base Systems." In *Proc. First Int'l. Conf. on Expert Database Systems*, Charleston, SC, April 1986, p. 353.

[Stonebraker 1986] M. Stonebraker. "Inclusion of New Types in Relational Database Systems." *Proc. of IEEE Data Eng. Conf.*, February 1986, pp. 262-269.

[Stonebraker and Rowe 1986] Stonebraker M. and Rowe L. "The Design of POSTGRES." In *Proc. of the ACM SIGMOD Conf.*, Washington D.C., May 1986, p. 350.

[Stonebraker et al. 1987] Stonebraker M., Anton J., Hanson E. "Extending a Database System with Procedures." In *ACM Transactions on Database Systems* **12, 3**, September 1987, p. 350.

[Stonebraker et. al 1990] Stonebraker M., Jhingran A., Goh J., Potamianos S. "On Rules, Procedures, Caching and Views in Data Base Systems." In *Proc. ACM SIGMOD Conference*, Atlantic City, NJ, May 1990, p. 281.

[Stonebraker, Rowe, and Hirohama 1990] Stonebraker M., Rowe L., Hirohama M. "The Implementation of POSTGRES." *IEEE Transactions on Knowledge and Data Eng.* **2, 1** (March 1990), p. 125.

[Stonebraker 1991] Stonebraker M. "Managing Persistent Objects in a Multi-Level Store." ACM-SIGMOD Int'l. Conf. on Management of Data, Denver, CO, May 1991, p. 2

[Stonebraker and Kemnitz 1991] Stonebraker M. and Kemnitz G. "The POSTGRES Next-Generation Database Management System." *Communications of the ACM, Special Section on Next-Generation Database Systems* **34, 10** (October 1991), p. 78.

[Straube and Ozsu 1990] Straube D.D. and Ozsu M.T. "Queries and Query Processing in Object-Oriented Database Systems." *ACM Transaction on Information Systems* **8, 4**, 1990, p. 387.

[Trinder 1992] Trinder P. "Comprehensions, a Query Notation for DBPLs." *Database Programming Languages: Bulk Types and Persistent Data*, pp 55–70, J.W. Schmidt, ed., Morgan Kaufmann, 1992.

[Vance 1991] Vance B. "An Object-Oriented Query Algebra Based on Standard ML." Technical Report Oregon Graduate Center, Beaverton, OR, CSE-91-008, April 1991.

[Vance 1992] Vance B. "Towards an Object-Oriented Query Algebra." Technical Report Oregon Graduate Center, Beaverton, OR, revised January 1992.

[Vandenberg and DeWitt 1991] Vandenberg S.L. and DeWitt D.J.. "Algebraic Support for Complex Objects with Arrays, Identity, and Inheritance." ACM-SIGMOD Int'l. Conf. on Management of Data, p. 158, Denver, CO, 1991.

[Wadler 1990] Wadler P. "Comprehending Monads." In *Proc. of the 1990 ACM Conf. on LISP and Functional Programming*, ACM Press, June 1990, pp. 61–78.

[Watt and Trinder 1991] Watt D.A. and Trinder P. "Towards a Theory of Bulk Types." FIDE Technical Report, June 1991.

[Wells et al. 1992] Wells D., Blakeley J.A., Thompson C.W. "Architecture of an Open Object-Oriented Database Management System." *IEEE Computer* **25, 10** (March 1990), p. 74.

[Wilkinson et al. 1990] K. Wilkinson, P. Lyngbaek, and W. Hasan. "The Iris Architecture and Implementation." *IEEE Trans. on Knowledge and Data Engineering* **2, 1**, March 1990, pp. 63–75. Special Issue on Prototype Systems.

[Wilms et al. 1988] Wilms, P., Schwartz, P., Schek, H. and Haas, L. "Incorporating Data Types in an Extensible Architecture." *Proc. of International Conf. on Data and Knowledge Bases*, pp. 180-192, 1988.

PART IV

Access Methods, Physical Design, and Performance Evaluation

13

A Survey of Indexing Techniques for Object-Oriented Database Management Systems

Elisa Bertino

Abstract

Indices are crucial in database systems to expedite the evaluation of queries that retrieve a small subset of data from a large database. Indexing techniques have been widely investigated in the framework of relational, and network databases and several organizations have been proposed. The most common way to implement an index is by a B-tree structure or hashing. The novel features of object-oriented (and semantic) data models pose, however, some requirements beyond conventional indexing techniques in order to efficiently support the types of queries that are possible in databases based on these advanced data models. In this paper we discuss some issues concerning advanced indexing techniques, we report results, and point out open research directions.

13.1
Introduction

Object-oriented database management systems (OODBMSs) represent one of the most promising directions in the database area towards meeting requirements posed by advanced applications, such as CAD/CAM, software engineering, office automation, and geographic information systems. These applications require effective support for the management of complex, possibly multimedia, objects. For example, hypermedia applications require handling of text, graphics, and bitmap pictures, while design applications very often require support for geometric objects. Other crucial requirements derive from the evolutionary nature of applications and include multiple versions of the same data and long-lived transactions. The usage of an object-oriented data model allows some of the previous issues to be solved easily. For example, an application's complex objects can be directly represented by the model, and therefore there is no need of flatten them into tuples, as when relational DBMSs are used. Moreover, the encapsulation property supports the integration of packages for multimedia handling. However, because of the increased complexity of the data model, and of the additional operational requirements, such as versions or long transactions, the design of an OODBMS poses several issues, both on the data model and languages, and on the architecture [Bertino 1991a, Joseph et al. 1991, Zdonik and Maier 1989].

Among the issues, an important question is the type of object access that must be supported [Joseph et al. 1991]. Many of the previous applications need navigational access based on object references. A typical example is represented by graph traversal. On the other hand, the experience of relational DBMSs has shown that high-level, declarative, efficient query languages are a key functionality. Therefore, most OODBMSs provide, in addition to navigational access, a query language. The two means of access are often complementary. A query selects a set of objects. The retrieved objects and their components are then accessed by using navigational capabilities [Bertino 1991b]. A brief summary of query languages will be presented in Section 13.2.

To expedite the execution of queries, DBMSs typically provide a secondary index using some variations of B-tree structures [Comer 1979] or some hashing techniques. An index is maintained on an attribute or combination of attributes of a relation. Since an object-oriented data model has many differences with respect to the relational model, suitable indexing techniques must be developed to efficiently support object-oriented query languages. In this paper we survey some of the issues associated with indexing techniques and we describe proposed approaches. The remainder of the paper is organized as follows. Section 13.2 presents an overview of the basic concepts of object-oriented data models, query languages, and query processing. For the purpose of the discussion, we consider an object-oriented database organized along two dimensions: aggregation, and inheritance. Indexing techniques for each of those dimensions are discussed in Section 13.3 and Section 13.4, respectively. Section 13.5 presents integrated organizations, supporting queries along both aggregation and inheritance graphs. Section 13.6 briefly discusses method precomputation and caching. Finally, Section 13.7 presents some conclusions.

13.2
Review of the Object-Oriented Data Model, Query Language, and Query Processing

An object-oriented data model is based on a number of concepts [Atkinson et al. 1989, Bertino 1991a, Zdonik and Maier 1989]:

- Each real-world entity is modeled by an object. Each object is associated with a unique *identifier* (called an OID) that makes the object distinguishable from other objects. OODBMSs provide objects with persistent and immutable identifiers: an object's identifier does not change even if the object modifies its state.

- Each object has a set of instance attributes and methods (operations); the value of an attribute can be an object or a set of objects. The set of attributes of an object and the set of methods represent the object structure and behavior, respectively.

- The attribute values represent the object's state. This state is accessed or modified by sending messages to the object to invoke the corresponding methods.

- Objects sharing the same structure and behavior are grouped into the same class. A class represents a template for a set of similar objects. Each object is an instance of some class. A class definition consists a set of instance attributes (or simply attributes) and methods. The domain of an attribute may be an arbitrary class. The definition of a class C results in a directed-graph (called *aggregation graph*) of the classes rooted at C. An attribute of any class on an aggregation graph is a nested attribute of the root of the graph. Objects, instances of a given class, have a value for each attribute defined by the class, and respond to all messages defined by the class.

- A class can be defined as a specialization of one or more classes. A class defined as specialization is called a subclass and inherits attributes, messages, and methods from its superclass(es). The specialization relationship among classes organizes them in an *inheritance graph* which is orthogonal to the aggregation graph.

Note that there are many variations with respect to these basic concepts, especially when comparing OODBMSs and object-oriented programming languages (OOPLs). However, despite all differences, it has been widely recognized that this paradigm offers several advantages, such as separation of object interfaces from implementations, re-usability, and so forth. In the database field, the object-oriented paradigm brings an important advantage, in addition to the previous ones, in that it allows *complex objects* to be directly represented by the model. Therefore, an object-oriented model allows a natural and direct representation of real world objects that in most cases are constructed from other component objects.

An example of object-oriented database schema, which will be used as running example, is presented in Figure 13.1. In the representation used in Figure 13.1, a box represents a class. Within each box there are the names of the attributes of the class. Names labeled with * denote multi-valued attributes. Two types of arcs are used in the representation. A simple arc from a class C to a class C' denotes that C' is domain of an attribute of C. A bold arc from a class C to a class C' indicates that C is a superclass of C'.

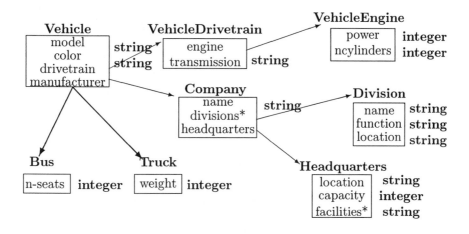

FIGURE 13.1
A database example

In the remainder of the discussion, we make the following assumptions. First, we consider classes as having the extensional notion of the set of their instances. Therefore, queries are made against classes. Note, that in several systems, such as for example GemStone [Bretl et al. 1989] and O_2 [Deux 1990], classes do not have mandatory associated extensions. Therefore, the users have to use collections, or sets, to group instances of the same class. Different collections may be defined on the same class. Therefore, increased flexibility is achieved, even if the data model becomes more complex. When collections are the basis for queries, indices are allocated on collections and not on classes [Maier and Stein 1986]. An open issue is whether all techniques and results that we will present in the remainder of this paper are also valid when collections are used. Second, we make the assumption that the extent of a class does not include the instances of its subclasses.

As we discussed earlier, most OODBMSs provide an associative query language [Cluet 1989, Kim 1989, Shaw and Zdonik 1989]. In general such languages are similar to relational ones; often, the former are derived as an evolution of the latter. Moreover, nested relational languages [Ozsoyoglu et al. 1987, Pistor and Traunmueller 1986, Roth et al. 1988, Schek and Scholl 1986] have many similarities with object-oriented query languages. However, there are some differences between relational and object-oriented query languages [Bertino 1991b]. In the following we summarize the aspects that most influence indexing techniques:

- Nested predicates
  Because of object's nested structures, most object-oriented query languages allow objects to be restricted by predicates on both nested and non-nested attributes of objects. An example of a query against the database schema of Figure 13.1 is:

  Retrieve all red vehicles manufactured by Fiat (Q1)

  This query contains the nested predicate 'manufactured by Fiat'. Nested predicates are often expressed using path-expressions. For example, the nested predicate in the above query can be expressed as Vehicle.manufacturer.name = 'Fiat'.

- Inheritance
  A query may apply to just a class, or to a class and to all its subclasses. An example of a query against the database schema of Figure 13.1 is:

  Retrieve all red instances of class Vehicle, including the instances of its subclasses

- Methods
  A method can used in a query as a *derived attribute method* or a *predicate method*. A derived attribute method has a function comparable to that of an attribute, in that it returns an object (or a value) to which comparisons can be applied. A predicate method returns the logical constants True or False. The value returned by a predicate method can then participate in the evaluation of the Boolean expression that determines whether the object satisfies the query.

A distinction often made in object-oriented query languages is between *implicit join* (called *functional joins* by other by other authors [Carey and De-Witt 1988]), deriving from the hierarchical nesting of objects, and the *explicit join*, similar to the relational join, where two objects are explicitly compared on the values of their attributes. Note that some query languages only support implicit joins. The motivation for this limitation is based on the argument that in relational systems joins are mostly used to recompose entities that were decomposed for normalization [Bretl et al. 1989] and to support relationships among entities. In object-oriented data models there is no need to normalize objects, since these models directly support complex objects. Moreover, relationships among entities are supported through object references; thus the same function that joins provide in the relational model to support relationships is provided more naturally by path-expressions. It therefore appears that in OODBMSs there is no strong need for explicit joins, especially if path-expressions are provided. An example of a path-expression (or simply path) is 'Vehicle.manufacturer.name' denoting the nested attribute 'manufacturer.name' of class Vehicle. The evaluation of a query with nested predicates may cause the traversal of objects along aggregation graphs. Examples of strategies for evaluations of these queries can be found in several papers [Bertino 1990, Jenq et al. 1989, Kim et al. 1988]. Therefore, we can expect that in OODBMSs most joins will be implicit joins along aggregation graphs based on object identities. It is therefore possible to take advantage of this fact by defining techniques that precompute implicit joins. We will discuss these techniques in Section 13.3

In order to discuss the various index organizations, we need to summarize some topics concerning query processing and execution strategies. As discussed by Kim, et al. [Kim et al. 1988], a query can be conveniently represented by a *query graph*. The query execution strategies vary along two dimensions. The first dimension concerns the strategy used to traverse the query graph. The second dimension is the technique used to retrieve instances of the classes that are traversed for the evaluation of nested predicates. Two basic traversal strategies can be devised:

- *Forward traversal*: the first class visited is the target class of the query (root of the query graph). The remaining classes are traversed starting from the target class in any depth-first order. The forward traversal strategy for query Q1 is (Vehicle Company).

- *Reverse traversal*: the traversal of the query graph begins at the leaves and proceeds bottom-up along the graph. The reverse traversal strategy for query Q1 is (Company Vehicle).

Another dimension in query processing is the strategy for accessing instances from a given class. There are two basic strategies for retrieving data from a visited class. The first strategy is called *nested-loop* and consists of instantiating separately each qualified instance of a class. The instance attributes are examined for qualification, if there are simple predicates on the instance attributes. If the instance qualifies, it is passed to its parent node (in the case of reverse traversal) or to its child node (in case of forward traversal). The second strategy is called *sort-domain* and consists of instantiating all qualified instances of a class at once. Then all qualifying instances are passed to their parent or child node (depending on the traversal strategy used). By combining the graph traversal strategies with instance retrieval strategies, four basic query execution strategies are obtained, namely nested-loop forward traversal (NLFT), nested-loop reverse traversal (NLRT), sort-domain forward traversal (SDFT), sort-domain reverse traversal (SDRT). When complex queries are concerned, these basic strategies can be combined generating more complex strategies. Consider for example a query made of the conjunction of two predicates $pred_n$ and $pred_m$ against two nested attributes A_n and A_m of a class C. Two possible complex strategies for this query are:

1. Executing an NLFT on the path leading to A_n in order to retrieve all instances of C satisfying $pred_n$; then another NLFT on the other path to evaluate $pred_m$ on each qualifying instance of the previous search; the set of instances retrieved by this second scan is the answer to the query.

2. Two NLRT on the two paths and then the intersections of the results.

13.3
Index Organizations for Aggregation Graphs

In this section, we first present some preliminary definitions from a previous paper by Bertino and Kim [Bertino and Kim 1989]. Then we present a number of indexing techniques that support efficient evaluations of implicit joins along aggregation graphs. Therefore, these indexing techniques can be used to efficiently implement class traversal strategies.

Definition. Given an aggregation graph H, a *path* $\mathcal{P}$ is defined as

$$C_1.A_1.A_2.\,.\,.\,.\,.A_n \quad (n \geq 1)$$

where:

- C_1 is a class in H;

- A_1 is an attribute of class C_1;

- A_i is an attribute of a class C_i in H, such that C_i is the domain of attribute A_{i-1} of class C_{i-1}, $1 < i \le n$;

with

- $\text{len}(\mathcal{P}) = n$ denotes the length of the path;

- $\text{class}(\mathcal{P}) = C_1 \bigcup \{C_i \ / \ C_i$ is domain of attribute A_{i-1} of class C_{i-1},

- with $1 < i \le n\}$ denotes the set of the classes along the path;

- $\text{dom}(\mathcal{P})$ denotes the class C domain of attribute A_n of class C_n.□

A path is simply a branch in a given aggregation graph. Examples of paths in the database schema in Figure 13.1 are:

- P_1: Vehicle.manufacturer.divisions.location
  $\text{len}(P_1)=3$ $\text{class}(P_1)=\{$Vehicle, Company, Division$\}$ $\text{dom}(P_1)=$string

- P_2: Vehicle.color $\text{len}(P_2)=1$ $\text{class}(P_2)=\{$Vehicle$\}$ $\text{dom}(P_2)=$string

- P_3: Vehicle.manufacturer.headquarters
  $\text{len}(P_3)=2$ $\text{class}(P_3) = \{$Vehicle, Company$\}$ $\text{dom}(P_3)=$string

A second concept that we will use is that of *path instantiation*. A path instantiation is a sequence of objects found by instantiating a path. The objects in Figure 13.2 are instances of the classes shown in Figure 13.1. The following are example instantiations of the path P_1:

- $PI_1=$ Vehicle[1].Company[11].Division[24].Milan
  (PI_1 is graphically illustrated in Figure 2)

- $PI_2=$ Vehicle[1].Company[11].Division[21].Bordeaux

- $PI_3=$ Vehicle[3].Company[10].Division[20].Turin

- $PI_4=$ Vehicle[3].Company[10].Division[22].Milan.

The previous path instantiations are all *complete*, that is, they start with an instance belonging to the first class of the path (i.e. Vehicle), contain an instance for each class found in the path, and end with an instance of the class domain of the path. It is possible that a path has also *partial instantiations*. In Figure 13.2, there are the following partial instantiations of path P_1:

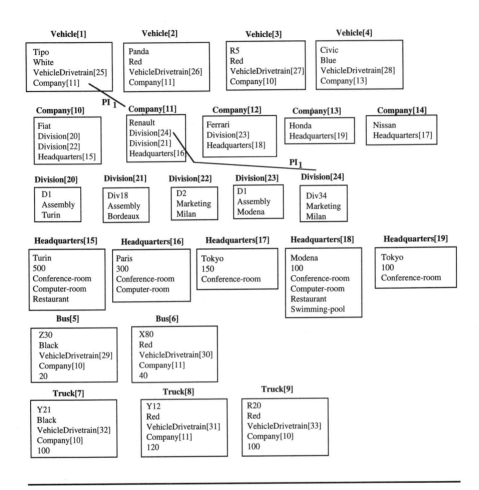

FIGURE 13.2

Instances of classes of Figure 1

- $PI_5 =$ Company[12].Division[23].Modena

- $PI_6 =$ Vehicle[4].Company[13]

- $PI_7 =$ Company[14]

In particular, PI_5 is a *left-partial instantiation*, that is, the first component of the path instantiation is not an instance of the first class of the path (Vehicle in the example), but rather an instance of a class following the first class along the path (Company in the example). PI_6 is a *right-partial instantiation*, since it ends with an object which is not an instance of the class that is the domain of the path. In other words, a right-partial instantiation is such that the last object in the instantiation contains a null value for the attribute referenced in the path. A path instantiation can be both left-partial and right-partial; an example is PI_7. Formal definitions of those concepts can be found in a previous paper by Bertino and Kim [Bertino and Kim 1989] (only for left-partial instantiations) and in a paper by Kemper and Moerkotte [Kemper and Moerkotte 1990].

Multi-index (Maier, and Stein [Maier and Stein 1986])

This organization is based on allocating an index on each class traversed by the path. Therefore, given a path $P = C_1.A_1.A_2.\ldots.A_n$, traversing n classes $C_1 C_2 \ldots C_n$, a multi-index is defined as a set of n simple indices (called *index components*) $I_1, I_2, ..., I_n$, where I_i is an index defined on $C_i.A_i$, $1 \leq i \leq n$. All indices $I_1, I_2, \ldots, I_{n-1}$ are *identity indices*, that is, they have as key values OIDs. Only the operators == (identical to) and $\sim\sim$ (not identical to) are supported on an identity index. The last index I_n can be either an identity index, or an *equality index* depending on the domain of A_n. An equality index is an index whose key values are primitive objects, such as numbers or characters. An equality index supports operators such as = (equal to), $\sim$ (different from), $<, \leq, >, \geq$.

As an example consider path $P_1 =$ Vehicle.manufacturer.divisions.location. There will be three indices allocated for this path. Example index entries for path P_1 are the following. Each index entry is represented as a pair, whose first element is a key-value, and whose second element is the set of OIDs of objects holding this key-value for the indexed attribute.

- First index I_1 on Vehicle.manufacturer

  - (Company[10], {Vehicle[3]})

- (Company[11], {Vehicle[1], Vehicle[2]})

- (Company[13], {Vehicle[4]})

- Second index I_2 on Company.divisions

  - (Division[20], {Company[10]})

  - (Division[22], {Company[10]})

  - (Division[24], {Company[11]})

  - (Division[21], {Company[11]})

  - (Division[23], {Company[12]})

  - (Null, {Company[13], Company[14]})

- Third index I_3 on Division.location

  - (Bordeaux, {Division[21]})

  - (Milan, {Division[22], Division[24]})

  - (Modena, {Division[23]})

  - (Turin, {Division[20]})

Note that in the second index (I_2) the special key-value Null is used to record a right-partial instantiation. Therefore, the index organization above allows determining all path instantiations having null values for some attributes along the path. By contrast, the determination of left-partial instantiations does not require any special key-value.

Under this organization, solving a nested predicate requires scanning a number of indices equal to the path-length. For example to select all vehicles with a manufacturer having a division located in Turin, the following steps are executed:

1. a look-up of index I_3 with key-value=Turin; the result is {Division[20]}

2. a look-up of index I_2 with the key-value=Divison[20]; the result is {Company[10]}

3. a look-up of index I_1 with the key-value=Company[10]; the result is {Vehicle[3]} which is the result of the query.

Therefore, under this organization the retrieval operation is performed by first scanning the last index allocated on the path. Then the results of this index lookup are used as keys for a search on the index preceding the last one in the path, and so forth until the first index is scanned. Therefore, this organization only supports reverse traversal strategies. The major advantage of this organization, compared to others we describe later on, is the low update cost.

Join index (Valduriez [Valduriez 1987b])

The notion of join index has been introduced to efficiently perform joins in the relational model. However, they have been used to efficiently implement complex objects. A binary join index is defined as follows:

Given two relations R and S and attributes A and B, respectively from R and S, a *binary join index* is

$$BJI = \{(r_i, s_k)|f(\text{tuple } r_i.A, \text{ tuple } s_k.B) \text{ is true}\}$$

where

- f is a Boolean function that defines the join predicate

- r_i denotes the surrogate of a tuple of R

- s_k denotes the surrogate of a tuple of S

- tuple r_i (tuple s_k) refers to the tuple having r_i (s_k) as surrogate.

(Note that a BJI can be generalized to non-binary join index when more than two relations are joined.) A BJI is implemented as a binary relation and two copies may be kept, one clustered on r and the other on s; each copy is implemented as a B$^+$-tree. In aggregation graphs, a sequence of BJIs can be used in a multi-index organization to implement the various index components along a given path. Example index entries for path P_1 are:

- First binary join index BJI_1 on Vehicle.manufacturer

    - copy clustered on OIDs of instances of Company
      (Company[10], {Vehicle[3]})
      (Company[11], {Vehicle[1],Vehicle[2]})
      (Company[13], {Vehicle[4]})

- copy clustered on OIDs of instances of Vehicle
  (Vehicle[1], {Company[11]})
  (Vehicle[2], {Company[11]})
  (Vehicle[3], {Company[10]})
  (Vehicle[4], {Company[13]})

- Second binary join index BJI_1 on Company.divisions

  - copy clustered on OIDs of instances of Division
    (Division[20], {Company[10]})
    (Division[21], {Company[11]})
    (Division[22], {Company[10]})
    (Division[23], {Company[12]})
    (Division[24], {Company[11]})
    (Null, {Company[13], Company[14]})

  - Copy clustered on OIDs of instances of Company
    (Company[10], {Division[20],Division[22]})
    (Company[11], {Division[24], Division[21]})
    (Company[12], {Division[23]})
    (Company[13], {Null})
    (Company[14], {Null})

- Third binary join index BJI_3 on Division.location

  - Copy clustered on OIDs of instances of Division
    (Division[20], {Turin})
    (Division[21], {Bordeaux})
    (Division[22], {Milan})
    (Division[23], {Modena})
    (Division[24], {Milan})

  - Copy clustered on OIDs (values) of instances of String
    (Bordeaux, {Division[21]})
    (Milan, {Division[22], Division[24]})
    (Modena, {Division[23]})
    (Turin, {Division[20]})

Note that with this structure, a multi-index on the same path is a subset of it. A BJI-multi-index organization supports both forward and reverse traversal strategies among classes when both copies are allocated for each binary join index. Reverse traversal is suitable for solving queries such as "Select all vehicles with a manufacturer having a division located in Turin." Forward traversal arises when given an object, all objects must be determined that are referenced directly or indirectly by this object. An example is "Determine the locations of the divisions of the company manufacturing Vehicle[1]." The reverse traversal is already supported by the simple multi-index organization [Maier and Stein 1986]. Forward traversal could be performed by directly accessing the objects, since each object stores in its attributes references to other objects. However, the usage of a sequence of BJIs may make forward traversal faster when object accesses are expensive (for example, very large objects, non-optimal clustering). Moreover, forward traversal supported by a sequence of BJIs may be useful in complex queries when objects at the beginning of the path have already been selected as the effect of another predicate in the query. An example of more complex query is "Select all red vehicles manufactured by a company with a division located in Turin." Suppose that an index is allocated on attribute 'color' and moreover a BJI-multi-index organization is allocated on the path P_1=Company.manufacturer.divisions.location. A possible query strategy could be to first select all red vehicles (using the index on attribute 'color'), and then to use the BJI-multi-index in forward traversal to determine the locations of the divisions of the vehicles selected by the first index scan. Note that the update costs of a BJI-multi-index organization have not been evaluated yet. We can expect the update costs to be double that of the simple multi-index organization, since in the BJI-multi-index organization there are two copies of each binary join index. However, depending on the access and update patterns, it is always possible to allocate a single copy of some binary join indexes along the path.

The usage of join indices in optimizing complex queries has been discussed by Valduriez [Valdureiz 1987a]. A major conclusion is that the most complex part (i.e. the joins) of a query can be executed through join indices, without accessing the base data. However, there are cases when traditional indexing (selection indices on join attributes) is more efficient than the usage of a join index. For example, a traditional index is more efficient than a join index when the query simply consists of a join preceded by a highly selective selection. The major conclusion is that join indices are more suitable for complex queries, that is, queries involving several joins.

Nested index (Bertino, and Kim [Bertino and Kim 1989])

Both the previous organizations require, when solving a nested predicate, to access a number of indices proportional to the path length. Different organizations have been proposed aiming at reducing the number of indices accessed. The first of these organizations is the nested index which provides a direct association between an object of a class at the end of a path and the corresponding instances of the class at the beginning of the path. Example index entries for path P_1 are

- (Bordeaux, {Vehicle[1],Vehicle[2]})

- (Milan, {Vehicle[1],Vehicle[2],Vehicle[3]})

- (Turin, {Vehicle[3]})

- (Null, {Vehicle[4]})

Note also that in this organization the Null key-value is used for right-partial instantiations. However, unlike the previous organizations, only the instances at the beginning of the right-partial instantiations are recorded in the nested index. Therefore, from the index it is not possible to determine whether the path instantiation starting with Vehicle[4] is right-partial because Vehicle[4] has a null value for the attribute 'manufacturer' or rather because the object that is value of the attribute 'manufacturer' of Vehicle[4] has a null value for attribute 'divisions' (and so forth). Moreover, note that the left-partial instantiations are not recorded in the index because the left-partial instantiations start with instances of classes different from the first class of the path. Since a nested index only associates instances of the first class of the path with the values of the attribute at the end of the path, instances at the beginning of left-partial instantiations are not recorded in the index.

Retrieval under this organization is quite fast, since a query such as "Select all vehicles with a manufacturer having a division located in Turin" is solved with only one index lookup. The major problem of this indexing technique is update operations that require access to several objects in order to determine the index entries to be updated. For example, suppose that Division[24] is removed from the set of divisions of Company[11]. To perform this update operation, the following steps must be executed:

1. access Division[24] and determine the value of attribute 'location'; result: Milan

2. determine all instances of class Vehicle having Company[11] as manufacturer; result: {Vehicle[1], Vehicle[2]}

3. remove {Vehicle[1], Vehicle[2]} from the index entry with key-value=
   Milan; after the removal the index entry is (Milan, {Vehicle[3]}).

From the example above, it may be seen that update operations in general require both forward and backward traversals of objects. Forward traversal is required to determine the value of the indexed attribute (that is, the value of the attribute at the end of the path) for the modified object. Reverse traversal is required to determine the instances at the beginning of the path. The OIDs of those instances will be removed (added) to the entry associated with the key value determined by the forward traversal. Note that reverse traversal is very expensive when there are no reverse references among objects. In such case, the nested index organization may not be usable.

Note that a nested index as defined above can only be used for performing reverse traversal strategies. However, it would be possible, as for the *BJI* organization, to allocate two copies of a nested index: the first having as key-values the values of attribute A_n at the end of the path (examples of entries of this copy for path P_1 would be the ones we have shown earlier); the second having as key-values the OIDs of the instances at the class at the beginning of the path. Therefore, for path P_1 this second copy would have the following entries:

- (Vehicle[1], {Bordeaux, Milan})

- (Vehicle[2], {Bordeaux, Milan})

- (Vehicle[3], {Milan, Turin})

- (Vehicle[4], {Null}).

The use of the above nested index would be more efficient than forward traversal using the object themselves.

Path index (Bertino, and Kim [Bertino and Kim 1989])

A path index is based on a single index, like the nested index. The difference is that a path index provides an association between an object O at the end of a path and the instantiations ending with O. Example index entries for P_1 are

- (Bordeaux,{Vehicle[1].Company[11].Division[21],
  Vehicle[2].Company[11].Division[21]})

- (Milan, {Vehicle[1].Company[11].Division[24],
  Vehicle[2].Company[11].Division[24],
  Vehicle[3].Company[10].Division[22]})

- (Modena, {Company[12].Division[23]})

- (Turin, {Vehicle[3].Company[10].Division[20]})

- (Null, {Vehicle[4].Company[13], Company[14]}).

Note that a path index records, in addition to complete instantiations, left-partial and right-partial instantiations.

Unlike the nested index, a path index can be used to solve nested predicates against all classes along the path. For example, the path index on P_1 can be used to determine all vehicles manufactured by a company with a division located in Turin, or simply to find the divisions located in Turin. This feature is also very useful when dealing with complex queries. In particular, it supports a special kind of projection, called *projection on path instantiation* [Bertino 1991d]. This operation allows retrieving OIDs of several classes along the path with a single index lookup. For example, suppose we wish to determine all vehicles manufactured by a company with a division located in Milan and headquarters in Turin. This query can be solved by first performing an index lookup with key-value equal Milan and then performing a projection on positions 1 and 2 on the selected index entries. That is, the first and second element of each path instantiation verifying the nested predicate are extracted from the index. Therefore, the results of this projection in the above example are: {(Vehicle[1], Company[11]), (Vehicle[2], Company[11]), (Vehicle[3], Company[10])}. Then the second element of each pair is extracted. The corresponding object is accessed and the predicate on attribute 'headquarters' is evaluated. If this predicate is satisfied, the first element of the pair is returned as query result. For example, given the three pairs above, Company[11] would be accessed to verify whether its headquarters is in Turin. Company[11] does not verify the predicate. Therefore Vehicle[1] and Vehicle[2] are discarded. Then, Company[10] would be accessed. Since Company[10] verifies the predicate on attribute 'headquarters', Vehicle[3] is returned as the query result. An analysis of query processing strategies using this operation is presented in a paper by Bertino and Guglielmina [Bertino 1992].

Updates on a path index are expensive, since forward traversals are required, as in the case of the nested index. However, no reverse traversals are required. Therefore, the path index organization can be used even when no reverse references among objects on the path are present. Suppose that Division[24] is removed from the set of divisions of Company[11]. To perform this update operation, the following steps must be executed:

1. access Division[24] and determine the value of attribute 'location'; result: Milan

2. remove from the index entry with key-value= Milan all path instantiations having Company[11] as second element and Division[24] as third element; after the removal, the index entry is (Milan,{Vehicle[3].Company[10].Division[22]}).

Access relation (Kemper, and Moerkotte [Kemper and Moerkotte 1990])

An access relation is an organization very similar to the path index in that it involves calculating all instantiations along a path and storing them in a relation. For path P_1, the access relation will contain the following tuples:

<Vehicle[1], Company[11], Division[21], Bordeaux>
<Vehicle[2], Company[11], Division[21], Bordeaux>
<Vehicle[1], Company[11], Division[24], Milan>
<Vehicle[2], Company[11], Division[24], Milan>
<Vehicle[3], Company[10], Division[22], Milan>
<Vehicle[3], Company[10], Division[20], Turin>
<Vehicle[4], Company[13], Null, Null>
<Null, Company[14], Null, Null>
<Null, Company[12], Division[23], Modena>.

Similarly to what is discussed by Bertino and Kim [Bertino and Kim 1989], a path may be split and different access relations allocated for each subpath. Moreover, it is possible to store incomplete path instantiations using null values in relations.

A Comparison

A comparison among multi-index, nested index and path index has been carried out by Bertino and Kim [Bertino and Kim 1989]. An important parameter in the evaluations is represented by the *degree of reference sharing*. Two objects share a reference if they reference the same object as value of an attribute. Therefore, this degree models the topology of references among objects. A more accurate model of reference topology was developed later by Bertino and Foscoli [Bertino 1991f].

The major results from the analysis by Bertino and Kim [Bertino and Kim 1989] can be summarized as follows. For retrieval the nested index has the lowest cost; the path index has in general lower cost than the multi-index. Note that the nested index has a better performance than the path index for retrieval, because a path index contains OIDs of instances of all classes along the path, while the nested index contains OIDs of instances of only the first class in the path. However, a single path index allows predicates to be solved for all classes along the path, while the nested index does not. For update the multi-index has the lowest cost. The nested index has a slightly lower cost than the path index for path length 2. For paths longer than 2, the nested index has a slightly lower cost than the path index if updates are on the first two classes of the path; otherwise the nested index has significantly higher cost than the path index. Note, however, that the update costs for the nested index are computed under the hypothesis that there are reverse references among objects. When there are no reverse references, update operations for the nested index became much more expensive.

For paths longer than 2, intermediate solutions are also possible based on splitting a path into several smaller subpaths, and allocating on each subpath either a nested index, a path index or a simple index. For example, path P_1=Vehicle.manufacturer.divisions.location could be split into two subpaths:

- P_{11}= Vehicle.manufacturer with a simple index allocated

- P_{12}=Company.divisions.location with a path index allocated.

An algorithm determining optimal configurations for paths has been defined by Bertino [Bertino 1991c]. The algorithm takes as input the frequency of operations of retrieval, insert, and delete for classes along the path. Moreover, it also takes into account whether reverse references exist among objects as well as all data logical and physical characteristics. The algorithm determines the optimal way of splitting a path into subpaths, and the organization to be used for each subpath. The algorithm also considers, for each subpath, the choice of allocating no index. An interesting result obtained by running the algorithm is that when the degrees of reference sharing along a path are very low (that is, close to 1) and reverse references are allocated among objects, the best index configuration consists of allocating no index on the path. This result shows that reverse references [Andrew and Harris 1987, Kim et al. 1989] among objects can be an access technique that in some situations can be used as alternative to indices. Some further evaluations concerning the usage of reverse references have been carried out and the results are presented in a technical report [Bertino 1991g].

13.4
Index Organizations for Inheritance Graphs

As we discussed in Section 13.2. an object-oriented query language offers the user the option to declare whether the scope of a query is a class C only or a class C and all its subclasses in the inheritance graph rooted at C. Since an attribute of C is inherited by all its subclasses, a first issue concerns how to evaluate a predicate against such an attribute efficiently when the scope of the query is the inheritance graph rooted at C.

A solution based on traditional indexing techniques requires building an index on the indexed attribute for each class in the graph. For example, let us consider the inheritance graph rooted at class Vehicle in Figure 13.1. If the attribute 'color' is often used in queries against this inheritance graph, this approach requires building three indices, one for each class in the graph. The evaluation of a predicate against the attribute 'color' would then require scanning the three indices and performing the union of the results. We will refer to an index that is maintained on an attribute of a single class as *non-inherited index*. As an example consider the instances in Figure 13.2. The three indices against the attribute 'color' for the classes in the graph rooted at class Vehicle will contain the following entries:

- Index on class Vehicle
  entries: (Blue, {Vehicle[4]}) (Red, {Vehicle[2], Vehicle[3]})
  (White, {Vehicle[1]})

- Index on class Truck
  entries: (Black, {Truck[7]}) (Red, {Truck[8], Truck[9]})

- Index on class Bus
  entries: (Black, {Bus[5]}) (Red, {Bus[6]})

A different approach has been proposed by Kim, et al. [Kim et al. 1989] that directly supports queries against inheritance graphs. The approach consists of maintaining one index on the common attribute for all classes in an inheritance graph. Therefore an index entry contains the identifiers of instances of any class in the graph. We will refer to this approach as *inherited index.* Under this organization, an index on the attribute 'color' for the inheritance graph rooted at class Vehicle will contain the following entries:

- (Black, (Truck, {Truck[7]}) (Bus, {Bus[5]}))

- (Blue, (Vehicle, {Vehicle[4]}))

- (Red, (Vehicle, {Vehicle[2], Vehicle[3]}) (Truck, {Truck[8], Truck[9]}) (Bus, {Bus[6]}))

- (White, (Vehicle, {Vehicle[1]})).

Note that the third entry contains three sets of OIDs. The first set contains the OIDs of the instances of Vehicle that are red, while the second set contains the trucks, and the third the buses.

A leaf node of an inherited index has a different format than a traditional non-inherited index. A leaf node in an inherited index consists of a key-value, a key-directory, and for each class in the inheritance graph the number of elements in the list of OIDs for instances of this class that hold the key-value in the indexed attribute, and the list of OIDs. The key-directory contains an entry for each class that has instances with the key-value in the indexed attribute. An entry for a class consists of the class identifier and the offset in the index record where the list of OIDs for the class is located. Figure 13.3 shows an example of a leaf node in an inherited index.

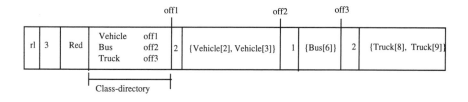

FIGURE 13.3
A leaf node record in an inherited index

In the inherited index, a predicate against the indexed attribute on a single class is evaluated as follows. Let C be the class against which the predicate is issued. The index is scanned to find the leaf-node record with the key-value satisfying the predicate. Then the key-directory is accessed to determine the offset in the index record where the list of OIDs of instances of C is located. If there is no entry for class C, then there are no instances of C satisfying the predicate. If the query is against more than one class in the indexed inheritance graph, the predicate is processed in the same way, except that the lookup in the key-directory is executed for each class involved in the query. Therefore, this access mechanism can be used when a query is applied only to some (not necessarily all) classes in the indexed graph. For example, given the inheritance graph rooted at class Vehicle and an inherited index on the attribute 'color', the index can be used to solve a predicate on the attribute 'color' for a query that applies only to the classes Vehicle and Bus.

In general, an inherited index is more efficient for queries whose access scope involves a significant subset of the classes in the indexed inheritance graph, while a non-inherited index should be more effective for queries against a single class. To quantify the performance, an extensive evaluation of these indexing techniques has been carried out by Kim, et al. [Kim et al. 1989]. An important parameter in the evaluation is the distribution of key values across the classes in the inheritance graph. In general, if each key value is taken by instances of only one class C (i.e. disjoint distribution), the inherited index is less efficient than the non-inherited index. Conversely, if each key value is taken by instances of several classes, the inherited index may perform better. Therefore, in the experiments different distributions of key-values across classes have been taken into account. The major conclusions are that for single-key predicates the inherited index is in general more efficient than a non-inherited index if the query involves at least two classes of the inheritance graph. For range-key predicates, the inherited index is more efficient if the query involves at least three classes.

13.5
Integrated Organizations

In this section we review an indexing technique defined by Bertino [Bertino 1991] that provides an efficient evaluation of nested predicates for both queries having as a target a single class and queries having as a target any number of classes in a given inheritance graph. Therefore, this technique provides an integrated treatment of indexing in the framework of both aggregation and inheritance graphs. The technique is defined as a combination of ideas from the nested index, the inherited index, and the join index techniques. Its main limitation is that it has been defined for paths having all single-valued attributes. However, it is currently being extended to support multi-valued attributes as well [Bertino 1991f]. In order to present the indexing technique, we need some additional definitions. To simplify the following discussion, we make the assumption that a class occurs only once in a path.

Given a class C_1, C_1^* denotes the set of classes in the inheritance hierarchy rooted at C_1. As an example, consider the object-oriented schema in Figure 13.1:

Vehicle* = {Vehicle, Bus, Truck}.

Given a path $\mathcal{P} = C_1.A_1.A_2.\ldots.A_n$ ($n \geq 1$), the *scope* of $\mathcal{P}$ is defined as the set $\bigcup_{C_i \in class(\mathcal{P})} C_i^*$. Class C_1 is the root of the scope. Given a class C in the scope of a path, the *position* of C is given by an integer i, such that C belongs to the inheritance hierarchy rooted at class C_i, [1] where $C_i \in class(\mathcal{P})$. The scope of a path simply represents the set of all classes along the path and all their subclasses. For example, consider the path $P=$ Vehicle.manufacturer.headquarters.location, scope(P)= {Vehicle, Bus, Truck, Company, Headquarters}. Vehicle is the root of P. Classes Vehicle, Bus, Truck have position one, class Company has position two, and class Headquarters has position three. In the remainder of the discussion, given an object O, we will use the term *parent object* to denote an object that references O. For example, the parents of Company[11] are Vehicle[1], Vehicle[2], Bus[6], Truck[8].

Given a path $\mathcal{P} = C_1.A_1.A_2 \ldots A_n$, the *nested-inherited index* associates with a value v of attribute A_n OIDs of instances of each class in the scope of $\mathcal{P}$ having v as value of the (nested) attribute A_n. A nested-inherited index on path $P=$Vehicle.manufacturer.headquarters.location associates with a given location all vehicles manufactured by a company located at that location. Similarly for all the other classes in the scope. Logically, the index will contain the following entries (in each entry the key-value is in boldface)

- (**Modena**, (Company, {Company[12]}), (Headquarters, {Headquarters[18]}))

- (**Paris**, (Vehicle, {Vehicle[1], Vehicle[2]}), (Bus, {Bus[6]}, (Truck, {Truck[8]}), (Company, {Company[11]}), (Headquarters, {Headquarters[16]}))

- (**Tokyo**, (Vehicle, {Vehicle[4]}), (Company, {Company[13],

---

[1] Note that if a class occurs at several points in a path, the class has a set of positions.

Company[14]}), (Headquarters, {Headquarters[19], Headquarters[17]}))

- (**Turin**, (Vehicle, {Vehicle[3]}), (Bus, {Bus[5]}), (Truck, {Truck[7], Truck[9]}), (Company, {Company[10]}), (Headquarters, {Headquarters[15]}))

The nested-inherited index, as the nested index and path index, supports fast retrieval operations. However, unlike those two organizations, the nested-inherited index does not require object traversals for update operations, because of some additional information that is also stored in the index. The format of nonleaf node has a structure similar to that of traditional indices based on B$^+$-tree. The record in a leaf node, called a *primary record*, has a different structure. It contains the following information:

- record-length

- key-length

- key-value

- class-directory

- for each class in the path scope, the number of elements in the list of OIDs for the objects that hold the key-value in the indexed attribute, and the list of OIDs.

The class-directory contains a number of entries equal to the number of classes having instances with the key-value in the indexed attribute. For each such class C_i, an entry in the directory contains:

- the class identifier

- the offset in the primary record where the list of OIDs of C_i instances are stored

- the pointer to an auxiliary record where the list of parents is stored for each instance of C_i. An auxiliary record is allocated for each class, except for the root class of the path and for its subclasses. An auxiliary record consists of a sequence of 4-tuples. A 4-tuple has the form:

  $(oid_i, \text{pointer to primary record}, \text{no-oids}, \{p - oid_{i_1}, \ldots, p - oid_{i_n}\})$.

  There are as many 4-tuples as the number of instances of C_i having the key-value in the indexed attribute. For an object O_i, the tuple contains the identifier of O_i, the pointer to the primary record, the number of parent objects of O_i, the list of parent objects. In the 4-tuple definition above, no-oids denotes the number of parent objects, and $p - oid_{i_j}$ denotes the j-th parent of O_i

Auxiliary records are stored in different pages than primary records. Given a primary record, there are several auxiliary records that are *connected* to it. A second B$^+$-tree is superimposed on the auxiliary records. The second B$^+$-tree indexes the 4-tuples based on the object-identifiers that appear as the first elements of 4-tuples. Therefore, the index organization actually consists of two indices. The first, called the *primary index*, is keyed on the values of attribute A_n. It associates with a value v of A_n the set of OIDs of instances of all classes relative to the path that have v as value of the (nested) attribute. The second index, called the *auxiliary index*, has OIDs as indexing keys. It associates with the OID of an object O the list of OIDs of the parents of O. Leaf-node records in the primary index contain pointers to the leaf-node records in the auxiliary index, and vice versa. The reason for the auxiliary index is to provide all information for updating the primary index without accessing the objects themselves. Recall that when updates are executed, the nested index may require object forward and reverse traversals, while the path index only requires forward traversals. By contrast, the nested inherited index does not require any access to the objects. The reason for this organization will be however more clear when discussing the operations.

Figure 13.4 provides an example of the partial index contents for the objects shown in Figure 13.2.

We now discuss how retrieval, insert, and delete operations are performed on the nested-inherited index. For ease of presentation, we will use examples to describe the operations. Formal algorithms are presented in a paper by Bertino and Foscoli [Bertino 1991f].

Retrieval

The nested inherited index supports a fast evaluation of predicates on the indexed attribute for queries having as target any class, or class hierarchy, in the scope of the path ending with the indexed attribute. As an example, suppose that a query is issued that retrieves all instances of class Bus manufactured by a company with headquarters in Turin. This query is executed by first executing a lookup on the primary index with key value equal to Turin. The primary record is then accessed. A lookup in the class directory is executed to determine the offset where the OIDs of Bus instances are stored.

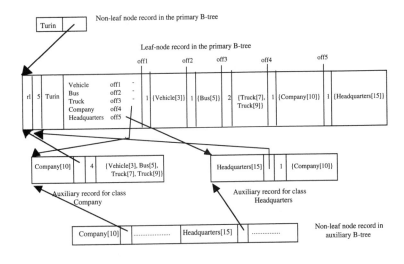

FIGURE 13.4

Example of index contents in a nested-inherited index

Then those OIDs are fetched and returned as the result of the query. We now consider a query like the previous one except that the query is on the class hierarchy rooted at class Vehicle. The same steps as before are executed. The only difference is that the class-directory lookup is executed for classes Vehicle, Bus, and Truck, and three different portions of the record are accessed, one for each offset obtained from the class-directory. Therefore, the retrieval operation is similar to retrieval in an inherited index [Kim et al. 1989]. The main difference, however, is that a nested-inherited index can be used for queries on all class hierarchies found along a given path. By contrast, the inherited index is allocated on a single class-hierarchy. Therefore, if a path has length n, the number of inherited indices allocated would be n.

Insert

Suppose that a new vehicle, Vehicle[100], is created having Company[10] as value of attribute 'manufacturer'. Vehicle[100] is therefore a new parent of Company[10]. The overall effect of the insertion in the index must be that Vehicle[100] is added to the primary record with key-value equal to 'Turin', and to the parent list of Company[10]. Note that no parent list needs to be allocated for Vehicle[100], since it is an instance of a class at the beginning of the path. The following steps are executed:

1. The auxiliary index is accessed with key-value equal to Company[10].

2. The 4-tuple of Company[10] is retrieved and modified by adding Vehicle[100] to the list of Company[10] parents.

3. From the 4-tuple of Company[10] the pointer to the primary record is determined.

4. The primary record is accessed.

5. A look-up is executed of the class directory in the primary record to determine the offset where OIDs of the class Vehicle are stored.

6. Vehicle[100] is added to the list of OIDs stored at the offset determined at the previous step.

Note that there is no need to execute a look-up of the primary index, since the address of the primary record can be directly determined from the auxiliary record. Moreover, note that if the instance to be inserted is an instance of a class C not at the beginning of the path, during step 5 the address of the auxiliary record for class C is also determined by the class directory. Then an additional step is executed after step 6 that accesses the auxiliary class record and inserts a 4-tuple for the newly inserted instance.

Delete

Suppose now that Company[10] is removed. The overall effect of this operation on the index must be that Company[10] and all instances referencing Company[10] (that is, Vehicle[3], Bus[5], Truck[7], and Truck[9]) be eliminated from the primary record with key-value equal to 'Turin'. Moreover, the 4-tuples for instances Company[10], Vehicle[3], Bus[5], Truck[7], and Truck[9] must be eliminated. Finally, Company[10] must be eliminated from the parent list of Headquarters[15]. Note that the update to the parent lists of Headquarters[15] may not be needed if Headquarters[15] is removed as well; in this case it may be better to accumulate several delete operations on the same index. However, we will include that update to exemplify the algorithm.

1. The value of attribute 'headquarters' of Company[10] is determined. This value is the OID Headquarters[15].

2. The auxiliary index is accessed with key-value equal to Headquarters[15].

3. The 4-tuple of Headquarters[15] is retrieved and modified by removing Company[10] from the list of parents of Headquarters[15].

4. From the 4-tuple of Headquarters[15] the pointer to the primary record is determined.

5. The primary record is accessed.

6. A look-up is executed on the class-directory in the primary record to determine the offset where the OIDs of the class Company are stored and the pointer to the auxiliary record for class Company.

7. Company[10] is removed from the list of OIDs stored at the offset determined at the previous step.

8. The auxiliary record of class Company is accessed and the 4-tuple containing as first element the OID Company[10] is determined. From this tuple, the OIDs of the Company[10] parents are determined. Those are Vehicle[3], Bus[5], Truck[7], and Truck[9]. Then the 4-tuple of Company[10] is removed.

9. A lookup is executed on the class-directory in the primary record to determine the offset where the OIDs of the class Vehicle are stored.

10. Vehicle[3] is removed from the list of OIDs stored at the offset determined at the previous step.

11. A lookup is executed on the class-directory in the primary record to determine the offset where the OIDs of class Bus are stored.

12. Bus[5] is removed from the list of OIDs stored at the offset determined at the previous step.

13. A lookup is executed on the class-directory in the primary record to determine the offset where the OIDs of class Truck are stored.

14. Truck[7] and Truck[9] are removed from the list of OIDs stored at the offset determined at the previous step.

The delete operation may appear rather costly. However, note that the primary record is accessed only once from secondary storage. Several modifications may be required on this record. However, the record can be kept in memory and written back after all modifications have been executed. Also note that the algorithm may require accessing several auxiliary records. However, they are all connected to the same primary record. Therefore, they are likely to be in the same page.

A preliminary comparison among the nested-inherited index and two other organizations has been carried out by Bertino [Bertino 1991]. The first is a multi-index organization and simply consists of allocating an index on each class in the scope of the path. In the example of path P=Vehicle.manufacturer.headquarters, five indices would be allocated. The second organization, called *inherited-multi-index* consists of allocating an inherited index on each inheritance graph found along the path. Therefore, the inherited-multi-index is a combination of the inherited index organization (defined for inheritance graphs) with the multi-index organization (defined for aggregation graph). For path P=Vehicle.manufacturer.headquarters, there would be an inherited index rooted at class Vehicle (thus, indexing Vehicle, Bus, and Truck), and two simple indices, one on class Company and another one on class Headquarters. Major results from the comparison are the following:

- the nested-inherited index has the best retrieval performance;

- the nested-inherited index has quite good performance for the insert operation, since it requires an additional cost of at most three I/O operations with respect to the other two organizations;

- the delete operation for the nested-inherited index has in the worst case an additional cost of $4 * i$ (where i is the position of the class in the path) with respect to the other organizations.

An accurate model of those costs has been recently developed by Bertino and Foscoli [Bertino 1991f].

13.6
Precomputation and Caching

The indexing techniques we discussed so far are based on object structures, that is, on object attributes. Another possibility is to provide indexing based on object behavior, that is, on method results [Bretl et al. 1989]. Techniques based on this approach have been proposed by Bertino [Bertino 1991h], Bertino and Quarati [Bertino 1991e], Jhingran [Jhingran 1991], Kemper, Kilger, and Moerkotte [Kemper et al. 1991]. Most techniques are based on precomputing or caching the results of method invocations. Moreover, these results are stored in an index, or other access structures, so that it is possible to efficiently evaluate queries containing the invocation of the method. A major issue of this approach is how to detect when the computed method results are no longer valid. In most approaches some *dependency information* is kept. This dependency information keeps track of which objects (and possibly which attributes of each object) have been used to compute a given method. When an object is modified, all method precomputed results that have used that object are invalidated. Different solutions can be devised to the problem of dependencies, also depending on the characteristics of the method. In the approach proposed by Kemper, Kilger, and Moerkotte [Kemper et al. 1991], a special structure (implemented as a relation) keeps track of these dependencies. A dependency has the format

$$< oid_i, \; method\_name, < oid_1, oid_2, ..., oid_k >> .$$

This dependency records the fact that the object whose identifier is oid_i has been used in computing the method of name *method_name* with input parameters $< oid_1, oid_2, ..., oid_k >$. Note that the input parameters include also the identifier of the object to which the message invoking the method has been send.

A more sophisticated approach has been proposed by Bertino and Quarati [Bertino 1991e]. If a method is *local*, that is, uses only the attributes of the object upon which it has been invoked, all dependencies are kept within the object itself. Those dependencies are coded as bit-strings, therefore they require a minimal space overhead. If a method is not local, that is, uses attributes of other objects, all dependencies are stored in a special object. All objects whose attributes have been used in the precomputation of a method, have a reference to this special object. This approach is similar to the one proposed by Kemper, Kilger, and Moerkotte [Kemper et al. 1991]. The main difference is that in the approach proposed by Bertino and Quarati, dependencies are stored not in a single data structure, rather they are distributed among several "special objects." The main advantage of this approach is that it provides a greater flexibility with respect to object allocation and clustering. For example, a "special object" may be clustered together with one of the object used in the precomputation of the method, depending on the expected update frequencies.

In order to further reduce the need of invalidation, it is important to determine the actual attributes used in the precomputation of a method. As noted by Kemper, Kilger, and Moerkotte [Kemper et al. 1991], not all attributes are used in executing all methods. Rather, each method is likely to require a small fraction of an object's attributes. Two basic approaches can be devised. The first approach is called *static* and it is based on inspecting the method implementation. Therefore, for each method the system keeps the list of attributes used in the method. In this way, when an attribute is modified, the system has only to invalidate a method if the method uses the modified attribute. Note, however, that an inspection of method implementations actually determines all attributes that can be possibly used when the method is executed. Depending on the method execution flow, some attributes may never be used in computing a method on a given object. This problem is solved by the *dynamic approach.* Under this approach, the attributes used by a method are actually determined only when the method is precomputed. Upon precomputation of the method, the system keeps track of all attributes actually accessed during the method execution. Therefore, the same method precomputed on different objects may use different sets of attributes for each one of these objects. Performance studies of method precomputation have been carried out by Jhingran [Jhingran 1991] and by Kemper, Kilger, and Moerkotte [Kemper et al. 1991].

13.7
Conclusions

In this paper, we have discussed a number of indexing techniques specifically tailored for object-oriented databases. We have first presented indexing techniques supporting an efficient evaluation of implicit joins among objects. There are several techniques developed. No one of them, however, is optimal from both retrieval and update costs. Techniques providing lower retrieval costs, such as path indices or access relations, have a greater update costs compared to techniques, such as multi-index, that, however have greater retrieval costs.

Then we have discussed indexing techniques for inheritance graphs. Finally, we have presented an indexing technique that provides integrated support for queries on both aggregation and inheritance graphs. This indexing technique is currently being extended to deal with multi-valued attributes [Bertino 1991f].

Overall, an open problem is to determine how all those indexing techniques perform for different types of queries. Studies along that direction have been carried out by Bertino [Bertino 1990] and Valduriez [Valdureiz 1987a]. Similar studies should be undertaken for all the other techniques. Another open problem concerns optimal index allocation.

In the paper we also briefly discussed the problem of indexing for methods. Efficient execution of queries with method invocations is an interesting problem that is peculiar to object-oriented databases (and in general, to advanced system supporting procedures or functions as part of the data model). However, few solutions have yet been proposed. Moreover, there is the need for comprehensive analytical models.

Bibliography

[Andrew and Harris 1987] Andrews, T., Harris, C. Combining language and database advances in an object-oriented development environment. *Proc. of the Second Int. Conference on Object-Oriented Programming Systems, Languages, and Applications*, Orlando (Florida), Oct. 1987.

[Atkinson et al. 1989] Atkinson, M., Bancilhon, F., DeWitt, D., Dittrich., K., Maier, D., Zdonik, S. The object-oriented database system manifesto. *Proceedings of the First Int. Conference on Deductive and Object-Oriented Databases*, Kyoto (Japan), Dec. 1989.

[Bertino and Kim 1989] Bertino, E., Kim, W. Indexing techniques for queries on nested objects. *IEEE Trans. on Knowledge and Data Engineering*, Vol. 1, No. 2 (1989), 196-214.

[Bertino 1990] Bertino, E. Query optimization using nested indices. *Proc. of the Second Int. Conference on Extending Database Technology (EDBT)*, Venice (Italy), March 1990, Lecture Notes in Computer Sciences 416, Springer-Verlag.

[Bertino 1991] Bertino, E. An indexing technique for object-oriented databases. *Proc. of the Seventh IEEE Int. Conference on Data Engineering*, Kobe (Japan), April 1991.

[Bertino 1991a] Bertino, E., Martino, L. Object-oriented database management systems: concepts and issues. *Computer* (IEEE Computer Society), Vol. 24, No. 4 (1991), 33-47.

[Bertino 1991b] Bertino, E., Negri, M., Pelagatti, G., Sbattella, L. Object-oriented query languages: the notion and the issues. *IEEE Trans. on Knowledge and Data Engineering*, Vol. 4, No. 3 (1992), 223-237.

[Bertino 1991c] Bertino, E. On index configuration in object-oriented databases. Submitted for publication, June 1991.

[Bertino 1991d] Bertino, E., Guglielmina, C. Optimization of object-oriented queries using path indices. *Proc. of Int. IEEE Workshop on Research Issues on Data Engineering: Transaction and Query Processing (RIDE-TQP)*, Phoenix (Ariz.), Feb. 1992.

[Bertino 1991e] Bertino, E., Quarati, A. An approach to support method invocations in object-oriented queries. *Proc. of Int. IEEE Workshop on Research Issues on Data Engineering: Transaction and Query Processing (RIDE-TQP)*, Phoenix (Ariz.), Feb. 1992.

[Bertino 1991f] Bertino, E., Foscoli, P. Index organizations for object-oriented databases. Submitted for publication, October 1991.

[Bertino 1991g] Bertino, E. Object-oriented query optimization using reverse references. Technical Report, University of Genova, August 1991.

[Bertino 1991h] Bertino, E. Method precomputation in object-oriented databases. *Proc. of ACM-SIGOIS and IEEE-TC-OA Int. Conference on Organizational Computing Systems (COCSU91)*, Atlanta (Georgia), Nov. 1991.

[Bertino 1992] Bertino, E., Guglielmina, C. Path-index: an approach to the efficient execution of object-oriented queries. Accepted for publication in *Data and Knowledge Engineering* (North-Holland), 1992 (to appear).

[Bretl et al. 1989] Bretl, R., et al. The GemStone data management system. *Object-Oriented Concepts, Databases, and Applications*, W. Kim and F. Lochovsky, eds., Addison-Wesley (1989), 283-308.

[Carey and DeWitt 1988] Carey, M., DeWitt, D. An overview of the EXODUS project. *Proc. of ACM-SIGMOD Conference on Management of Data*, Chicago (Ill.), June 1988.

[Cluet 1989] Cluet, S., et al. Reloop, an algebra based query language for an object-oriented database system. *Proc. of the First Int. Conference on Deductive and Object Oriented Databases*, Kyoto (Japan), Dec. 1989.

[Comer 1979] Comer, D. The ubiquitous B-tree. *ACM Comput. Surveys*, Vol. 11, No. 2 (1979), 121-137.

[Deux 1990] Deux, O. The story of O_2. *IEEE Trans. on Knowledge and Data Engineering*, Vol. 2, No. 1 (1990), 91-108.

[Jenq et al. 1989] Jenq, P., Woelk, D., Kim, W., Lee, W.L. Query processing in distributed ORION. MCC Technical Report, No. ACA-ST-035-89, January 1989.

[Jhingran 1991] Jhingran, A. Precomputation in a complex object environment. *Proc. Seventh IEEE Int. Conference on Data Engineering*, Kobe (Japan), April 1991.

[Joseph et al. 1991] Joseph, J., Thatte, S., Thompson, C., Wells, D. Object-oriented databases: design and implementation. *IEEE Proceedings*, Vol. 79, No. 1 (1991), 42-64.

[Kemper and Moerkotte 1990] Kemper, A., Moerkotte, G. Access support in object bases. *Proc. of the ACM-SIGMOD Conference on Management of Data*, Atlantic City (N.J.), May 1990.

[Kemper et al. 1991] Kemper, A., Kilger, C., Moerkotte, G. Function materialization in object bases. *Proc. of the ACM-SIGMOD Conference on Management of Data*, Denver (Colorado), May 1991.

[Kim et al. 1988] Kim, K.C., Kim, W., Woelk, D., Dale, A. Acyclic query processing in object-oriented databases. *Proc. of ER Conference*, Rome, Nov. 1988, also MCC Technical Report, No.ACA-ST-287-88, Sept. 1988.

[Kim et al. 1989] Kim, W., Kim, K.C., Dale, A. Indexing techniques for object-oriented databases. *Object-Oriented Concepts, Databases, and Applications*, W. Kim, and F. Lochovsky, eds., Addison-Wesley, 1989.

[Kim 1989] Kim, W. A model of queries for object-oriented databases. *Proc. of the 15th Int. Conference on Very Large Data Bases (VLDB)*, Amsterdam, Aug. 1989.

[Kim et al. 1989] Kim, W., Bertino, E., Garza, J.F. Composite objects revisited. *Proc. of ACM-SIGMOD Conference on Management of Data*, Portland (Oreg.), June 1989.

[Maier and Stein 1986] Maier, D., Stein, J. Indexing in an object-oriented database. *Proc. of IEEE Workshop on Object-Oriented DBMSs*, Asilomar (Calif.), Sept. 1986.

[Ozsoyoglu et al. 1987] Ozsoyoglu, M., et al. Extending relational algebra and relational calculus with set-valued attributes and aggregate functions. *ACM Trans. on Database Systems*, Vol. 12, No. 4 (1987), 566-592.

[Pistor and Traunmueller 1986] Pistor, P., Traunmuller, R. A database language for sets, lists, and tables. *Information Systems*, Vol. 11, No. 4 (1986), 323-336.

[Roth et al. 1988] Roth, M.A., Korth, H.F., Silberschatz, A. Extended algebra and calculus for nested relational databases. *ACM Trans. on Database Systems*, Vol. 13, No. 4 (1988), 389-417.

[Schek and Scholl 1986] Schek, H.J., and Scholl, M.H. The relational model with relational-valued attributes. *Information Systems*, Vol. 11, No. 2 (1986), 137-147.

[Shaw and Zdonik 1989] Shaw, G.B., Zdonik S.B. An object oriented query algebra. *Proc. of the Second Int. Workshop on Database Programming Languages*, Portland (Oreg.), June 1989.

[Valdureiz 1987a] Valduriez, P. Optimization of complex database queries using join indices. MCC Technical Report, No. ACA-ST-265-87, August 1987.

[Valduriez 1987b] Valduriez, P. Join indices. *ACM Trans. on Database Systems*, Vol. 12, No. 2, (1987), 218-246.

[Zdonik and Maier 1989] Zdonik, S., Maier, D. Fundamentals of object-oriented databases. *Readings in Object-Oriented Database Management Systems*, D.Maier, and S.Zdonik, eds., Morgan Kaufmann, 1989.

14

Physical Database Design for an Object-Oriented Database System

Marc H. Scholl

Abstract

Object-oriented database systems typically offer a variety of structuring capabilities to model complex objects. This flexibility, together with type (or class) hierarchies and computed "attributes" (methods), poses a high demand on the physical design of object-oriented databases. Similar to traditional databases, it is hardly ever true that the conceptual structure of the database is also a good, that is, efficient, internal one. Rather, data representing the conceptual objects may be structured completely different, for performance reasons. Database systems providing a reasonable amount of data independence allow a physical design that differs from the logical structure significantly. Hence, the performance of the system can be tailored to the overall transaction load faced. The paper presents choices for physical designs that make use of a complex storage model, an extended nested relational model. A first prototype of a physical design optimizer is also presented.

14.1
Introduction

Object-oriented database management systems (OODBMSs) typically offer a variety of structuring capabilities to model complex objects: objects may be hierarchically composed of subobjects, several objects may share common subobjects, objects may appear as (attribute) values of other objects, different objects can be related to each other by functions, methods, or relationships. Type (or class) hierarchies introduce another dimension of object interrelation: an object of one class also "appears" in all its superclasses; again, with multiple inheritance, this need not be a strict hierarchical inclusion. Computed values (attributes, methods) may be used to derive, rather than store, data that are associated with objects. Obviously, it is not at all trivial to find good, that is, efficient, storage structures that support the variety of operations on objects reasonably well.

Two of the standard approaches to implementing such object-oriented data models are to either (i) map everything to an underlying relational database system (RDBMS), or (ii) implement an advanced storage server that offers more complex structures than flat relations.

The first approach offers the advantage that one can build on established, matured technology and, because of standards, that this seems to be a portable solution: it is not necessarily tied to one particular RDBMS.

On the other hand, the typical disadvantages of such "front-end" solutions are that without being able to internally tune the RDBMS to that application, it is unlikely to obtain good performance, since the complex structures of the object-oriented database schema have to be broken into small pieces in order to be stored in (flat) relations. As a consequence, queries to the object-oriented schema have to be mapped into large joins queries against the relational database. Of course, one might improve on the state-of-the-art in commercial RDBMSs by including advanced access support, such as join indices, link fields, or materialized functions, in order to make the relational implementation more feasible. We discuss such extensions under the second approach in a more general context.

The second approach has the obvious disadvantage that one has to implement a new storage manager with more powerful capabilities for complex structured data, which requires a major effort in terms of design and implementation. On the other hand, the potential benefit of such an endeavor is superior performance due to a more flexible physical database organization that allows for more efficient query processing algorithms. Over the last decade, there have been numerous attempts to come up with new DBMS architectures based on advanced storage managers (see [Carey et al. 1986, Batory 1987, Haas et al. 1990, Haerder et al. 1987] for some examples). The DASDBS project[1] is one of these attempts [Paul et al. 1987, Schek et al. 1990], where the storage manager implements *nested relations*, that is, a hierarchical data structure where attribute values can either be atomic or embedded (sub-) relations. The idea is that nested relations serve as a high-level, abstract description of internal storage structures. It was shown in [Scholl et al. 1987] that nested relations can in fact be used to model all schema-driven clustering strategies. That is, all storage schemes that are described by static information. For example, a physical design that stores all employee records adjacent to "their" department record is a schema-driven strategy (which is naturally represented by a nested department relation with an employee sub-relation). In contrast, a physical design that locates employee records either with "their" department record or with "their" manager record, depending on which of these related records was "current" at the time of the creation of the employee record, represents a dynamic clustering strategy, which is partially, but not completely, schema-driven. An example of a fully dynamic, schema-independent clustering strategy is "always append at the end of the database". Schema-driven clustering techniques are both, practically important (they re-

---

[1]**D**armstadt **D**atabase **K**ernel **S**ystem

semble but largely extend the current state-of-the-art) and theoretically interesting (they give rise to powerful algebraic query optimizations). The latter was shown in [Scholl et al. 1987, Scholl 1986] in a context where (flat) relational schemas were internally represented as nested relations. Both, the transformations of the structures and that of the operations can be expressed in a nested relational algebra, so query optimization can mostly operate on an algebraic level.

In this paper, we discuss the problem of physical database design—that is, given a logical DB schema and a transaction load, we want to determine what the internal DB layout with the least overall cost of transaction execution is—in the context of DASDBS as the storage manager. Therefore, all relational database designs are subsumed by this approach, while more flexibility is introduced by taking hierarchical clustering strategies into account. For example, tuples of two "related" tables might as well be stored together in one *nested relational tuple*, containing for each tuple of the first table all the "matching" tuples from the second as a "subrelation". The intuition behind such an organization is that the larger nested tuple is stored consecutively (that is, together with its subtuples) in one or as few as possible page(s) on disk (see [Paul et al. 1987, Schek et al. 1990, Deppisch et al. 1987] for details). Other options to accelerate the execution of "implicit" or "functional joins" include "link fields", that is, references (in the form of object identifiers (OIDs) or addresses) to objects, that may be stored together with the referencing object tuple or separately from it. We will show that, with the extended nested relational interface of the DASDBS storage manager (the extension consists in the availability of physical tuple addresses), we can express a wide variety of physical design alternatives. Furthermore, the high-level (i.e., relational) description of these choices allows the query optimizer to apply algebraic transformations in order to exploit these storage structures when mapping logical level query expressions to the physical level.

The placement trees of O_2 [Benzaken 1990] pursue a similar purpose: objects that are related via super- and subobject relationships or via methods can be clustered hierarchically by defining appropriate placement trees. A placement tree is a hierarchical structure whose nodes are O_2-classes. Upon generation of a new object of some class, the system searches for placement trees that contain the object's class and places the new object on the same page as its parent object, if such a placement tree is found and if the new object is related to an instance of the parent class in that tree. Multiple placement trees may contain the same class, in which case the algorithm for determining the storage location of a newly generated object becomes more complex. In contrast to our approach, placement trees are more a dynamic clustering strategy, because the clustering strategy expressed there is not guaranteed, it is used as a "guideline" rather. In our approach, the definition of a certain clustering strategy (in terms of a nested relational storage relation) precisely determines where object tuples will be stored. While being less flexible on the one hand, our approach has the advantage that the query processor can rely on the information represented in the storage hierarchies, whereas the O_2 optimizer makes no use of this information (yet?). Rather, O_2 expects performance gains to result from increased hit ratios in the buffer pool.

The paper is structured as follows: Section 14.2 describes our notation for the object model as well as the nested relational description of storage clusters. Section 14.3 presents the alternatives that are offered when mapping object schemas to DASDBS, and discusses their pros and cons in terms of which operations benefit and which incur extra costs. In Section 14.4 we describe a first physical database design tool that we have implemented to select a good (ideally the best) database layout for a given object schema and load description. Some remarks about query optimization are given in Section 14.6 together with a summary and outline of future work.

14.2
Notation and Terminology

Before entering the technical exposition, we introduce the notation and terminology used throughout this paper. We first describe the COCOON object model used at the logical level for the schema description; then we set up the framework for the physical level, the extended nested relations available at the interface of the DASDBS storage manager.

14.2.1   The COCOON Object Model

There is no universal consensus on a specific object-oriented data model (OODM), however, many of the features in any of the proposals seem to approach a mature state. For example, support for complex structures, including shared subobjects, and some form of inheritance hierarchies. Like many others, we have contributed to the field by proposing one such model, called COCOON [Scholl and Schek 1990a, Scholl and Schek 1990b]. In this paper, we do not depend heavily on the particular flavor of the OODM used for the logical database schema, so we use our notation and terminology mostly because *we* are most familiar with this model. For the reader, however, it should be straightforward to translate into his or her model of choice.

COCOON is a so-called "object-function" model, as is IRIS [Wilkinson et al. 1990], for example. This means, *objects* are pure abstractions, in the sense of the well-known abstract data type (ADT) approach. Particularly, none of the descriptive information "associated with" an object is considered to be "part of" the object in any sense. Rather, *functions* (or methods) are used as the uniform abstraction of stored fields, computed attributes, and relationships. In an even more general interpretation, "functions" can also be taken as an abstraction of retrieval *and update* methods, that is, the ADT-specific operators. Throughout the rest of the paper, we do not consider functions with side-effects, that is, update methods. Therefore, the term "function" refers to type-specific operators without side-effects. Intentionally, we do not distinguish between stored and computed or derived functions here, considering it as a higher level of data independence to hide this distinction from the logical database schema. In order express general relationships, functions may be set-valued. Furthermore, two functions may be defined as being inverses of each other.

In terms of other OODMs that do distinguish between attributes (stored) or instance variables on the one hand and methods on the other, just think of database schemas where all attributes are hidden (encapsulated) behind access functions (retrieval methods). The point behind our more abstract view is that we want to leave it up to the process of physical database design to make the decisions on what to store and what to derive. Of course, there are restrictions to these decisions, so we can mainly decide to materialize derived functions, trading update effort for retrieval speed.

In COCOON, like in most other OODMs, objects are instances of *types*, which are arranged in an inheritance hierarchy (actually, due to multiple inheritance, this is not a strict hierarchy). A type describes the set of functions that can be applied to its instances. COCOON's query language is strongly typed, that is, a type checker (statically) guarantees that only type-valid expressions are ever executed. The *subtype hierarchy* essentially represents the superset relationship between the sets of functions defined on the subtype as compared to its supertype(s). A subtype inherits all the functions from all its supertypes and adds new functions. Also, all instances of a subtype are also instances of the supertype(s).

A less common characteristic of the COCOON model is its separation between types and *classes*. A type describes the common interface of all instances, whereas a class represents a collection of objects of a given type (or subtypes thereof). Therefore, we can have more than one collection of a given type, for example distinguished by different membership predicates. Each class, C, is characterized by two properties: the type of its member objects, mtype(C), and its current set of member objects, extent(C).

Classes can also be arranged in a (non-strict) hierarchy, representing the subset relationships between their extents, that is, the extent of a subclass is necessarily a subset of the extents of all its superclasses.[2]

Other OODMs that do not distinguish between types and classes would map into COCOON by defining exactly one class per type. Notice that O_2, for example, uses both terms, however, with different semantics: O_2-types are *data*-types, O_2-classes are *object*-types. The O_2-clause "with extent" indicates that an explicit extent should be kept for that particular O_2-class. (In our terminology: O_2-classes are types, and "with extent" defines a class with the same name as the type.)

EXAMPLE 14.1
[Logical DB Schema]   In the following discussions we will refer back to this example database as the logical level DB schema. The database contains information about companies, employees and cities [Scholl and Schek 1990a].

```
define database SampleDB;

    define type city =
        name : string,
        zip : string,
        pop : integer,
        has_comp : set of company inverse location;

    define type person =
        name : string,
        bdate : date,
        addr : city;
```

---

[2]An analysis of object algebra operators, such as selection and projection, shows that the separation of types and classes is necessary in order to define "object-preserving" queries, because the subtype relationship between types and the subset relationship between classes need not always correspond to each other [Scholl and Schek 1990a, Heuer and Scholl 1991, Beeri 1990]. Details of this aspect, however, are not relevant for the purpose of this paper. Just keep in mind that we want to allow the maintenance of more than one "type extent."

```
define type company =
   name : string,
   budg : integer,
   loc : set of city inverse has_comp,
   pres : chief,
   staff : set of employee inverse works_for;

define type employee isa person =
   hired : date,
   ssec : integer,
   sal : integer,
   works_for : company inverse staff;

define class City : city;
define class Pers : person;
define class Comp : company;
define class Empl : employee some Pers;
```

end.

The phrase "some Pers" in the definition of class "Empl" states that (i) Empl is a subclass (i.e., subset) of Pers, and (ii) that inclusion of person objects in the subclass has to be specified explicitly by the user. (In contrast, "all Pers where P" would define a class whose members are automatically determined from the superclass and the predicate P.)

14.2.2   Nested Relations as a Description of Storage Structures

In this section we introduce our notation for physical database designs. We use nested relations to describe the physical clustering strategy on disk blocks. That is, if we say that data from the conceptual database schema is stored in a particular nested relation on the physical level, we assume that the nested tuples are directly mapped to disk blocks in a depth-first fashion: for each nesting level, we will first find all the atomic attribute values followed by the representations of all tuples of the first subrelation, then followed by the representations of all tuples of the second subrelations, and so on, recursively, until no more subrelations exist. This way, one nested tuple is implemented on as few pages as possible. Furthermore, this implementation gives efficient access to complete nested tuples as well as to parts thereof. For the latter to work, the storage manager has to keep structural information that helps figuring out which pages belonging to a nested tuple actually have to be read in from disk in order to process a given request. One implementation technique for this purpose, the one used by DASDBS, is described in detail in [Paul et al. 1987, Deppisch et al. 1987].

As usual, we denote the schema of a nested relation by recursively giving the name of the (sub-) relation followed by a list of attributes enclosed in parentheses: $Dept(dno, dname, budget, Empl(eno, ename, salary))$ is a two-level nested relation $Dept$ with three atomic attributes and one subrelation, $Empl$, that itself has three atomic attributes. In the sequel, when talking about *relations* (on the physical level), we always mean "relations used to store some information about objects" (object-relations). In order to describe *physical level* nested relations we introduce the following additional conventions:

$@R$ for a given relation R denotes the *physical address* of R-tuples, e.g. tuple identifiers (TID). We can use $@R$ either as a (virtual) attribute of relation R, or as a (stored) attribute in any other relation, S (not necessarily distinct from R), in order to describe the fact that the stored S-tuples contain a physical reference to an R-tuple (a "link field").

$\#R$ for a given relation R, representing a conceptual object type R, denotes the unique *object identifier* (OID). This is a stored value used to represent the object itself, a surrogate value that is given to the object by the system upon creation.

Notice that we do not a priori assume that we use the physical address of the tuple representing an object as the object's identifier. Given that we use tuple identifiers (TIDs) as the physical addressing scheme, we could have chosen to do so, since TIDs are guaranteed to be stable. Let us explain why we chose to separate the issues. First, even with TIDs as the physical addressing scheme, it might be necessary to have logical OIDs that are never (not even in case of DB reorganizations) changed or re-used—for example, if OIDs are given to users for some reasons (we do not do this!. Second, and more importantly, we do not exclude redundant storage schemes, where objects may be represented in more than one tuple. This might be useful as a "decomposed" storage strategy, for example, when different object properties have very inhomogeneous access frequencies. Furthermore, we may gain overall performance from object replication. In the latter case, we certainly need a unique OID that is independent from physical tuple addresses.

The use of nested relations to describe a wide variety of physical database designs has been discussed extensively in the context of flat relations as the conceptual model in [Scholl et al. 1987]. Essentially, the choices that we have now, for an object-oriented model at the conceptual level, are largely the same. A relational schema together with the key-to-foreign-key relationships might be considered a "Complex Object" schema, without generalization. Therefore, we repeat the basic ideas here using a few examples.

EXAMPLE 14.2

[Physical storage structures described with nested relations]
A logical "relationship" can be supported in a variety of ways at the physical level, ranging from no particular support, via several kinds of indexes or link fields, through physical neighborhood of related tuples (clustering). Some of these, particularly clustering, can only be applied to $1 : n$-relationships without incorporating redundancy. Basically, all the options for $n : m$-relationships can be tracked down to a specific choice for any of the two hierarchical directions embodied in the $n : m$-relationship.

Assume two relations R and S are related through some predicate P (which might just be equality on a common attribute, some more complex condition, a function in the COCOON object model, or whatever). Physical database design may provide

No specific support: Relations R and S are stored separately:

$$R \quad (\#R, \dots \ some \ attributes \dots)$$
$$S \quad (\#S, \dots \ some \ attributes \dots)$$

Upon retrieval, both have to be traversed (possibly in a nested loops fashion) in order to evaluate the predicate P on every pair of R- and S-tuples. (Alternatively, an index could be used, if present. Here and in the following, we do not take indexes into account, since this is an orthogonal issue. Indexes can be useful in all the designs discussed here.)

An embedded reference: Assuming that each R-tuple is related to at most one S-tuple, we could store the address of that S-tuple with each R-tuple. That is, upon insertion of the R-tuple, we evaluate the predicate P on relation S for that R-tuple, find the matching

S-tuple (if any), and store its physical address ($@S$), or its OID ($\#S$), or both, in the R-tuple:

$$S \quad (\#S, \dots \text{ some attributes} \dots)$$

$$\text{and} \quad R \quad (\#R, \#S, \dots \text{ some attributes} \dots)$$

$$\text{or} \quad R \quad (\#R, @S, \dots \text{ some attributes} \dots)$$

$$\text{or} \quad R \quad (\#R, \#S, @S, \dots \text{ some attributes} \dots)$$

In the case where the predicate P is actually a function relating objects on the conceptual level, we will *have to* store at least the OID of the referenced object.

An embedded reference set: Similarly, if an R-tuple can be related to more than one S-tuple, we can store a whole set of references (OIDs and/or TIDs) within each R-tuple, in a nested subrelation, $SRef$ (for "references to S"):[3]

$$S \quad (\#S, \dots \text{ some attributes} \dots)$$

$$\text{and} \quad R \quad (\#R, SRef(\#S), \dots \text{ some attributes} \dots)$$

$$\text{or} \quad R \quad (\#R, SRef(@S), \dots \text{ some attributes} \dots)$$

$$\text{or} \quad R \quad (\#R, SRef(\#S, @S), \dots \text{ some attributes} \dots)$$

This storage structure corresponds to CODASYL pointer arrays.

A "join index":   The pointers linking related objects could also be stored separately from the object-tuples, thus resembling the idea of join indices [Valduriez 1987]:

$$R \quad (\#R, \dots \text{ some attributes} \dots)$$

$$S \quad (\#S, \dots \text{ some attributes} \dots)$$

$$\text{plus} \quad JI_1 \quad (@R, SRef(@S))$$

$$\text{and} \quad JI_2 \quad (@S, RRef(@R))$$

Notice that we have grouped (nested) one set of addresses in each of the two parts of the join index. Furthermore, we can be more flexible in that physical addresses (TIDs) can be accompanied by or replaced with OIDs, independently form each other in any of the two parts of the join index.

---

[3]The notation "$SRef(\dots)$" inside the schema of relation R denotes a subrelation with name "$SRef$" and subattributes "$(\dots)$".

Physical clustering: The strongest way of supporting fast access "along" the predicate P is to physically cluster related R and S tuples. This is only possible without replication if it is a $1 : n$-relationship, though:

$$R \ (\#R, \ldots \ R\text{-}attributes \ldots, \ S(\#S, \ldots \ S\text{-}attributes \ldots))$$

In this storage scheme, all S-tuples related to a given R-tuple are stored within that R-tuple, so no extra I/O is necessary once we have the R-tuple.

Given a logical database schema, it is the task of the physical database design process to select one of these choices for each "relationship" between objects in the logical schema. The choice is based on cost estimates for all types of operations on all the different storage structures. Heuristics (such as an experienced DBA or even some automated tool) can be used to find a good design for a given transaction load (see Section 14.4).

The choices indicated in the example above all refer to the implementation of "relationships" between objects, such as via functions in COCOON. Decisions have to be taken for other choices too, for example, how to implement the inheritance hierarchy, and how to deal with computed functions. We present the alternatives considered in our context next.

14.3
Alternatives for Physical DB Design

This section presents the alternatives for mapping object-oriented database schemas from the conceptual level to nested relations at the physical level. We proceed by stepping through the basic concepts of the COCOON object model, and showing the implementation choices. Since the choices for each of the concepts combine orthogonally, a large decision space is spanned that is later on investigated by the physical database design tool (next section).

14.3.1   Implementing Objects

According to the object-function paradigm of COCOON, an object itself is sufficiently implemented by a unique identifier (OID), which is generated by the system. All data related to an object in one way or the other will refer to this identifier (see below). Following the conventions set up above, we denote, for each object type T, attributes of internal relations containing the OID of objects of type T by $\#T$.

14.3.2   Implementing Functions

In COCOON, functions are the basic way of associating information (data values or other objects) to objects. In principle, we can think of each function being implemented as a binary relation, with one attribute for the argument OID and the other for the result value (data item or OID). In the case of set-valued functions the second attribute will actually be a subrelation of unary subtuples, containing one result (OID or data value) each. So, in principle, a single-valued function $f_s : T_1 \rightarrow T_2$ and a multi-valued function $f_m : T_1 \rightarrow \mathbf{set}(T_3)$ could be implemented by two binary relations:

$$f_s \quad (\#T_1, \#T_2)$$
$$f_m \quad (\#T_1, T_3 Ref(\#T_3))$$

There are some obvious choices (such as: Do we really store each function in a separate binary relation or do we combine several of them into a "wider" relation?), and also some more subtle alternatives (such as: Shall we include physical pointers?).

The decision space as far as function implementations are concerned includes the following alternatives in our current approach:

Bundled vs. Decoupled: Each function f defined on a given domain object type T might either be stored in a separate (binary) relation f as shown above: we call this the *decoupled* mode. Alternatively, we can *bundle* the function f (possibly with other functions) together with the relation T implementing the type T (see below).

Notice the restriction: the set of all functions defined on the same domain type are partitioned into bundled functions (that are all stored together in one internal relation) and decoupled functions (that are all stored in separate tables, one each). More flexible function partitioning schemes are possible and certainly useful. However, we currently limit our optimization process to the restricted choice for tractability reasons.

In the example above, the bundled implementation of both, f_s and f_m would yield the following type table for T_1:

$$T_1 \quad (\#T_1, f_s\#, f_m\#Set(\#T_3))$$

Notice the naming convention: attributes are named after the function they implement, a suffix "#" indicates a (logical, OID) reference, a suffix "Set" indicates a multi-valued function (a subrelation).

Logical vs. Physical Reference: A function returning a (set of) object(s), not (a) data value(s), can be implemented by storing just OIDs (*logical reference*) of result objects or by including a TID (*physical reference*) as well. In the latter case, relations for single-valued functions become 3-attribute relations, those for multi-valued functions now have pairs in the subrelation.

Continuing on the example above (bundled), inclusion of physical references for both, f_s and f_m, would result in:

$$T_1 \quad (\#T_1, f_s\#, f_s@, f_m\#Set(\#T_3, @T_3))$$

Oneway vs. Bothway References: A function f from type T to (possibly a set of) type S can be implemented by a forward reference only (*oneway*), or it can be implemented with backpointers (*bothway*). Again, backward pointers, if any, can be implemented with just logical references or with physical references. Notice that COCOON includes the specification of *inverse functions*. If an inverse functions is defined in the conceptual schema, then the "backward" reference is present anyway. Therefore, this option is only considered for functions that have no inverse in the object schema.[4] Whenever the inverse function is not given explicitly in the schema, we have to assume that back references are multi-valued.

For decoupled functions, the backward references will also be decoupled. Therefore, decoupled functions with backpointers result in the "join indices" shown in the previous section. For bundled functions, back references are also bundled with the corresponding type table.

In our (bundled) example above, assuming a (logical only) backpointer for function f_s would make the type table for type T_2 look like:

$$T_2 \quad (\#T_2, f_s^{-1}\#, \dots \ other \ attributes \dots)$$

Reference vs. Materialized: Functions returning (sets of) objects, not data values, can be implemented by the various forms of references discussed up to now. Alternatively, however, we can directly *materialize* the object-tuple(s) representing the result object(s) within the object-tuple

---

[4]Backpointers might be useful, because COCOON's query language allows traversing functions backwards even if the inverse is not given explicitly in the schema.

representing the argument tuple. That is, we can store the resulting object-tuple "in-place". This strategy achieves physical clustering.

In our example, the decision to materialize the function f_m would generate a nested type table for T_1 that contains the type table for T_3 as a subrelation:

$$T_1 \quad (\#T_1, f_s\#, f_s@, f_m Set(\#T_3, \ldots \text{ other } T_3\text{-attributes} \ldots))$$

Obviously, we need no backward references in this case. Furthermore, this alternative is free of redundancy only if the materialized function is $1:n$, that is, its inverse is single-valued.

As shown in the example, materialization is considered only in conjunction with bundling in our current optimizer. More generally, it may be optimal to materialize decoupled functions as well. Then we would actually partition the objects of the result type according to this function.

Computed vs. Materialized: Finally, an additional option is to materialize derived (computed) functions. Assuming that some function f on type T can be computed, we could nonetheless decide to internally materialize it, if retrieval on f dominates updates to the underlying base information significantly. The more retrieval dominates updates, and the more costly the computation is, the more likely is the case that materialization pays off. For example, with geometric object descriptions, one typically uses a "bounding box" function to filter objects coarsely in spatial queries. Obviously, the bounding box is derived from the actual geometry of objects. But computing the bounding box incurs quite some effort, and if object shapes rarely change, materializing the bounding box function clearly is a good strategy (see also [Kemper and Moerkotte 1990a, Kemper and Moerkotte 1990b]).

Let us repeat that choosing how to implement functions (retrieval methods) for an object-oriented database schema is essentially the same problem as physical database design for network (CODASYL) databases, or for "Complex Object" databases (in the sense of [Abiteboul and Beeri 1988, Abiteboul et al. 1989]), or even for relational databases (where the 'structure' stems from key-foreign key relationships).

14.3.3 Implementing Types, Classes, and Inheritance

Some new aspects in physical database design, however, originate from data modeling concepts not typically found in 'pre-object-oriented" models:

inheritance hierarchies. In the context of the COCOON object model, we are dealing with two such hierarchies: one between types (organizing structural, function inheritance), and one between classes (organizing set inclusion).

Before going into the details of these hierarchies, there is one more basic question to be answered: how to implement types and classes. In general, our approach to physical design is schema-driven (as opposed to fully dynamic or instance-driven). That is, we analyze and optimize the physical DB layout based on schema-level information (types, classes, functions) rather than for individual objects. In our model, this raises the question whether we do the design for types of objects, or for individual classes. Since classes are always bound to a particular (member-) type, physical design for types is the larger grain approach, whereas design for individual classes would be the finer grain approach (remember, there may be more than one class per type).

Currently, we do the physical design on a type basis, that is, all objects of a given type are physically represented in the same way (even if they belong to several classes). The argument for doing so is that it is easier, because it gives fewer choices. Furthermore, if typical database schemas have roughly one class per type, the difference as compared to a class-based physical design is only marginal. Classes are implemented as views over their underlying type table. If classes are defined by a predicate, this predicate is used as a selection condition, user-defined classes (whose members are explicitly added/removed by query language operators) require an additional boolean attribute in the type table.

The inheritance hierarchy for types introduces two further degrees of freedom for physical design: first, if functions are bundled, shall we include inherited functions in the type tables of subtypes? Second, shall objects be represented in an object-tuple only for the most specific subtype's table, or in several object-tuples, one per supertype? These choices have sometimes been called horizontal versus vertical partitioning of objects or properties.

Currently, we allow only very limited choices with respect to types, classes, and inheritance:

Types: Each object type T is mapped to a type table T with at least one attribute, $\#T$, containing the OID. Additional attributes are present in case of any bundled functions and/or materializations of object functions. The type table T may itself be a subrelation of some other table S, if type T was materialized w.r.t. a function returning T-objects. (In the latter case, a dummy object tuple has to be added to S that collects T-objects not related to any S-object, that is, if the function used for materialization is not *onto T*.)

Classes: Each class C is implemented as a view over its underlying type table. If the class is defined by a predicate ("all"-classes and views in COCOON), this predicate is used as the selection condition. If the class is defined to include manually added member objects ("some"-classes in COCOON, see [Scholl and Schek 1990a, Scholl et al. 1991]), the underlying type table is extended by a boolean attribute C that is set to true if and only if the object is a member of this class C.

Inheritance: Subtyping is implemented by having one type table per sub-type. Two possibilities are considered:

- an object-tuple is included in each supertype's table. In case there are any bundled or materialized functions, these are not repeated in the subtypes' tables.

  In this case, object-tuple in subtype tables might optionally include physical references to supertype tuples. Using this option, physical references to object tuples always point to an object tuple *in a specific type table*. So, there is yet another degree of freedom: which one to point to? When choosing this option, we always point to the object tuple in the type table that implements the range type of the function under consideration.

- an object-tuple is included in only one type's table, that of the most specific subtype. In case of any bundled or materialized functions in supertypes, these are also included in the subtype's table.

Therefore, function values are never kept redundantly, while OIDs may be replicated in all supertypes.

Subclassing is implemented without redundancy, because all classes are views anyway.

Future plans include the consideration of classes instead of types as the basis for physical design, and potential redundancy with respect to inheritance.

14.3.4 Indexes

Obviously, among the most important decisions that have to made during physical database design for any database is the selection of appropriate indexes. All the classical indexing techniques, such as B^+-trees, will be considered. Furthermore, several specialized index structures have been proposed that are designed to support OODB-specific kinds of operations, such as path traversals [Bertino 1990]. In order to evaluate the advantages and costs of using a complex record (DASDBS) instead of a flat record (RDBMS) storage manager, though, indexes play only a supporting role. The main emphasis is on the effects of hierarchical clustering and embedded references. Therefore, we do currently not consider index selection.

In the future, we plan to take indexes into account, particularly because DASDBS allows the implementation of very powerful index structures, such as nested or path indexes.

14.3.5   The Default Physical Design

In order to have a starting point for both the physical database design tool described in the next section, and the implementation of COCOON on top of DASDBS, we have identified a default physical design that includes the following choice of implementation strategies:

Functions: All functions are *bundled* with their type table, so as to cluster all object properties together. *Object-valued* functions are implemented as *references* (potentially shared subobjects), *with physical references and backpointers* (efficient access, also for inverse direction). Multi-valued functions become subrelations.

Inheritance: Objects are present in all supertype tables (efficient access to all instances at all levels), inherited functions are not repeated in subtype tables (non-redundant storage scheme). No backpointers to supertype tuples are included (fast access via index is assumed).

For the conceptual schema given in Example 14.1, the default physical design would be (a backpointer for a function f is called $f^{-1}\ldots$, names of set-valued functions are suffixed by "$\ldots Set$"):

$$
\begin{aligned}
City \quad & (\#City, pop, name, zip, \\
& \quad has\_compSet(Comp\#, Comp@), addr^{-1}Set(Pers\#, Pers@)) \\
Comp \quad & (\#Comp, name, budg, pres\#, pres@, \\
& \quad locSet(City\#, City@), staffSet(Emp\#, Emp@)) \\
Pers \quad & (\#Pers, name, bdate, addr\#, addr@) \\
Empl \quad & (\#Empl, sal, hired, ssno, works\_for\#, works\_for@, \\
& \quad pres^{-1}Set(Comp\#, Comp@))
\end{aligned}
$$

Notice that an employee object's OID (Empl#) is actually the same as the corresponding person object's OID (Pers#).

14.4
A Physical Design Tool

In this section, we present a preliminary physical database design tool that considers some of the alternatives above and produces an internal nested relational schema for use with DASDBS, derived from a conceptual COCOON schema, a load description, and a cost model.

14.4.1 General Approach

One of the main objectives of the COCOON project is to investigate the architecture of OODBMSs. Therefore, three implementation platforms are currently being used: a commercial relational DBMS (Oracle), a commercial OODBMS (Ontos), and the DASDBS prototype. The relational and the nested relational "storage managers" will be used for extensive performance experiments to evaluate the pros and cons of the different storage alternatives. While the physical design alternatives presented above were developed mainly for implementation on top of DASDBS, some of them can be mapped to Oracle, too. For example, nested relations with only two levels of nesting (i.e., all subrelations are flat) can be simulated quite exactly by means of Oracle's "Clusters" [ORACLE 1990].

In order to assist the DBA in selecting a good physical design for a given conceptual database schema and anticipated transaction load (which may be estimated, observed, or "guesstimated"), we have implemented a first prototype of a physical database design tool (DBDesigner). The system was developed in one master thesis [Gross 1991] and is implemented in PROLOG. It uses a simplified version of a cost model for DASDBS operations developed earlier [Brauburger and Deußer 1987, Paul 1988].

14.4.2 Load Description

The transaction load is given to DBDesigner as a collection of *abstractions of COCOON operations* together with their frequencies. That is, a load description is a collection of entries of the form

```
/f/operation-specification;
```

The operation specifications consist of the following:

- For *selections* we record what the attributes in the predicate are, and the general form of the predicate. The specific predicate used is not included. Furthermore, the estimated selectivity of the predicate is also given in the load description (as an absolute cardinality or as a relative fraction).

As an example, consider the following two entries:

```
/100/select/0.3/[(name(manufacturer)) mul (name(owner))]
  (Vehicle);
/30/select/150/[address rel location(works_for)](Employee);
```

The first entry states that 100 times a selection of Vehicles returning 30% of all member objects of that class is issued. The predicate involves names of manufacturers and names of owners, these two parts are conjunctively ("mul") combined. The second entry indicates that 30 selections on the Employee class are issued that return about 150 objects each. The predicate compares the address of the Employee with the location of his or her employer (using a set comparator, as indicated by "rel").

- For *projections*, of which COCOON's query language actually has two forms, an object-preserving operator "project" and a tuple-generating operator "extract", we record only **extract**, since **project** is a type-cast operation that is "executed" completely at compile-time (used for type checking purposes). Since **extract**'s can be nested to produce nested sets of tuples, the load description for extracts records the "path traversals" that are performed by these operations.

For example, if 50 extracts of Company data together with (nested) Employee data are contained in the mix, the load description will have the following line:

```
/50/extract[cname,budget,extract[name,salary](staff)]
(Company);
```

This basically conveys the information, what parts of the accessed objects are read for output.

- For *extend* operations that define new derived functions and can also be used to simulate joins (see [Scholl and Schek 1990a]), the load description currently contains no entries. The query compiler will substitute

the defining expressions for the function names, so in the first DBDesigner prototype we expect this substitution to be done before the load
description.

Set operations, such as union, difference, and intersection, are currently
excluded from the load description. The reason is mainly to reduce the
problem space (and also, that we expect them to be less frequent and
crucial).

- For *update* operations, the main information is frequencies and what
  functions get updated. The following three lines are used to describe
  two update operations that occur 30 and 4 times, respectively.

```
/30/update[produces := select/430/[id](Vehicle)](Company);
/4/newemployer := select/1/[name](Company);
/4/update[works_for := newemployer](Employee);
```

The first update sets the 'produces' function to a new value for a Company. The new value for 'produces' is obtained by a query (selection)
against the Vehicle class (that returns 430 objects on the average). The
second update proceeds in two steps: first, a variable is assigned the
result of a selection on Companies (returning only 1 object), then this
Company is made the new value of the 'works_for' function of an Employee object.

Notice that frequency information for update statements can be interpreted in two ways: either single object updates are performed that
often, or that many objects are updated at once. For the cost calculation there is no difference.

14.4.3 Statistical Information

In order to compute the cost of operations, the design optimizer should
actually cooperate with the query optimizer of the execution engine. In the
current development phase of the COCOON–DASDBS mapping, however,
this part is not yet completed (see Section 14.5). Therefore, DBDesigner uses
its own set of statistics and cost formulae. The statistics used by physical
designer are:

- cardinalities of types (how many objects of that type are in the DB?)[5]

---

[5]Accumulation for supertypes is done by the tool, based on the assumption that different
subtypes of one type have disjoint extents.

- (average) cardinalities of set-valued functions

- (average) sizes of all atomic values

No information about value distributions is needed, since selectivities are included in the load description.

14.4.4   The Optimization Process

The optimization algorithm of DBDesigner uses a branch-and-bound method. From the given load description we first generate a "transaction graph" (TG) that will be used for enumerating the design alternatives. The TG consists of vertices representing the types in the conceptual database schema, directed edges connect types if there is a "traversal" in the corresponding direction in the load. Traversals can, for example, occur in selection conditions: whenever a selection on a class over type T_1 uses a function that returns objects of type T_2, there will be an edge from node T_1 to node T_2 in the TG. Other possibilities for such traversal are projections (extract) and 'information flow' in update statements (where do the values assigned come from?). Finally, use of inherited functions also leads to an edge from the subtype node to the supertype node.

The next step is to add a weight to the edges in the TG. This weight represents the accumulated traffic across this link, that is, from the load description we computes the sum of the frequencies of all operations that incur the traversal represented by the edge.

The current version of DBDesigner has the following restriction: usually, multiple connections may be present in the conceptual schema between two types. For example, several functions might connect two types. This is not permitted in schemas that can be optimized by DBDesigner. As a consequence, if the conceptual schema does contain such cases, the range type of such functions has to be specialized into subtypes, such that the functions map objects of the domain type to different range types.

After the construction of the TG, the optimization can actually begin. Starting from the default physical design (see above), the optimizer selects the most promising (that is, heaviest) edge from the TG and tries to improve performance by materializing the corresponding function (physical clustering) or by repeating the inherited attributes in the subtype's object-table. The total cost of the new design is compared with the old cost. The next step depends on how these costs compare. If the transformation of the physical design led to an improvement, we proceed with this design, otherwise we try the 2nd heaviest edge, and so on. The search is always continued at the currently best alternative, as long as it still contains some immediate potential for improvement. An alternative has no immediate potential, if either

- no more transformations can be applied, or

- all possible transformations have already been tested, but they have all led to no improvement.

Notice that an alternative without immediate potential could still lead to the optimal solution. So, immediate potential is only used as the criterion where to continue the search next. If no alternatives with immediate potential are left, we continue with the best alternative that allows transformations until no more transformations are possible.

The search can further be limited by the user by giving a maximum number of final designs to evaluate. A design is final if it has no immediate potential.

14.4.5 Experiences and Extensions

We have tested DBDesigner with a couple of (rather small) sample databases, with only a modest complexity in the transaction load. Larger scale experiments are planned, but have not yet been carried out. With the small test cases, as expected, the performance was good and PROLOG has not (yet?) turned out to be a big penalty.

The first prototype has already been extended to allow dynamic modifications in either the transaction load or the database schema. The objective here is to avoid complete re-iteration of the optimization process, for two reasons: one is to avoid duplicate work. The other, more challenging one is that the new physical design should not be too different from the old one in case we already have a big populated database. Otherwise we would have to reorganize the existing data. Particular emphasis was put on the inclusion of view definitions in the schema description. For this specific case we have added redundant storage strategies to the optimizer's repertoire: a view can be materialized in a separate internal relation or just kept as a virtual (computed) class.

14.5
Query Optimization

In this section we briefly discuss the transformation and optimization of queries that are given to the system in terms of the conceptual database schema. It is the task of the query optimizer to map these COCOON queries down to the physical level by: (i) transforming them to the nested relational model and algebra as available at the DASDBS kernel interface, and (ii) selecting a good (if not the best) execution strategy.

Because COCOON's query language, COOL, is pretty similar to a nested relational algebra, a straightforward transformation from COOL expressions down to a nested relational algebra expression against a fixed implementation at the internal level (e.g., the default physical design) is done rather easily. Complications arise from the fact that the mapping of data structures is quite flexible, and that, depending on the chosen design, operations have to be optimized substantially.

Originally, we planed to investigate two competitive approaches to query transformation and optimization. The first would have been a purely algebraic one, comparable to what we did with the relational to nested relational mapping [Scholl et al. 1987, Scholl 1986]: COCOON classes would be defined as 'views' over the stored nested relations, COOL queries would be transformed to the nested relational level by 'view substitution', and finally, algebraic transformations within the nested relational algebra could be applied, so as to eliminate redundant subexpressions. Quite a few redundant joins would have to be removed in case we materialized functions (hierarchical clustering). This has exactly been the problem addressed in [Scholl 1986].

The second approach is to transform the given COOL query into a nested algebra query using a class connection graph, similar to the one used in [Lanzelotte et al. 1991]. The class connection graph is somewhat similar to the transaction graph used in DBDesigner, edges are labeled by the implementation strategy. For example, whether a pointer (in case of a physical reference) has to be followed, whether a join has to be performed (in case of a logical reference), or whether a subrelation has to be accessed (in case of a materialized function), is represented by corresponding labels. Each label identifies the particular algebraic (sub-) expression that is generated when the nested algebra query is recursively constructed for the COOL query. This results in a correct, but not necessarily optimal, access plan in terms of stored relations. The remaining work is to determine the best execution order and implementation strategy of the operators, but no redundant joins are created in this transformation. The latter part of the optimization is done by a program that was generated using the EXODUS optimizer generator [Graefe and DeWitt 1987]. This first prototype of a COOL-to-DASDBS optimizer is operational, it succeeds in finding the right plans (at least w.r.t. the clustering strategy chosen in the physical design), and it is integrated with the DASDBS-based implementation of COCOON. What remains to be done in the next months is to run performance experiments with queries exploiting the hierarchical clustering capabilities of DASDBS and compare them to an Oracle-based implementation of COCOON.

14.6
Conclusion

In this paper, we have presented an approach to the implementation of object-oriented databases that uses a 'complex record' data manager, the DASDBS kernel system. This system offers nested relations as the interface to its storage subsystem. The key ideas of using such an advanced storage service is that data used to represent the objects of the conceptual database schema (expressed in some OODB model) can be clustered much more flexible than with typical relational DBMSs. Particularly interesting for us is the opportunity to hierarchically cluster data that represent objects that are interrelated through (possibly set-valued) functions (methods).

Throughout, we used the terminology and notation of our object model, COCOON, an object-function model. However, in spite of their differences, virtually all OODB models agree on the fact that objects may be arranged in some complex form. Therefore, the principal alternatives discussed should be applicable for other object models as well. We presented alternatives for the implementation of functions (with emphasis on clustering options) as well as inheritance hierarchies. A first prototype of a physical database design aid (DBDesigner) was outlined, which implements an optimization algorithm to select among some of the choices that were discussed before. Finally, we commented on query transformation and optimization, which is essential, if the variety of physical design alternatives should be utilized efficiently.

Acknowledgements

The work reported here was done while the author was with ETH Zurich, Department of Computer Science. Hans-Jörg Schek, Peter Scheuermann and the editors of this volume provided useful hints for improvements of the draft.

Bibliography

[Abiteboul and Beeri 1988] S. Abiteboul and C. Beeri. *On the power of languages for the Manipulation of Complex Objects.* Technical Report 846, INRIA, Paris, May 1988.

[Abiteboul et al. 1989] S. Abiteboul, P. C. Fischer, and H.-J. Schek, editors. *Nested Relations and Complex Objects in Databases.* LNCS 361, Springer Verlag, Heidelberg, 1989.

[Batory 1987] D. S. Batory. *A molecular database systems technology.* Technical Report TR-87-23, University of Texas at Austin, Austin, Texas, June 1987.

[Beeri 1990] C. Beeri. *A formal approach to object-oriented databases.* Data & Knowledge Engineering, 5:353–382, October 1990.

[Benzaken 1990] V. Benzaken. *An evaluation model for clustering strategies in the O_2 object-oriented database system.* In *ICDT '90 – Proc. Int'l. Conf. on Database Theory*, pages 126–140, Paris, December 1990. LNCS 470, Springer Verlag, Heidelberg.

[Bertino 1990] E. Bertino. *Optimization of queries using nested indices.* In *Advances in Database Technology (Proc. EDBT '90)*, pages 44–59, Venice, March 1990. LNCS 416, Springer Heidelberg.

[Brauburger and Deußer 1987] D. Brauburger and P. Deußer. *Design and implementation of a cost estimator and physical database DESIGNER for DASDBS.* Diploma Thesis, Dept. of Computer Science, TU Darmstadt, 1987. In German.

[Carey et al. 1986] M.J. Carey, D.J. DeWitt, J.E. Richardson, and E.J. Shekita. *Object and file management in the EXODUS extensible database system.* In *Proc. Int. Conf. on Very Large Databases*, Kyoto, 1986.

[Deppisch et al. 1987] U. Deppisch, H.-B. Paul, H.-J. Schek, and G. Weikum. *Managing complex objects in the Darmstadt database kernel system.* In A. Buchmann, U. Dayal, and K. R. Dittrich, editors, *Object-Oriented Database Systems.* Topics in Information Systems, Springer Verlag, Heidelberg, 1987.

[Graefe and DeWitt 1987] G. Graefe and D.J. DeWitt. *The EXODUS optimizer generator.* In *Proc. ACM SIGMOD Conf. on Management of Data*, pages 160–172, San Francisco, May 1987. ACM.

[Gross 1991] R. Gross. *Physical database design for object-oriented databases.* Diploma Thesis, Department of Computer Science, ETH Zurich, March 1991.

[Haas et al. 1990] L.M. Haas, W. Chang, G.M. Lohman, J. McPherson, P.F. Wilms, G. Lapis, B. Lindsay, H. Pirahesh, M.J. Carey, and E. Shekita. *Starburst mid-flight: As the dust clears. IEEE Trans. on Knowledge and Data Engineering*, 2(1):143–160, March 1990. Special issue on Database Prototype Systems.

[Haerder et al. 1987] T. Haerder, K. Meyer-Wegener, B. Mitschang, and A. Sikeler. *PRIMA – a DBMS prototype supporting engineering applications.* In *Proc. Int. Conf. on Very Large Databases*, pages 433–442, Brighton, September 1987.

[Heuer and Scholl 1991] A. Heuer and M.H. Scholl. *Principles of object-oriented query languages.* In H.-J. Appelrath, editor, *Proc. GI Conf. on Database Systems for Office, Engineering, and Scientific Applications*, pages 178–197, Kaiserslautern, March 1991. IFB 270, Springer Verlag, Heidelberg.

[Kemper and Moerkotte 1990a] A. Kemper and G. Moerkotte. *Access support in object bases.* In *Proc. ACM SIGMOD Conf. on Management of Data*, pages 364–374, Atlantic City, NJ, May 1990. ACM, New York.

[Kemper and Moerkotte 1990b] A. Kemper and G. Moerkotte. *Advanced query processing in object bases using access support relations.* In *Proc. Int. Conf. on Very Large Databases*, pages 294–305, Brisbane, August 1990. Morgan Kaufmann, Los Altos, Ca.

[Lanzelotte et al. 1991] R. Lanzelotte, P. Valduriez, M. Ziane, and J.J. Cheiney. *Optimization of nonrecursive queries in OODBs.* In *Proc. Int'l*

Conf. on Deductive and Object-Oriented Databases (DOOD), pages 1–21, Munich, December 1991. LNCS 566, Springer Heidelberg.

[ORACLE 1990] Oracle Corporation. *ORACLE Version 6.0 Database Administrator's Guide*. Oracle Corporation, Redwood Shores, CA, October 1990.

[Paul et al. 1987] H.-B. Paul, H.-J. Schek, M.H. Scholl, G. Weikum, and U. Deppisch. *Architecture and implementation of the Darmstadt database kernel system*. In *Proc. ACM SIGMOD Conf. on Management of Data*, San Francisco, 1987. ACM, New York.

[Paul 1988] H.-B. Paul. DAS Database Kernel System for Standard and Non-standard Applications—Architecture, Implementation, Applications. PhD thesis, Dept. of Computer Science, TU Darmstadt, 1988. (in German).

[Schek et al. 1990] H.-J. Schek, H.-B. Paul, M.H. Scholl, and G. Weikum. *The DASDBS project: Objectives, experiences and future prospects. IEEE Trans. on Knowledge and Data Engineering*, 2(1):25–43, March 1990. Special Issue on Database Prototype Systems.

[Scholl 1986] M.H. Scholl. *Theoretical foundation of algebraic optimization utilizing unnormalized relations*. In *ICDT '86: Int. Conf. on Database Theory*, pages 380–396, Rome, Italy, September 1986. LNCS 243, Springer Verlag, Heidelberg.

[Scholl and Schek 1990a] M.H. Scholl and H.-J. Schek. *A relational object model*. In *ICDT '90 – Proc. Int'l. Conf. on Database Theory*, pages 89–105, Paris, December 1990. LNCS 470, Springer Verlag, Heidelberg.

[Scholl and Schek 1990b] M.H. Scholl and H.-J. Schek. *A synthesis of complex objects and object-orientation*. In *Proc. IFIP TC2 Conf. on Object Oriented Databases (DS-4)*, Windermere, UK, July 1990. North-Holland. To appear.

[Scholl et al. 1987] M.H. Scholl, H.-B. Paul, and H.-J. Schek. *Supporting flat relations by a nested relational kernel*. In *Proc. Int. Conf. on Very Large Databases*, pages 137–146, Brighton, September 1987. MK.

[Scholl et al. 1991] M.H. Scholl, C. Laasch, and M. Tresch. *Updatable views in object-oriented databases*. In *Proc. Int'l Conf. on Deductive and Object-Oriented Databases (DOOD)*, pages 189–207, Munich, December 1991. LNCS 566, Springer, Heidelberg.

[Valduriez 1987] P. Valduriez. *Join indices. ACM Transactions on Database Systems*, 12(2):218–246, June 1987.

[Wilkinson et al. 1990] K. Wilkinson, P. Lyngbaek, and W. Hasan. *The Iris architecture and implementation. IEEE Trans. on Knowledge and Data Engineering*, 2(1):63–75, March 1990. Special Issue on Prototype Systems.

15

An Analysis of a Dynamic Query Optimization Scheme for Different Data Distributions

C.A. van den Berg

M.L. Kersten

Abstract

Query processing in parallel database systems is commonly based on the assumption that reliable estimates can be made for the sizes of intermediate results and the load distribution in the system. However, for increasingly complex DBMS to support non-standard applications, reliable estimates are difficult to make. In this paper, we describe a distributed query processing architecture, which is adaptive to the data and load distribution. In particular, we determine the impact of different data distributions on the effectiveness of a dynamic query optimization technique, called *task elimination*, to reduce the total amount of work. A probabilistic model is developed to determine the reduction obtained and the effect on the total processing cost.

15.1
Introduction

Exploiting distributed processing capacities provided by large multiprocessor systems has been used in many database machine projects to improve the performance of database management systems [Boral et al. 1990, DeWitt et al. 1990, Kersten and Apers et al. 1988]. Although each prototype has demonstrated a performance improvement over centralized systems, they are mostly based on the same hidden assumptions, which may still block a potential leap in performance for large multiprocessors.

Namely, the query optimizers of these systems determine a single query evaluation plan based on estimates about the data distribution and the sizes of intermediate results. Furthermore, upon allocation of the subqueries to the available processors, the query optimizer assumes that the query runs in isolation. The effect of concurrently running queries, which may hold an exclusive lock on a relation fragment or which may increase the load of one of the participating processors, is not taken into account. As a consequence, if the estimates on the data distribution and selectivity of the operations turn out to be wrong, or the load on the available processors changes during query evaluation, the query evaluation plan will be far from optimal.

Dynamic query processing alleviates these problems by adjusting the allocation of query tasks to processors and by adjusting the query plan at run time. In recent years a number of papers have been published on task allocation and dynamic query optimization, which indicate some of the problems and gains to be expected.

Lu and Carey [Lu and Carey 1986] presented a task allocation algorithm aimed at balancing the system load and minimizing the communication cost for a query evaluation plan. It showed that load balancing leads to significant reductions in the average time a query task waits for I/O and CPU resources.

In [Bodorik and Riordon 1988] and [Nguyen 1981] a scheme based on a *threshold* mechanism is proposed. In this scheme the query plan is corrected when the actual size of a partial result exceeds the estimated size by a certain threshold value.

Graefe and Ward [Graefe and Ward 1989] introduced the notion of Dynamic Query Evaluation Plans to solve the problem of producing query plans for parameterized queries. Query execution involves evaluating a decision procedure for the actual query constants and the data distribution and linking the components of an access module into an optimal query plan.

Murphy [Murphy 1989] considered the problem of increasing the performance of query execution on shared memory multiprocessors using a minimal number of processors and a limited amount of database buffer space. The method was based on scheduling page reads and page join operations efficiently.

In our approach, the allocation of query tasks, (partial) optimization of the query plan, and data distribution are performed at run time. Like Murphy, we consider query evaluation as a scheduling problem. First, a program is constructed which solves the query for a single processor. Second, the relations involved in the query are partitioned into segments small enough, so that the constructed program can evaluate the query for a combination of segments in main memory. Finally, combinations of these segments form query tasks, which are distributed over the available processors by a centralized scheduler. The query scheduler controls the load balancing and logical query optimization using up-to-date information on the execution of query tasks and the availability of segments.

In a previous article [van den Berg, Kersten and Shair-Ali 1991] we focussed on load balancing and load control algorithms for this architecture. We observed a rapid increase of performance towards a maximum that depends on the inherent parallelism in the query only. The overhead incurred by using a centralized scheduler to manage the load control turned out to be negligible in our distributed store environment.

This paper presents an overview of the query architecture and focuses on one dynamic query optimization technique: task elimination. In particular the effectiveness of this technique is determined using a probabilistic model.

The remainder of this report is organized as follows. In Section 15.2, we describe the architecture for our dynamic query processing scheme. Section 15.3 describes the dynamic query optimization scheme of the architecture. In Section 15.4 we give an analysis of the task reduction technique for different data distributions. Section 15.5 determines the resulting total processing cost. And Section 15.6 concludes this paper, with a summary and future research objectives.

15.2
The Dynamic Query Processing Architecture

The query architecture described here is part of an experimental distributed OODBMS, which is developed in the Goblin project for supporting advanced applications, such as astronomy, robotics, CIM, and geography [Kersten 1991, Kersten and van den Berg 1991]. This OODBMS is built on top of a large message-passing multiprocessor, where each processor has enough resources to execute a subquery over a reasonable partition of the database in main memory. The Goblin architecture aims at bulk object management, because it is the operation on bulk data with order independence that has proved to be a decisive factor in the exploitation of parallelism. Furthermore, for efficient manipulation, the objects will generally be decomposed at the physical storage level into a collection of flat- and set-valued objects with references. Instead of using a navigational approach to query evaluation, the selection on attribute values are performed in parallel followed by join operations to combine the selection results. Join processing remains therefore in our view also for OODBMS an important issue.

Furthermore, the Goblin DBPL allows the specification of arbitrary complex operations. As a result the cost and the selectivity of an operation is unknown at query compilation time. Our Dynamic Query Processing scheme tries to alleviate this problem. In this paper we concentrate on a dynamic query optimization strategy. For the sake of discussion we limit ourselves in this paper to the subset of flat objects with the common relational operations.

The query evaluation is based on first partitioning the relations R_i involved into n_i segments $R_i = \bigcup_{j=1}^{n_i} S_{ij}$. Partitioning functions are, for instance, a range selection on attribute values or a hash function over an attribute value. Then using the commutative and distributive properties of the relational operations, the query Q over the relations $R_1, \ldots, R_k$ can be transformed into a collection of subqueries over the segments, such as:

$$Q = RelExpr(R_1, \ldots, R_k) \longrightarrow Q = \bigcup_{1 \leq j_1 \leq n_1} RelExpr'(S_{1j_1}, \ldots, S_{nj_k})$$

$$\vdots$$

$$1 \leq j_k \leq n_k$$

Furthermore, several query plans can be generated for the subqueries using the algebraic properties of the operations [Chu and Hurley 1982]. All actions that form part of the feasible query plans, such as scans, hash tables to be constructed, and join algorithms to be applied, are then combined into an event-driven query program.

Now query evaluation involves the execution of the query program for all the possible segment combinations, called tasks. The final union is calculated at the processing site running the application. If all the k relations R_i are all partitioned into q segments this results in q^k tasks. Depending on the query this number can be reduced by choosing a suitable partitioning function. For instance, using hash based partitioning for the operands of an equi-join operation reduces the number of subquery evaluations to $\lceil \frac{n_1}{h} \rceil \lceil \frac{n_2}{h} \rceil$, where h is the number of hash buckets. Other optimizations based on the run-time behavior of the query are presented in Section 15.3.

Our architecture is based on two kinds of processes: *query dependent* and *schema dependent*. The query-dependent processes are called the Query Scheduler (QS) and the Query Processor (QP). Typically, during query processing there will be a single QS and several QP processes active. The schema-dependent process is the Class Manager (CM). The query-dependent processes are generated for a specific query. The schema-dependent processes are generated for a specific relation or view. In the following we will discuss briefly their functionality as it pertains to our query processing scheme. Figure 15.1 illustrates the communication pattern between the components and the application program.

15.2.1   The Class Manager

The Class Managers provide a persistent storage and retrieval facility for a single relation. Upon receiving an *openCM* request from the Query Scheduler, the CM starts a subtransaction to partition the relation into segments according to the partition function. Whenever it receives a *nextSeg* request it caches the partitioned segments and returns the corresponding segment identifiers to the QS.

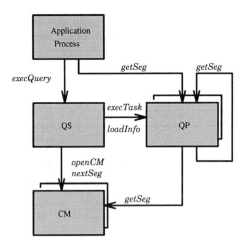

FIGURE 15.1
The basic system communication pattern

When the segment data has been cached, a Query Processor can subsequently retrieve this data by sending a *getSeg* message to the CM. The CM then transports the data over the network to the QP. The CM can not only deliver the raw data from disk, but it can also apply selection and projection operations on the data directly.

15.2.2 The Query Processor

The Query Processors form the query evaluation engine. The global architecture is shown in Figure 15.2. The Query Scheduler translates the query over the relations into a batch of queries over the relation segments, called tasks. The Query Processors evaluate these tasks to form the partial results. The final query result is obtained by taking the union of the partial results produced at the QP.

For each task the QP collects the segments involved into its cache. In the basic architecture the segments are retrieved from the CM caches. In the extended architecture, the segments can also be obtained directly from other QP caches, thereby reducing the load on the CM. A detailed analysis of these two approaches can be found in [van den Berg, Kersten and Shair-Ali 1991].

In contrast with a pipelined execution model, the execution order of the

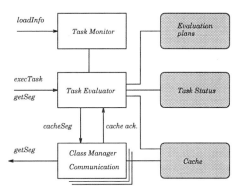

FIGURE 15.2
The Query Processor

individual operations within the query is not fixed at compile time. Instead, all evaluation plans are included in the query program. The task evaluator selects a plan depending on availability of the segments, or based on suggestions from the QS. For instance, if the QS requests a QP to calculate $R_1 \bowtie S_2 \bowtie T_1$, and segments S_2 and T_1 are already present, it will first calculate $S_2 \bowtie T_1$, and store the intermediate result in its cache for further use. When segment R_1 arrives, it continues the join operation and it informs the QS that the (R_1, S_2, T_1) task has been completed.

A task monitor keeps a record of the average task execution time, and of events of interest for dynamic query optimization, such as the occurrence of empty intermediate results (see also Section 15.3). This information is made available to the QS through the *loadInfo* operation.

15.2.3   The Query Scheduler

The QS is built around a data structure called the *Tasktable*. The *Generator*, *Allocator* and *Optimizer* use this data structure to store task descriptions, select tasks for execution, and to change or remove task descriptions, respectively. Figure 15.3 presents the global structure of the QS.

The Generator initiates and drives the query execution process. It is started by the *execQuery* call and then initiates the query evaluation process by initializing the necessary CMs with *openCM* calls, followed by subsequent *nextSeg* calls to let them prepare segments. The segment identifiers of the

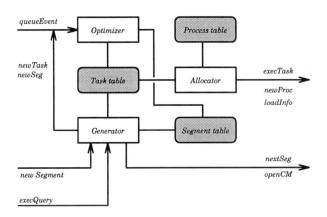

FIGURE 15.3
The main components of the Query Scheduler

segments prepared by the CM are returned to the Generator through the *newSegment* function. It stores these identifiers with the segment statistics in the *Segmenttable* and adds new tasks that can be formed with the new segment identifiers to the *Tasktable*.

The Generator suspends execution if the *Tasktable* is full. If all the *newSegment* calls fail (because the last segment has been formed), the Generator terminates.

The Allocator is responsible for the load control, load balancing, and physical optimization of the query evaluation. It selects tasks from the *Tasktable* and assigns these tasks to the available processors. For task selection, the Allocator can use the distribution information of segment copies over the QP caches. For the selection of the processor site, the current load and load distribution of each QP is taken into account. This information is maintained in the *processTable*. With the *loadInfo* call, the Allocator obtains information on the current processor load from a QP. The Allocator initializes new QP processes with the *newProc* function.

The Optimizer performs logical optimizations of the query at run time. Similar to an ordinary query optimizer, it uses the operator semantics to change the query evaluation process, but the optimization is driven by observed statistical properties of task executions rather than heuristic values for cost and selectivity of operations. In the Goblin architecture query modification boils down to modification or removal of tasks from the *Tasktable*.

The Optimizer is event-driven. Interesting events from a logical query optimization point of view are, for instance, the creation of a new task by the Generator, statistical information on new segments or statistical information on tasks executions.

The considerations and algorithms for the optimizer are described in more detail next.

15.3
Dynamic Query Optimization

The naive approach of evaluating a query as a Cartesian product over all combinations of relation partitions, results in a potentially large task table. As mentioned before (Section 15.2), the number of tasks can be reduced considerably by a clever choice of the partition function.

In this paper we present a run-time optimization, which adapts the query evaluation to the data distribution. This optimization is based on the assumption that the tuples, that partake in the query result are, in general, not uniformly distributed over the product space of the relations involved; instead, they often exhibit some clustering. For example consider the following query:

```
SELECT *
FROM P IN Persons, C IN Cities, F IN Factories
WHERE P.address = C.name and C.name = F.location
```

Since not all the cities have factories and the number of factories in a city is variable, there will be many (City, Factory) pairs that do not contribute to the query result. Consequently, a large number of (Person, City, Factory) combinations do not have to be considered either.

The dynamic query optimizer performs logical optimizations using knowledge about the actual dependencies between the operators in a query task. The optimizations are triggered by feedback information from the task executions and distribution information about the relations. In the following sections we consider an optimization that reduces the number of query tasks (task elimination). Several techniques can be used for dynamic optimization. Here we discuss only the task elimination technique, because this technique is generally applicable and is still analytically tractable.

15.4
Task elimination

Task elimination uses the occurrence of empty intermediate (partial) results to reduce the number of outstanding tasks. For instance, if for the query $S \bowtie R \bowtie T$ the Query Processor discovers that the intermediate result $S_1 \bowtie R_2$ is empty, it reports this observation to the Query Scheduler, which then removes all remaining tasks of the form $S_1 \bowtie R_2 \bowtie T_i$ from the task table.

In this section we determine the potential savings that can be obtained by task elimination. The effectiveness of this technique is determined by the fraction of empty intermediate results and how the Query Processor evaluates the tasks. The fraction of empty intermediate results, or *elimination factor* e, strongly depends on the relational operation and the attribute distribution of the participating relations. The expected value of the elimination factor for a binary operation $\otimes$ between two fragmented relations A and B can be expressed in the probability distribution $P(i, j)$ for empty intermediate results and the number of segments of the relations n_A and n_B. $P(i, j)$ is defined as the probability that the result of $A_i \otimes B_j$ is empty. Thus:

$$P(i, j) \quad = \quad Prob\{A_i \otimes B_j = \emptyset\}$$

$$E[e] \quad = \quad \tfrac{1}{n_A n_B} \sum_{i,j} P(i, j)$$

It is interesting to determine how the segment size influences the elimination factor for the different data distributions. We expect the elimination factor to increase as the segment size decreases, because the probability of an empty result increases. Furthermore, the segment size determines the processing cost of a task and the communication cost for transporting the segments to the Query Processors. For reasons of brevity, we have restricted ourselves to equi-join queries. For a description of a general cost model we refer to [Yao 1979]. The results of this exercise can be found in Section 15.5.

In the following, the elimination factor is determined for an equi-join operation $A \bowtie_{A.a=B.b} B$. Attribute a is a key attribute of relation A and assumes values in the range $[1, \cdots, c_A]$. The relation A is range partitioned over its key attribute a into n_a segments A_i containing p tuples each, so that the key attribute a of segment A_i ranges over the values $[pi + 1, \cdots, p(i + 1)]$. The relation B is also range partitioned on its key attribute. We assume that the distribution of the key attribute of B and its non-key attribute b are independent. The segments B_j also contain p tuples each. The attribute value b is distributed according to a certain probability distribution function $\pi(b)$.

To determine the elimination factor $E[e]$, we first express the probability distribution $P(i,j)$ in terms of the probability distribution $\pi(b)$. The probability $P_m(i,j) = Prob\{A_i \bowtie B_j \neq \emptyset\}$ that the attribute b of segment B_j lies within the range of key attributes $[pi+1, \cdots, p(i+1)]$ of segment A_i is independent of the B segment, thus:

$$P_m(i,j) = P_m(i) \quad = \quad \int_{pi+1}^{p(i+1)} \pi(b)db$$

Because $P_m(i)$ is the same for all the segments of B, we find the following expressions for $P(i,j)$ and $E[e]$:

$$P(i,j) = P(i) \quad = \quad (1 - P_m(i))^p$$

$$E[e] \quad = \quad \frac{1}{n_A n_B} \sum_{i,j} P(i,j) = \frac{1}{n_A} \sum_i P(i)$$

In the following paragraphs we have calculated the elimination factor for the situation where the foreign key attribute $B.b$ follows the Uniform, Normal and Zipf distribution. Because the query is an equi-join operation on a key attribute, the query result has the same cardinality as the referencing relation B. The elimination factor calculated can therefore be used to compare the optimization technique for different data distributions. To show the clustering property of the data distributions, we have calculated equi-join queries for these data distributions on two relations containing 10.000 tuples divided over 100 segments, and presented the result in scatterplots (Figures 15.5, 15.6, 15.7). Each dot represents a non-empty task result.

Uniform distribution

The uniform distribution gives the worst case behavior for the dynamic query optimization. The reason is that the data contributing to the query result is not clustered, which implies a low task elimination factor for moderately sized segments. The probability distribution function of the uniform distribution is $\pi(x) = \frac{1}{c_A}$. From this distribution we can derive the following:

$$P_m(i) \quad = \quad \int_{pi+1}^{p(i+1)} \frac{1}{c_A} db = \left[\frac{b}{c_A}\right]_{pi+1}^{p(i+1)} = \frac{p+1}{c_A}$$

$$P(i) \quad = \quad \left(1 - \frac{p+1}{c_A}\right)^p$$

$$E[e] \quad = \quad \left(1 - \frac{p+1}{c_A}\right)^p$$

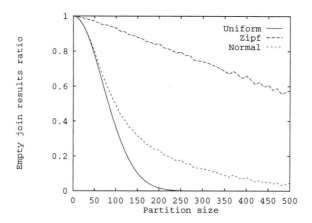

FIGURE 15.4

$E[e]$ as a function of segment size

In Figure 15.4 the function $E[e]$ is displayed for $c_A = 10,000$. Note that when the segment size is small the elimination factor is large. However, making segments too small leads to expensive processing due to communication setup overhead.

In Figure 15.5 the distribution of the tasks contributing to the query result are displayed. Each dot represents a non empty task result.

Normal distribution

The Normal distribution is also used in [Schneider and DeWitt 1989]. This attribute distribution could occur in scientific databases for attributes that represent measurement data. The distribution function of the normal distribution $N : \mu, \sigma$ is:

$$\pi(x) = \frac{1}{\sigma\sqrt{2\pi}} \exp \frac{-(x-\mu)^2}{2\sigma^2}$$

This results in the following expressions for $P_m(i)$, $P(i)$ and $E[e]$.

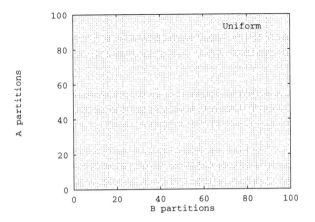

FIGURE 15.5

Join index ($B.b$ Uniform distribution)

$$P_m(i) \quad = \quad \int_{pi+1}^{p(i+1)} \frac{1}{\sigma\sqrt{2\pi}} \exp \frac{-(x-\mu)^2}{2\sigma^2} dx$$

$$P(i) \quad = \quad (1 - P_m(i))^p$$

$$E[e] \quad = \quad \frac{1}{n_A} \sum_{i=0}^{n_A - 1} \left((1 - P_m(i))^p \right)$$

The expression for $E[e]$ can not be simplified further. We have therefore made a numerical approximation of the function. Figure 15.4 displays the fraction of empty join results for a $c_A = 10,000$, $\mu = 5000$ and $\sigma = 1667$.

Figure 15.6 shows the distribution of task participating in the query result. It shows that the tasks are clustered in a well defined band.

Zipf distribution

In actual databases, the attribute distribution will more likely follow the Zipf distribution [Salza and Terranova 1989]. The probability distribution function of the Zipf distribution $Z : c$ is:

$$\pi(x) = cx^{-c}$$

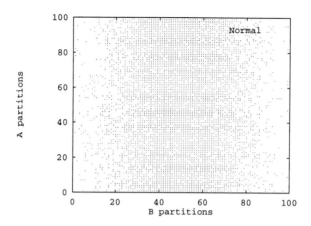

FIGURE 15.6

Join index ($B.b$ Normal distribution)

This distribution results in the following expressions for $P_m(i)$, $P(i)$ and $E[e]$.

$$P_m(i) \ = \ \int_{pi+1}^{p(i+1)}(cx^{-c-1})dx = [-x^{-c}]_{pi+1}^{p(i+1)} = (pi+1)^{-c} - (pi+p)^{-c}$$

$$P(i) \ = \ (1 - P_m(i))^p$$

$$E[e] \ = \ \sum_{i=0}^{n_A-1}(1 - P_m(i))^p$$

In Figure 15.4 the function $E[e]$ is displayed for $c_A = 10.000$, $c = 0.5$. Over a large range of segment sizes the elimination factor for the Zipf distribution is reasonable. Furthermore, because of the steepness of the Zipf distribution, the elimination factor almost a linear function of the segment size. Figure 15.7 shows the data distribution.

15.5
Multiple join evaluation

In a multiple join operation, the occurrence of an empty partial join result will also result in the removal of tasks. In this section the total task

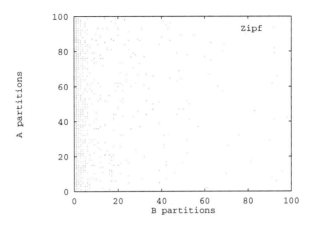

FIGURE 15.7

Join index ($B.b$ Zipf distribution)

elimination E_k of an k-way equi-join is determined given the elimination factors e_i of the $(k-1)$ partial joins. First an expression for the elimination factor for the multiple join is formulated which is then used to calculate the total processing cost for a specific 3-way and 4-way equi-join.

The evaluation order of the join operations has a strong influence on the total elimination factor. We considered two different evaluation methods: *sequential evaluation*, which corresponds to the traditional left-deep and right-deep query tree, and our own method *parallel bottom-up evaluation*.

In the following paragraphs formulas are derived for a general k-way equi-join query. In the analysis each joined relation R_i is partitioned into n_i fragments. For each method we derive a formula for the number of tasks N_k that are removed by the task elimination technique. The total task elimination factor of the join query is obtained through division by the total number of tasks N_{task}:

$$E_k \;=\; \frac{N_k}{N_{task}} \tag{15.1}$$

$$N_{task} \;=\; \prod_{i=1}^{k} n_i \tag{15.2}$$

Sequential evaluation

In the sequential evaluation method the query is either represented by a left-deep or a right-deep join tree. The intermediate result at each stage of evaluation can be empty (Figure 15.8).   Thus the Query Processor sends

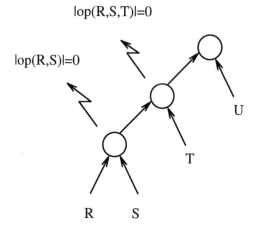

FIGURE 15.8
Sequential evaluation

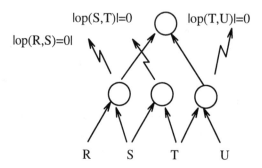

FIGURE 15.9
Parallel bottom up evaluation

the Query Scheduler information that combinations of two, three or more fragments result in an empty query result. For a combination of two fragments a large number of tasks can be removed. However, if the combination is more specific, less tasks can be removed. For instance, for a 4-way join, the event $|R_1 \bowtie S_1| = 0$ results in the removal of $n_3 n_4$ tasks[1]. Whereas the event $|R_1 \bowtie S_1 \bowtie T_1| = 0$ reduces the number of tasks only with n_4 tasks. The number of eliminated tasks for a 3-way and 4-way join operation are given by:

$$
\begin{aligned}
N_3 &= e_1 n_1 n_2 (n_3 - 1) \\
N_4 &= e_1 n_1 n_2 (n_3 n_4 - 1) + (1 - e_1) e_2 n_1 n_2 n_3 (n_4 - 1)
\end{aligned}
$$

Generally, of a k-way join $e_1 n_1 n_2$ tasks result in empty $R_1 \bowtie R_2$ combinations, because of the first join operation. This results in $e_1 N_{task}$ task eliminations. The next operation results in $(1 - e_1) e_2 N_{task}$ eliminations, caused by $(1 - e_1) e_2 n_1 n_2 n_3$ empty task results. Summing all terms until the $(k - 2)$-th join operation we find for N_k, the number of tasks that are not evaluated:

$$
N_k = \sum_{i=1}^{k-2} \left(\prod_{j<i} (1 - e_j) \right) e_i \prod_{l=1}^{k} n_l - \\
\sum_{i=1}^{k-2} \left\{ \left(\prod_{j<i} (1 - e_j) \right) e_i \prod_{l=1}^{k-1-i} n_i \right\} \tag{15.3}
$$

Parallel bottom-up evaluation

In the parallel bottom-up evaluation method, all possible join combinations are evaluated in parallel and the results are subsequently combined (Figure 15.9). The scheduler is informed if the result of a join for any combination of two fragments is empty. If such an event occurs, the scheduler removes the tasks containing this fragment combination. The number of eliminated tasks for a 3-way and 4-way join operation is thus given by:

$$
\begin{aligned}
N_3 &= (e_1 + (1 - e_1) e_2) n_1 n_2 n_3 n_4 - \max(n_1 n_2, n_2 n_3) \\
N_4 &= e_1 n_1 n_2 n_3 n_4 + (1 - e_1) e_2 n_1 n_2 n_3 n_4 \\
&\quad + (1 - e_1)(1 - e_2) n_1 n_2 n_3 n_4 - \max(n_1 n_2, n_2 n_3, n_3 n_4)
\end{aligned}
$$

If we generalize this for the k-way equi-join we find the following expression for N_k, the number of eliminated tasks:

---

[1] Note that at least one task had to be executed to generate this event.

$$N_k = \sum_{i=1}^{k-1} \left(\prod_{j<i}(1 - E_j) \right) E_i \prod_{l=1}^{k} n_l - $$
$$\max(n_1 n_2, \cdots, n_{k-2} n_{k-1}) \qquad (15.4)$$

Because all join combinations are evaluated, more work is done than actually required. However, the idea is that the additional work invested in a single subquery evaluation will result in a higher total elimination factor and, thereby, in a reduction of the total amount of work.

Comparison of the evaluation techniques

Using equations (15.1) and (15.2) and the expressions for the number of eliminated tasks (15.3) and (15.4) we have calculated the elimination factor for a 3 and a 4-way equi-join for the Normal and Zipf distribution for both evaluation techniques (See Figures 15.10 and 15.11). These graphs show that for all distributions the parallel bottom-up evaluation results in a larger elimination factor than sequential elimination.

Calculation of the elimination factor for other multi-join queries show that the range of fragment sizes for which the task elimination is effective does not depend on the number of joins, but only on the distribution parameters. However, within this range, the elimination factor increases with the number of joins.

15.5.1   Multiple join processing cost

The total elimination factor can now be used to calculate the total processing cost for a multiple-join query. In the cost model the assumption is made that the tasks are evaluated by a single Query Processor. Therefore it gives an upper bound on the total query cost. When more Query Processors are added to the architecture, tasks can be evaluated in parallel, which results in a lower total processing cost. Adding Query Processors influences the effectiveness of the dynamic query optimization technique only slightly. It could be that one QP is evaluating a task, which would be eliminated by the outcome of a task evaluation by another QP. The probability that this situation occurs is small, and can even be avoided by evaluating only those tasks in parallel, which do not use the same segment. Considering this, the following simple cost model is sufficient to measure the effectiveness.

The total query processing cost C_{query} for this architecture is equal to the product of the fraction of tasks remaining after task elimination $(1 - E_k)$

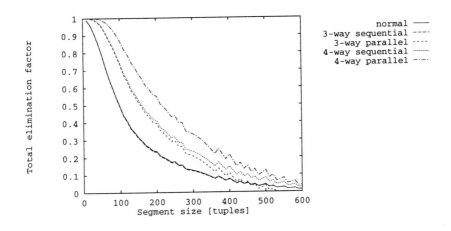

FIGURE 15.10

E for the Normal distribution as a function of segment size

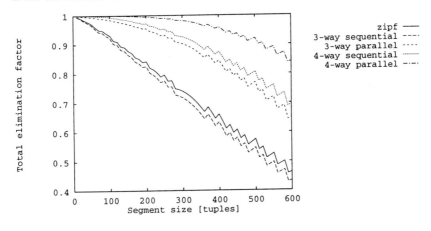

FIGURE 15.11

E for the Zipf distribution as a function of segment size

C_{access}	operating system overhead	1 msec
C_{copy}	data transfer rate	1msec/1k
C_{hash}	hash join cost	100μsec
N_{bytes}	tuple size	0.5 k

TABLE 15.1

The parameter setting for MicroVax systems running Amoeba

and the total processing cost without dynamic optimization C_{total}. The total processing cost can be expressed in the number of tasks N_{task} and the cost per task C_{task}.

As all the tasks are executed on a single Query Processor and every segment must be transported from the data store to the Query Processor, each task execution for a k-way join requires at most k segment transports $C_{com}(p)$ and a single join execution $C_{join}(p)$. These latter factors depend on the segment size p.

$$
\begin{aligned}
C_{query} &= (1 - E_k)C_{total} \\
C_{total} &= N_{task}C_{task} \\
C_{task} &= kC_{com}(p) + C_{join}(p)
\end{aligned}
$$

Segment transport requires a constant cost for network access and OS overhead C_{access} and a cost linear in the size of the segment C_{copy} for copying the data from the network to the processors memory.

For the execution cost of the join operation we only give an upper bound. Each of the $k - 1$ equi-join operations results in at most p combinations. Assuming that a hash join algorithm is used we find that the join cost is also linear in the segment size. In the first phase of the algorithm a hash table is constructed for one of the join operands, and in the second phase this hash table is probed for each join attribute value of the second operand.

$$
\begin{aligned}
C_{com}(p) &= pN_{bytes}C_{copy} + C_{access} \\
C_{join}(p) &= (k - 1)pC_{hash}
\end{aligned}
$$

Table 15.1 gives the parameter values for our target architecture, consisting of MicroVax workstations, using the Amoeba distributed operating system.

Evaluation of the formulas for these two evaluation methods on a 4-way equi-join operation results in the total query processing cost as shown

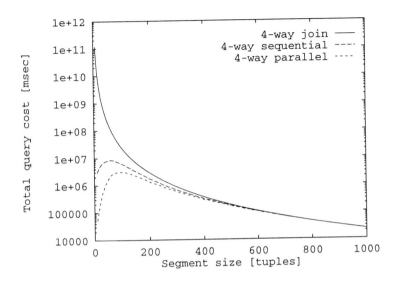

FIGURE 15.12

C_{query} for a 4-way join and Normal distribution

in Figures 15.12 and 15.13. These graphs present the total query processing cost using a logarithmic scale as a function of the segment size for the Normal distribution and the Zipf distribution. The elimination factors were obtained using the formulas of Section 15.4, and the cardinality of the relations was set to 10,000.

The result of the calculation shows that as the segment size increases the total query processing cost decreases. Although we saw that the task elimination technique becomes more effective for smaller segment sizes, it can not undo the effect of the exponential growth in the number of tasks. Only if the data follows the Zipf distribution, the total query processing cost is reasonable over a large range of segment sizes. Furthermore, the parallel bottom-up evaluation method turns out to be far more effective than the sequential evaluation method.

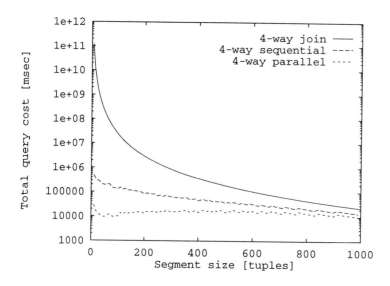

FIGURE 15.13

C_{query} for a 4-way join and Zipf distribution

15.6
Conclusions

This paper describes the query processing scheme of the Goblin object-oriented database system. Furthermore, a probabilistic model has been developed to estimate the potential gains of dynamic query optimization for different data distributions. Although the analysis was restricted to equi-join queries, we belief that the results can be carried over to object oriented database systems in general. The reason is that object oriented database systems with a focus on bulk data processing, such as Goblin, will decompose the database objects into partitions, enabling a parallel manipulation of attribute values. Query evaluation then requires efficient join processing to reconstruct the objects at the receiving site.

Our analysis shows that the task elimination technique can lead to significant reductions in the number of query tasks that have to be processed. The task elimination technique is particularly effective for a 'real life' Zipf attribute distribution. The total query evaluation cost for a three way equi-join query was reasonable over a large range of segment sizes. However, more research is required to show the effectiveness of these techniques in more general queries and to show their validity in a real database system implementation.

Bibliography

[Bodorik and Riordon 1988] P. Bodorik and J. S. Riordon. "A threshold mechanism for distributed query processing." In *Proc. of the 16-th Annual ACM Computer Science Conference*, pp. 616–625, 1988.

[Boral et al. 1990] H. Boral et al. "Prototyping Bubba, a highly parallel database system." *IEEE Transactions On Knowledge and Data Engineering*, **2(1)**, pp. 4–24.

[Chu and Hurley 1982] Wesley W. Chu and Paul Hurley. "Optimal query processing for distributed database systems." *IEEE Transactions on Computers*, **C-31(9)**, pp. 835–850.

[DeWitt et al. 1990] D. J. DeWitt, S. Ghadeharizadeh, D.A. Schneider, A. Bricker, H. Hsiao, and R. Rasmussen. "The GAMMA database machine project." *IEEE Transactions On Knowledge and Data Engineering*, **2(1)**, pp. 44–51.

[Graefe and Ward 1989] G. Graefe and K. Ward. "Dynamic query evaluation plans." In *Proceedings of the 1989 SIGMOD conference*, pp. 358–366.

[Kersten 1991] M. L. Kersten. "Goblin, a DBPL designed for advanced database applications." In *Proceedings of the 2nd International Conference of Database and Expert System Applications*.

[Kersten and Apers et al. 1988] M. L. Kersten, P. M. G. Apers, M. A. W. Houtsma, E. J. A. van Kuyk, and R. L. W. van de Weg. "A distributed, main-memory database machine; research issues and a preliminary architecture." In *Database Machines and Knowledge Base Machines*, pp. 353–369.

[Kersten and van den Berg 1991] M. L. Kersten and C. A. van den Berg. "Parallel processing of a class of geographical queries." In *Proceedings of the International Workshop on Database Management Systems for Geographical Applications*, pp. 274–288.

[Lu and Carey 1986] H. Lu and M. J. Carey. "Load balanced task allocation in locally distributed computer systems." In *Proceedings of the 1986 conference on parallel processing*, pp. 1037–1039.

[Murphy 1989] M. C. Murphy. "Effective resource utilization for multiprocessor join execution." In *Proc. of the fifteenth VLDB Conference*, pp. 67–75.

[Nguyen 1981] G. T. Nguyen. "Distributed query management for a local network." In *Proceedings of the 2nd International Conference on Distributed Computing Systems*, pp. 188–196.

[Salza and Terranova 1989] S. Salza and M. Terranova. "Evaluating the size of queries on relational databases with non uniform distribution and stochastic dependence." In *Proc. of the 1989 ACM SIGMOD conference*, pp. 8–14.

[Schneider and DeWitt 1989] D. A. Schneider and D. J. DeWitt. "A performance evaluation of four parallel join algorithms in a shared-nothing multiprocessor environment." In *Proc. of the 1989 ACM SIGMOD conference*, pp. 110–122.

[van den Berg, Kersten and Shair-Ali 1991] C. A. van den Berg, M. L. Kersten, and S. Shair-Ali. *Dynamic parallel query processing*. Technical Report CS-R9112, CWI, February 1991.

[Yao 1979] S. Bing Yao. "Optimization of query evaluation algorithms." *ACM Transactions on Database Systems*, **4(2)**, pp. 133–155.

List of Authors

1. Peter M.G. Apers
   University of Twente
   Computer Science Department
   Postbus 217
   NL-7500 AE Enschede
   The Netherlands
   apers@cs.utwente.nl

2. Jonathan Bauer
   Digital Equipment Corporation
   55 Northeastern Blv.
   Nashua, NH 03062-3191
   bauer@quill.enet.dec.com

3. Carel van den Berg
   CWI
   Kruislaan 413
   NL-1098 SJ Amsterdam
   The Netherlands
   Carel.van.den.Berg@cwi.nl

4. Elisa Bertino
   Dipartimento di Matematica
   Universita di Genova
   Via L.B. Alberti, 4
   I-16132 Genova, Italy
   bertino@igecuniv.bitnet

5. Sophie Cluet
   I.N.R.I.A
   B.P 105
   78153 Le Chesnay Cedex
   France
   cluet@inria.fr

6. Richard L. Cole
   University of Colorado
   Dept. of Computer Science
   Boulder, CO 80309-0430
   cole@cs.Colorado.edu

7. Diane L. Davison
   University of Colorado
   Dept. of Computer Science
   Boulder, CO 80309-0430
   davison@cs.Colorado.edu

8. Umeshwar Dayal
   Hewlett-Packard Labs.
   1501 Page Mill Road, 3U-4
   Palo Alto, CA 94304-1120
   dayal@hplud.hpl.hp.com

9. Claude Delobel
   Univ. Paris-Sud Orsay
   L.R.I (Bat 490)
   91405 Orsay Cedex
   delobel@inria.fr

10. Birgit Demuth
Technische Universität Dresden
Fakultät Informatik
Inst. für Datenbanken und KI
Mommsenstraße 13
O-8027 Dresden, FRG

11. Johann Christoph Freytag
Database Systems Research
Group/Munich
Digital Equipment GmbH
Rosenheimerstr. 116b
W-8000 München 80, FRG
freytag@dunant.enet.dec.com

12. Andreas Geppert
Institut für Informatik
Universität Zürich
Winterthurerstr. 190
CH-8057 Zürich, Switzerland

13. Thorsten Gorchs
Siemens-Nixdorf
Gustav-Meyer-Allee 1
W-1000 Berlin 65, FRG
gorchs.bln@sni.de

14. Götz Graefe
University of Colorado
Dept. of Computer Science
Boulder, CO 80309-0430
graefe@cs.Colorado.edu

15. Dirk Van Gucht
Computer Science Department
Indiana University
Bloomington, IN 47405-4101
vgucht@iuvax.cs.indiana.edu

16. Marc Gyssens
Dept. of Computer Science
University of Limburg
B-3610 Diepenbeek, Belgium
gyssens@ccu.uia.ac.be

17. Manfred Jeusfeld
Universität Passau
Postfach 2540
W-8390 Passau, FRG
jeusfeld@andorfer.fmi.
uni-passau.de

18. Mike Kelley
Digital Equipment Corporation
55 Northeastern Blv.
Nashua, NH 03062-3191
m_kelley@credit.enet.dec.com

19. Martin Kersten
CWI
Kruislaan 413
NL-1098 SJ Amsterdam
The Netherlands
mk@cwi.nl

20. Alfons Kemper
RWTH Aachen
Ahornstr. 55
D-5100 Aachen, Germany
kemper@ira.uka.de

21. Krishna Kulkarni
Database Systems Research
301 Rockrimmon Boulevard
Colorado Springs, CO 80919
kulkarni@cookie.enet.dec.com

22. Georg Lausen
    Praktische Informatik III
    Universität Mannheim
    Seminargebäude A5
    W-6800 Mannheim, FRG
    lausen@pi3.informatik.
    uni-mannheim.de

23. David Maier
    Oregon Graduate Institute
    Dept. of Computer Science
    19600 von Neumann Dr.
    Beaverton, OR 97006
    maier@cse.ogi.edu

24. Beate Marx
    Praktische Informatik III
    Universität Mannheim
    Seminargebäude A5
    W-6800 Mannheim, FRG
    marx@pi3.informatik.
    uni-mannheim.de

25. William J. McKenna
    University of Colorado
    Dept. of Computer Science
    Boulder, CO 80309-0430
    mckenna@cs.Colorado.edu

26. Jim Melton
    Mailstop CX02-1/7I
    301 Rockrimmon Boulevard
    Colorado Springs, CO 80919
    melton@cookie.enet.dec.com

27. Bernhard Mitschang
    Universität Kaiserslautern
    Fachbereich Informatik
    Erwin-Schrödinger-Str.
    W-6750 Kaiserslautern, FRG
    mitsch@informatik.uni-kl.de

28. Guido Moerkotte
    IPD
    Fakultät für Informatik
    Universität Karlsruhe
    W-7500 Karlsruhe, FRG
    moer@ira.uka.de

29. Hamid Pirahesh
    IBM Almaden Res. Center
    650 Harry Road
    San Jose, CA 95120-6099
    pirahesh@ibm.com

30. Lawrence V. Saxton
    University of Regina
    Computer Science Department
    Regina, Saskatchewan S4S 0A2,
    Canada
    saxton@mercury.cs.uregina.ca

31. Harald Schöning
    Universität Kaiserslautern
    Fachbereich Informatik
    Postfach 3049
    W-6750 Kaiserslautern, FRG
    schoenin@informatik.uni-kl.de

32. Marc Scholl
    Universität Ulm
    Fachbereich Informatik
    Oberer Eselsberg
    D-7900 Ulm, Germany
    scholl@informatik.uni-ulm.de

33. Martin Staudt
Universität Passau
Postfach 2540
W-8390 Passau, FRG
staudt@andorfer.fmi.
uni-passau.de

34. Hennie J. Steenhagen
University of Twente
Computer Science Department
Postbus 217
NL-7500 AE Enschede
The Netherlands
hennie@cs.utwente.nl

35. Gottfried Vossen
Lehrst.für Angewandte
Mathematik
RWTH Aachen
Ahornstr. 55
W-5100 Aachen, FRG
vossen@informatik.
rwth-aachen.de

36. Richard H. Wolniewicz
University of Colorado
Dept. of Computer Science
Boulder, CO 80309-0430
wolniewicz@cs.Colorado.edu

Index